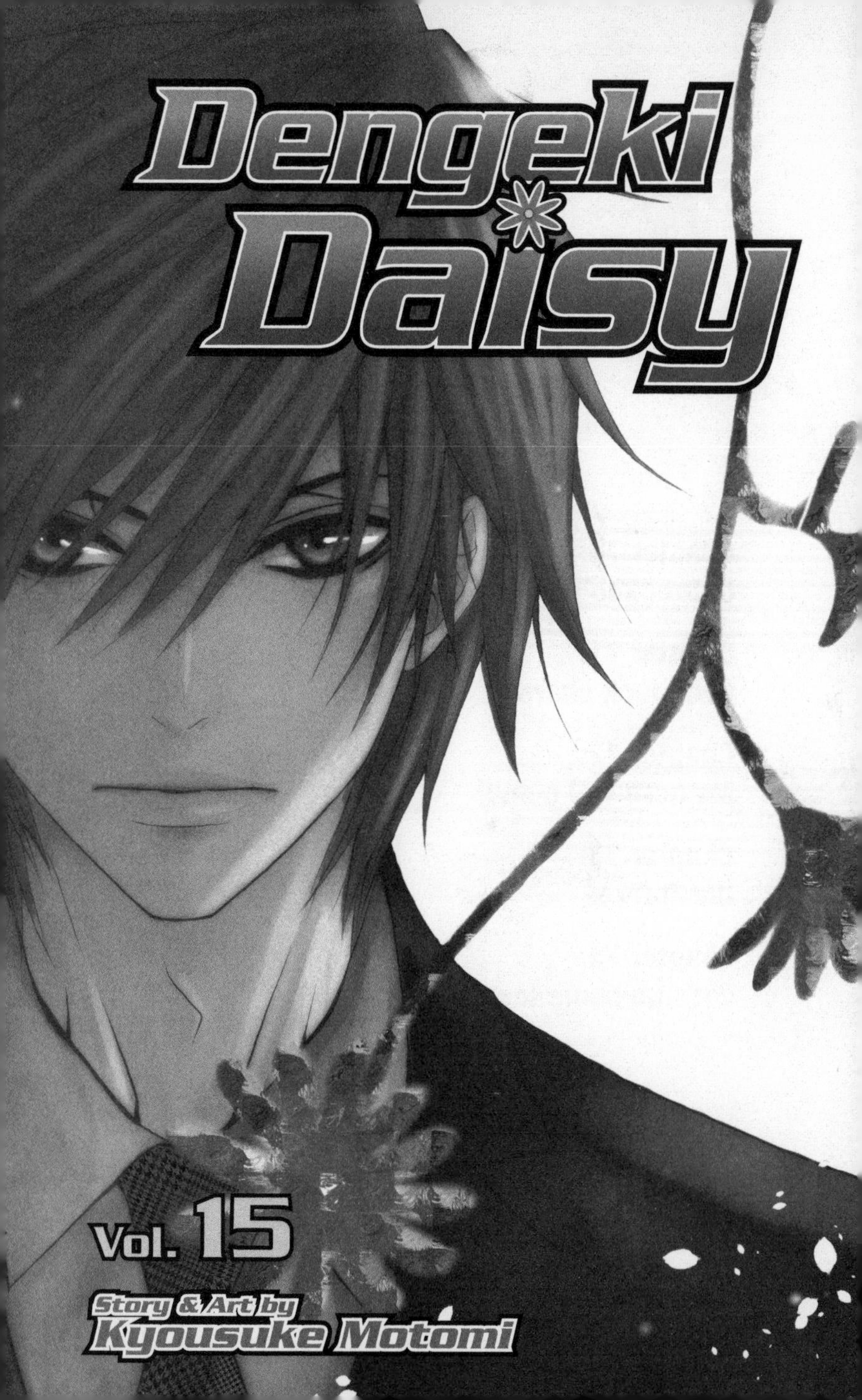
Dengeki Daisy
Vol. 15
Story & Art by
Kyousuke Motomi

Dengeki Daisy

Volume 15 CONTENTS

DENGEKI DAISY
QUESTION CORNER

(RELOCATED)

BALDLY ASK!!!

YES! THIS CORNER IS HERE BECAUSE OF YOU, THE READERS! THANK YOU ALWAYS! ONCE AGAIN, WE BRING YOU SILLINESS AT ITS FULLEST!! ①

IN VOLUME 11, CHAPTER 52, TERU WEARS A SWIM CAP DURING A SNOWBALL FIGHT WITH EVERYONE. THAT SWIM CAP HAS "1-2" WRITTEN ON IT.
BUT IN VOLUME 13, CHAPTER 63, SHE SAYS SHE WAS IN CLASS 3 DURING HER FIRST YEAR OF HIGH SCHOOL. WHAT'S GOING ON? PLEASE EXPLAIN.

(I LOVE GACHAPINKU, FUKUOKA PREFECTURE)

ACK! WHAT AN ASTUTE QUESTION! THE HONEST TRUTH IS THAT IT WAS THE AUTHOR'S MISTAKE. THIS WASN'T HER HIGH SCHOOL SWIM CAP, IT WAS HER SWIM CAP FROM MIDDLE SCHOOL. IT WAS MY INTENTION TO COORDINATE IT WITH THE SCHOOL SWIMSUIT THAT SHE APPEARED IN A LONG TIME AGO, BUT THAT SCHOOL SWIMSUIT SAID "3-2." SORRY ABOUT THAT. LET ME THINK... KUROSAKI MUST BE KEEPING THE CAP WITH "3-2" ON IT UNDER STRICT LOCK AND KEY ALONG WITH THE SWIMSUIT. THAT'S WHY TERU HAD NO CHOICE BUT TO WEAR HER CAP FROM HER FIRST YEAR IN MIDDLE SCHOOL. I'M REALLY SORRY ABOUT THAT. I FIGURE I'D BLAME IT ON KUROSAKI'S PERVERSION.

IN CHAPTER 70, KUROSAKI, RIKO AND BOSS ARE COSTUMED AS THE KIND OF DOCTORS AND NURSE YOU WOULDN'T WANT TO GET TREATED BY. IF YOU WERE TO ADD IN ANDY, TERU AND KIYOSHI TO THE MIX, WHAT COSTUMES WOULD THEY WEAR? DO YOU THINK ANDY WOULD DRESS AS A PATIENT BECAUSE HE LIKES TO BE TOUCHED?

(DANCING PRINCESS ☆, OITA PREFECTURE)

I BELIEVE SO. ANDY WOULD LOOK GOOD WITH A CAST OR BANDAGES. HE LOOKS LIKE HE MIGHT ENJOY BONDAGE. KIYOSHI, I THINK, WOULD LOOK GOOD IN A BEN CASEY-STYLE WHITE UNIFORM. AS FOR TERU... WELL, SHE LOOKS GOOD IN ANYTHING...SO LET'S PUT HER IN A HAZMAT SUIT.

TERU
↓

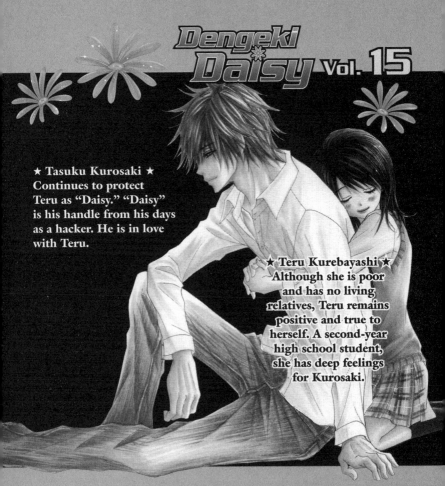

Dengeki Daisy Vol. 15

★ **Tasuku Kurosaki** ★ Continues to protect Teru as "Daisy." "Daisy" is his handle from his days as a hacker. He is in love with Teru.

★ **Teru Kurebayashi** ★ Although she is poor and has no living relatives, Teru remains positive and true to herself. A second-year high school student, she has deep feelings for Kurosaki.

★ Teru discovers that Kurosaki is Daisy, the mysterious person who supported and encouraged her after her brother Soichiro's death. Thinking that there must be a reason why Kurosaki has chosen to hide his identity, Teru decides to keep this knowledge to herself.

★ During this time, Teru's life is threatened, and strange incidents involving Teru and Kurosaki occur. Kurosaki decides to disclose the truth to Teru, but Akira beats him to it and tells her about Kurosaki's past "sin." Learning what Akira has done, Kurosaki disappears from sight. Seeing Teru so despondent, the Director and Riko tell her about Kurosaki's past.

★ Teru learns that Kurosaki's father was involved with the development of a top-secret government code, and his death was shrouded in mystery. Kurosaki became a hacker to clear his father's

CHARACTERS...

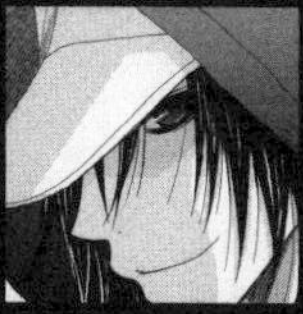

★ Akira ★
A mathematical genius and Chiharu Mori's partner-in-crime. He continues to stalk Teru and Kurosaki.

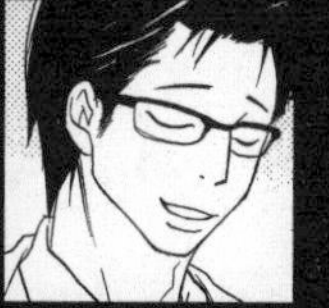

★ Takeda ★
Soichiro's former coworker. He is the owner of Kaoruko, a Shiba dog.

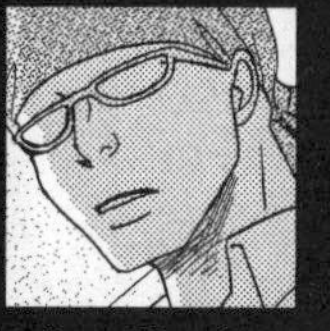

★ Boss (Masuda) ★
Currently runs the snack shop "Flower Garden" but has connections to the Ministry of Internal Affairs.

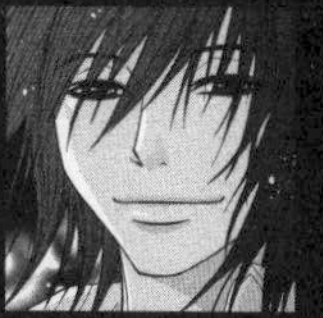

★ Soichiro Kurebayashi ★
Teru's older brother and a genius systems engineer. He died after leaving Teru in Kurosaki's care.

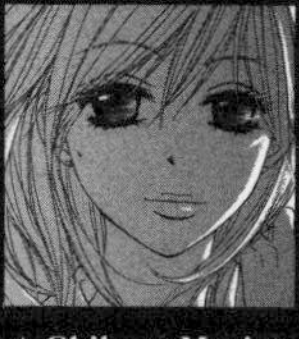

★ Chiharu Mori ★
She used to work at Teru's school. Teaming up with Akira, she continues to target Teru and Kurosaki.

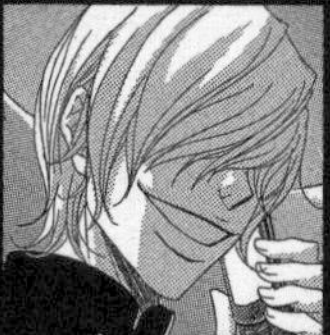

★ Antler ★
He tricked Kurosaki into creating the "Jack Frost" virus.

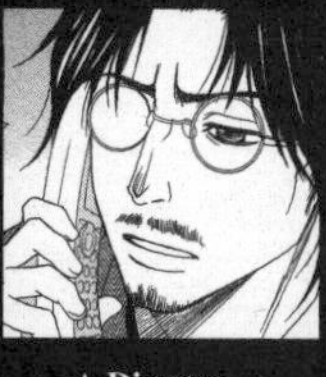

★ Director (Kazumasa Ando) ★
He used to work with Soichiro and is currently the director of Teru's school.

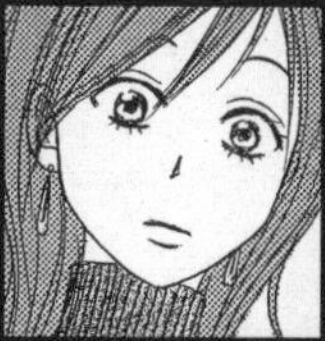

★ Riko Onizuka ★
She was Soichiro's girlfriend and is now a counselor at Teru's school.

STORY...

name and created the code virus known as "Jack Frost." In order to save Kurosaki from being charged with a "Jack Frost"-related murder, Soichiro worked nonstop to decipher the code and died in the process. Teru accepts this newfound knowledge about Kurosaki. She thanks him for all that he has done for her and asks him to stay by her side.

★ Kurosaki and friends learn that M's Last Testament isn't Professor Midorikawa's will—it's actually a trap to lure out and kill Akira. They rush to decipher the data so that they can help save him. Meanwhile, Kurosaki confesses his feelings for Teru for the first time on her birthday, and the two finally become a couple. But then Teru is abducted by Kono from the Ministry of Internal Affairs...!

DENGEKI DAISY QUESTION CORNER

RELOCATED

BALDLY ASK!!! ②

TERU APPEARS WEARING AN APRON MANY TIMES IN THE STORY, BUT DOES SHE USE THE PURE WHITE APRON THAT HARUKA AND FRIENDS GAVE HER ALONG WITH THE RED-BEAN RICE IN VOLUME 2, CHAPTER 5? DID YOSHI END UP TAKING IT?

(SUZUSHIRO, KANAGAWA PREFECTURE)

GYA HA HA HA! YOU LOOK SO GROSS!

HAVE A LOOK AT VOLUME 13, CHAPTER 60. WHILE IT'S NOT EXACTLY THE SAME, TERU IS WEARING A WHITE APRON. THINK OF IT AS THE ALL-WHITE APRON YOSHI GAVE HER BUT REDONE BY RIKO, WHO LOVES TO SEW. (THE APRON FROM CHAPTER 5 JUST WOULDN'T HAVE LOOKED RIGHT ON TERU.)

I DID THAT FOR MY OWN PERSONAL SATISFACTION, AND THAT WOULD'VE BEEN THE END OF IT HAD SOMEONE NOT REMEMBERED. I'M GLAD SOMEONE DID, SO I'VE DECIDED TO EXPLAIN IT HERE.

HERE WE GO! KIR ROYALE AND ...
...BAGUETTE WITH DUCK PÂTÉ.

IS THERE SOMETHING THAT TERU WOULD LIKE KUROSAKI TO DO OR STOP DOING?

(MA-CHAN)

HMM. I THINK SHE MIGHT WANT HIM TO STOP SMOKING SOMEDAY. ASIDE FROM THAT—EVEN THOUGH THIS SERIOUS ANSWER GOES AGAINST WHAT THIS CORNER IS ABOUT—THERE IS ONE THING THAT TERU ABSOLUTELY DOES NOT WANT KUROSAKI TO DO: "DISAPPEAR SUDDENLY, WITHOUT A WORD." ALSO, KUROSAKI HAS A HABIT OF NOT PUTTING THE TOILET SEAT DOWN. TERU GETS FURIOUS WHEN HER TUSH PLOPS DOWN DIRECTLY ON THE BARE TOILET RIM.

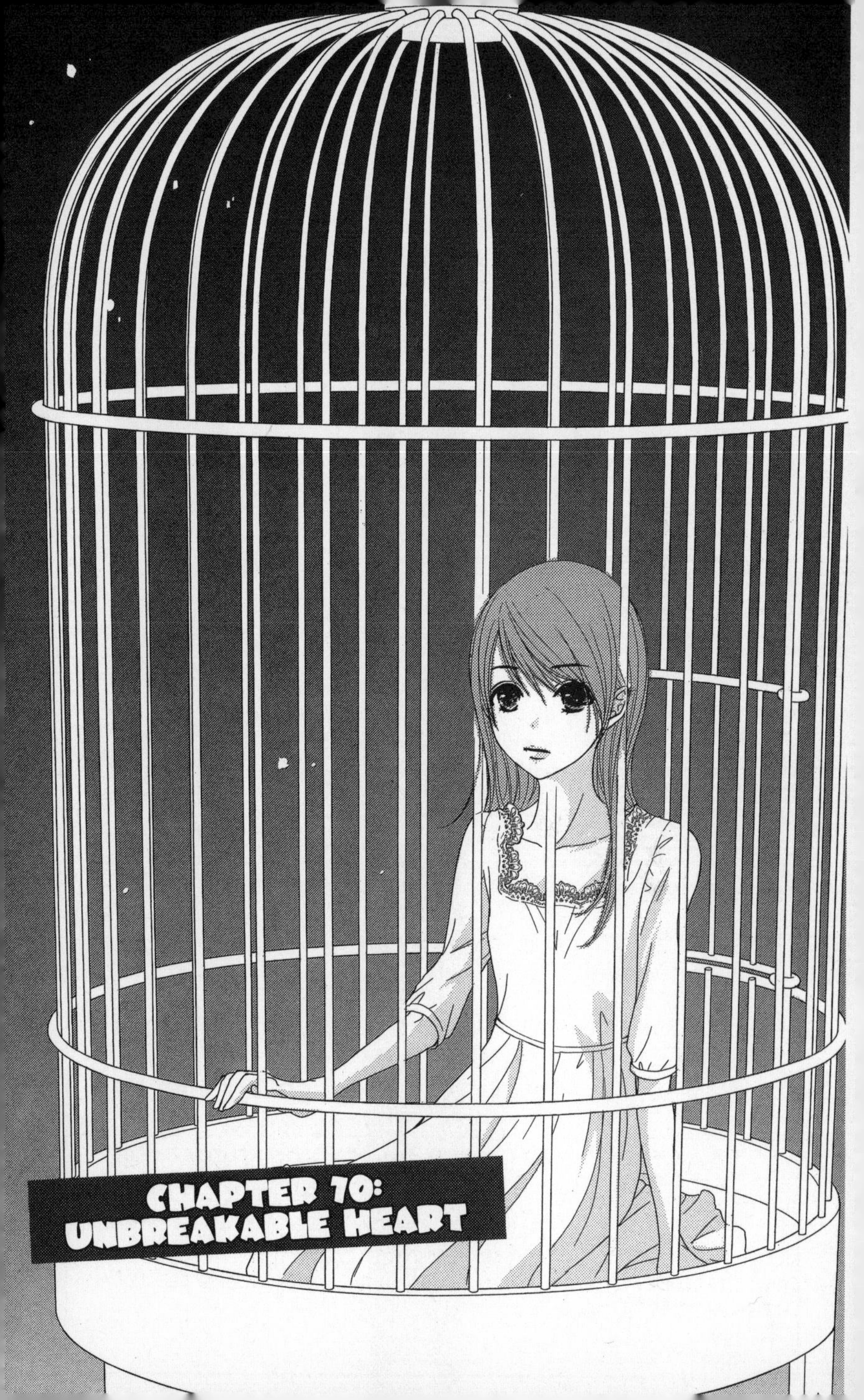
CHAPTER 10:
UNBREAKABLE HEART

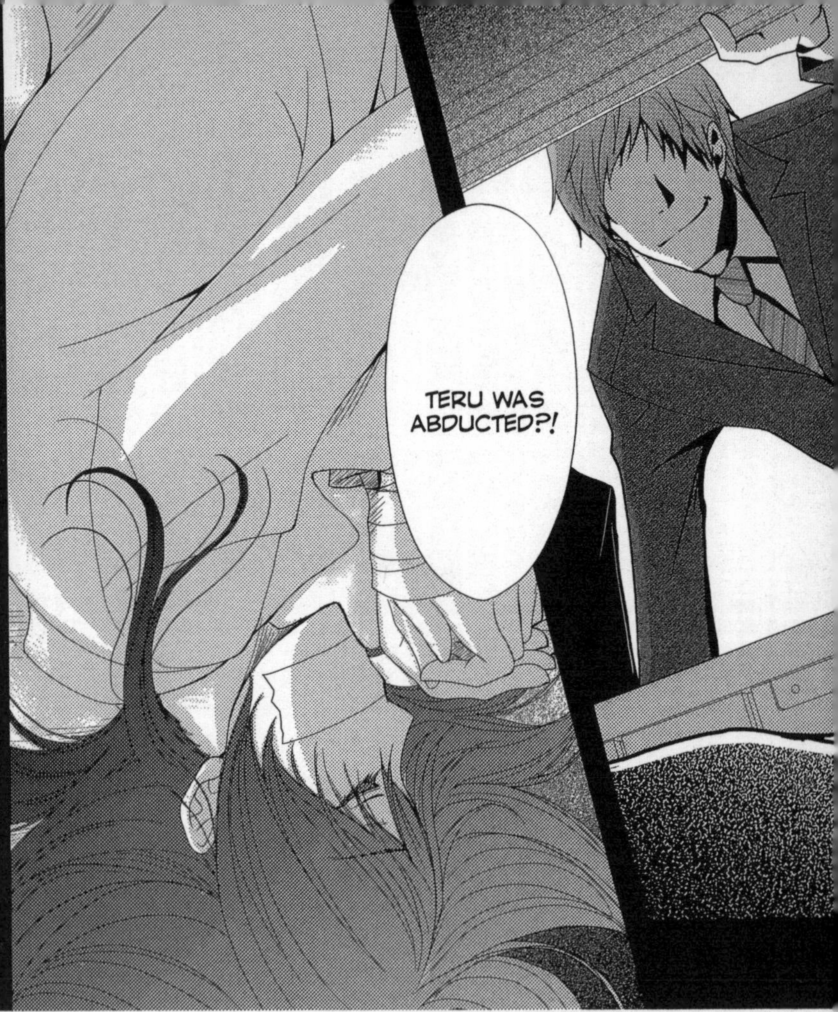
TERU WAS ABDUCTED?!

HI THERE, EVERYONE!! IT'S KYOUSUKE MOTOMI. *DENGEKI DAISY* HAS REACHED VOLUME 15. THANK YOU VERY MUCH. I OWE IT ALL TO YOU, THE READERS. THIS VOLUME IS JUST AS IMPORTANT AS ALL THE ONES BEFORE IT, SO I HOPE YOU'LL ENJOY IT JUST AS MUCH.

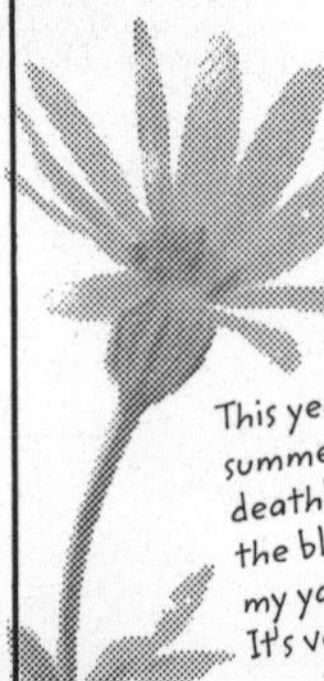

This year's summer was deathly hot, but the blue daisy in my yard survived. It's very strong!!!

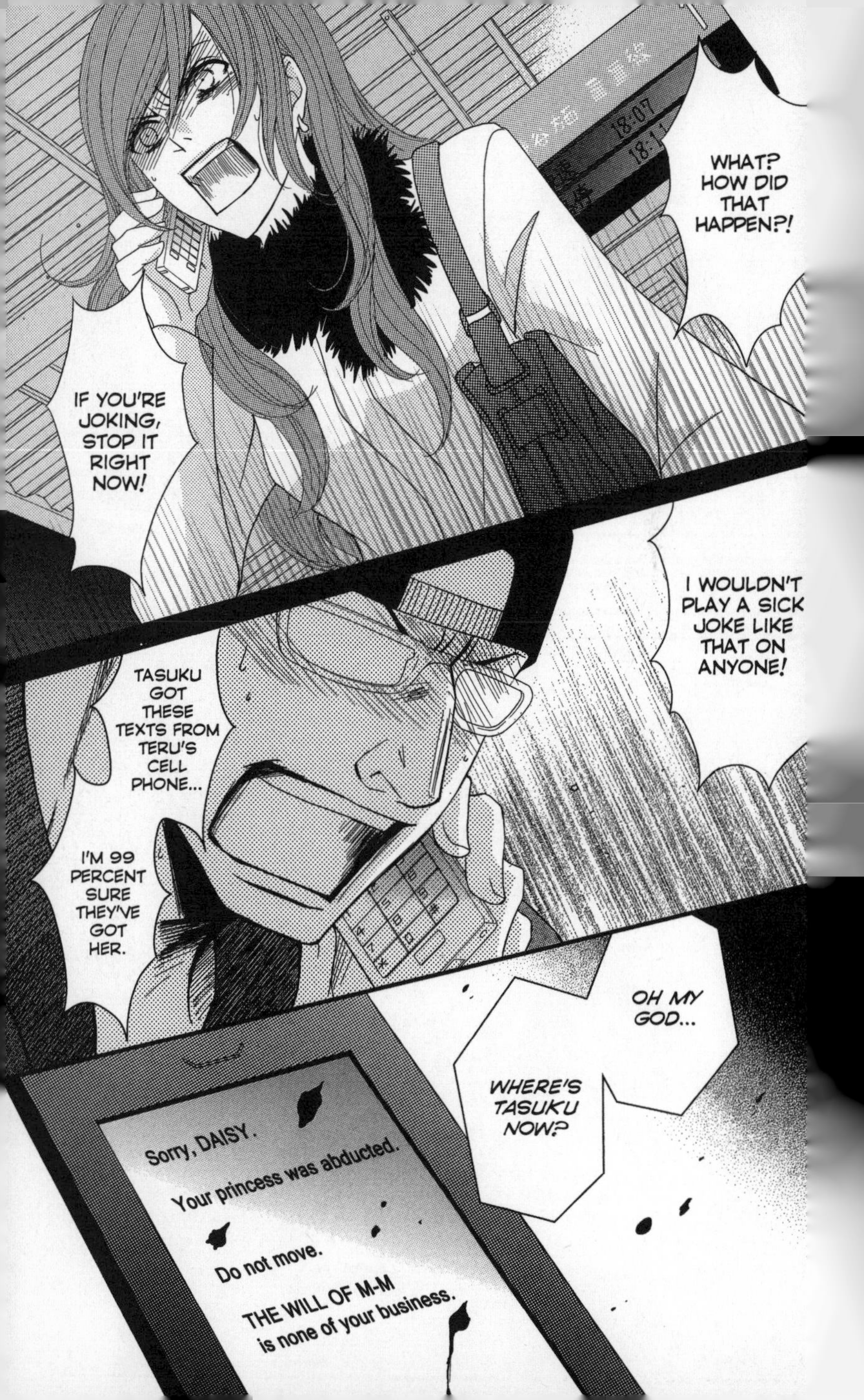
WHAT? HOW DID THAT HAPPEN?!
IF YOU'RE JOKING, STOP IT RIGHT NOW!
I WOULDN'T PLAY A SICK JOKE LIKE THAT ON ANYONE!
TASUKU GOT THESE TEXTS FROM TERU'S CELL PHONE...
I'M 99 PERCENT SURE THEY'VE GOT HER.
OH MY GOD...
WHERE'S TASUKU NOW?
Sorry, DAISY.
Your princess was abducted.
Do not move.
THE WILL OF M-M is none of your business.

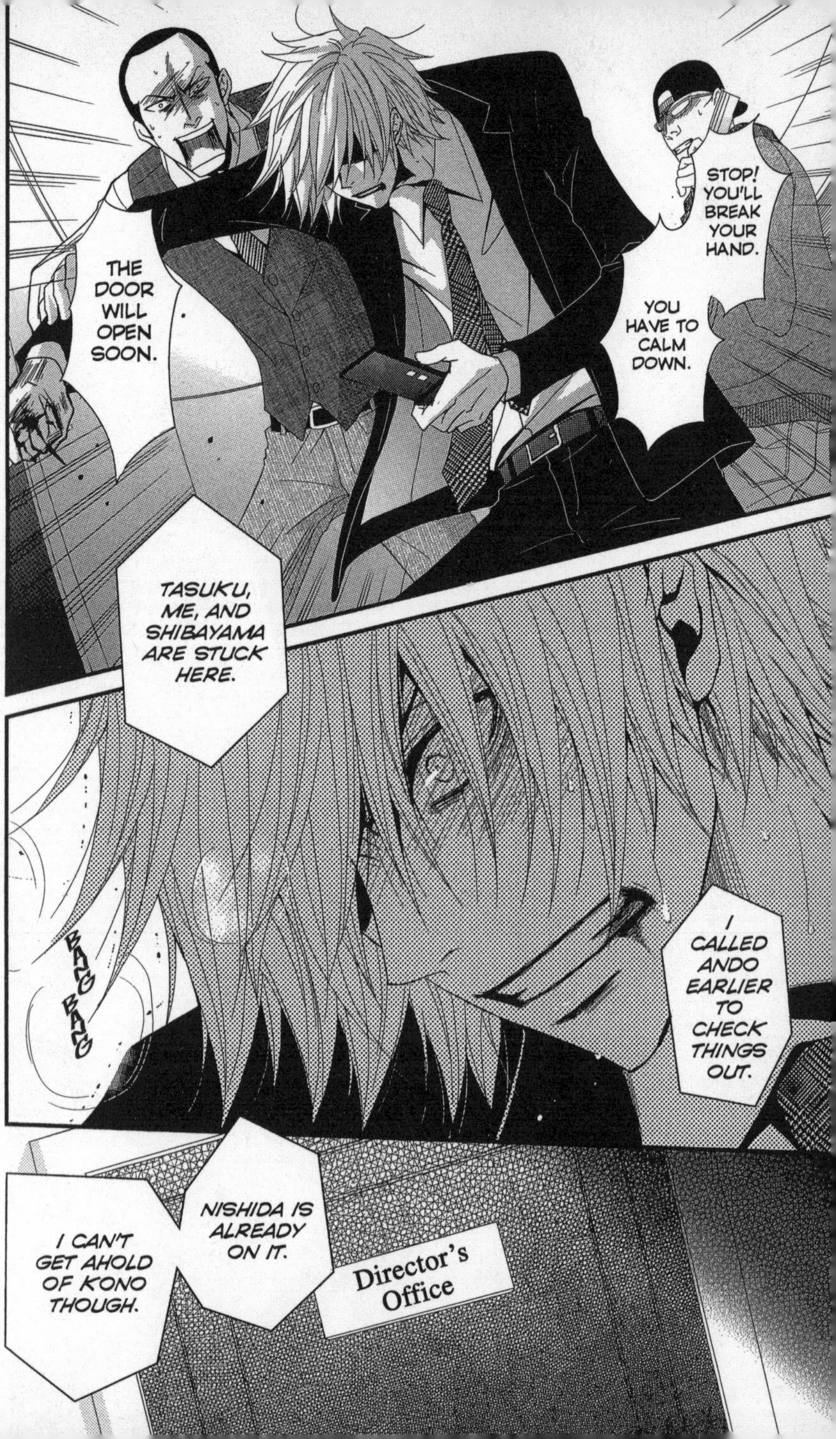
STOP! YOU'LL BREAK YOUR HAND.
YOU HAVE TO CALM DOWN.
THE DOOR WILL OPEN SOON.
TASUKU, ME, AND SHIBAYAMA ARE STUCK HERE.
I CALLED ANDO EARLIER TO CHECK THINGS OUT.
BANG BANG
NISHIDA IS ALREADY ON IT.
Director's Office
I CAN'T GET AHOLD OF KONO THOUGH.

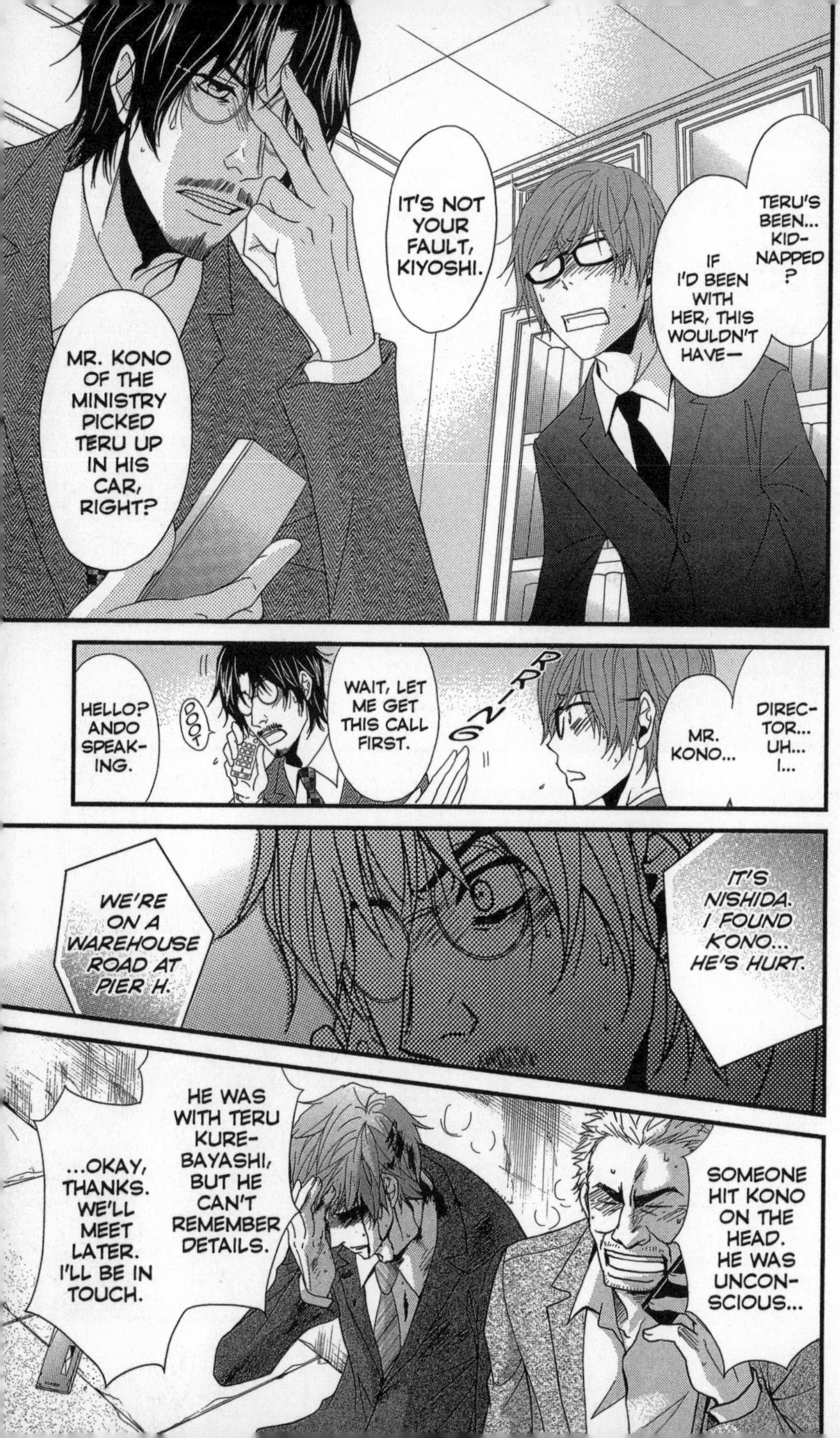
TERU'S BEEN... KID-NAPPED?
IF I'D BEEN WITH HER, THIS WOULDN'T HAVE—
IT'S NOT YOUR FAULT, KIYOSHI.
MR. KONO OF THE MINISTRY PICKED TERU UP IN HIS CAR, RIGHT?
DIRECTOR... UH... I...
MR. KONO...
RRING
WAIT, LET ME GET THIS CALL FIRST.
DOOT
HELLO? ANDO SPEAKING.
IT'S NISHIDA. I FOUND KONO... HE'S HURT.
WE'RE ON A WAREHOUSE ROAD AT PIER H.
SOMEONE HIT KONO ON THE HEAD. HE WAS UNCONSCIOUS...
HE WAS WITH TERU KURE-BAYASHI, BUT HE CAN'T REMEMBER DETAILS.
...OKAY, THANKS. WE'LL MEET LATER. I'LL BE IN TOUCH.

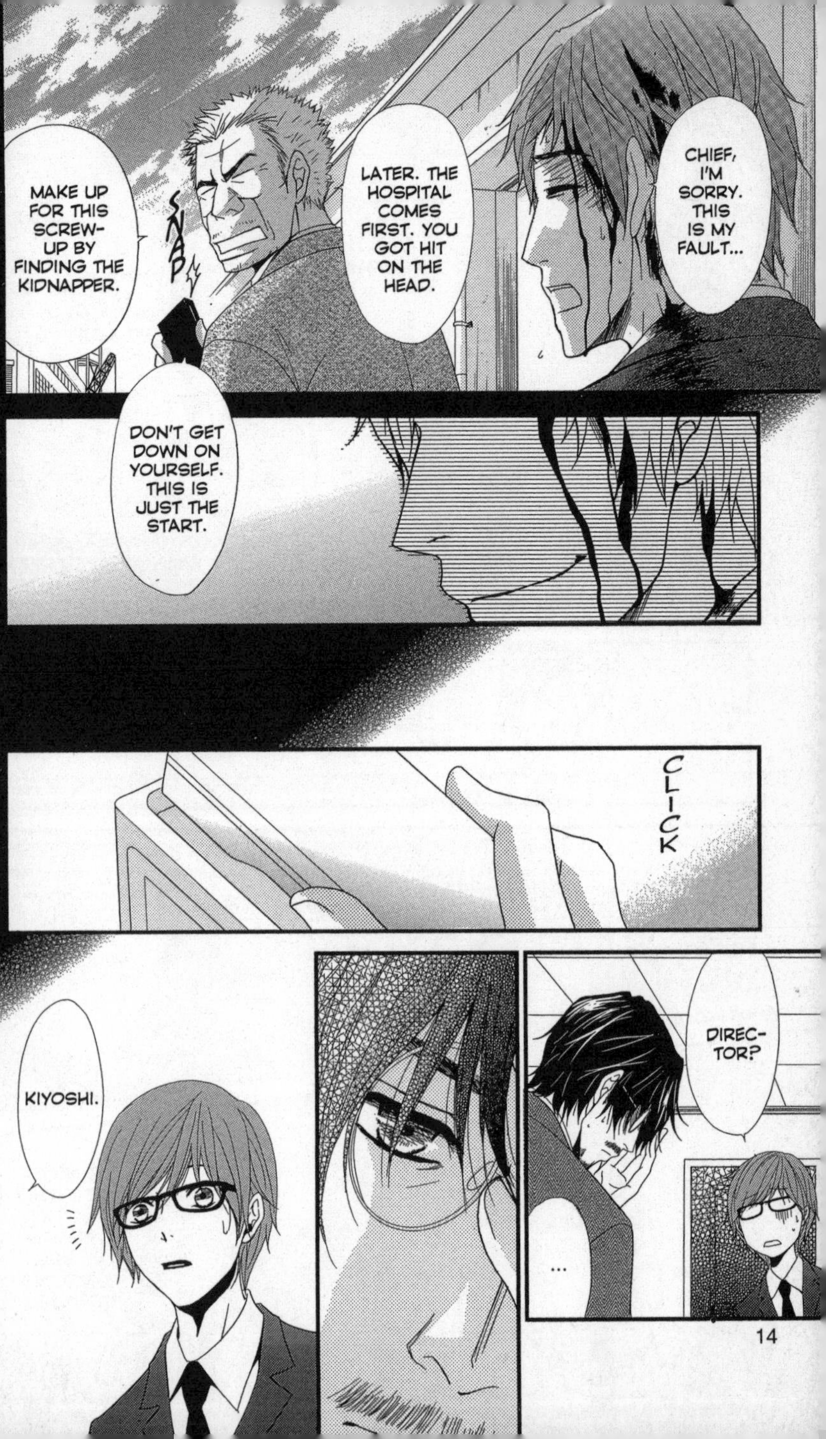
CHIEF, I'M SORRY. THIS IS MY FAULT...
LATER. THE HOSPITAL COMES FIRST. YOU GOT HIT ON THE HEAD.
SNAP
MAKE UP FOR THIS SCREW-UP BY FINDING THE KIDNAPPER.
DON'T GET DOWN ON YOURSELF. THIS IS JUST THE START.
CLICK
DIREC-TOR?
...
KIYOSHI.

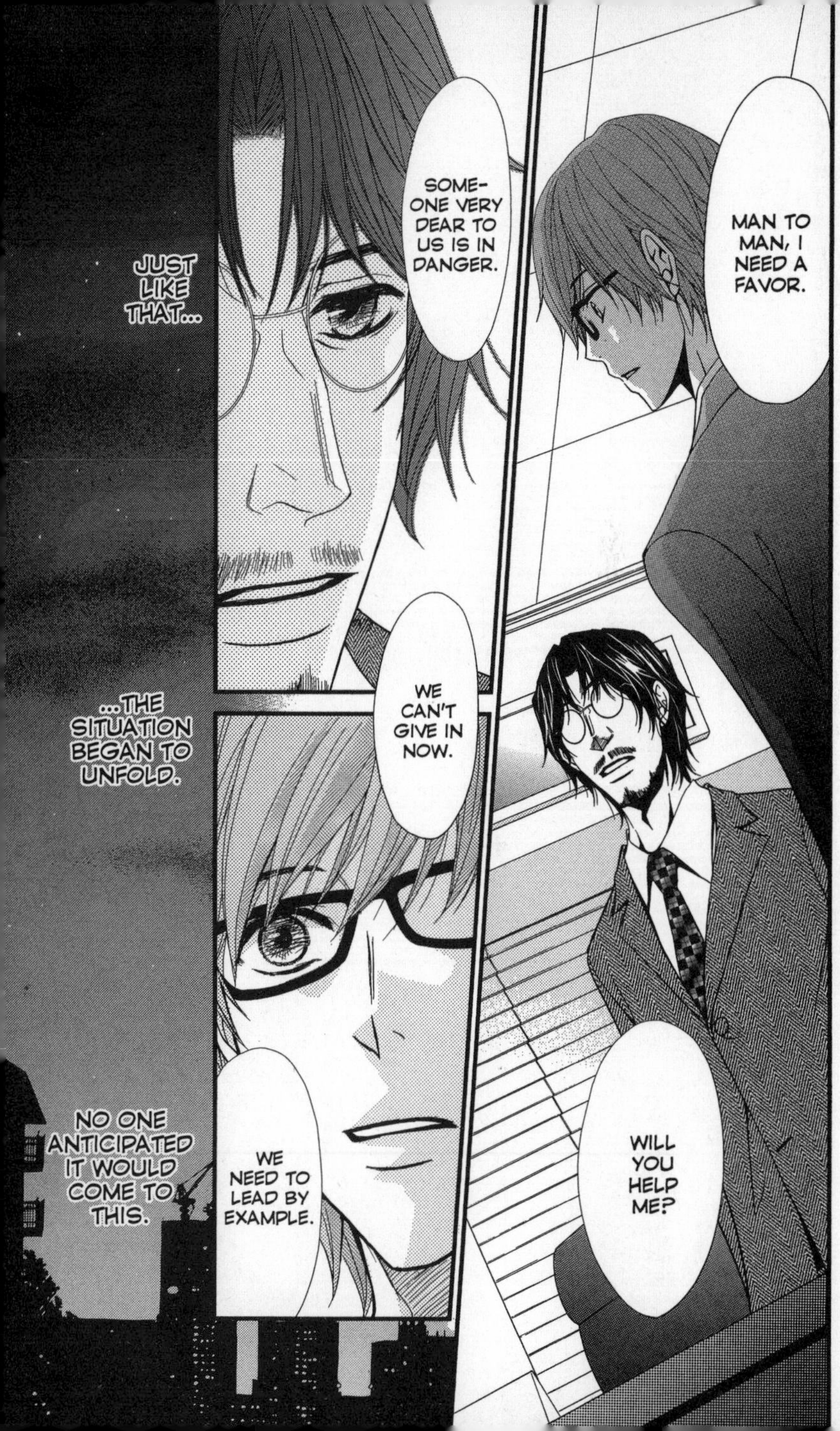
MAN TO MAN, I NEED A FAVOR.
WILL YOU HELP ME?
SOME-ONE VERY DEAR TO US IS IN DANGER.
WE CAN'T GIVE IN NOW.
WE NEED TO LEAD BY EXAMPLE.
JUST LIKE THAT...
...THE SITUATION BEGAN TO UNFOLD.
NO ONE ANTICIPATED IT WOULD COME TO THIS.

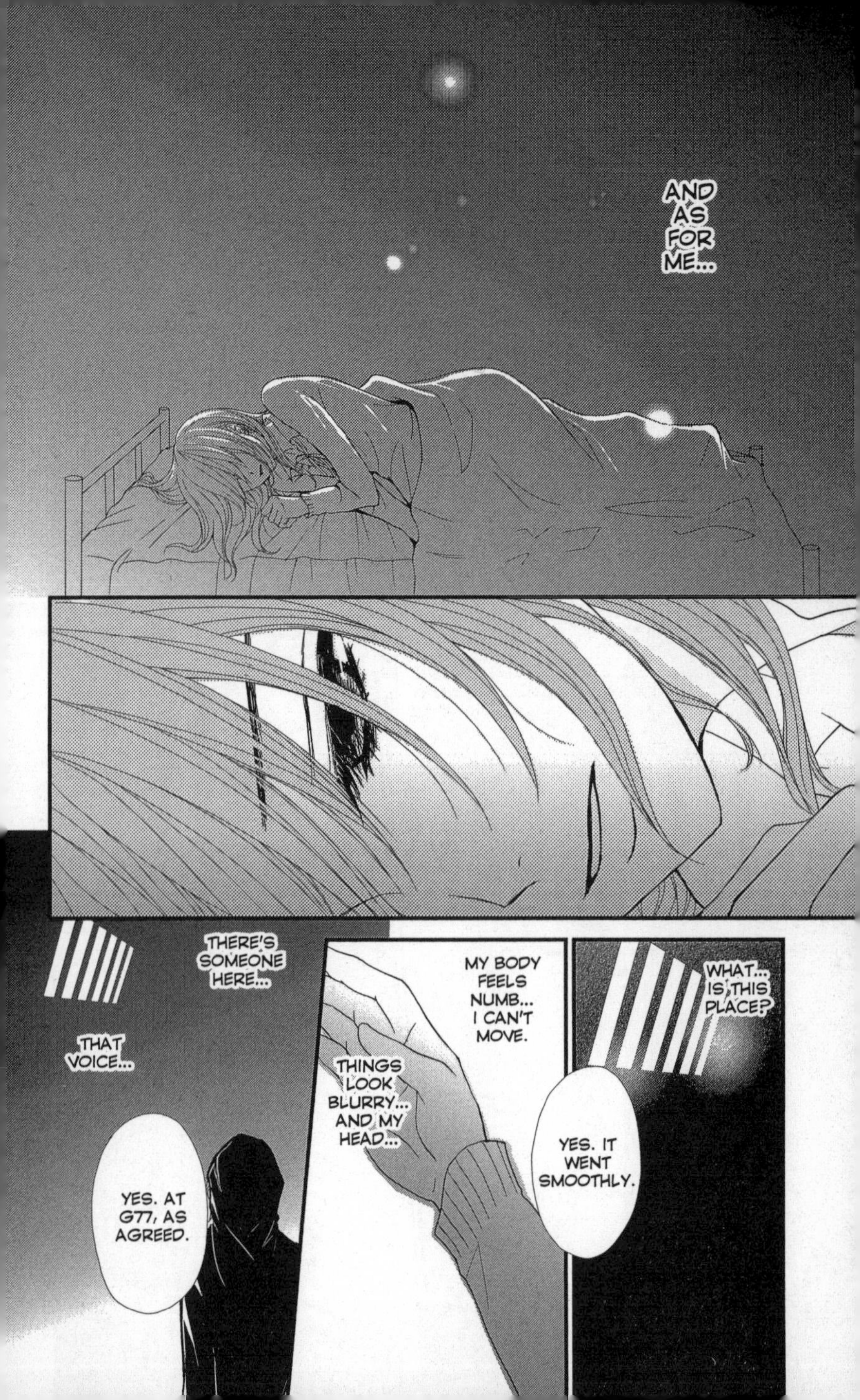
AND AS FOR ME...
WHAT... IS THIS PLACE?
YES. IT WENT SMOOTHLY.
MY BODY FEELS NUMB... I CAN'T MOVE.
THINGS LOOK BLURRY... AND MY HEAD...
THERE'S SOMEONE HERE...
THAT VOICE...
YES. AT G77, AS AGREED.

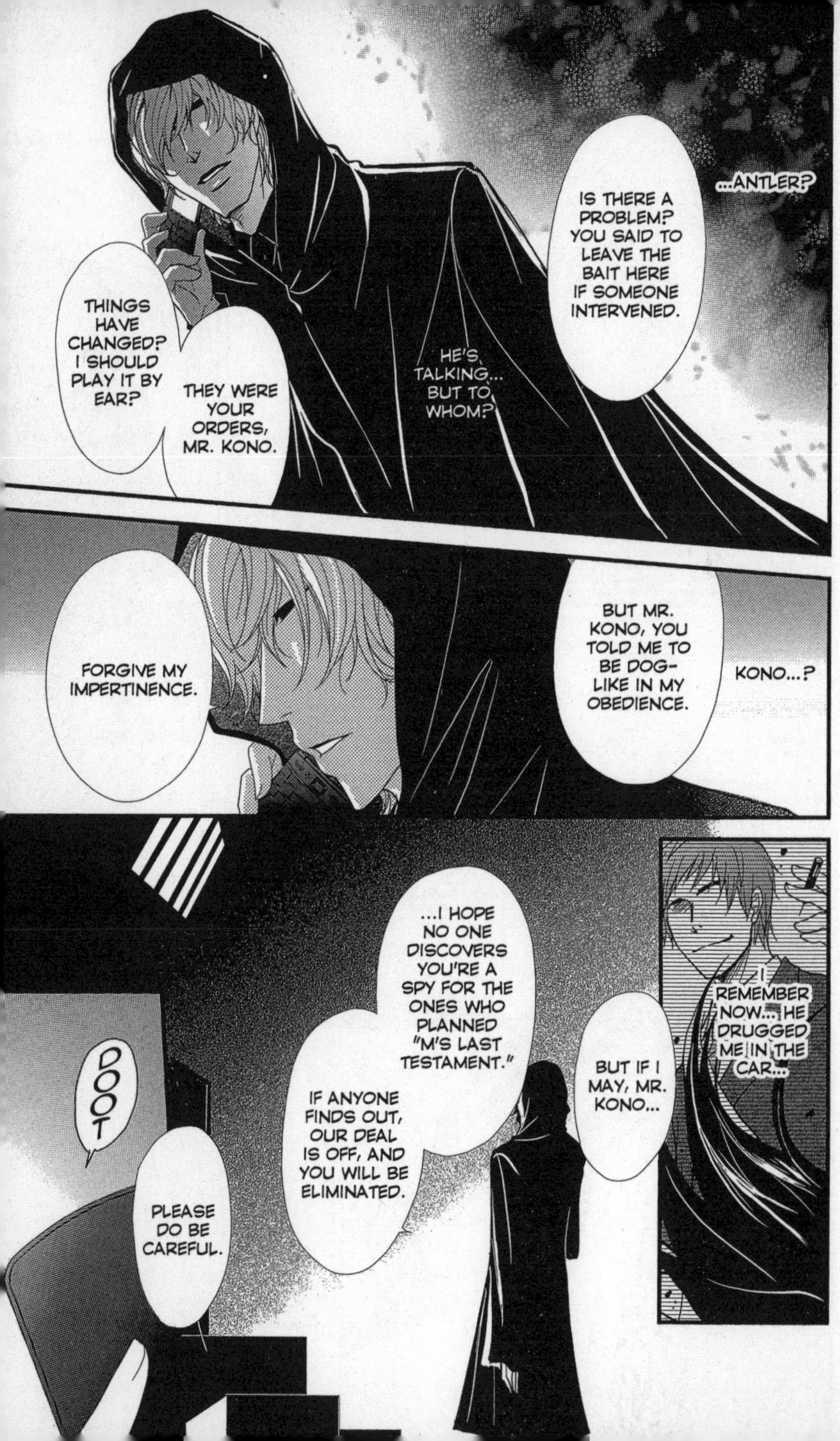
...ANTLER?
IS THERE A PROBLEM? YOU SAID TO LEAVE THE BAIT HERE IF SOMEONE INTERVENED.
HE'S TALKING... BUT TO WHOM?
THEY WERE YOUR ORDERS, MR. KONO.
THINGS HAVE CHANGED? I SHOULD PLAY IT BY EAR?
KONO...?
BUT MR. KONO, YOU TOLD ME TO BE DOG-LIKE IN MY OBEDIENCE.
FORGIVE MY IMPERTINENCE.
I REMEMBER NOW... HE DRUGGED ME IN THE CAR...
BUT IF I MAY, MR. KONO...
...I HOPE NO ONE DISCOVERS YOU'RE A SPY FOR THE ONES WHO PLANNED "M'S LAST TESTAMENT."
IF ANYONE FINDS OUT, OUR DEAL IS OFF, AND YOU WILL BE ELIMINATED.
PLEASE DO BE CAREFUL.
DOOT

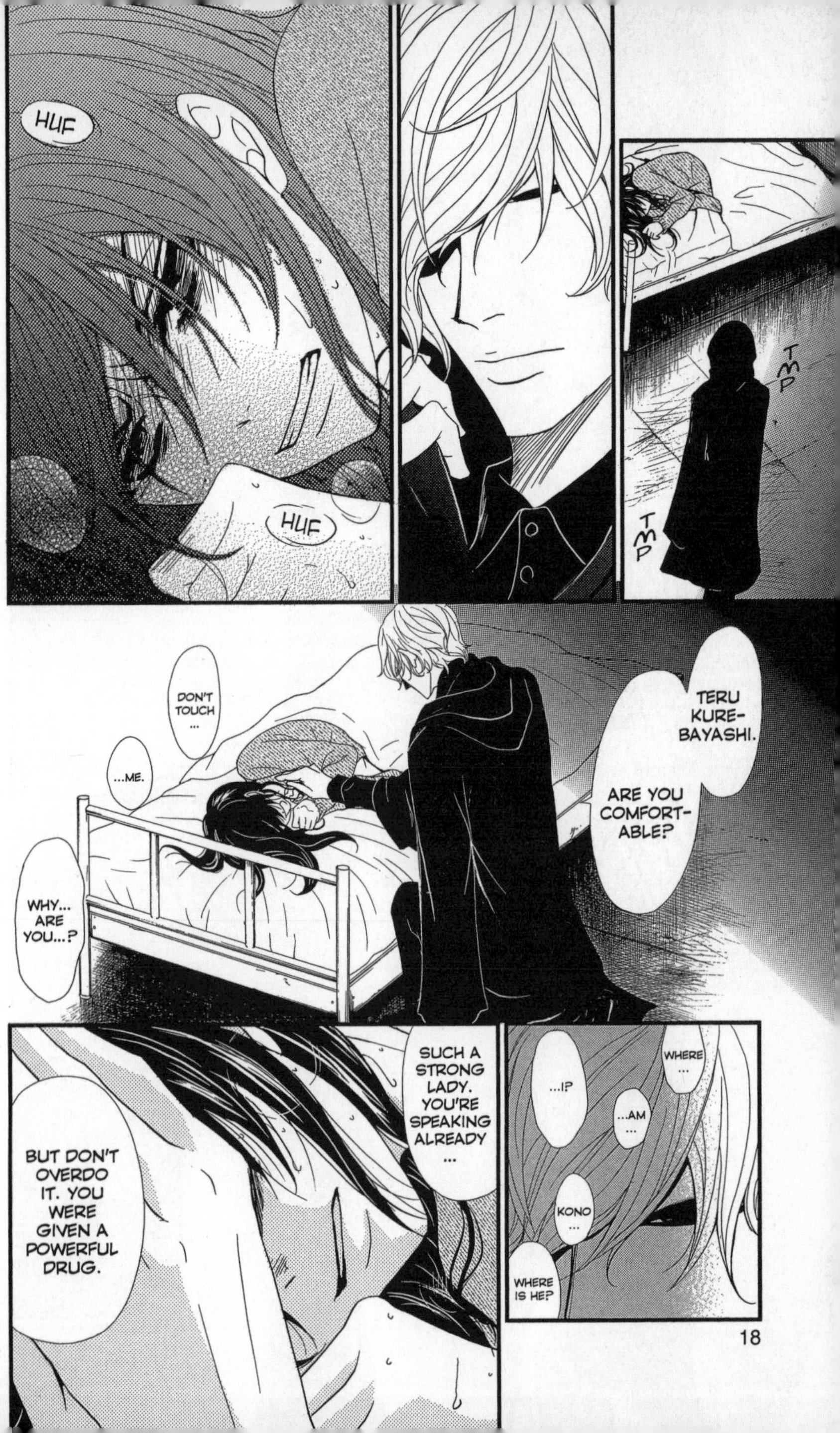
TMP
TMP
HUF
HUF
TERU KURE-BAYASHI.
ARE YOU COMFORT-ABLE?
DON'T TOUCH...
...ME.
WHY... ARE YOU...?
WHERE...
...AM...
...!?
KONO...
WHERE IS HE?
SUCH A STRONG LADY. YOU'RE SPEAKING ALREADY...
BUT DON'T OVERDO IT. YOU WERE GIVEN A POWERFUL DRUG.

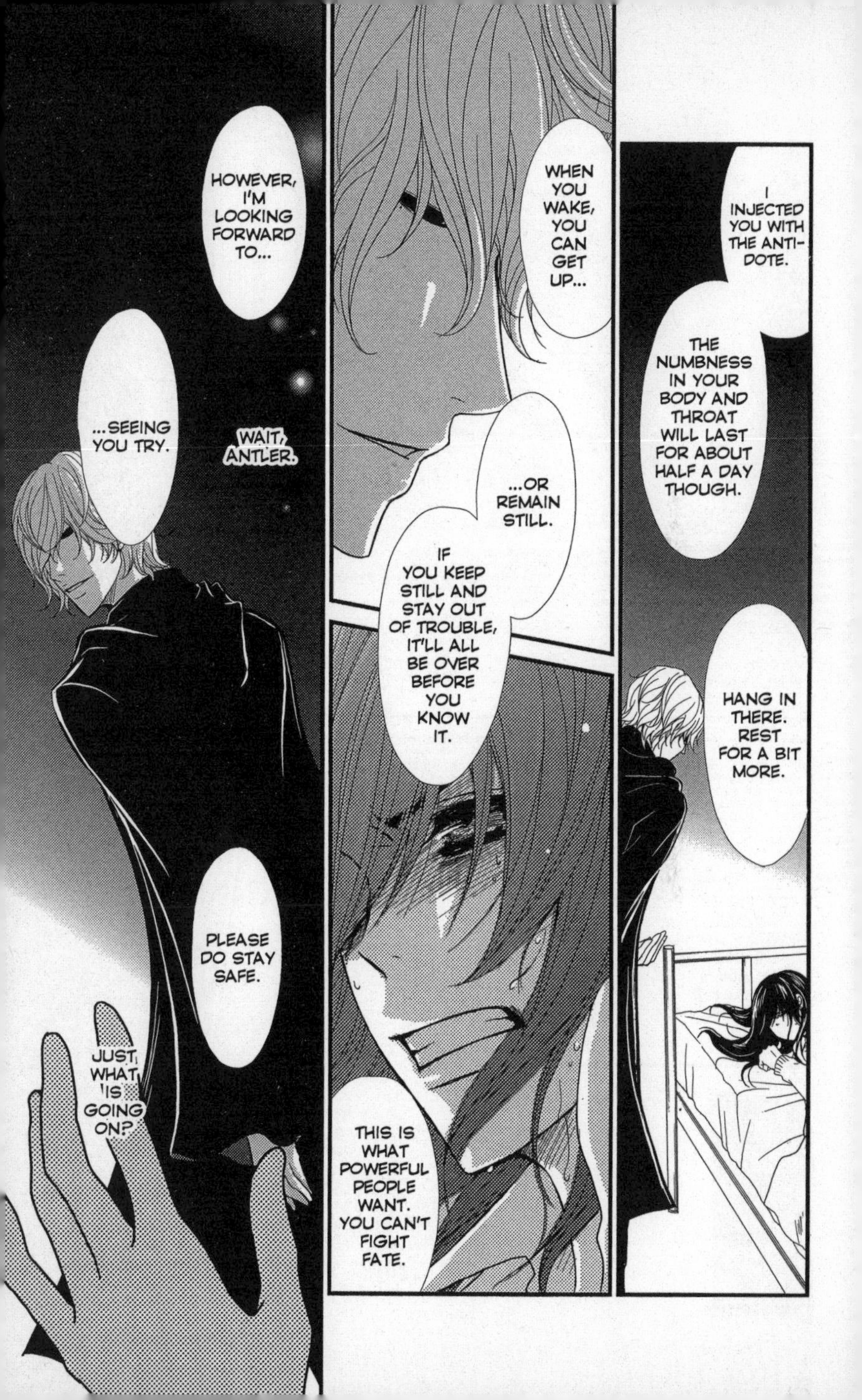
I INJECTED YOU WITH THE ANTI-DOTE.
THE NUMBNESS IN YOUR BODY AND THROAT WILL LAST FOR ABOUT HALF A DAY THOUGH.
HANG IN THERE. REST FOR A BIT MORE.
WHEN YOU WAKE, YOU CAN GET UP...
...OR REMAIN STILL.
IF YOU KEEP STILL AND STAY OUT OF TROUBLE, IT'LL ALL BE OVER BEFORE YOU KNOW IT.
THIS IS WHAT POWERFUL PEOPLE WANT. YOU CAN'T FIGHT FATE.
HOWEVER, I'M LOOKING FORWARD TO...
...SEEING YOU TRY.
WAIT, ANTLER.
PLEASE DO STAY SAFE.
JUST WHAT IS GOING ON?

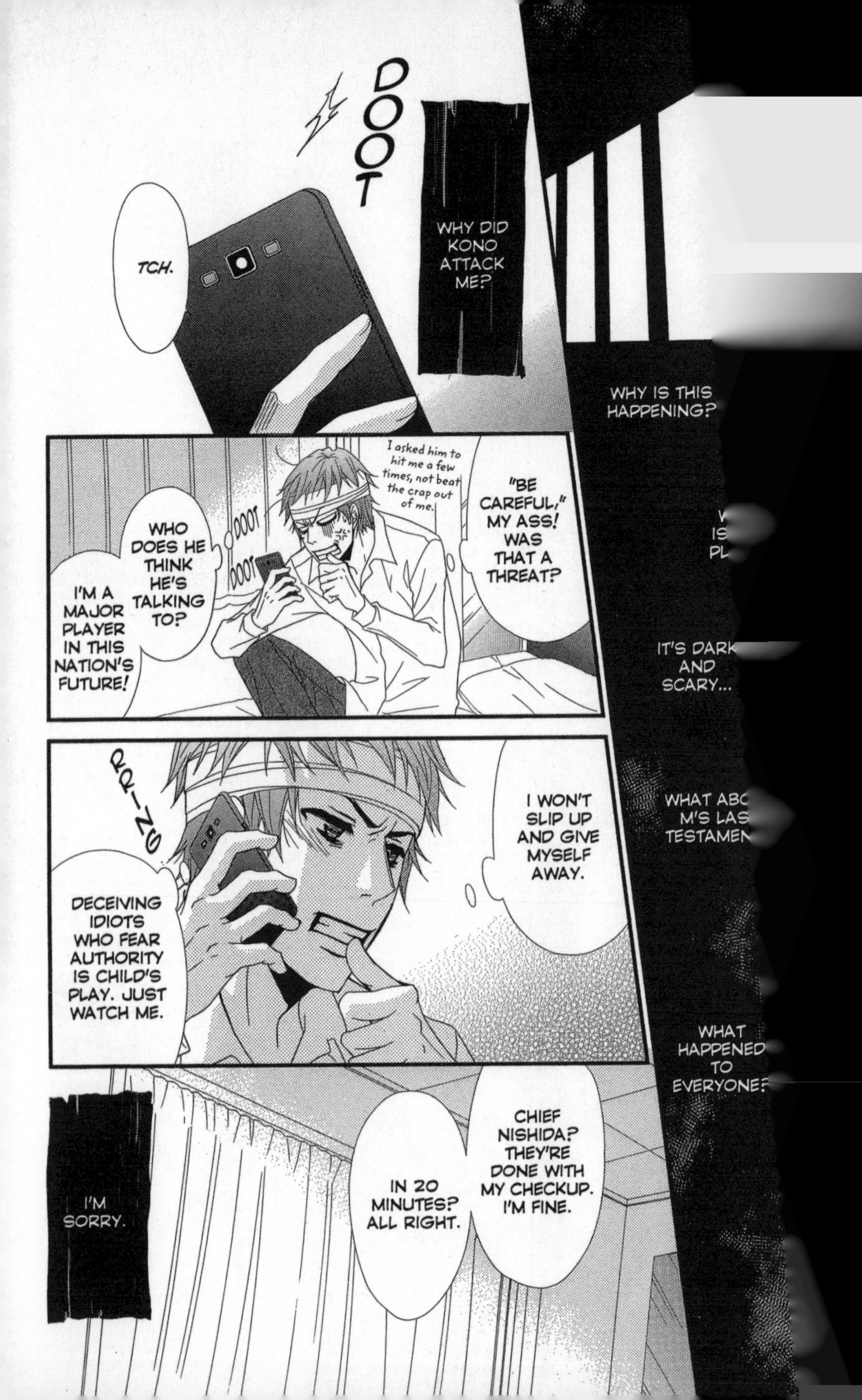
WHY IS THIS HAPPENING?
IT'S DARK AND SCARY...
WHAT ABC M'S LAS TESTAMEN
WHAT HAPPENED TO EVERYONE?
DOOT DOOT
WHY DID KONO ATTACK ME?
TCH.
"BE CAREFUL," MY ASS! WAS THAT A THREAT?
I asked him to hit me a few times, not beat the crap out of me.
DOOT DOOT
WHO DOES HE THINK HE'S TALKING TO?
I'M A MAJOR PLAYER IN THIS NATION'S FUTURE!
RR-ZU
I WON'T SLIP UP AND GIVE MYSELF AWAY.
DECEIVING IDIOTS WHO FEAR AUTHORITY IS CHILD'S PLAY. JUST WATCH ME.
CHIEF NISHIDA? THEY'RE DONE WITH MY CHECKUP. I'M FINE.
IN 20 MINUTES? ALL RIGHT.
I'M SORRY.

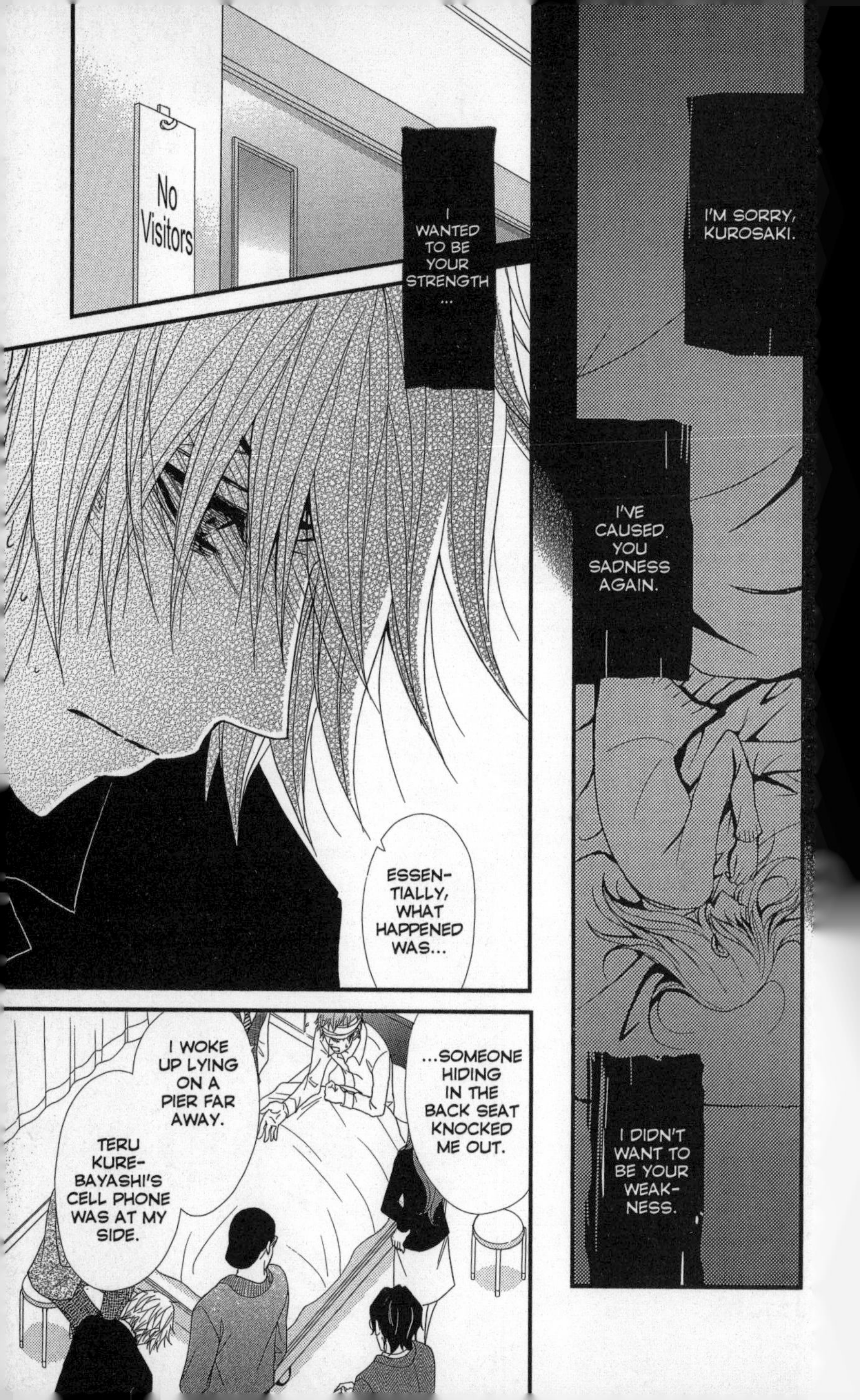
I'M SORRY, KUROSAKI.
I'VE CAUSED YOU SADNESS AGAIN.
I DIDN'T WANT TO BE YOUR WEAK-NESS.
No Visitors
I WANTED TO BE YOUR STRENGTH...
ESSEN-TIALLY, WHAT HAPPENED WAS...
...SOMEONE HIDING IN THE BACK SEAT KNOCKED ME OUT.
I WOKE UP LYING ON A PIER FAR AWAY.
TERU KURE-BAYASHI'S CELL PHONE WAS AT MY SIDE.

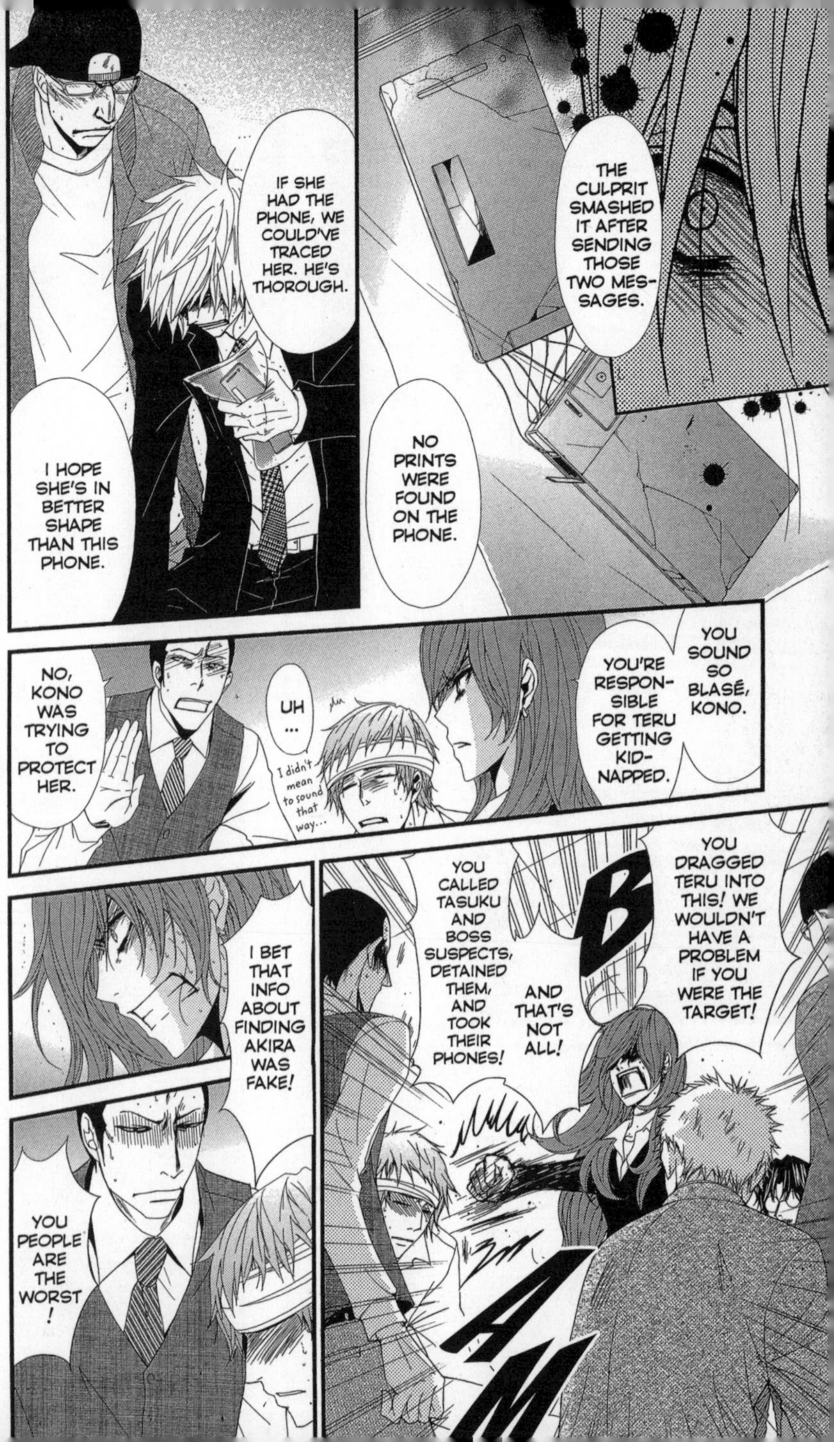
THE CULPRIT SMASHED IT AFTER SENDING THOSE TWO MESSAGES.
NO PRINTS WERE FOUND ON THE PHONE.
IF SHE HAD THE PHONE, WE COULD'VE TRACED HER. HE'S THOROUGH.
I HOPE SHE'S IN BETTER SHAPE THAN THIS PHONE.
YOU SOUND SO BLASÉ, KONO.
YOU'RE RESPONSIBLE FOR TERU GETTING KIDNAPPED.
UH ...
I didn't mean to sound that way...
NO, KONO WAS TRYING TO PROTECT HER.
YOU DRAGGED TERU INTO THIS! WE WOULDN'T HAVE A PROBLEM IF YOU WERE THE TARGET!
YOU CALLED TASUKU AND BOSS SUSPECTS, DETAINED THEM, AND TOOK THEIR PHONES!
AND THAT'S NOT ALL!
BAM
I BET THAT INFO ABOUT FINDING AKIRA WAS FAKE!
YOU PEOPLE ARE THE WORST!

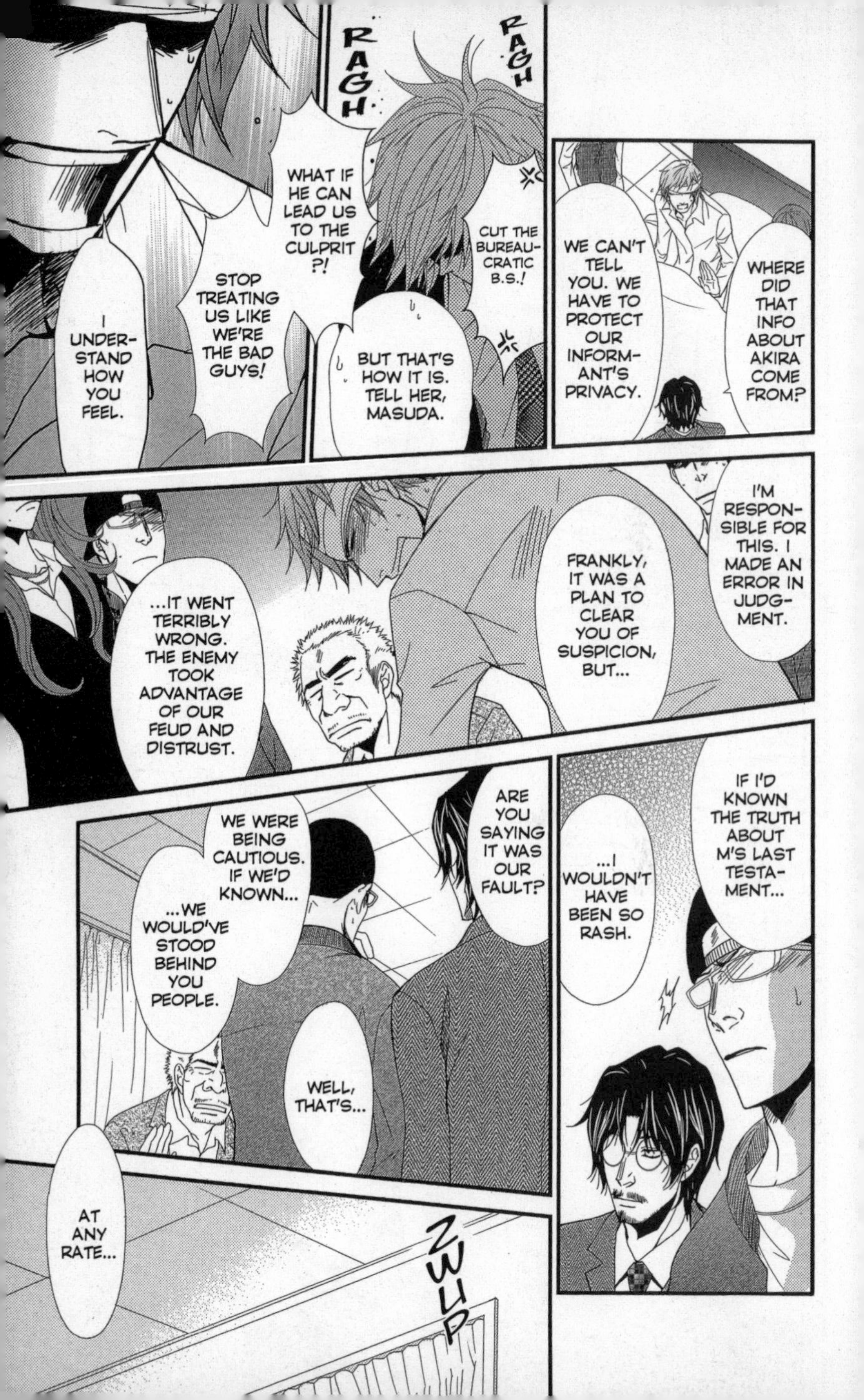
RAGH
RAGH
WHERE DID THAT INFO ABOUT AKIRA COME FROM?
WE CAN'T TELL YOU. WE HAVE TO PROTECT OUR INFORMANT'S PRIVACY.
CUT THE BUREAUCRATIC B.S.!
WHAT IF HE CAN LEAD US TO THE CULPRIT?!
BUT THAT'S HOW IT IS. TELL HER, MASUDA.
STOP TREATING US LIKE WE'RE THE BAD GUYS!
I UNDERSTAND HOW YOU FEEL.
I'M RESPONSIBLE FOR THIS. I MADE AN ERROR IN JUDGMENT.
FRANKLY, IT WAS A PLAN TO CLEAR YOU OF SUSPICION, BUT...
...IT WENT TERRIBLY WRONG. THE ENEMY TOOK ADVANTAGE OF OUR FEUD AND DISTRUST.
IF I'D KNOWN THE TRUTH ABOUT M'S LAST TESTAMENT...
...I WOULDN'T HAVE BEEN SO RASH.
ARE YOU SAYING IT WAS OUR FAULT?
WE WERE BEING CAUTIOUS. IF WE'D KNOWN...
...WE WOULD'VE STOOD BEHIND YOU PEOPLE.
WELL, THAT'S...
ZWUP
AT ANY RATE...

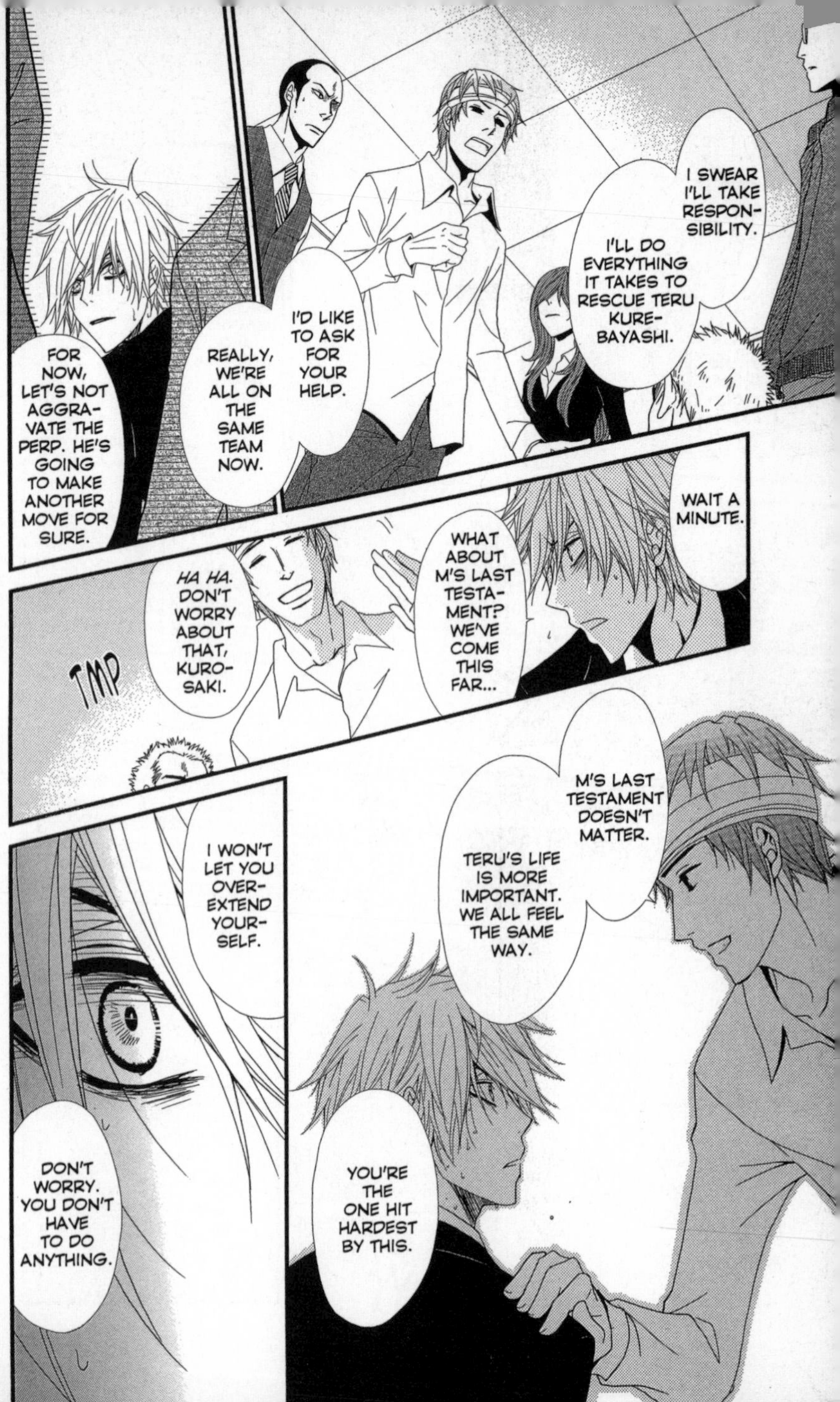

I SWEAR I'LL TAKE RESPONSIBILITY.
I'LL DO EVERYTHING IT TAKES TO RESCUE TERU KUREBAYASHI.
I'D LIKE TO ASK FOR YOUR HELP.
REALLY, WE'RE ALL ON THE SAME TEAM NOW.
FOR NOW, LET'S NOT AGGRAVATE THE PERP. HE'S GOING TO MAKE ANOTHER MOVE FOR SURE.
WAIT A MINUTE.
WHAT ABOUT M'S LAST TESTAMENT? WE'VE COME THIS FAR...
HA HA. DON'T WORRY ABOUT THAT, KUROSAKI.
TMP
M'S LAST TESTAMENT DOESN'T MATTER.
TERU'S LIFE IS MORE IMPORTANT. WE ALL FEEL THE SAME WAY.
YOU'RE THE ONE HIT HARDEST BY THIS.
I WON'T LET YOU OVEREXTEND YOURSELF.
DON'T WORRY. YOU DON'T HAVE TO DO ANYTHING.

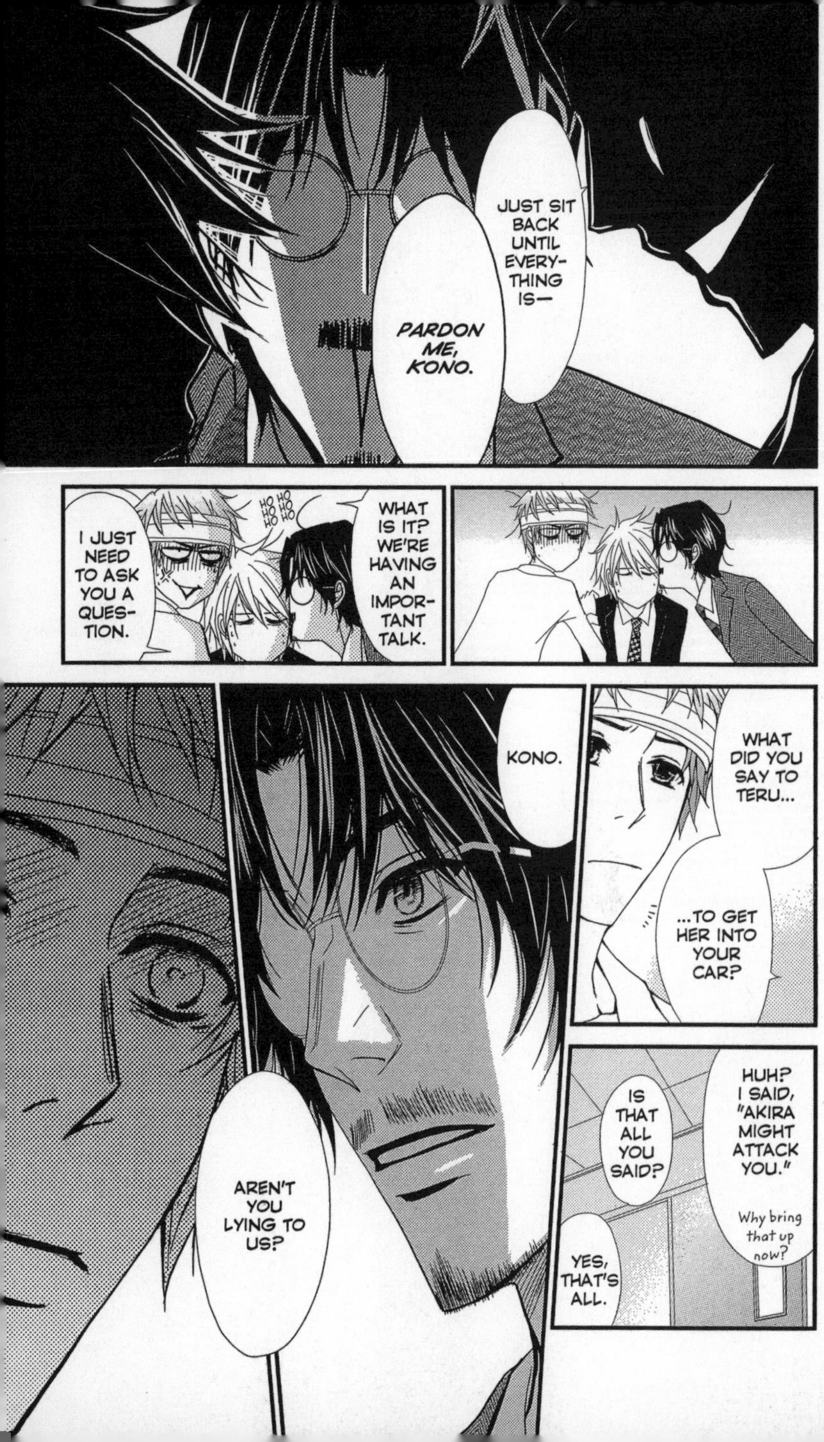
JUST SIT BACK UNTIL EVERYTHING IS—
PARDON ME, KONO.
WHAT IS IT? WE'RE HAVING AN IMPORTANT TALK.
HO HO HO HO HO HO
I JUST NEED TO ASK YOU A QUESTION.
WHAT DID YOU SAY TO TERU...
...TO GET HER INTO YOUR CAR?
HUH? I SAID, "AKIRA MIGHT ATTACK YOU."
Why bring that up now?
IS THAT ALL YOU SAID?
YES, THAT'S ALL.
KONO.
AREN'T YOU LYING TO US?

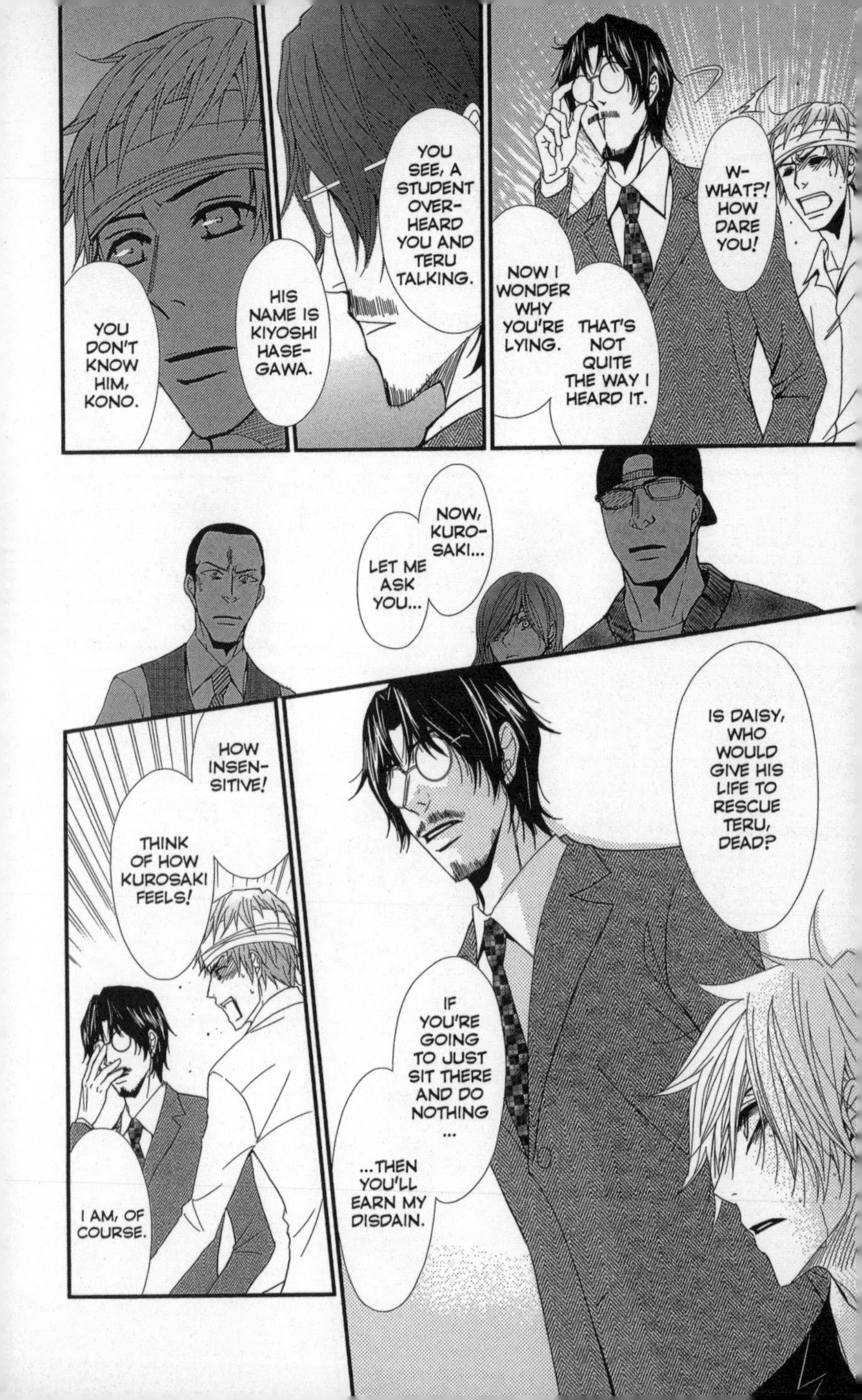
W-WHAT?! HOW DARE YOU!
THAT'S NOT QUITE THE WAY I HEARD IT.
NOW I WONDER WHY YOU'RE LYING.
YOU SEE, A STUDENT OVERHEARD YOU AND TERU TALKING.
HIS NAME IS KIYOSHI HASEGAWA.
YOU DON'T KNOW HIM, KONO.
NOW, KUROSAKI...
LET ME ASK YOU...
IS DAISY, WHO WOULD GIVE HIS LIFE TO RESCUE TERU, DEAD?
IF YOU'RE GOING TO JUST SIT THERE AND DO NOTHING...
...THEN YOU'LL EARN MY DISDAIN.
HOW INSENSITIVE!
THINK OF HOW KUROSAKI FEELS!
I AM, OF COURSE.

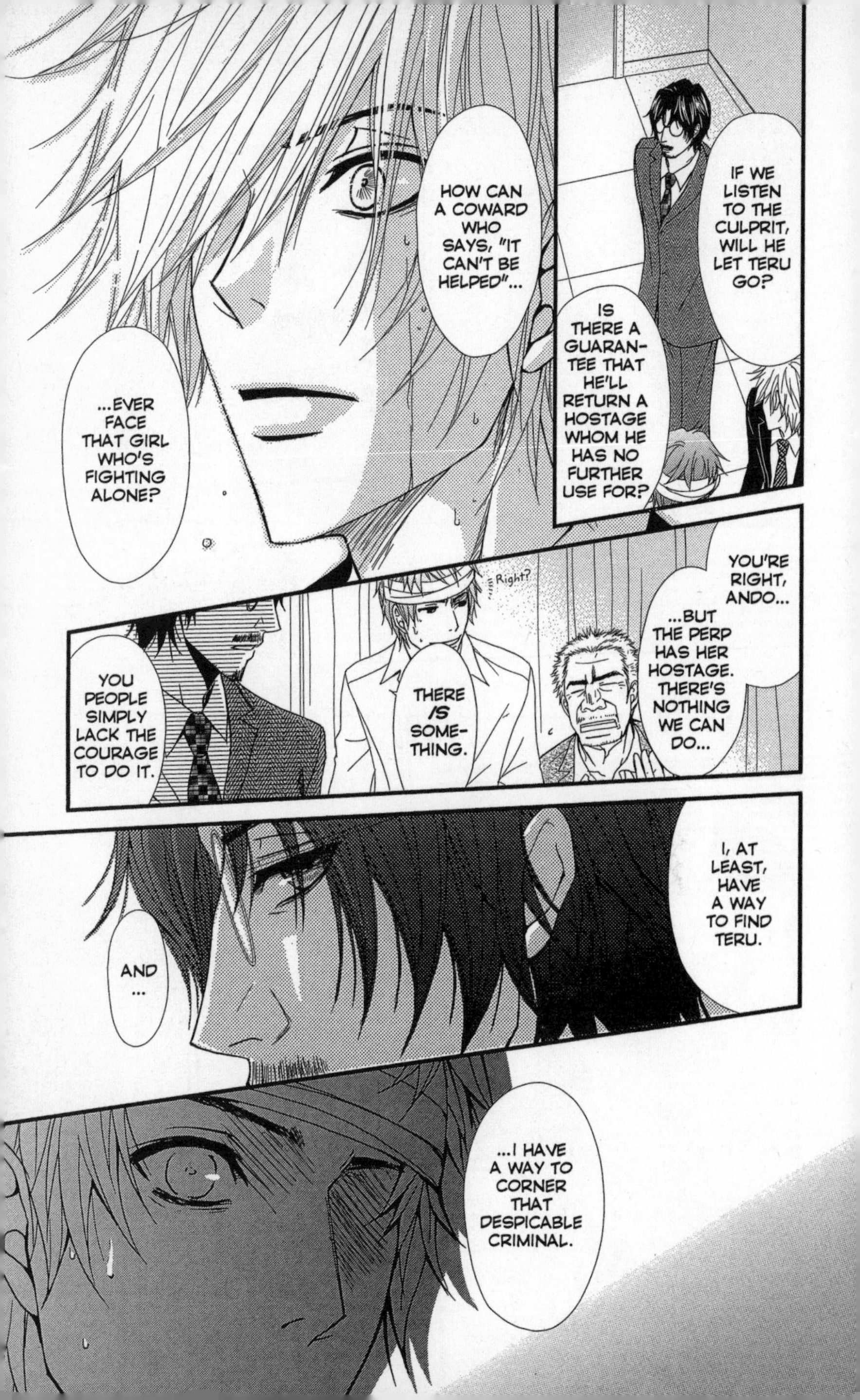
IF WE LISTEN TO THE CULPRIT, WILL HE LET TERU GO?
IS THERE A GUARANTEE THAT HE'LL RETURN A HOSTAGE WHOM HE HAS NO FURTHER USE FOR?
HOW CAN A COWARD WHO SAYS, "IT CAN'T BE HELPED"...
...EVER FACE THAT GIRL WHO'S FIGHTING ALONE?
YOU'RE RIGHT, ANDO...
...BUT THE PERP HAS HER HOSTAGE. THERE'S NOTHING WE CAN DO...
Right?
THERE *IS* SOMETHING.
YOU PEOPLE SIMPLY LACK THE COURAGE TO DO IT.
I, AT LEAST, HAVE A WAY TO FIND TERU.
AND ...
...I HAVE A WAY TO CORNER THAT DESPICABLE CRIMINAL.

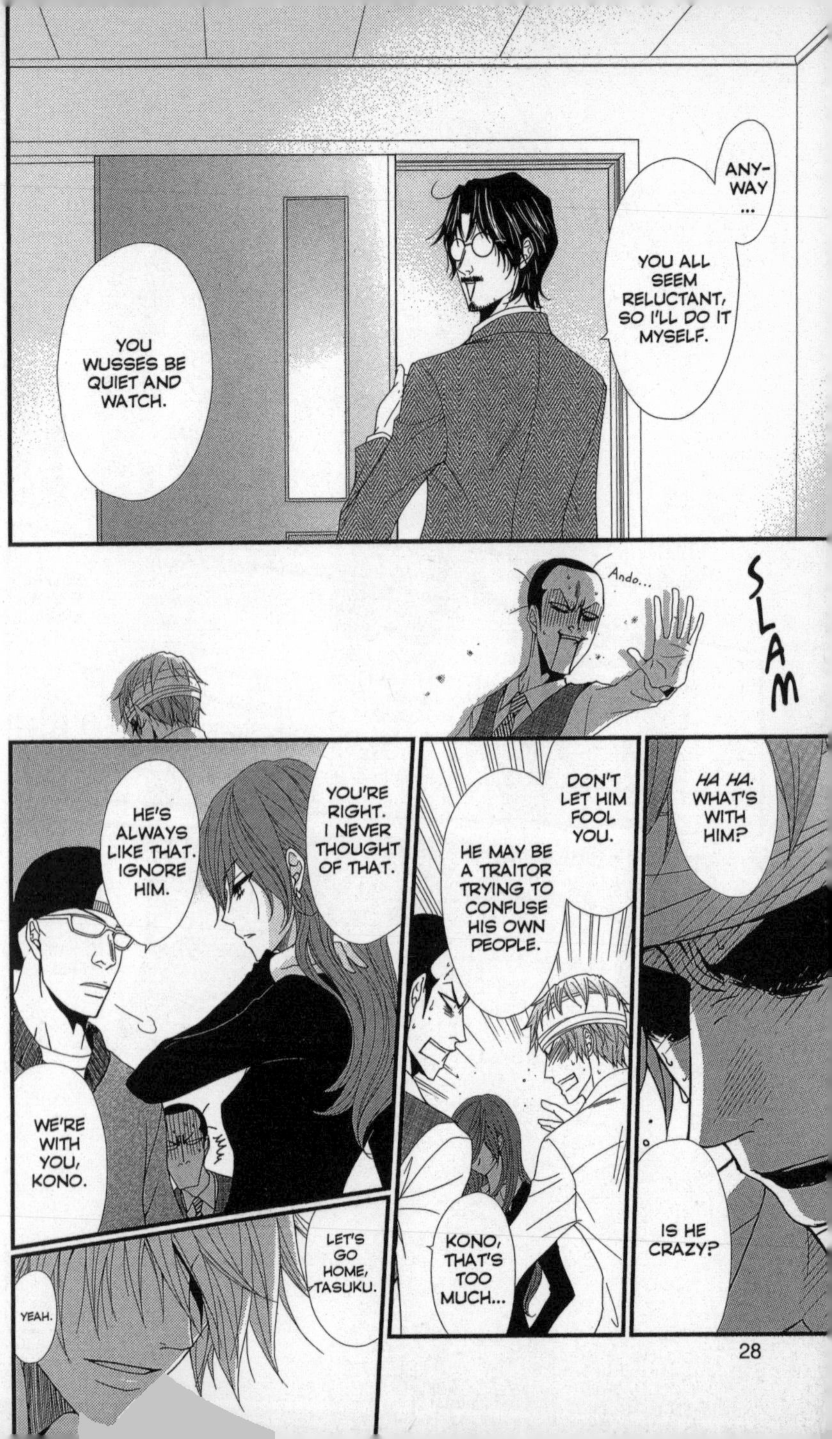
ANY-WAY ...
YOU ALL SEEM RELUCTANT, SO I'LL DO IT MYSELF.
YOU WUSSES BE QUIET AND WATCH.
SLAM
Ando...
HA HA. WHAT'S WITH HIM?
IS HE CRAZY?
DON'T LET HIM FOOL YOU.
HE MAY BE A TRAITOR TRYING TO CONFUSE HIS OWN PEOPLE.
KONO, THAT'S TOO MUCH...
YOU'RE RIGHT. I NEVER THOUGHT OF THAT.
HE'S ALWAYS LIKE THAT. IGNORE HIM.
WE'RE WITH YOU, KONO.
LET'S GO HOME, TASUKU.
YEAH.

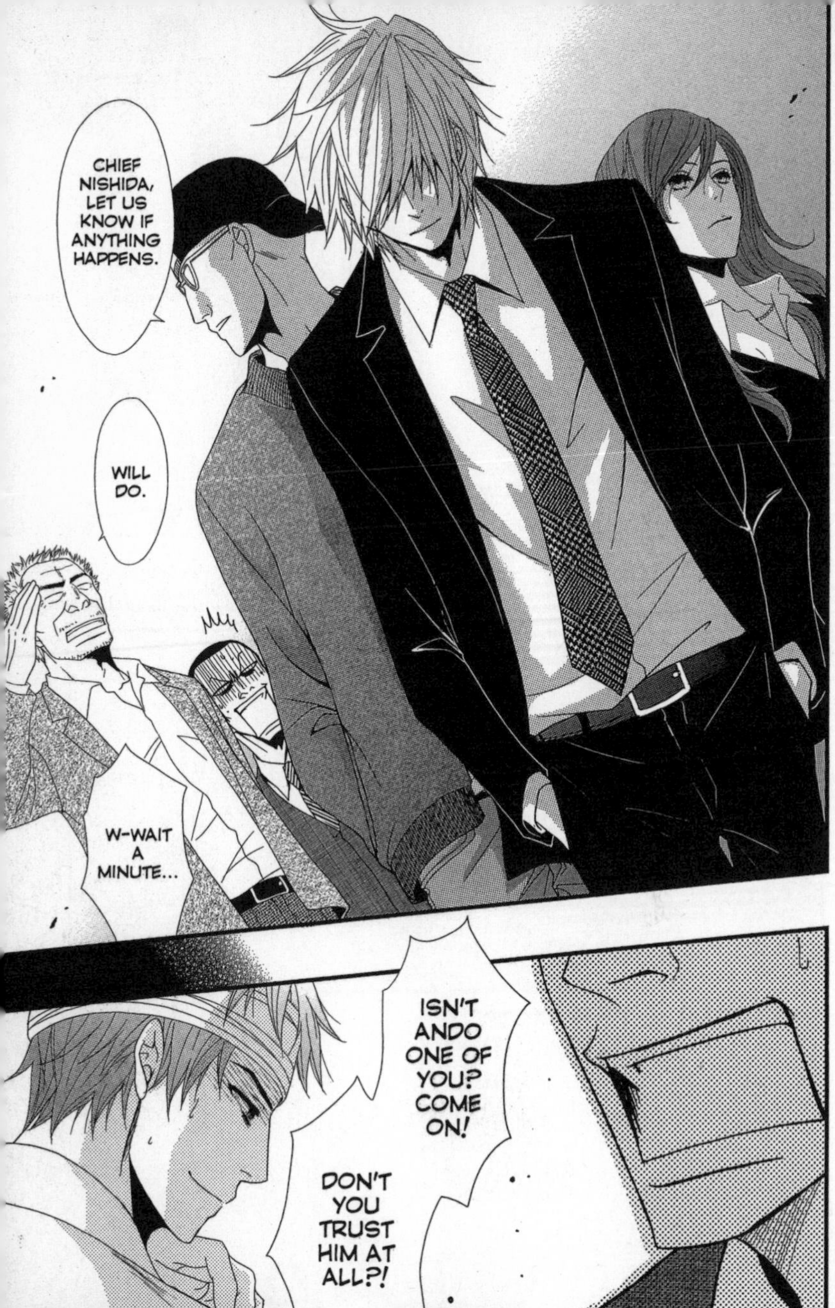
CHIEF NISHIDA, LET US KNOW IF ANYTHING HAPPENS.
WILL DO.
W-WAIT A MINUTE...
ISN'T ANDO ONE OF YOU? COME ON!
DON'T YOU TRUST HIM AT ALL?!

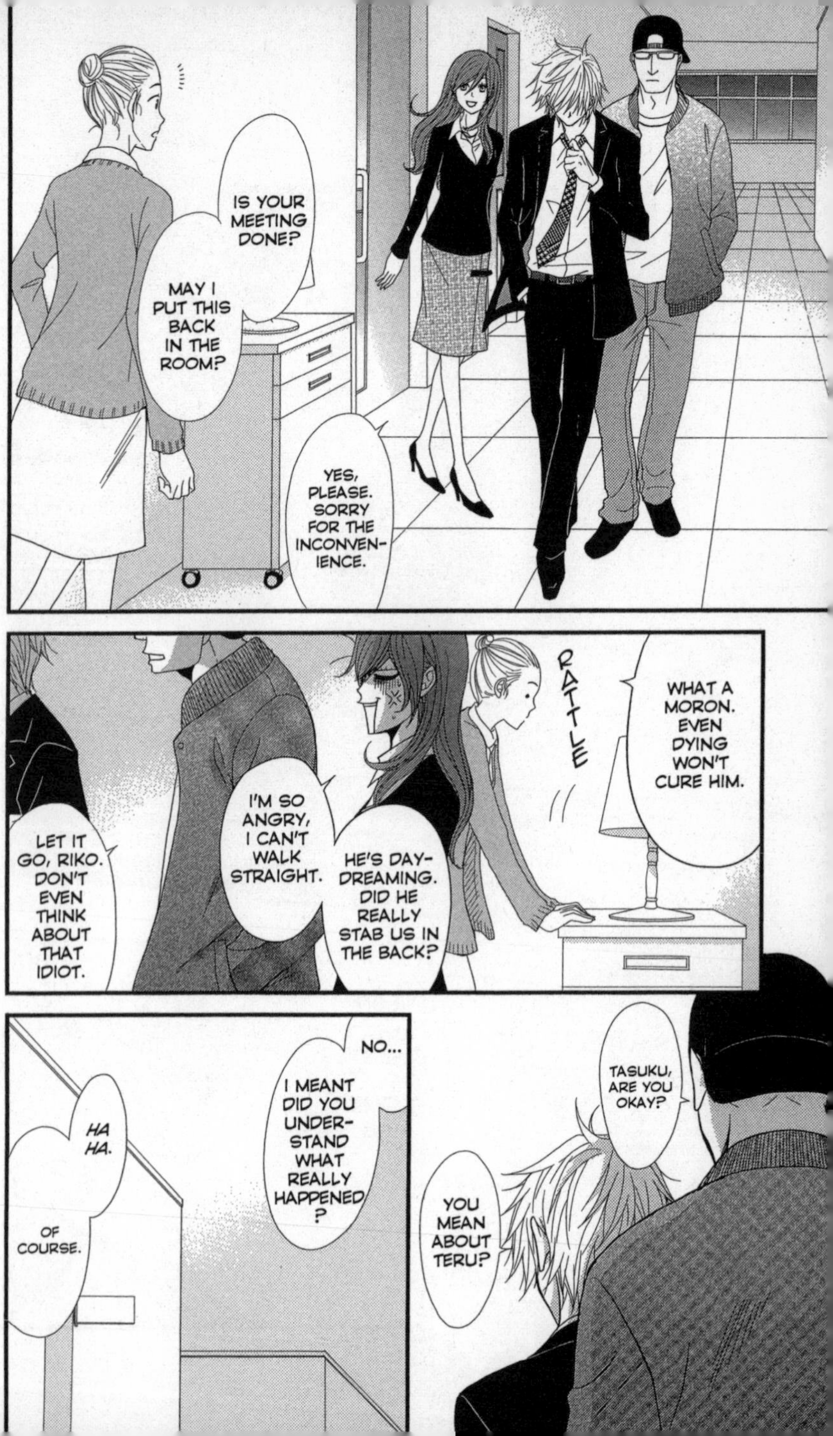
IS YOUR MEETING DONE?
MAY I PUT THIS BACK IN THE ROOM?
YES, PLEASE. SORRY FOR THE INCONVEN-IENCE.
WHAT A MORON. EVEN DYING WON'T CURE HIM.
RATTLE
HE'S DAY-DREAMING. DID HE REALLY STAB US IN THE BACK?
I'M SO ANGRY, I CAN'T WALK STRAIGHT.
LET IT GO, RIKO. DON'T EVEN THINK ABOUT THAT IDIOT.
TASUKU, ARE YOU OKAY?
YOU MEAN ABOUT TERU?
NO...
I MEANT DID YOU UNDER-STAND WHAT REALLY HAPPENED?
HA HA.
OF COURSE.

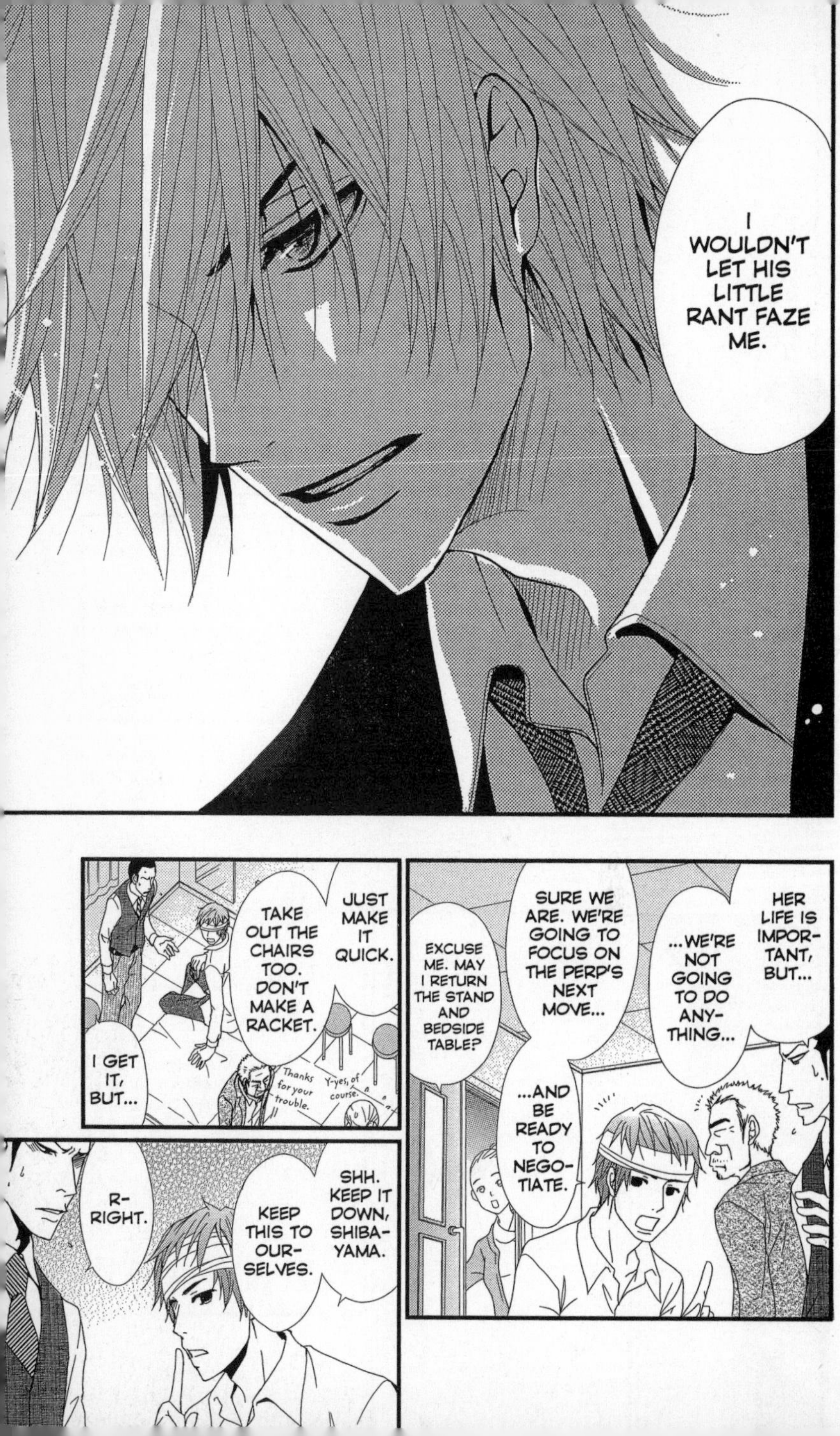
I WOULDN'T LET HIS LITTLE RANT FAZE ME.
HER LIFE IS IMPORTANT, BUT...
...WE'RE NOT GOING TO DO ANYTHING...
SURE WE ARE. WE'RE GOING TO FOCUS ON THE PERP'S NEXT MOVE...
...AND BE READY TO NEGOTIATE.
EXCUSE ME. MAY I RETURN THE STAND AND BEDSIDE TABLE?
JUST MAKE IT QUICK.
TAKE OUT THE CHAIRS TOO. DON'T MAKE A RACKET.
Y-yes, of course.
Thanks for your trouble.
I GET IT, BUT...
SHH. KEEP IT DOWN, SHIBAYAMA.
KEEP THIS TO OURSELVES.
R-RIGHT.

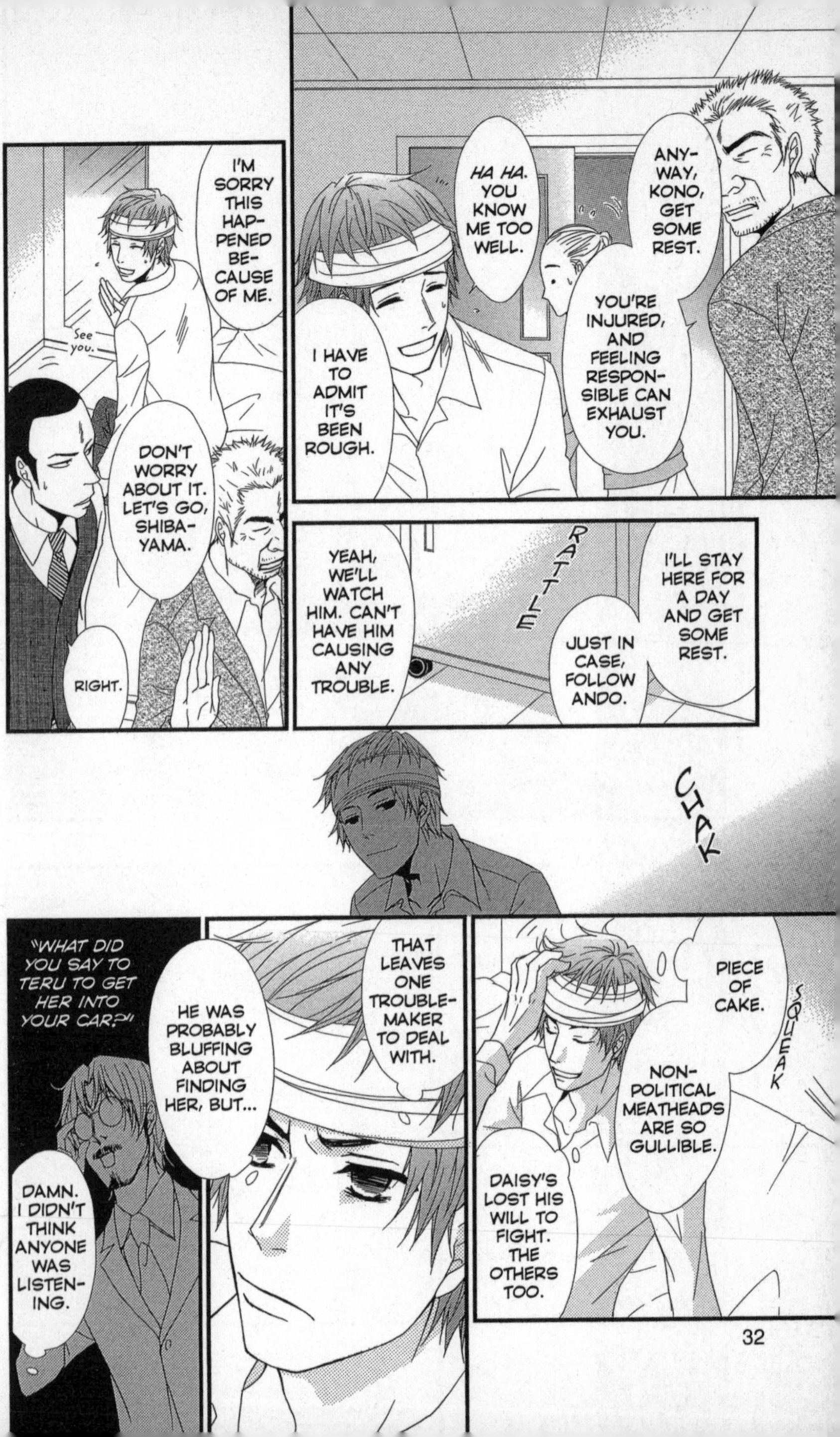
ANYWAY, KONO, GET SOME REST.
YOU'RE INJURED, AND FEELING RESPONSIBLE CAN EXHAUST YOU.
HA HA. YOU KNOW ME TOO WELL.
I HAVE TO ADMIT IT'S BEEN ROUGH.
RATTLE
I'LL STAY HERE FOR A DAY AND GET SOME REST.
JUST IN CASE, FOLLOW ANDO.
YEAH, WE'LL WATCH HIM. CAN'T HAVE HIM CAUSING ANY TROUBLE.
I'M SORRY THIS HAPPENED BECAUSE OF ME.
See you.
DON'T WORRY ABOUT IT. LET'S GO, SHIBAYAMA.
RIGHT.
CHAK
SQUEAK
PIECE OF CAKE.
NON-POLITICAL MEATHEADS ARE SO GULLIBLE.
DAISY'S LOST HIS WILL TO FIGHT. THE OTHERS TOO.
THAT LEAVES ONE TROUBLEMAKER TO DEAL WITH.
HE WAS PROBABLY BLUFFING ABOUT FINDING HER, BUT...
"WHAT DID YOU SAY TO TERU TO GET HER INTO YOUR CAR?"
DAMN. I DIDN'T THINK ANYONE WAS LISTENING.

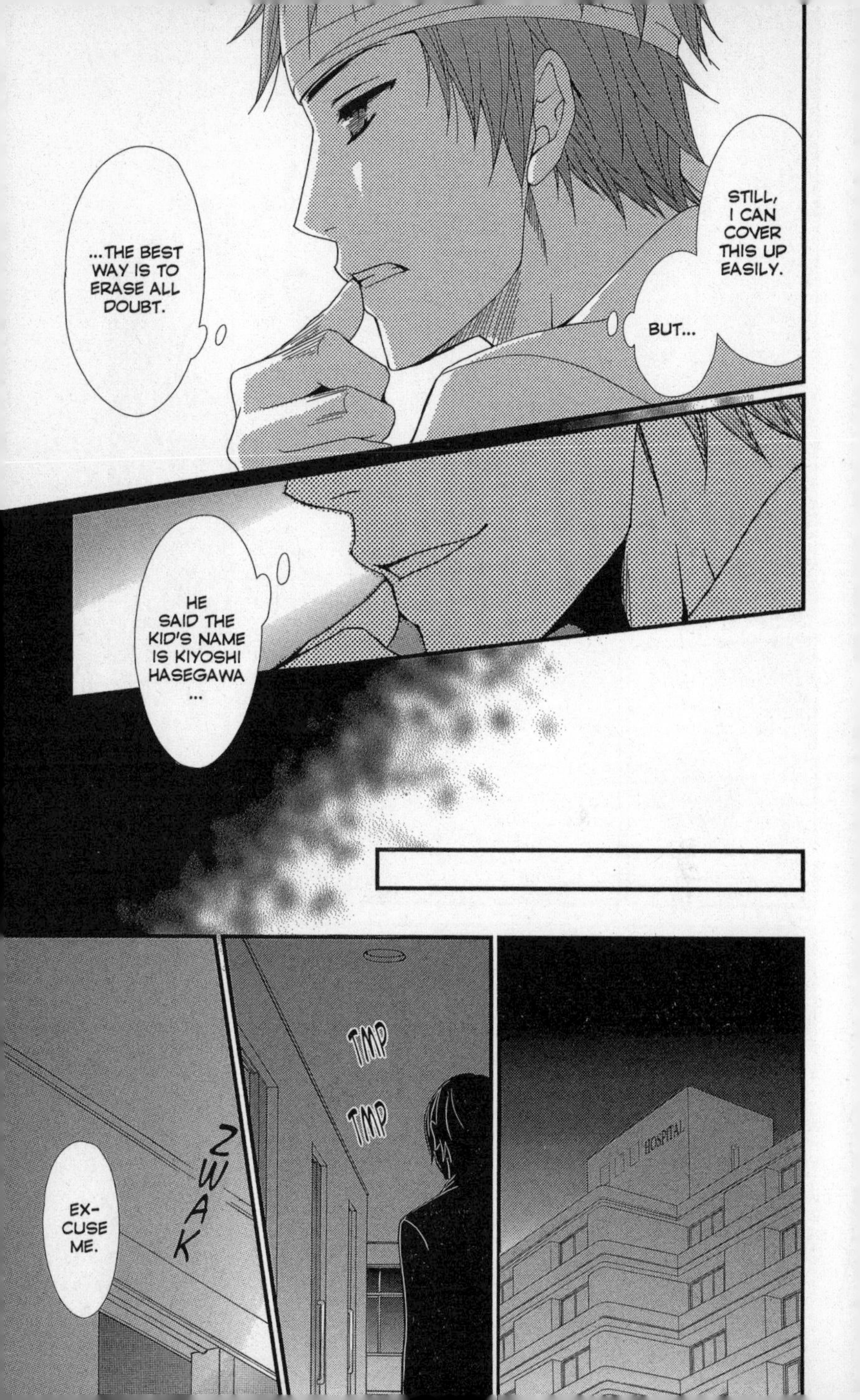
STILL, I CAN COVER THIS UP EASILY.
BUT...
...THE BEST WAY IS TO ERASE ALL DOUBT.
HE SAID THE KID'S NAME IS KIYOSHI HASEGAWA ...
HOSPITAL
TMP
TMP
ZWAK
EX-CUSE ME.

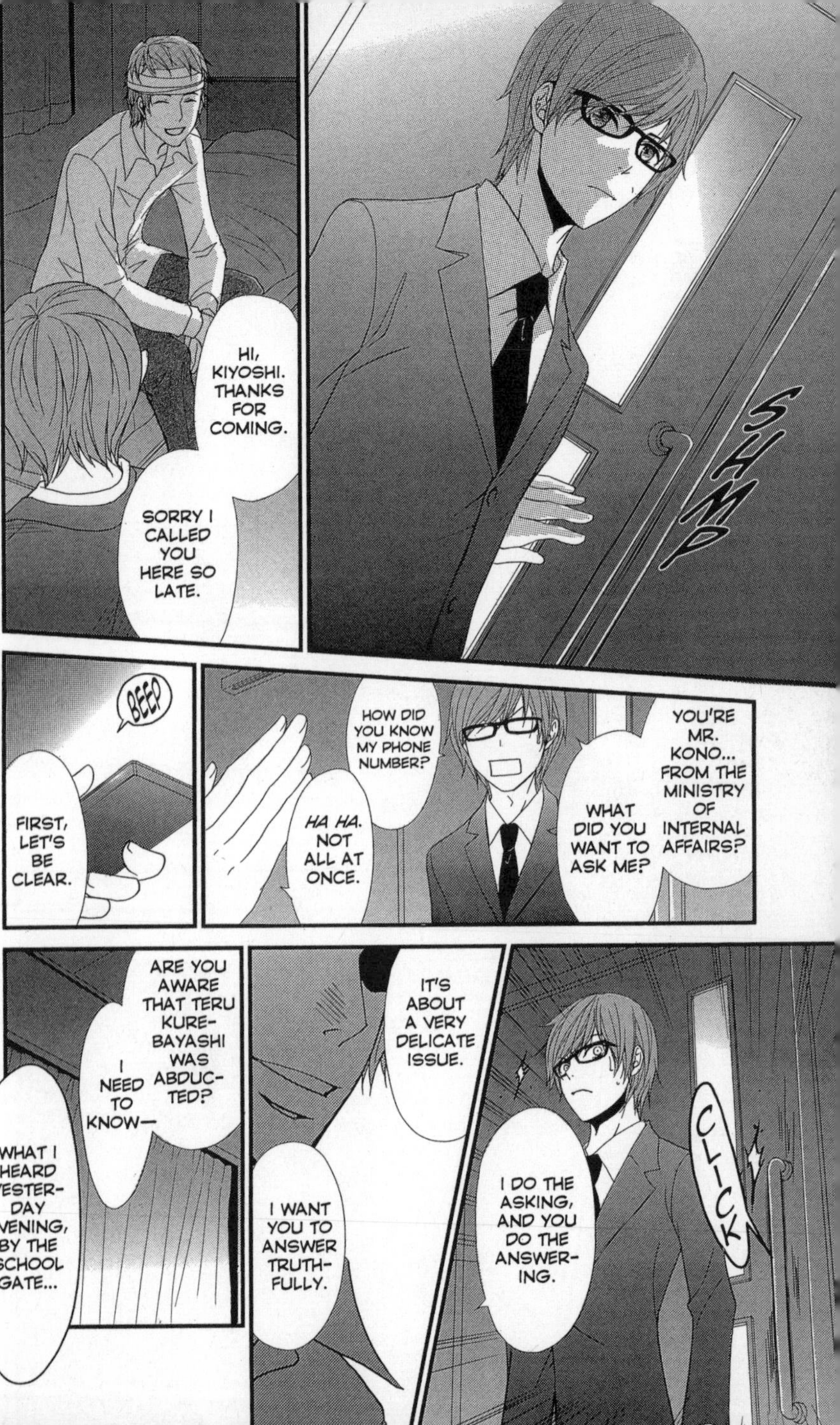
SHMP
HI, KIYOSHI. THANKS FOR COMING.
SORRY I CALLED YOU HERE SO LATE.
YOU'RE MR. KONO... FROM THE MINISTRY OF INTERNAL AFFAIRS?
WHAT DID YOU WANT TO ASK ME?
HOW DID YOU KNOW MY PHONE NUMBER?
HA HA. NOT ALL AT ONCE.
BEEP
FIRST, LET'S BE CLEAR.
CLICK
I DO THE ASKING, AND YOU DO THE ANSWER-ING.
IT'S ABOUT A VERY DELICATE ISSUE.
I WANT YOU TO ANSWER TRUTH-FULLY.
ARE YOU AWARE THAT TERU KURE-BAYASHI WAS ABDUC-TED?
I NEED TO KNOW—
WHAT I HEARD YESTER-DAY EVENING, BY THE SCHOOL GATE...

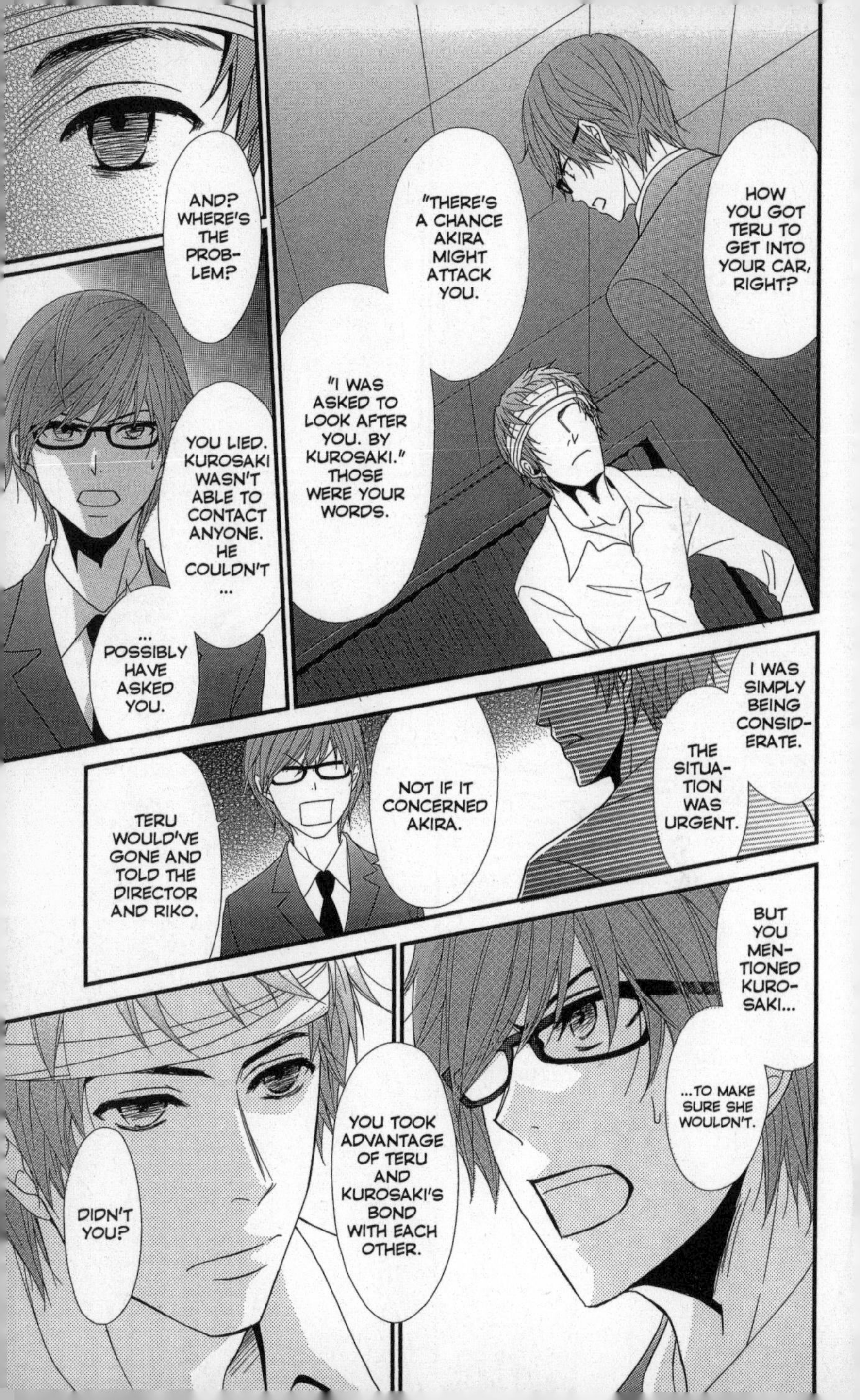
HOW YOU GOT TERU TO GET INTO YOUR CAR, RIGHT?
"THERE'S A CHANCE AKIRA MIGHT ATTACK YOU.
"I WAS ASKED TO LOOK AFTER YOU. BY KUROSAKI." THOSE WERE YOUR WORDS.
AND? WHERE'S THE PROB-LEM?
YOU LIED. KUROSAKI WASN'T ABLE TO CONTACT ANYONE. HE COULDN'T ...
... POSSIBLY HAVE ASKED YOU.
I WAS SIMPLY BEING CONSID-ERATE.
THE SITUA-TION WAS URGENT.
NOT IF IT CONCERNED AKIRA.
TERU WOULD'VE GONE AND TOLD THE DIRECTOR AND RIKO.
BUT YOU MEN-TIONED KURO-SAKI...
...TO MAKE SURE SHE WOULDN'T.
YOU TOOK ADVANTAGE OF TERU AND KUROSAKI'S BOND WITH EACH OTHER.
DIDN'T YOU?

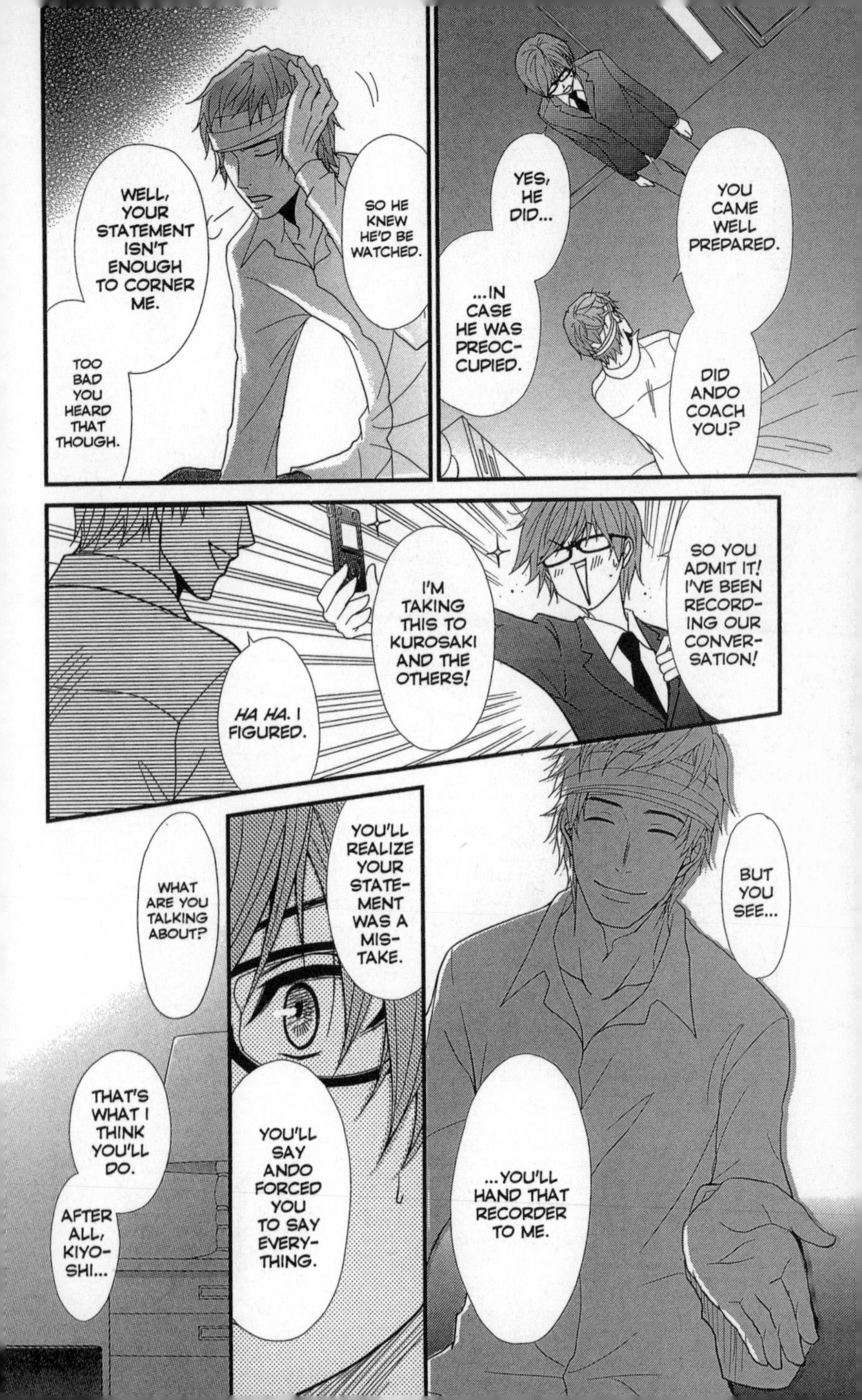
YOU CAME WELL PREPARED.
DID ANDO COACH YOU?
YES, HE DID...
...IN CASE HE WAS PREOC-CUPIED.
SO HE KNEW HE'D BE WATCHED.
WELL, YOUR STATEMENT ISN'T ENOUGH TO CORNER ME.
TOO BAD YOU HEARD THAT THOUGH.
SO YOU ADMIT IT! I'VE BEEN RECORD-ING OUR CONVER-SATION!
I'M TAKING THIS TO KUROSAKI AND THE OTHERS!
HA HA. I FIGURED.
BUT YOU SEE...
...YOU'LL HAND THAT RECORDER TO ME.
YOU'LL REALIZE YOUR STATE-MENT WAS A MIS-TAKE.
YOU'LL SAY ANDO FORCED YOU TO SAY EVERY-THING.
WHAT ARE YOU TALKING ABOUT?
THAT'S WHAT I THINK YOU'LL DO.
AFTER ALL, KIYO-SHI...

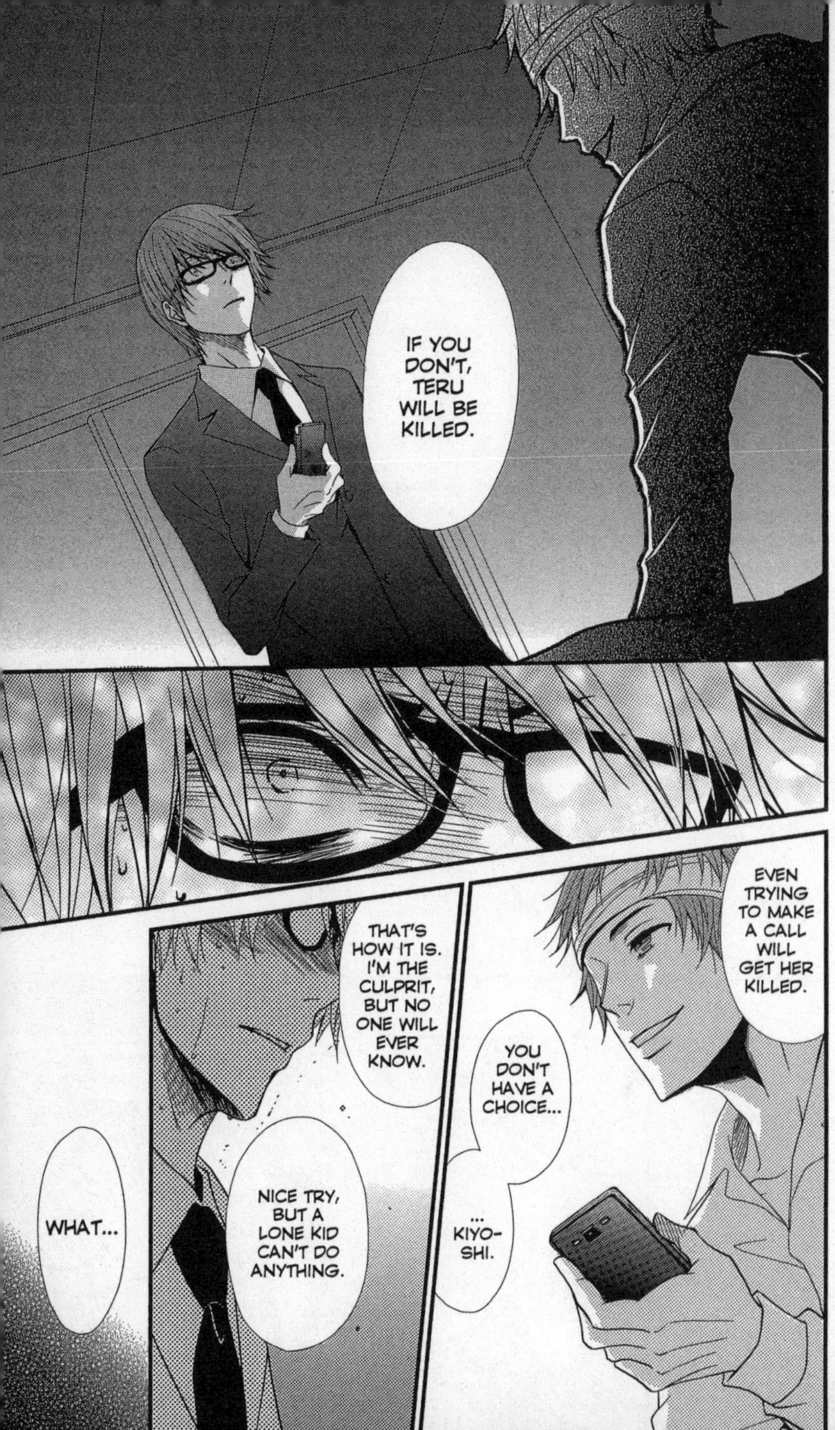
IF YOU DON'T, TERU WILL BE KILLED.
EVEN TRYING TO MAKE A CALL WILL GET HER KILLED.
YOU DON'T HAVE A CHOICE...
... KIYOSHI.
THAT'S HOW IT IS. I'M THE CULPRIT, BUT NO ONE WILL EVER KNOW.
NICE TRY, BUT A LONE KID CAN'T DO ANYTHING.
WHAT...

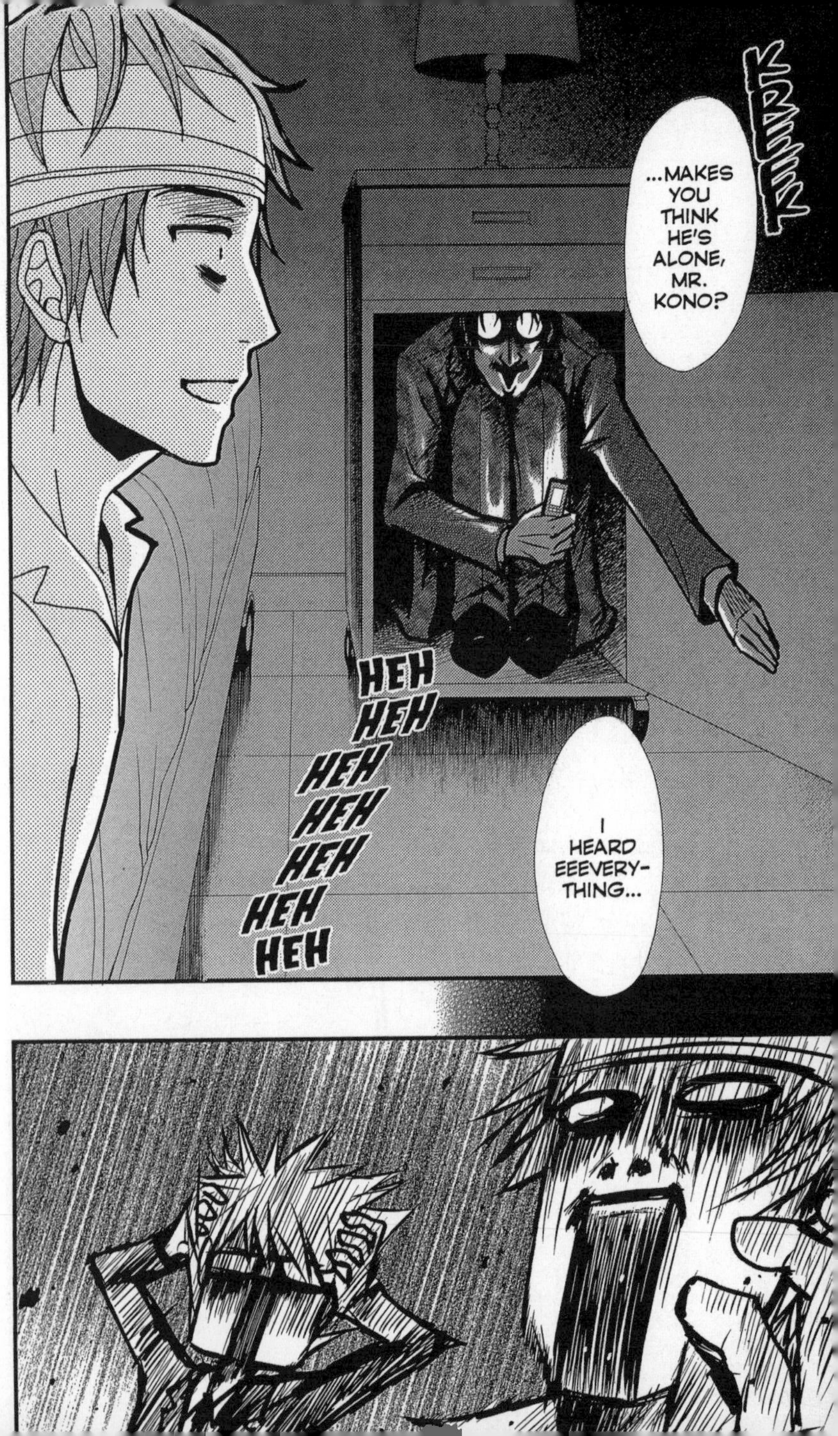
...MAKES YOU THINK HE'S ALONE, MR. KONO?
I HEARD EEEVERY-THING...
HEH HEH HEH HEH HEH HEH HEH

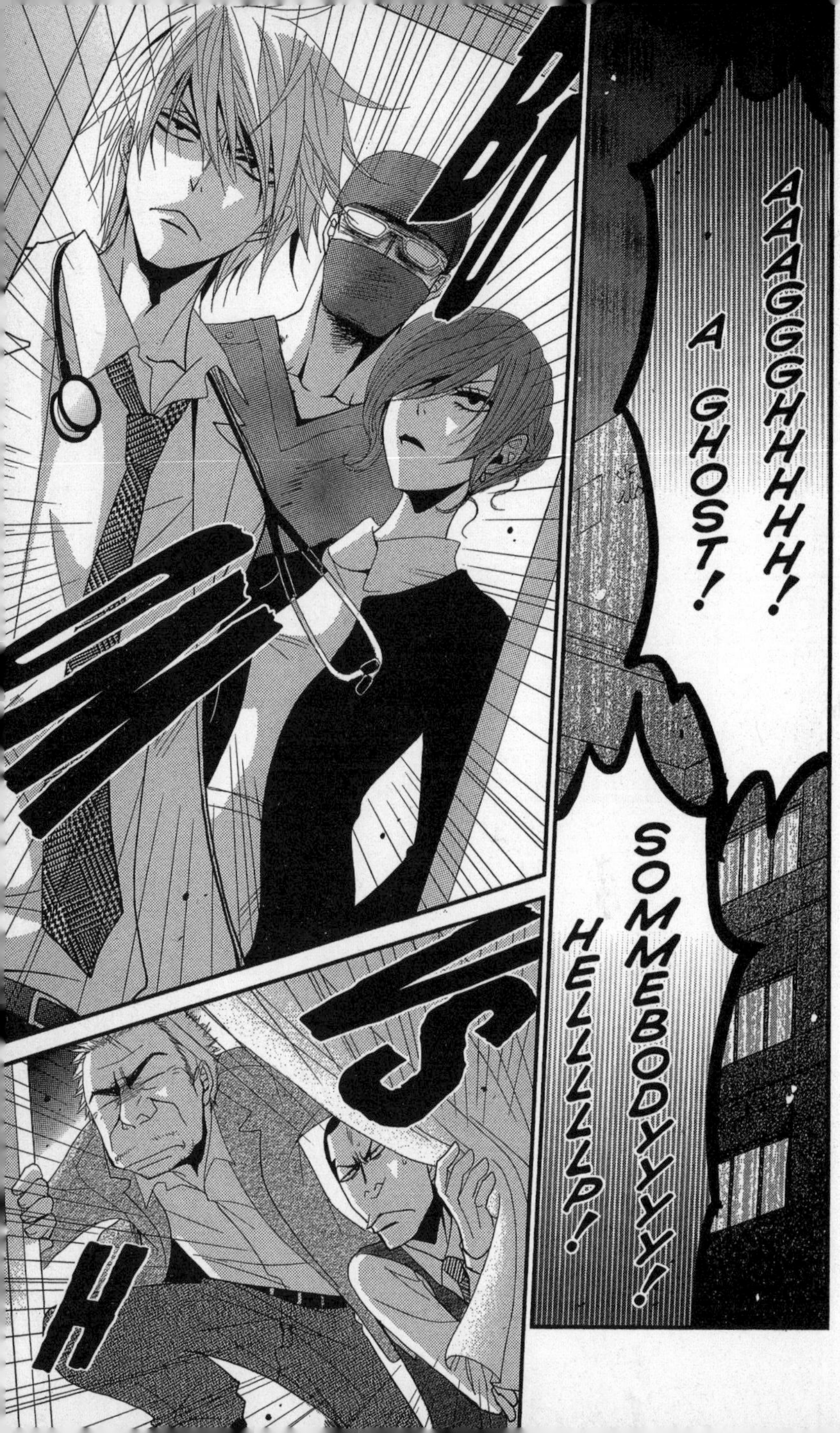
AAAAGGGHHHHH!
A GHOST!
SOMMEBODYYYY!
HELLLLLP!

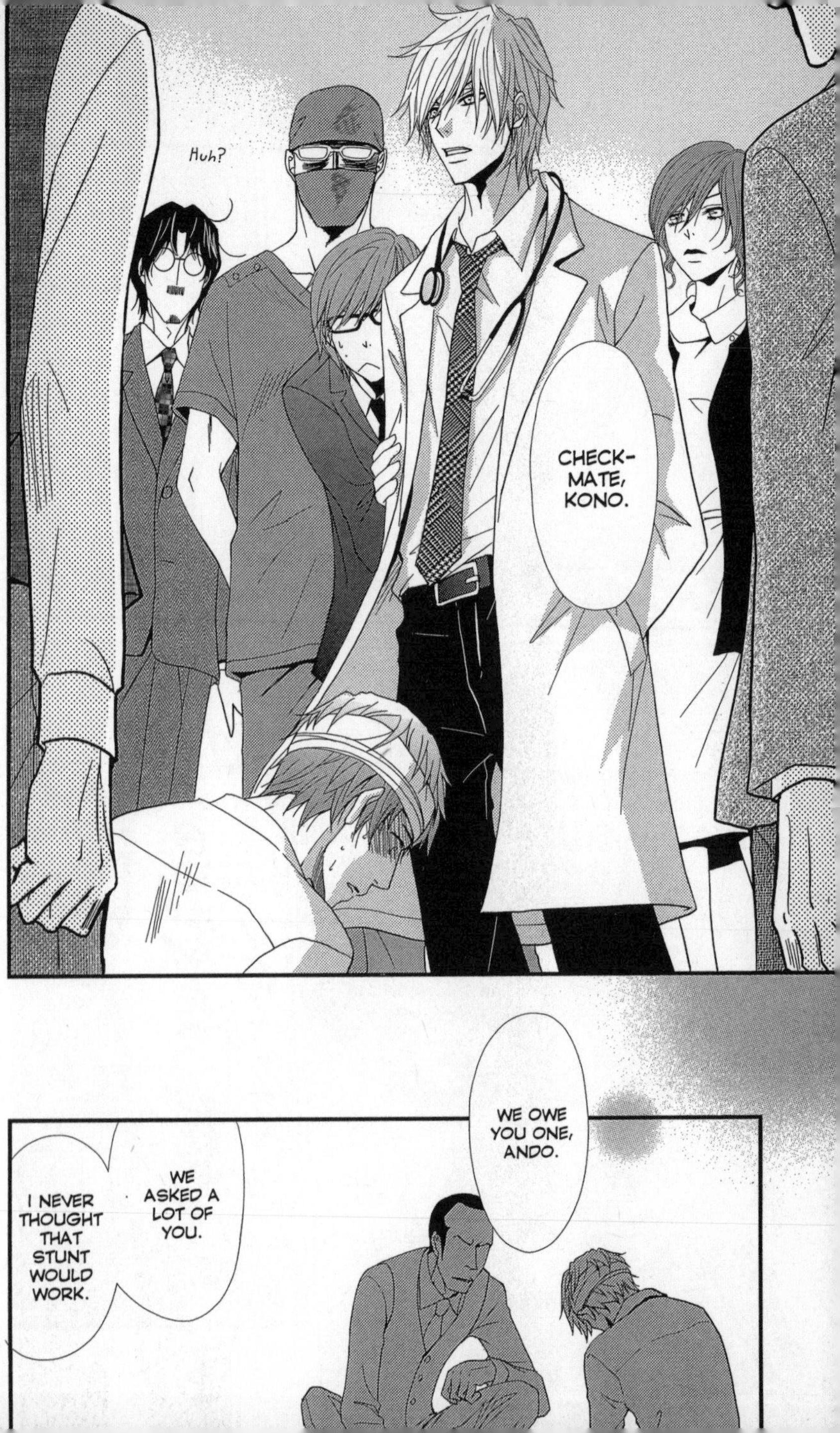
CHECK-MATE, KONO.
Huh?
WE OWE YOU ONE, ANDO.
WE ASKED A LOT OF YOU.
I NEVER THOUGHT THAT STUNT WOULD WORK.

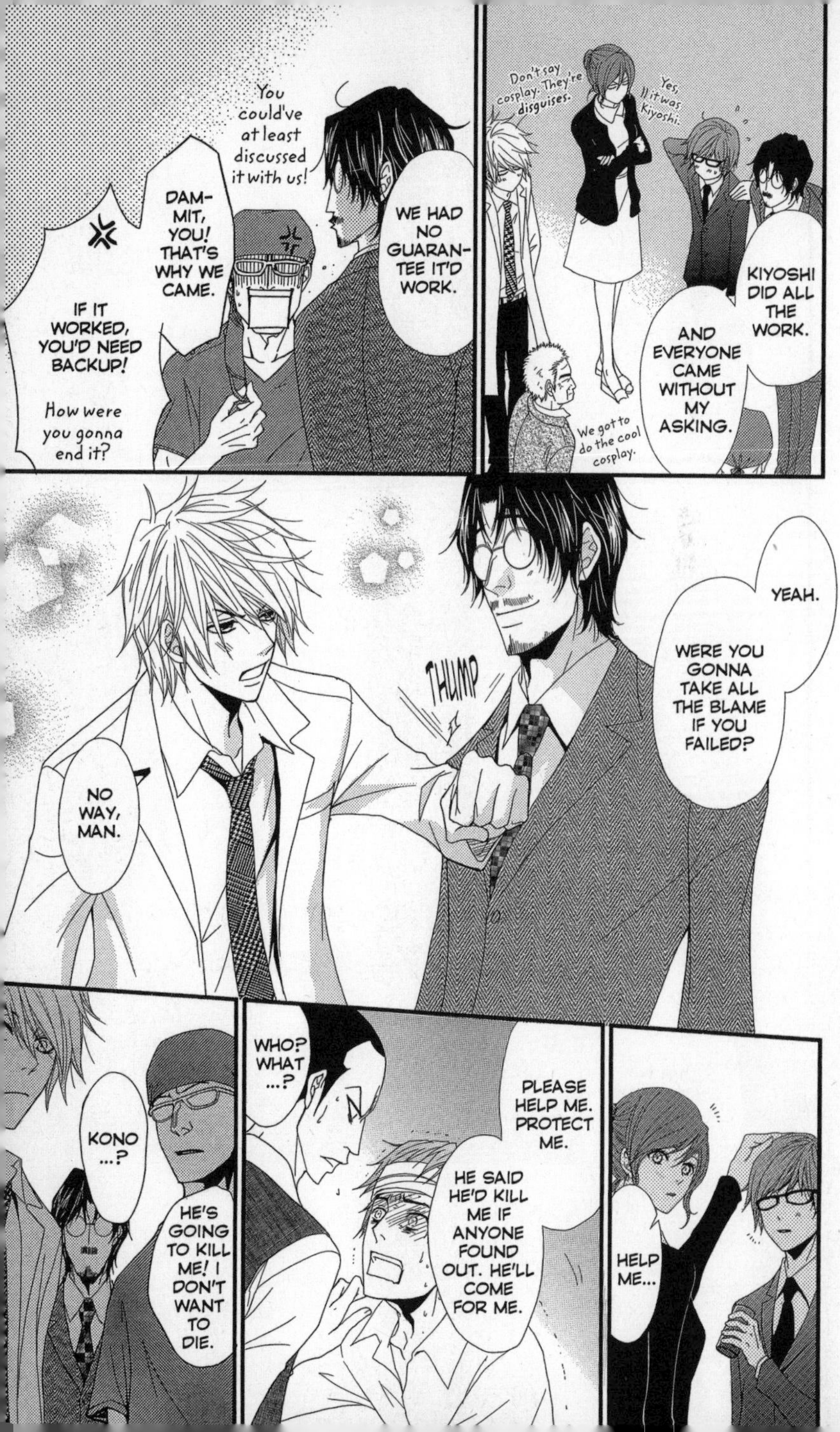
Yes, it was Kiyoshi.
Don't say cosplay. They're disguises.
KIYOSHI DID ALL THE WORK.
AND EVERYONE CAME WITHOUT MY ASKING.
We got to do the cool cosplay.
WE HAD NO GUARANTEE IT'D WORK.
You could've at least discussed it with us!
DAMMIT, YOU! THAT'S WHY WE CAME.
IF IT WORKED, YOU'D NEED BACKUP!
How were you gonna end it?
YEAH.
WERE YOU GONNA TAKE ALL THE BLAME IF YOU FAILED?
THUMP
NO WAY, MAN.
HELP ME...
PLEASE HELP ME. PROTECT ME.
HE SAID HE'D KILL ME IF ANYONE FOUND OUT. HE'LL COME FOR ME.
WHO? WHAT ...?
KONO ...?
HE'S GOING TO KILL ME! I DON'T WANT TO DIE.

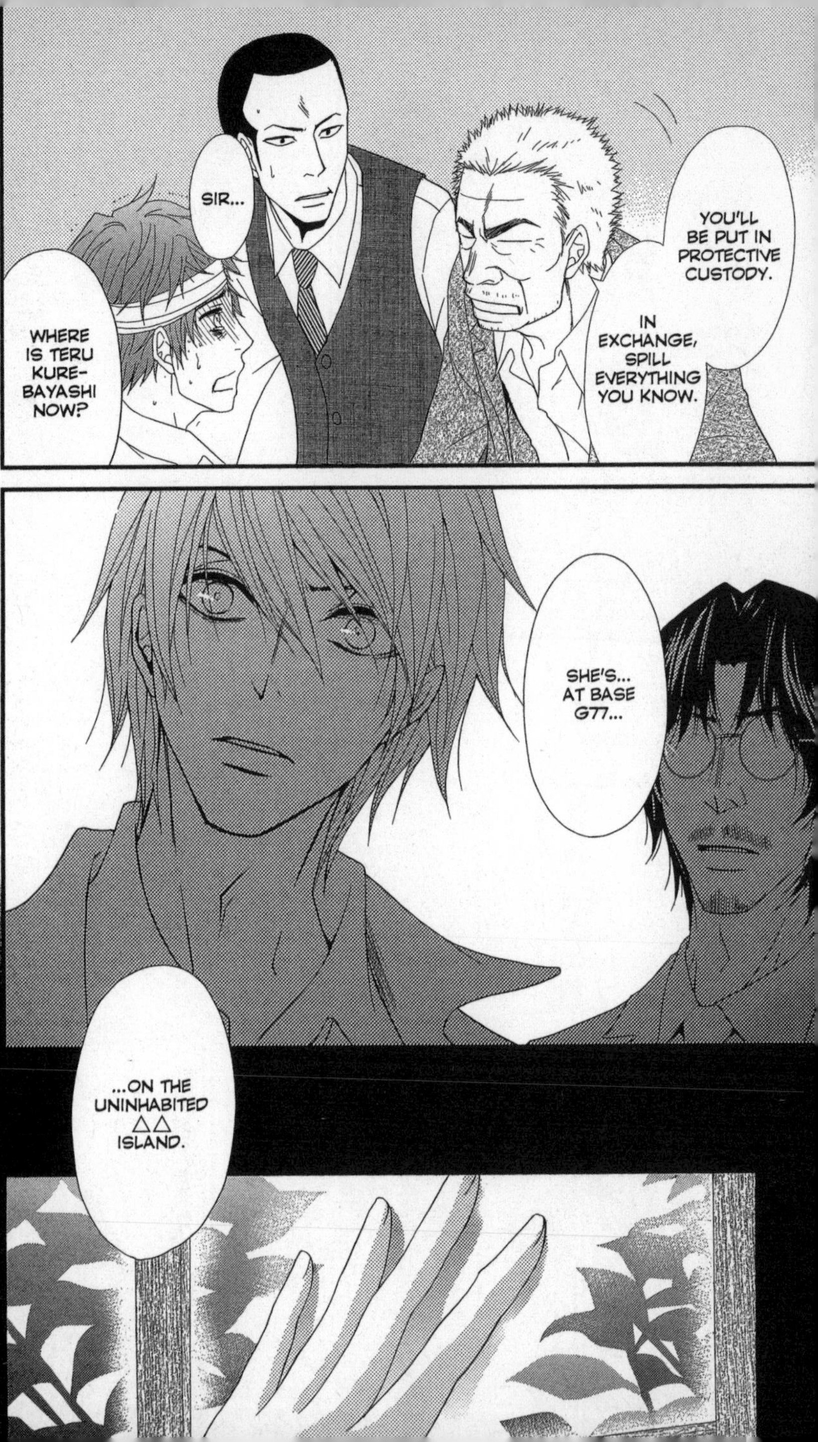
YOU'LL BE PUT IN PROTECTIVE CUSTODY.
IN EXCHANGE, SPILL EVERYTHING YOU KNOW.
SIR...
WHERE IS TERU KURE-BAYASHI NOW?
SHE'S... AT BASE G77...
...ON THE UNINHABITED △△ ISLAND.

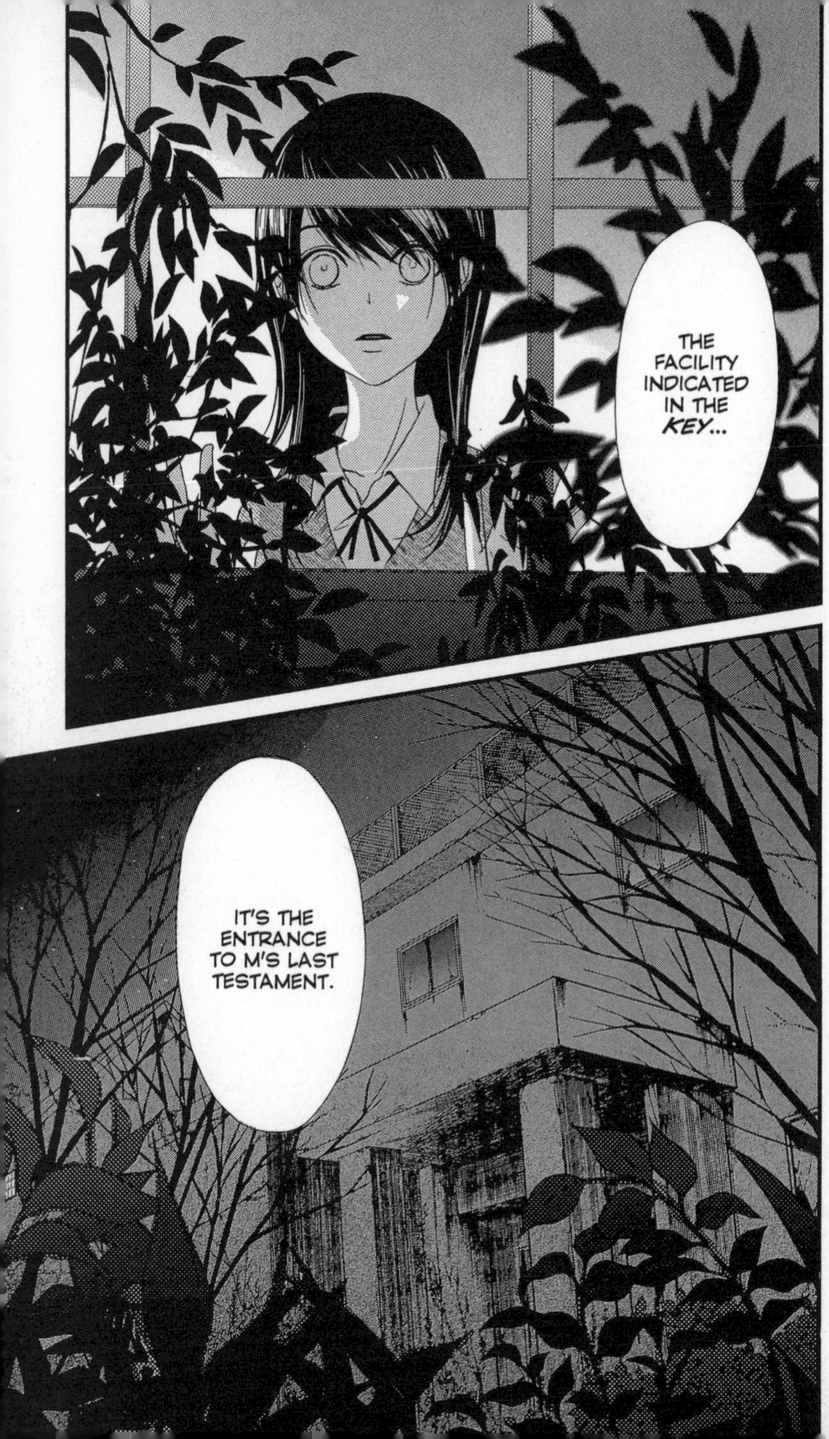
THE FACILITY INDICATED IN THE *KEY*...
IT'S THE ENTRANCE TO M'S LAST TESTAMENT.

DENGEKI DAISY QUESTION CORNER

RELOCATED

BALDLY ASK!!! ③

THANK YOU FOR WORKING SO HARD EVERY DAY! ALLOW ME TO BALDLY ASK. TERU APPEARS TO BE THE BEST STUDENT IN HER GRADE, BUT WHAT WAS KUROSAKI'S CLASS RANK WHEN HE WAS IN HIGH SCHOOL? WAS HE SMART?

IF YOU WOULDN'T MIND, PLEASE CREATE AN ACADEMIC RANKING OF THE *DENGEKI DAISY* CHARACTERS. I'VE JUST ENTERED THE 10TH GRADE. PLEASE PRAY THAT MY LOVE COMES TO FRUITION.

(KOUGA, MIYAZAKI PREFECTURE)

KUROSAKI LOST HIS FATHER WHILE HE WAS IN MIDDLE SCHOOL. HE WENT THROUGH A LOT, SO HE DIDN'T ATTEND HIGH SCHOOL. I THINK HE WAS ONE OF THE BETTER STUDENTS IN MIDDLE SCHOOL, THOUGH. IF I WERE TO RANK THE CHARACTERS OTHER THAN KUROSAKI BY HOW WELL THEY ARE DOING (DID) IN HIGH SCHOOL, IT WOULD PROBABLY GO LIKE...

TERU, KIYOSHI, ANDY, RENA > TAKEDA, BOSS, RIKO, HARUKA, KAKO, MEI > KEN, YOSHI >> SOICHIRO

I SORT OF FEEL THAT UNTIL HE HAD AN EPIPHANY SOMEWHERE ALONG THE WAY, SOICHIRO DISDAINED SCHOOLWORK AND DIDN'T STUDY AT ALL. HE REGRETTED IT A LITTLE WHEN HE BECAME AN ADULT, SO HE MADE TERU STUDY HARD.

"GOOD IN SCHOOL" DOESN'T NECESSARILY EQUATE TO "SMART." THERE ARE, OF COURSE, A LOT OF OTHER IMPORTANT THINGS. BUT THE "EARNESTNESS" NEEDED TO STUDY IS AN ABILITY THAT WILL SURELY SUPPORT A PERSON'S LIFE IN THE FUTURE.

YOU SHOULD TRAIN YOUR MIND WELL WHILE YOU HAVE THE CHANCE! GOOD LUCK TO ALL OF YOU IN YOUR STUDIES!

AND IN OTHER THINGS, TOO! EARNESTLY PURSUE YOUR 10TH GRADE LOVE.

GOOD LUCK!

In a world of "what if," college student Kurosaki might have tutored middle school student Teru...

CHAPTER 71: GOOD LUCK CHARM

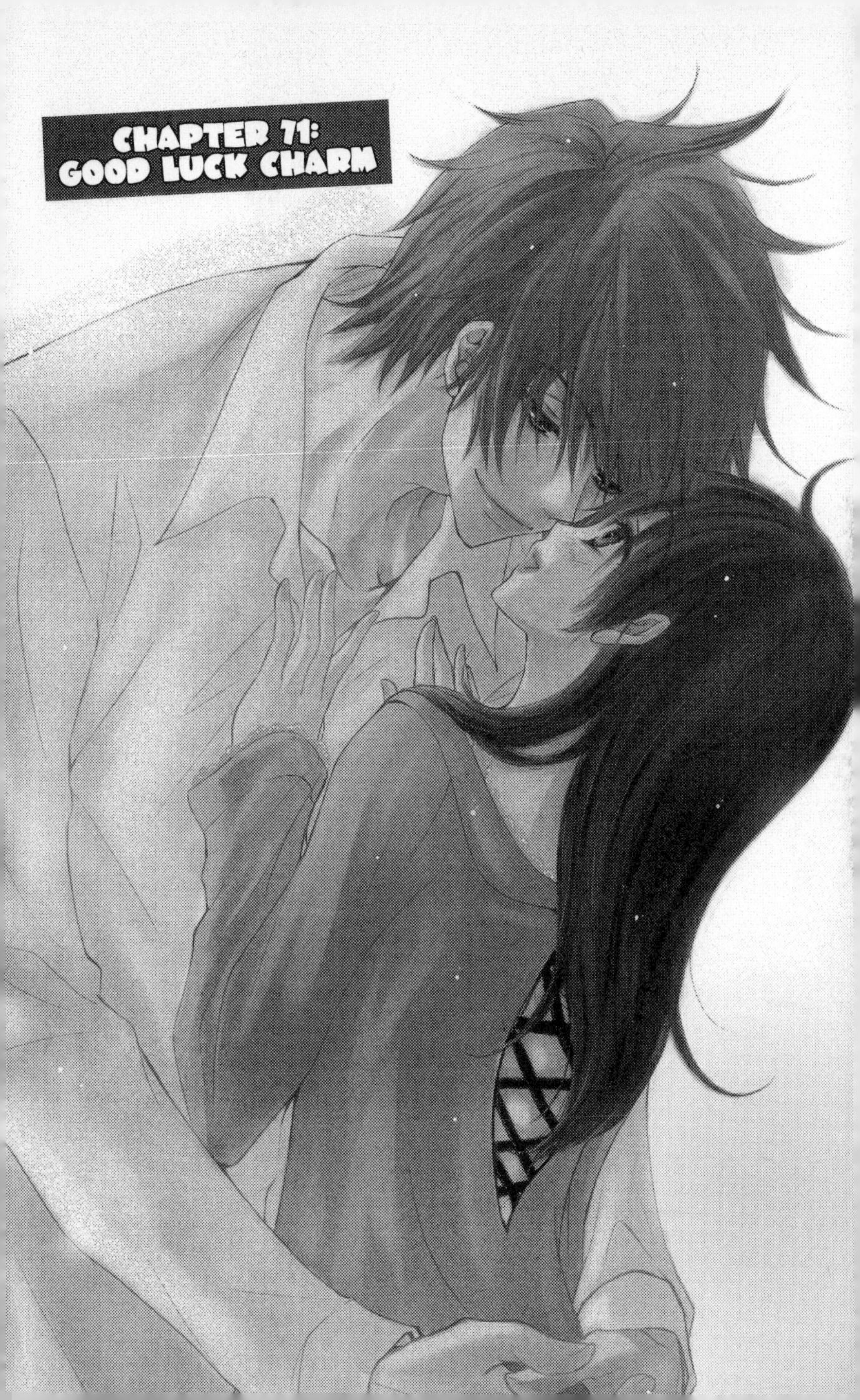

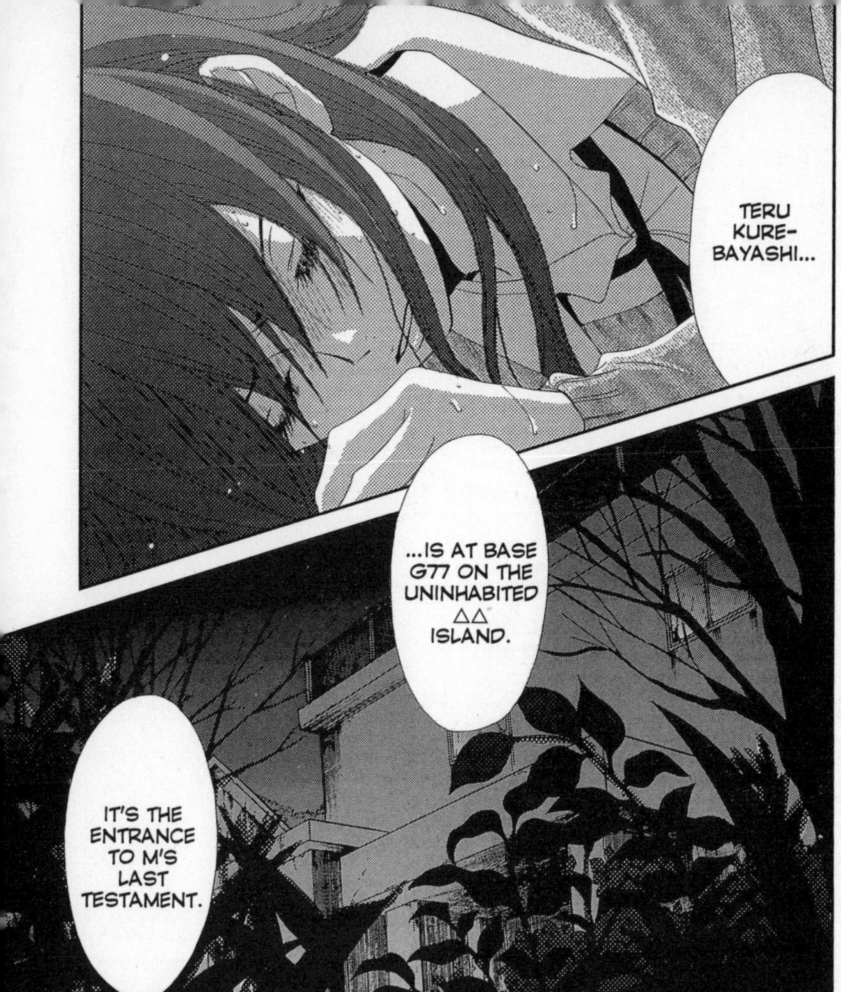
TERU KURE-BAYASHI...
...IS AT BASE G77 ON THE UNINHABITED △△ ISLAND.
IT'S THE ENTRANCE TO M'S LAST TESTAMENT.

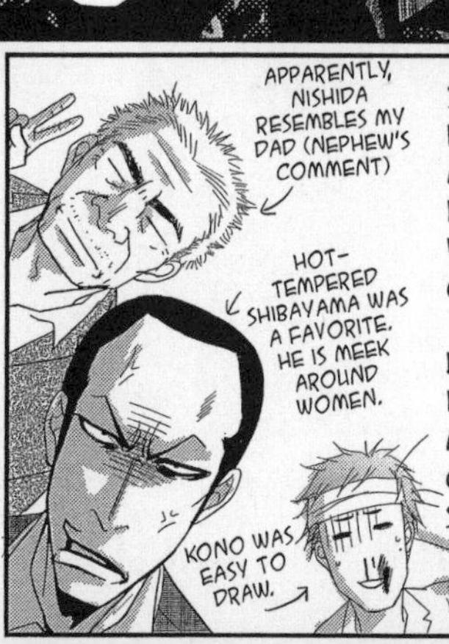
APPARENTLY, NISHIDA RESEMBLES MY DAD (NEPHEW'S COMMENT)
HOT-TEMPERED SHIBAYAMA WAS A FAVORITE. HE IS MEEK AROUND WOMEN.
KONO WAS EASY TO DRAW.

I FELT IT WOULDN'T BE APPROPRIATE TO DIVULGE WHICH OF THE THREE FROM THE MINISTRY WAS THE BAD GUY, SO I REFRAINED FROM TELLING. BUT MAYBE IT WAS OBVIOUS? MY DEPICTIONS OF BAD GUYS ALWAYS FOLLOW THE SAME PATTERN.

BEING THE AUTHOR, I WANTED TO REVEAL HIM EARLIER AND HAVE HIM DO A LOT MORE, BUT HAVING MORE OF THESE OLD GUYS WOULD ONLY DETRACT FROM THE SHOJO MANGA FEEL, SO I THINK I DID THE RIGHT THING.

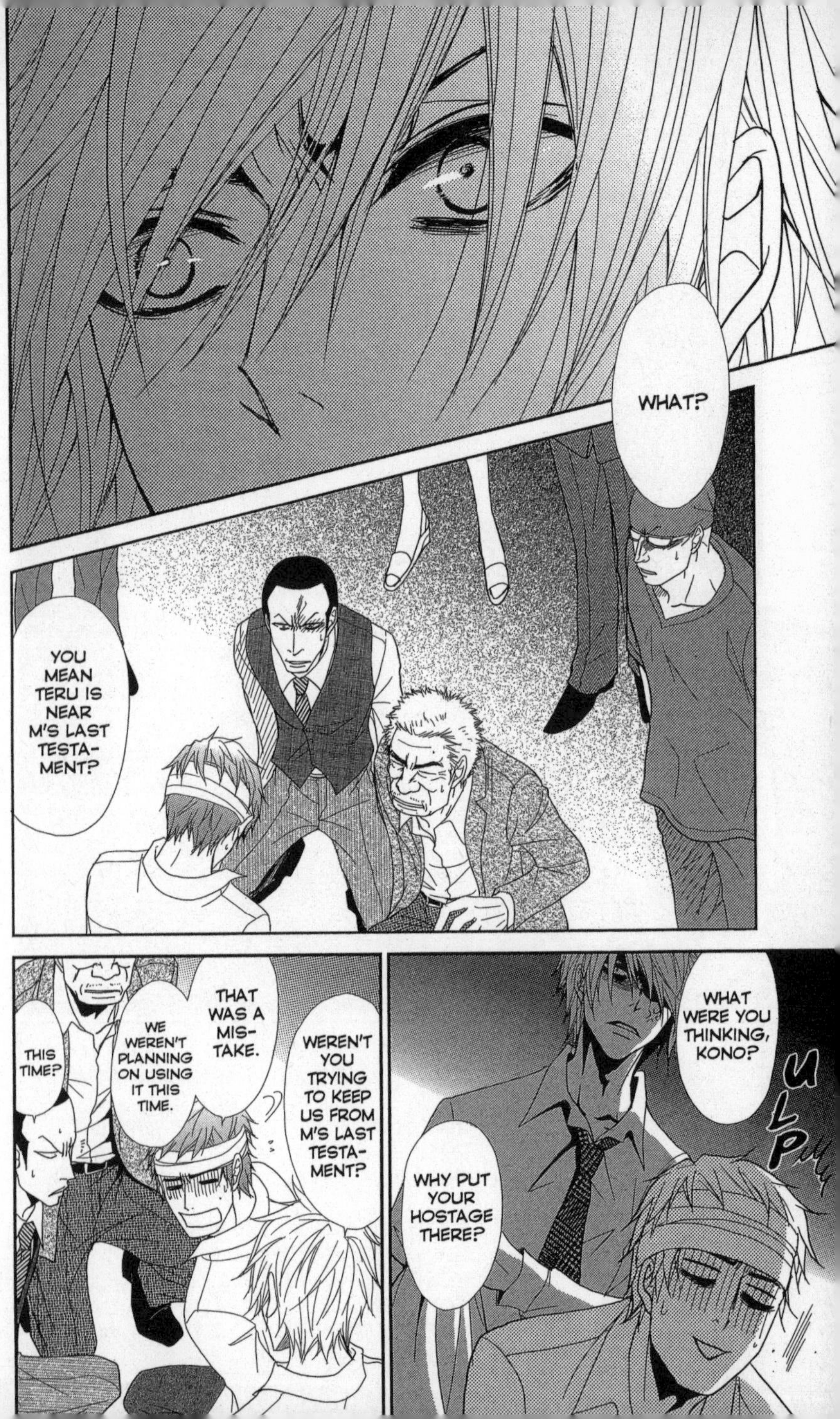
WHAT?
YOU MEAN TERU IS NEAR M'S LAST TESTA-MENT?
WHAT WERE YOU THINKING, KONO?
ULP
WHY PUT YOUR HOSTAGE THERE?
WEREN'T YOU TRYING TO KEEP US FROM M'S LAST TESTA-MENT?
THAT WAS A MIS-TAKE.
WE WEREN'T PLANNING ON USING IT THIS TIME.
THIS TIME?

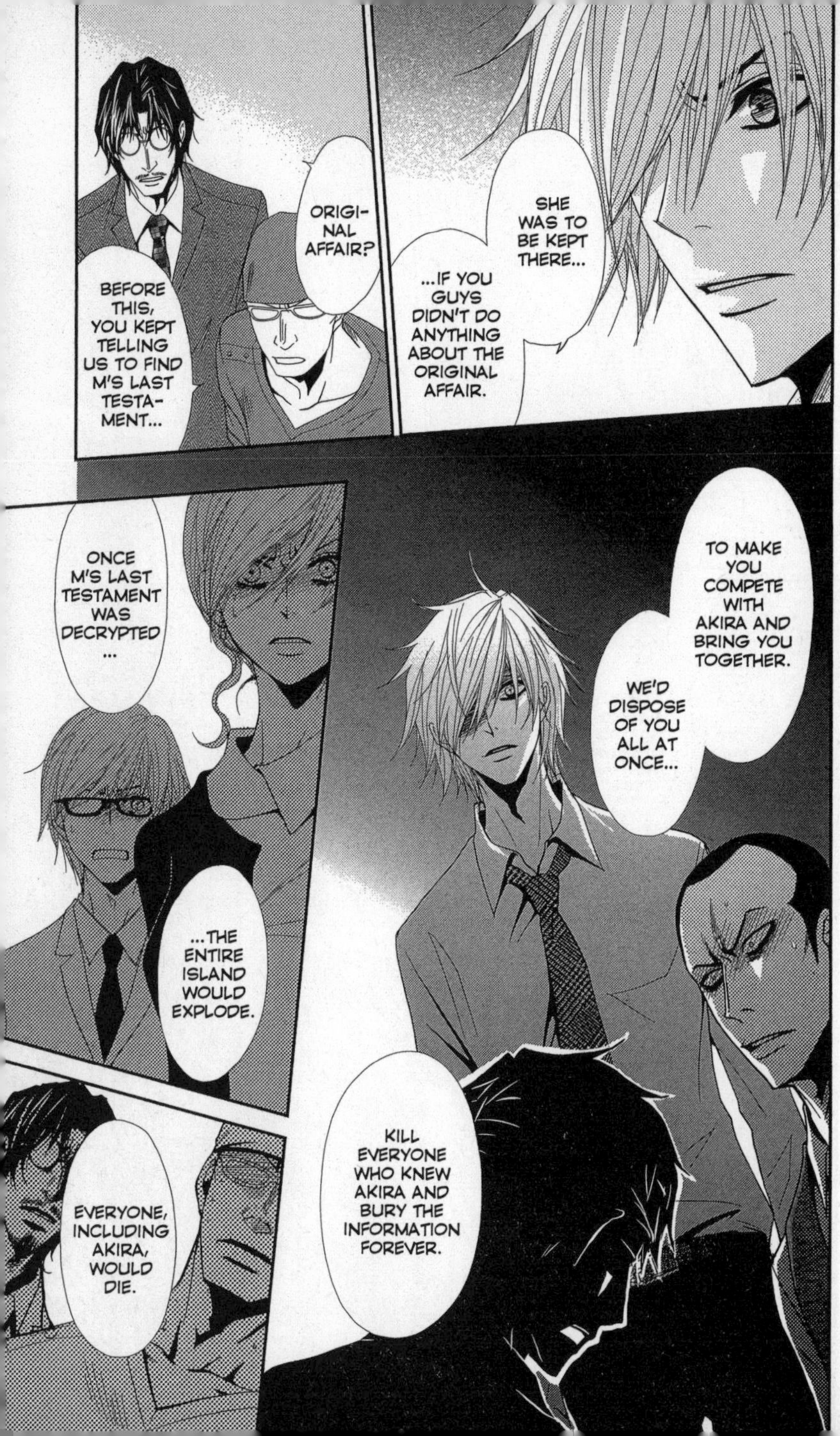
SHE WAS TO BE KEPT THERE...
...IF YOU GUYS DIDN'T DO ANYTHING ABOUT THE ORIGINAL AFFAIR.
ORIGI-NAL AFFAIR?
BEFORE THIS, YOU KEPT TELLING US TO FIND M'S LAST TESTA-MENT...
TO MAKE YOU COMPETE WITH AKIRA AND BRING YOU TOGETHER.
WE'D DISPOSE OF YOU ALL AT ONCE...
KILL EVERYONE WHO KNEW AKIRA AND BURY THE INFORMATION FOREVER.
ONCE M'S LAST TESTAMENT WAS DECRYPTED...
...THE ENTIRE ISLAND WOULD EXPLODE.
EVERYONE, INCLUDING AKIRA, WOULD DIE.

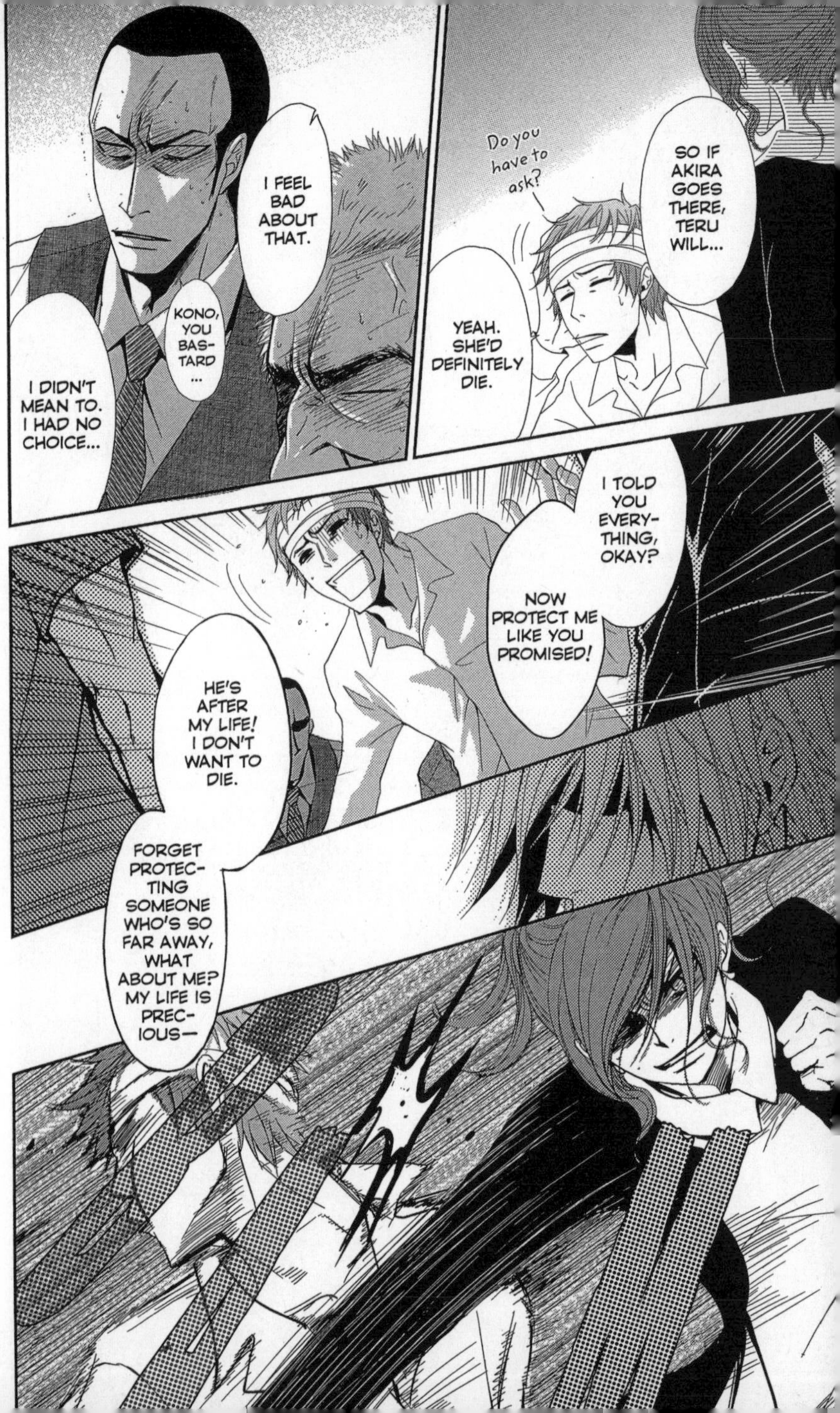
SO IF AKIRA GOES THERE, TERU WILL...
Do you have to ask?
YEAH. SHE'D DEFINITELY DIE.
I FEEL BAD ABOUT THAT.
KONO, YOU BASTARD...
I DIDN'T MEAN TO. I HAD NO CHOICE...
I TOLD YOU EVERYTHING, OKAY?
NOW PROTECT ME LIKE YOU PROMISED!
HE'S AFTER MY LIFE! I DON'T WANT TO DIE.
FORGET PROTECTING SOMEONE WHO'S SO FAR AWAY, WHAT ABOUT ME? MY LIFE IS PRECIOUS—

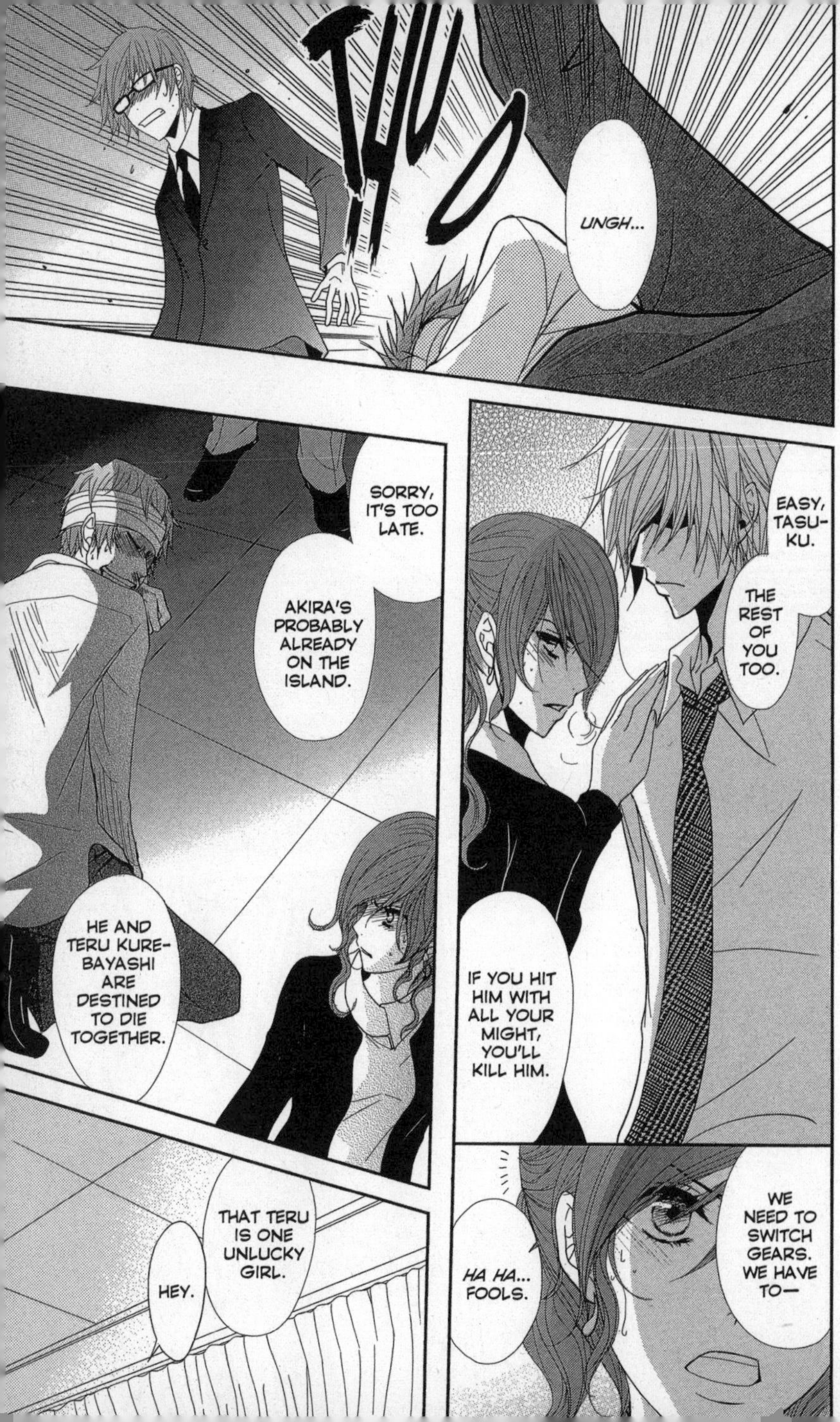
THUD
UNGH...
EASY, TASUKU.
THE REST OF YOU TOO.
IF YOU HIT HIM WITH ALL YOUR MIGHT, YOU'LL KILL HIM.
SORRY, IT'S TOO LATE.
AKIRA'S PROBABLY ALREADY ON THE ISLAND.
HE AND TERU KUREBAYASHI ARE DESTINED TO DIE TOGETHER.
WE NEED TO SWITCH GEARS. WE HAVE TO—
HA HA... FOOLS.
THAT TERU IS ONE UNLUCKY GIRL.
HEY.

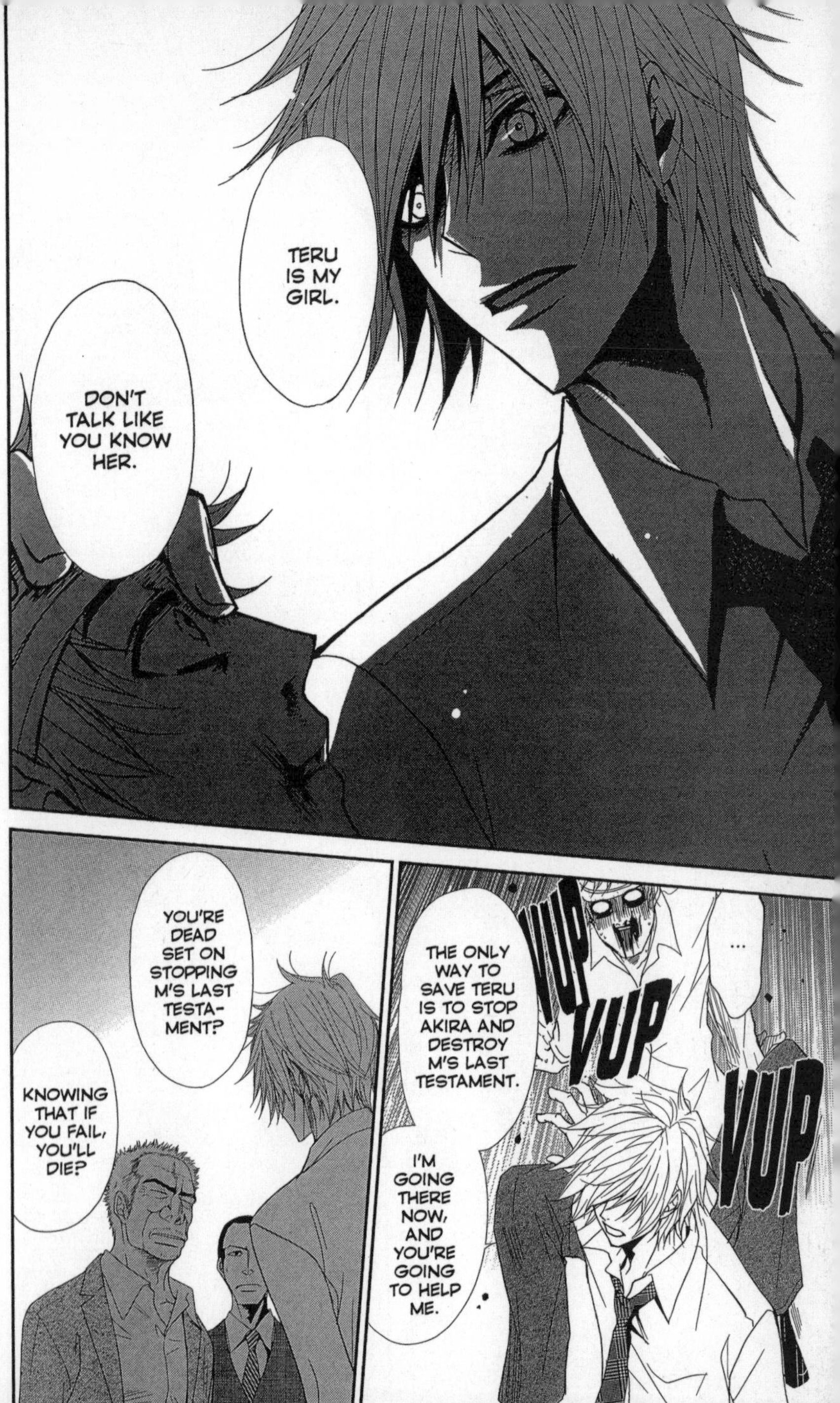
TERU IS MY GIRL.
DON'T TALK LIKE YOU KNOW HER.
...
THE ONLY WAY TO SAVE TERU IS TO STOP AKIRA AND DESTROY M'S LAST TESTAMENT.
VUP
VUP
VUP
I'M GOING THERE NOW, AND YOU'RE GOING TO HELP ME.
YOU'RE DEAD SET ON STOPPING M'S LAST TESTA-MENT?
KNOWING THAT IF YOU FAIL, YOU'LL DIE?

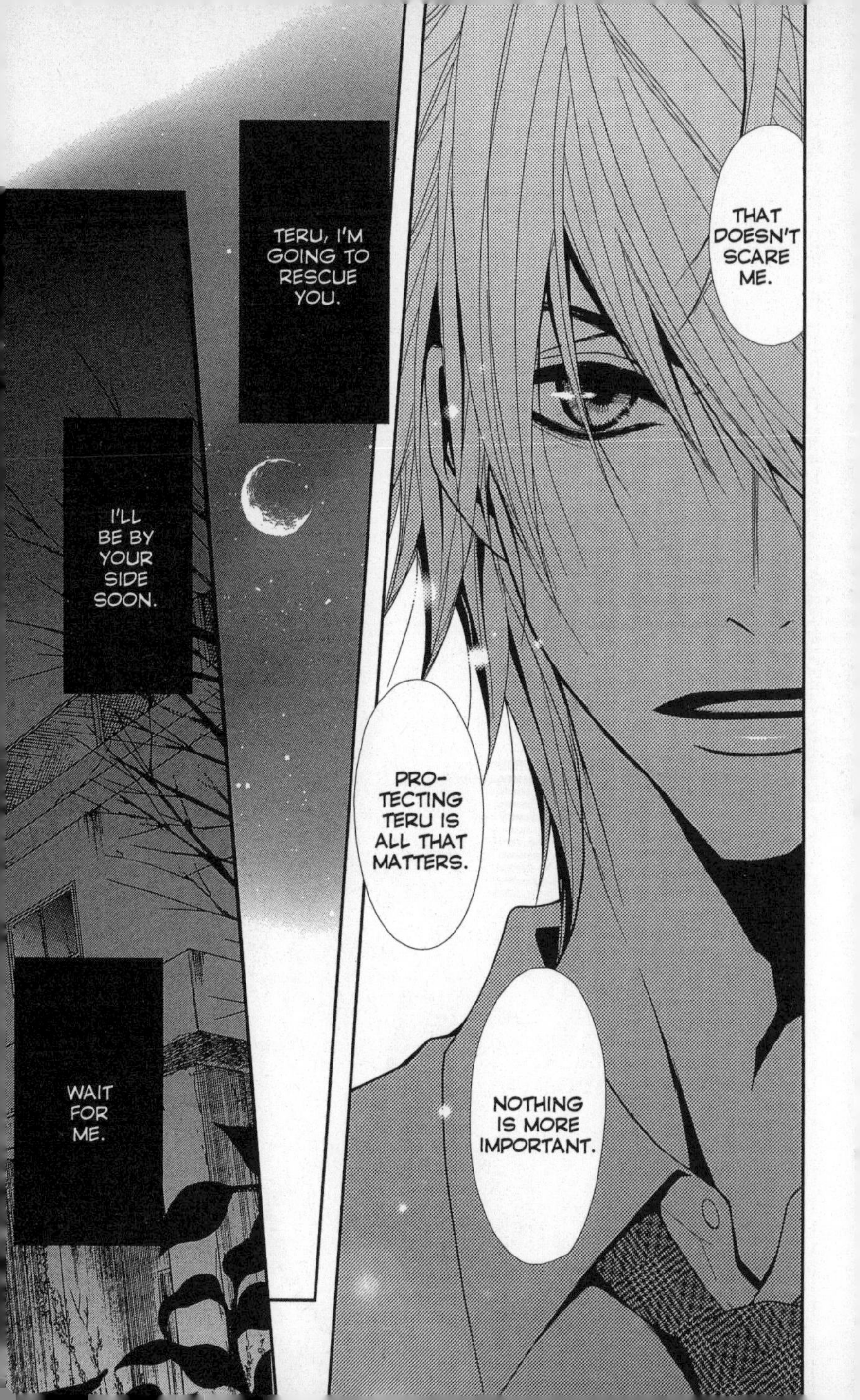
THAT DOESN'T SCARE ME.
PROTECTING TERU IS ALL THAT MATTERS.
NOTHING IS MORE IMPORTANT.
TERU, I'M GOING TO RESCUE YOU.
I'LL BE BY YOUR SIDE SOON.
WAIT FOR ME.

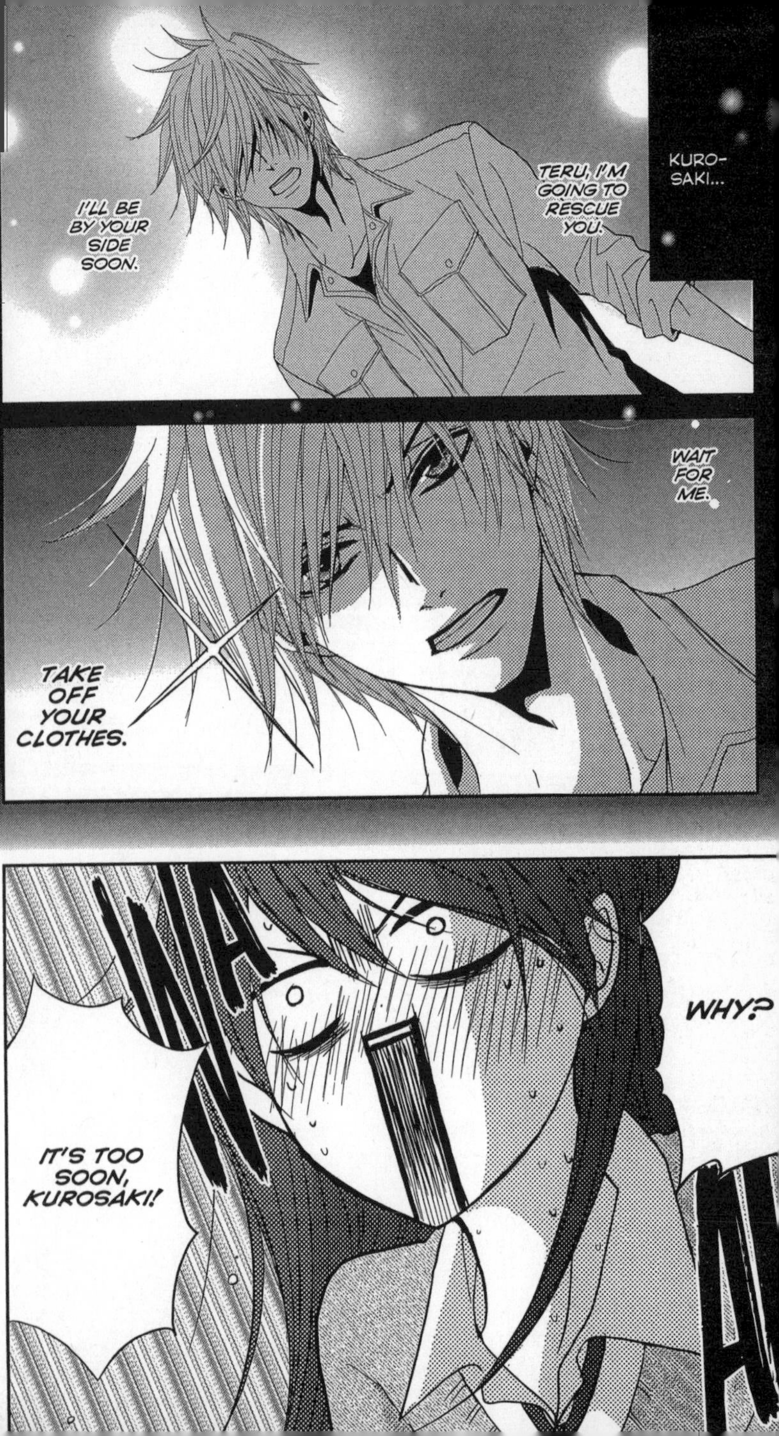
KURO-SAKI...
TERU, I'M GOING TO RESCUE YOU.
I'LL BE BY YOUR SIDE SOON.
WAIT FOR ME.
TAKE OFF YOUR CLOTHES.
WHY?
IT'S TOO SOON, KUROSAKI!

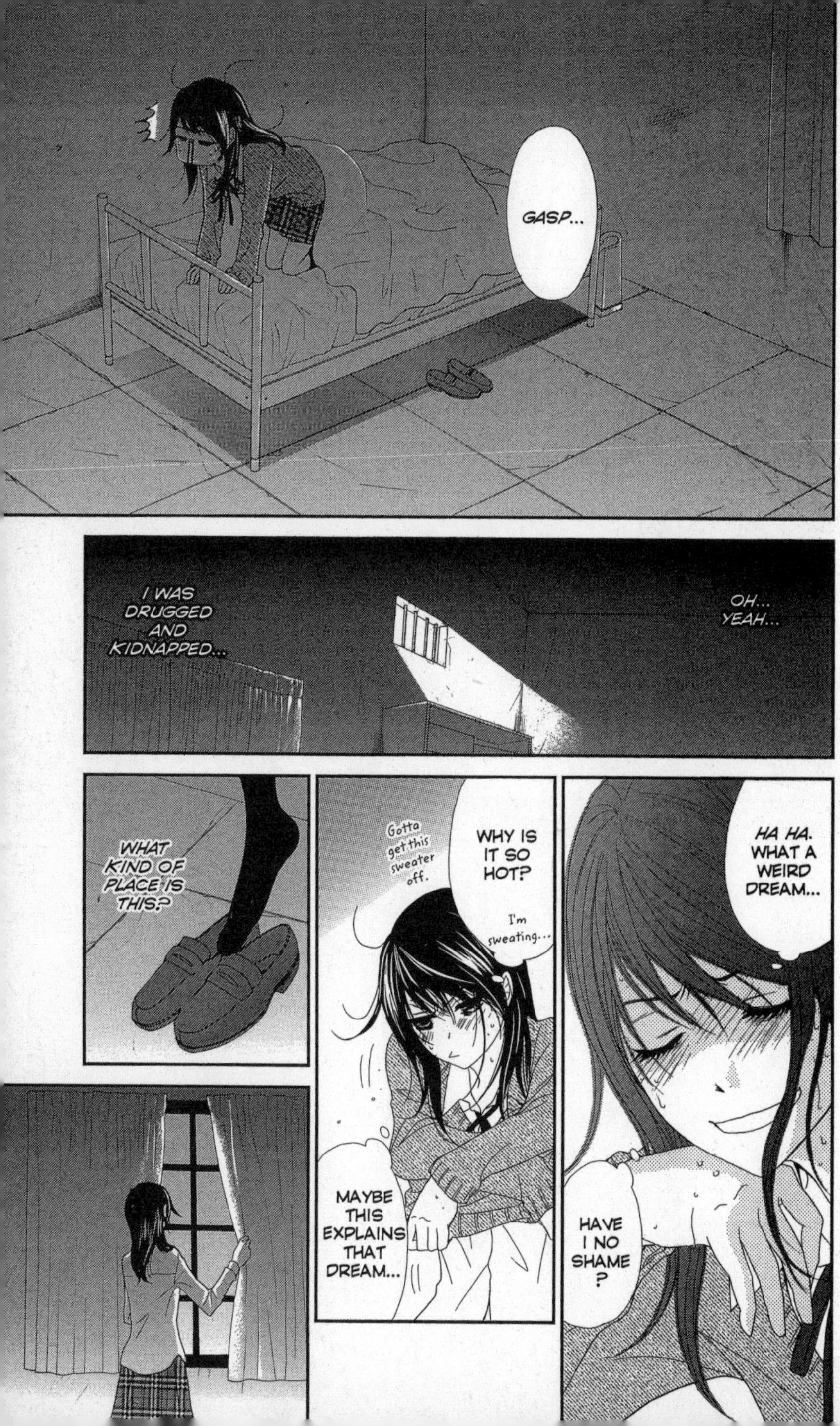
GASP...
OH... YEAH...
I WAS DRUGGED AND KIDNAPPED...
HA HA. WHAT A WEIRD DREAM...
HAVE I NO SHAME?
WHY IS IT SO HOT?
I'm sweating...
Gotta get this sweater off.
MAYBE THIS EXPLAINS THAT DREAM...
WHAT KIND OF PLACE IS THIS?

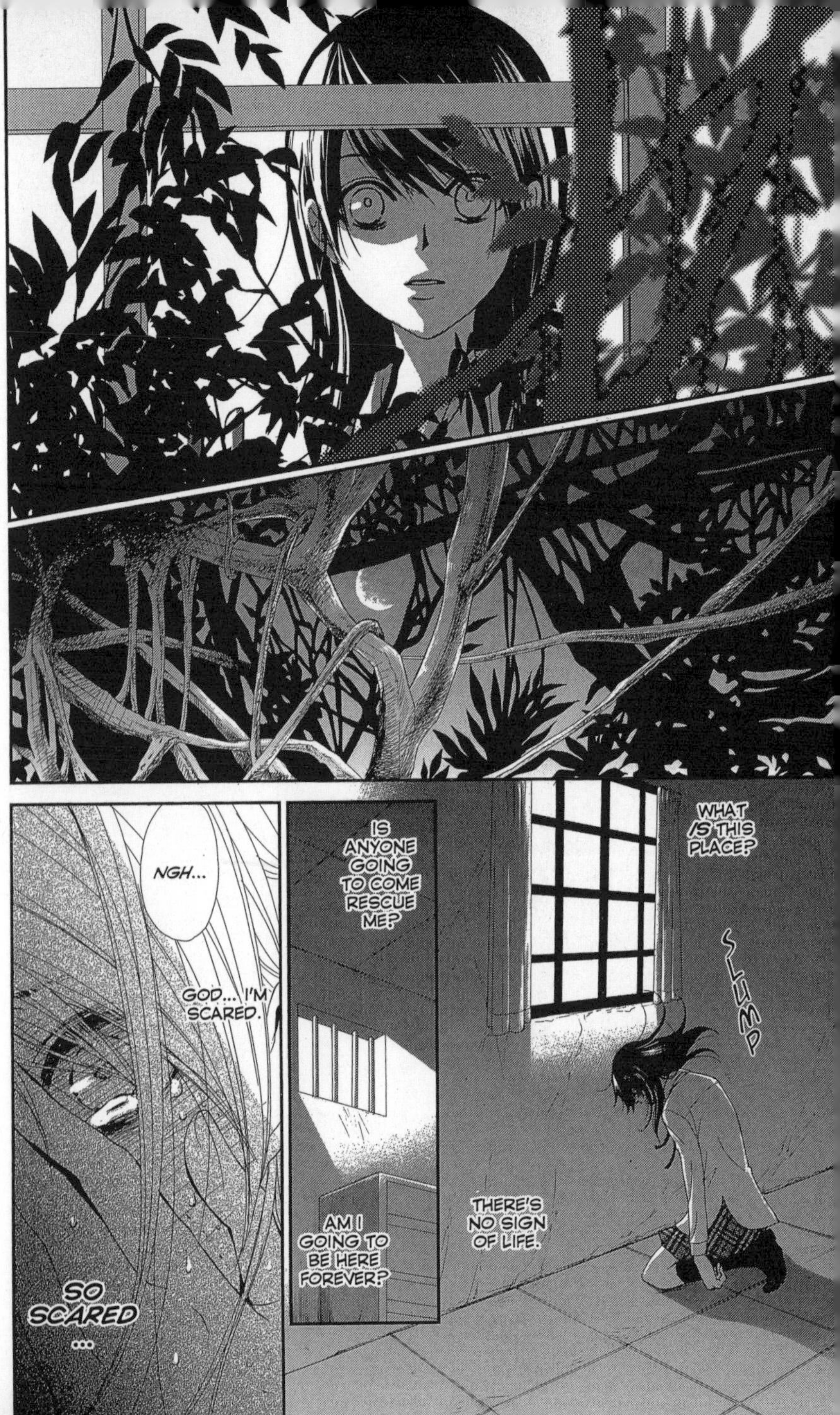
WHAT IS THIS PLACE?
SLUMP
THERE'S NO SIGN OF LIFE.
IS ANYONE GOING TO COME RESCUE ME?
AM I GOING TO BE HERE FOREVER?
NGH...
GOD... I'M SCARED.
SO SCARED...

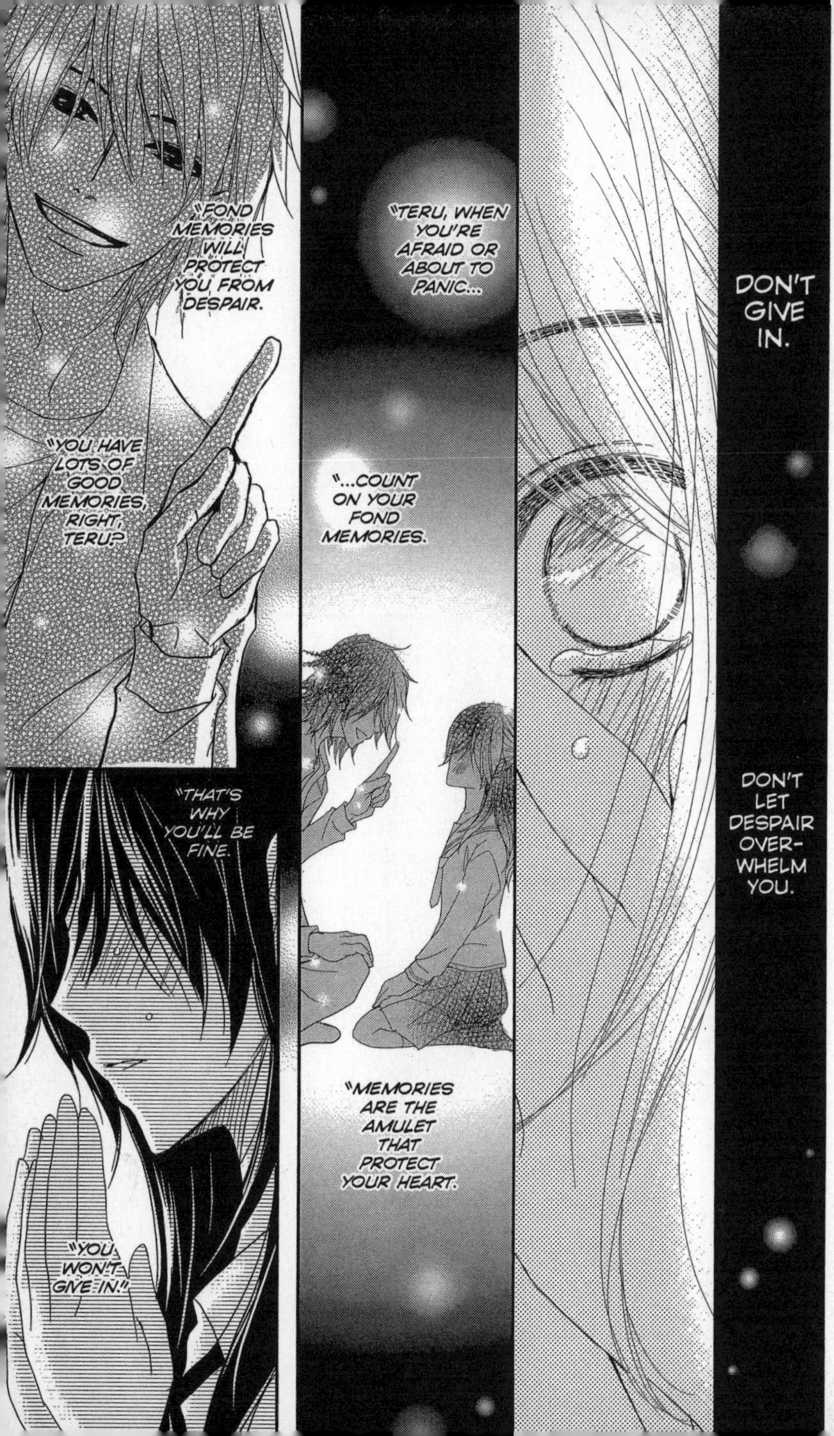
DON'T GIVE IN.
DON'T LET DESPAIR OVER-WHELM YOU.
"TERU, WHEN YOU'RE AFRAID OR ABOUT TO PANIC...
"...COUNT ON YOUR FOND MEMORIES.
"MEMORIES ARE THE AMULET THAT PROTECT YOUR HEART.
"FOND MEMORIES WILL PROTECT YOU FROM DESPAIR.
"YOU HAVE LOTS OF GOOD MEMORIES, RIGHT, TERU?
"THAT'S WHY YOU'LL BE FINE.
"YOU WON'T GIVE IN."

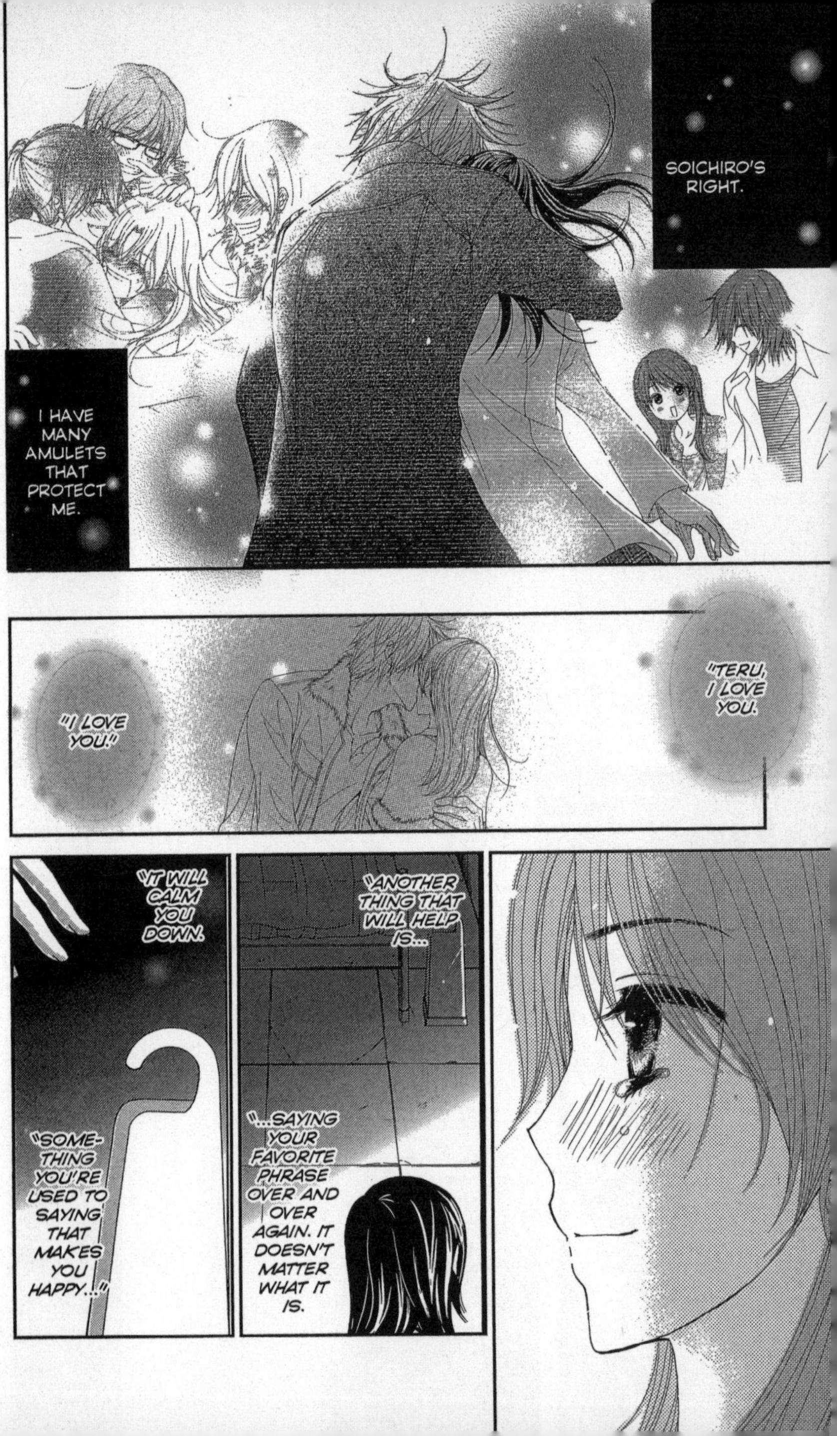
SOICHIRO'S RIGHT.
I HAVE MANY AMULETS THAT PROTECT ME.
"TERU, I LOVE YOU.
"I LOVE YOU."
"ANOTHER THING THAT WILL HELP IS...
"...SAYING YOUR FAVORITE PHRASE OVER AND OVER AGAIN. IT DOESN'T MATTER WHAT IT IS.
"IT WILL CALM YOU DOWN.
"SOME-THING YOU'RE USED TO SAYING THAT MAKES YOU HAPPY..."

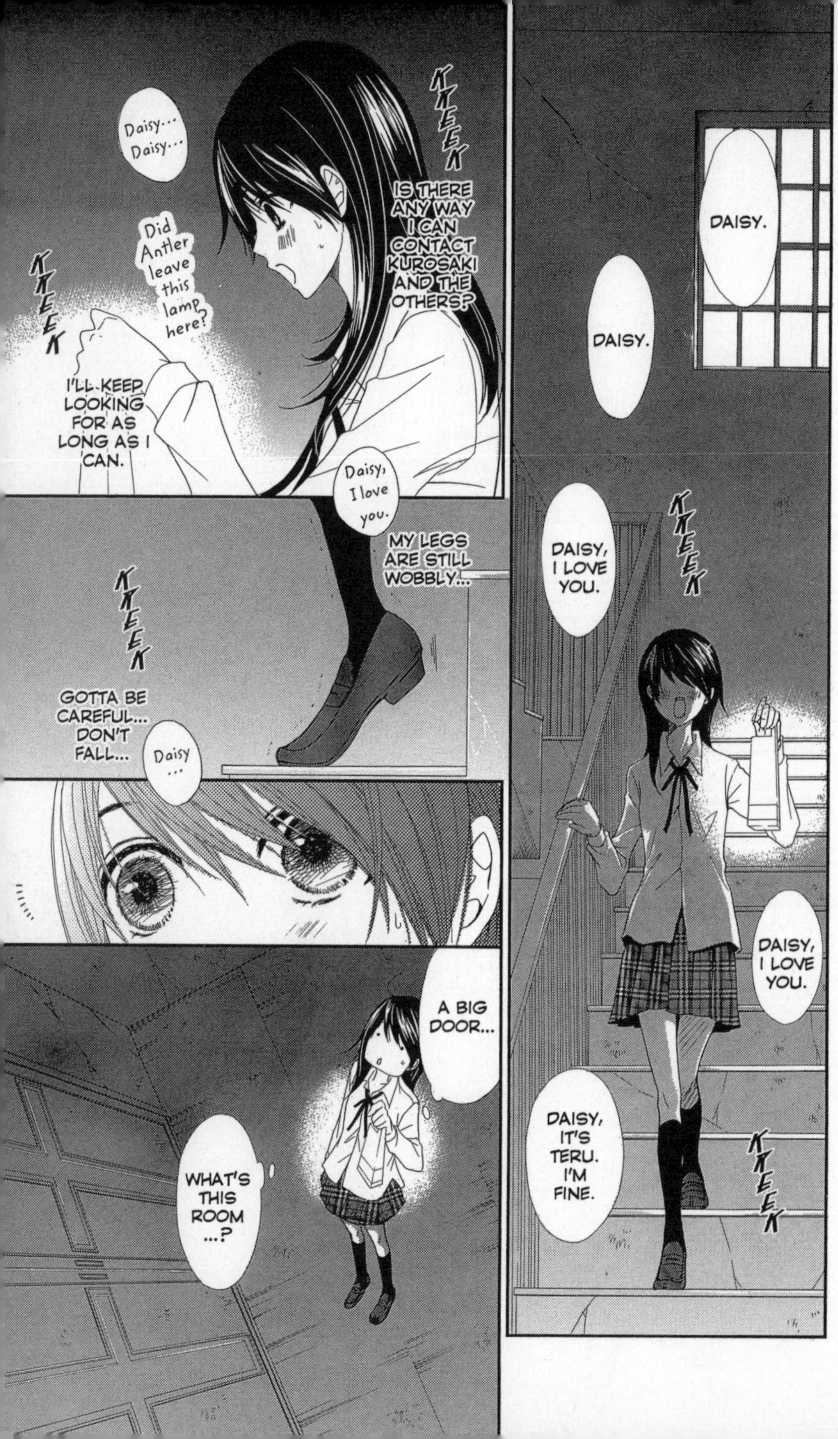
DAISY.
DAISY.
DAISY, I LOVE YOU.
KREEK
DAISY, I LOVE YOU.
DAISY, IT'S TERU. I'M FINE.
KREEK
KREEK
IS THERE ANY WAY I CAN CONTACT KUROSAKI AND THE OTHERS?
Daisy... Daisy...
Did Antler leave this lamp here?
KREEK
I'LL KEEP LOOKING FOR AS LONG AS I CAN.
Daisy, I love you.
MY LEGS ARE STILL WOBBLY...
KREEK
GOTTA BE CAREFUL... DON'T FALL...
Daisy ...
...
A BIG DOOR...
WHAT'S THIS ROOM ...?

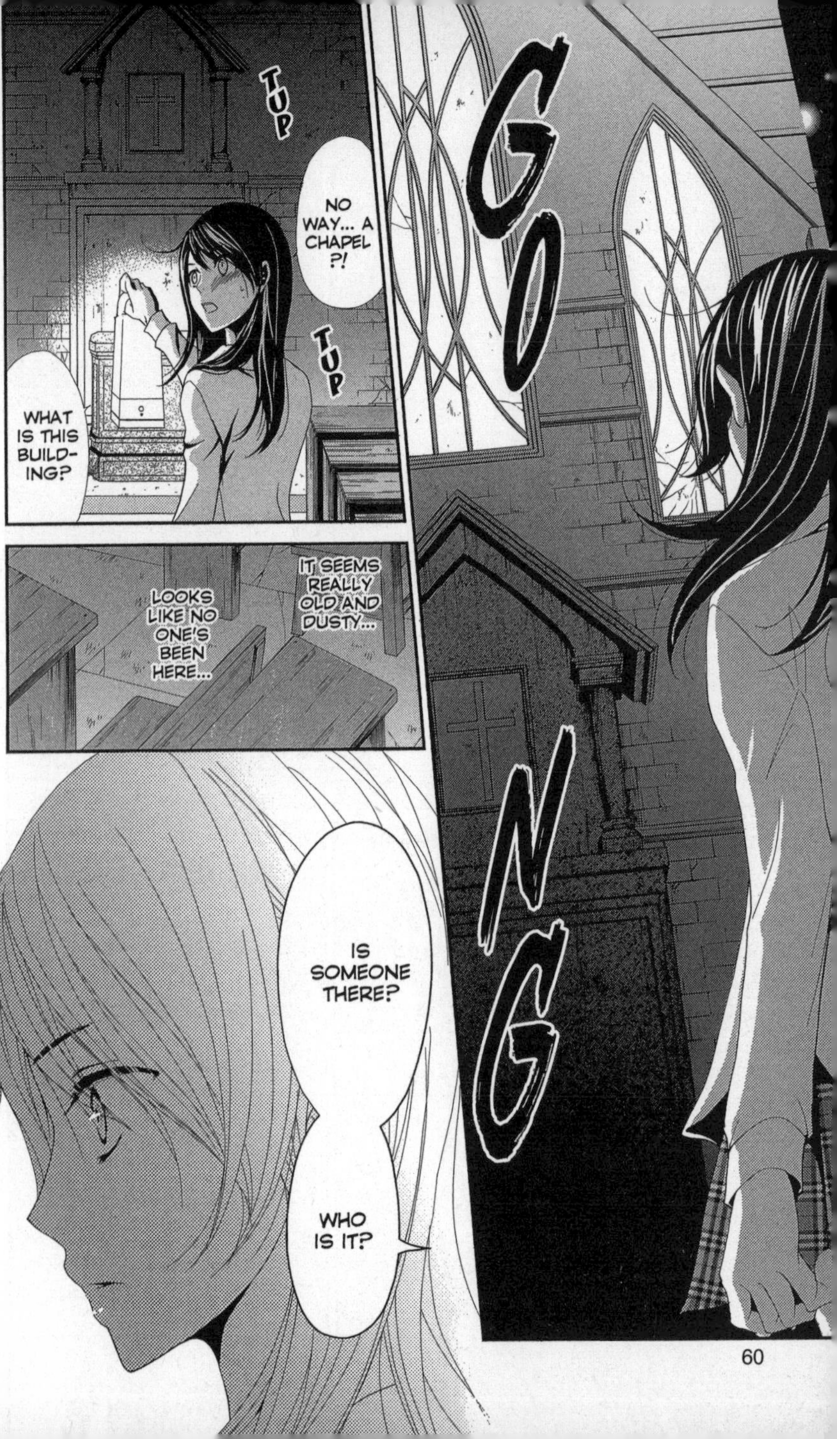
GONG
TUP
NO WAY... A CHAPEL?!
TUP
WHAT IS THIS BUILD-ING?
IT SEEMS REALLY OLD AND DUSTY...
LOOKS LIKE NO ONE'S BEEN HERE...
IS SOMEONE THERE?
WHO IS IT?

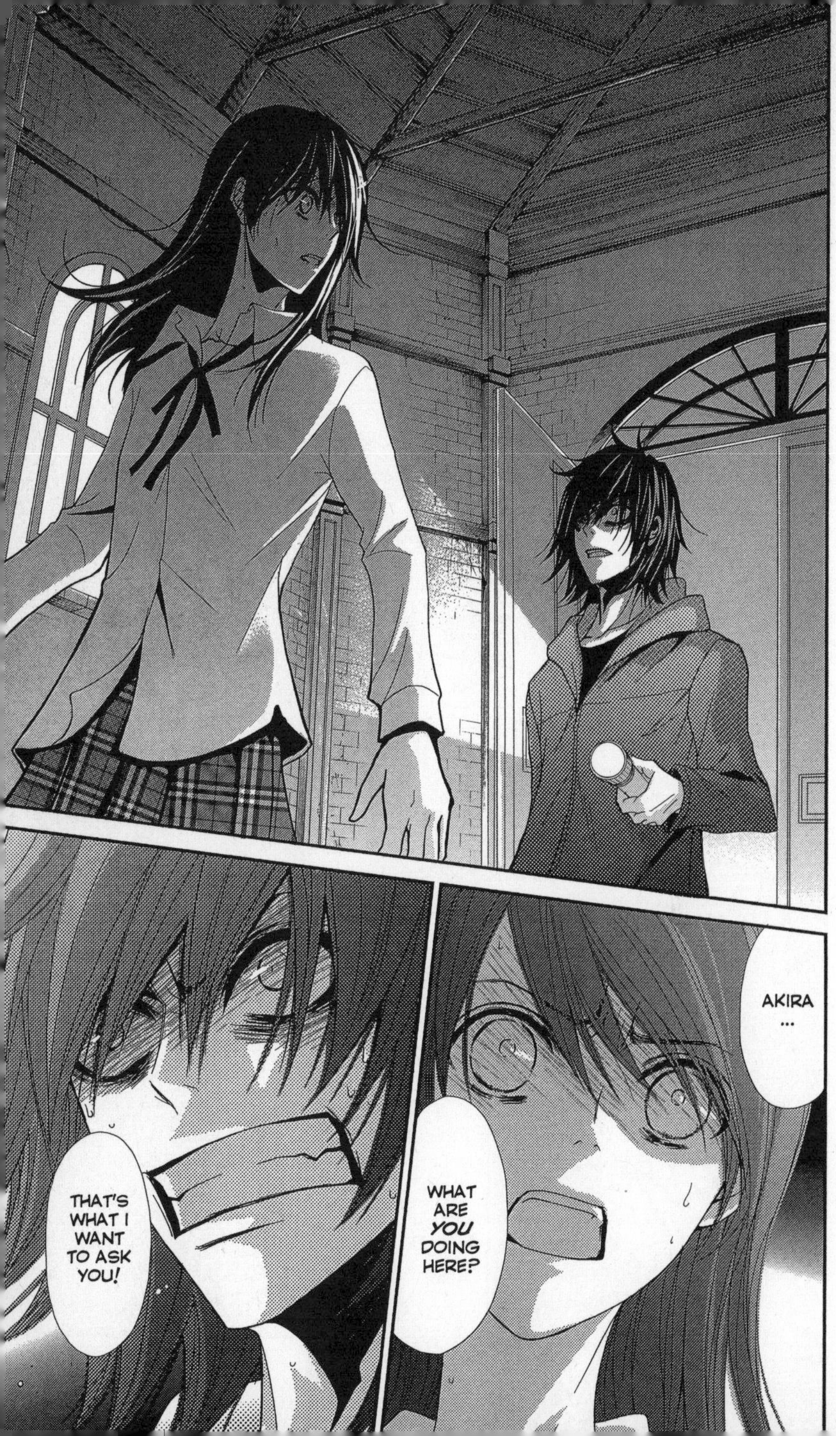
AKIRA ...
WHAT ARE *YOU* DOING HERE?
THAT'S WHAT I WANT TO ASK YOU!

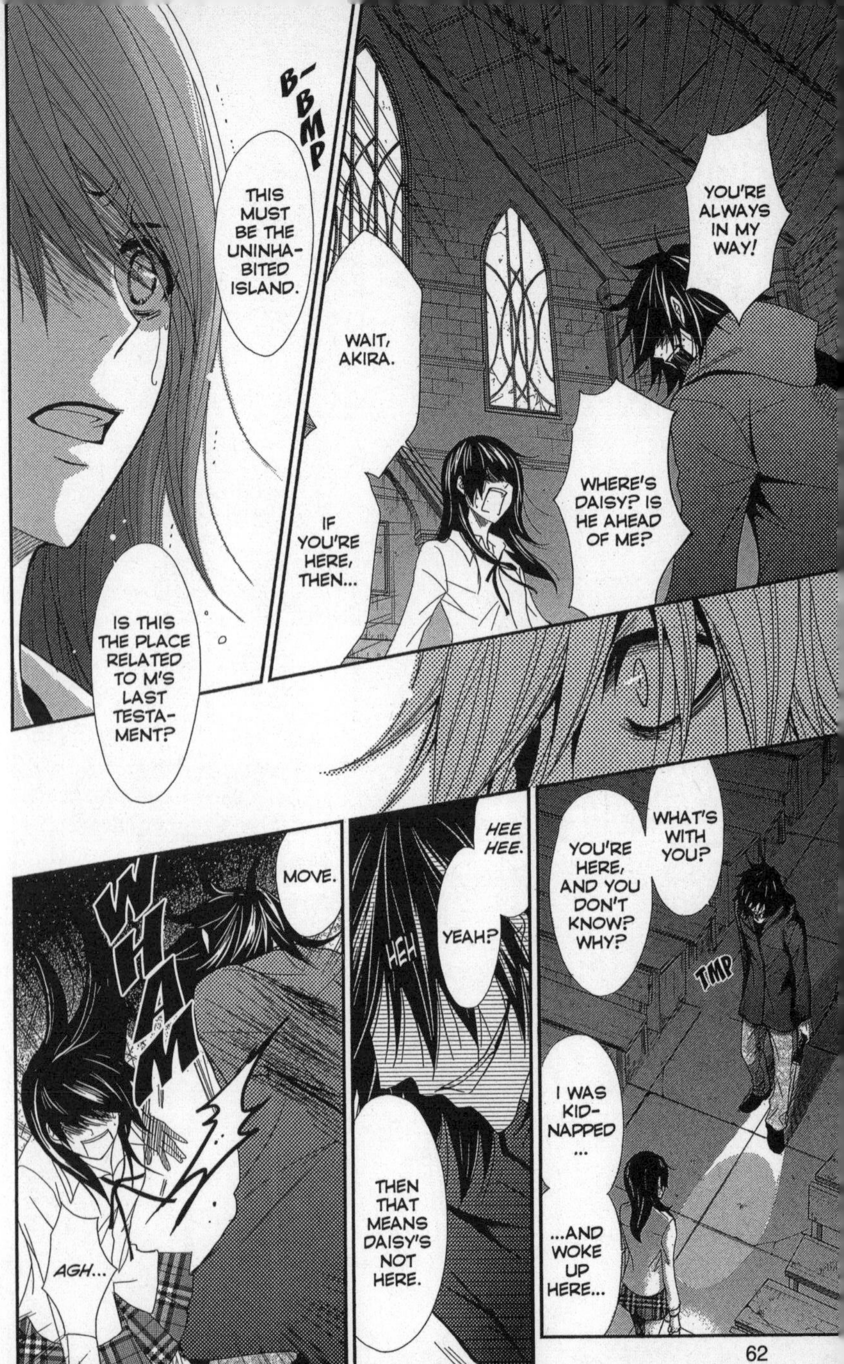
YOU'RE ALWAYS IN MY WAY!
WHERE'S DAISY? IS HE AHEAD OF ME?
WAIT, AKIRA.
IF YOU'RE HERE, THEN...
B-BMP
THIS MUST BE THE UNINHA-BITED ISLAND.
IS THIS THE PLACE RELATED TO M'S LAST TESTA-MENT?
WHAT'S WITH YOU?
YOU'RE HERE, AND YOU DON'T KNOW? WHY?
TMP
I WAS KID-NAPPED ...
...AND WOKE UP HERE...
HEE HEE.
YEAH?
HEH
THEN THAT MEANS DAISY'S NOT HERE.
MOVE.
WHAM
AGH...

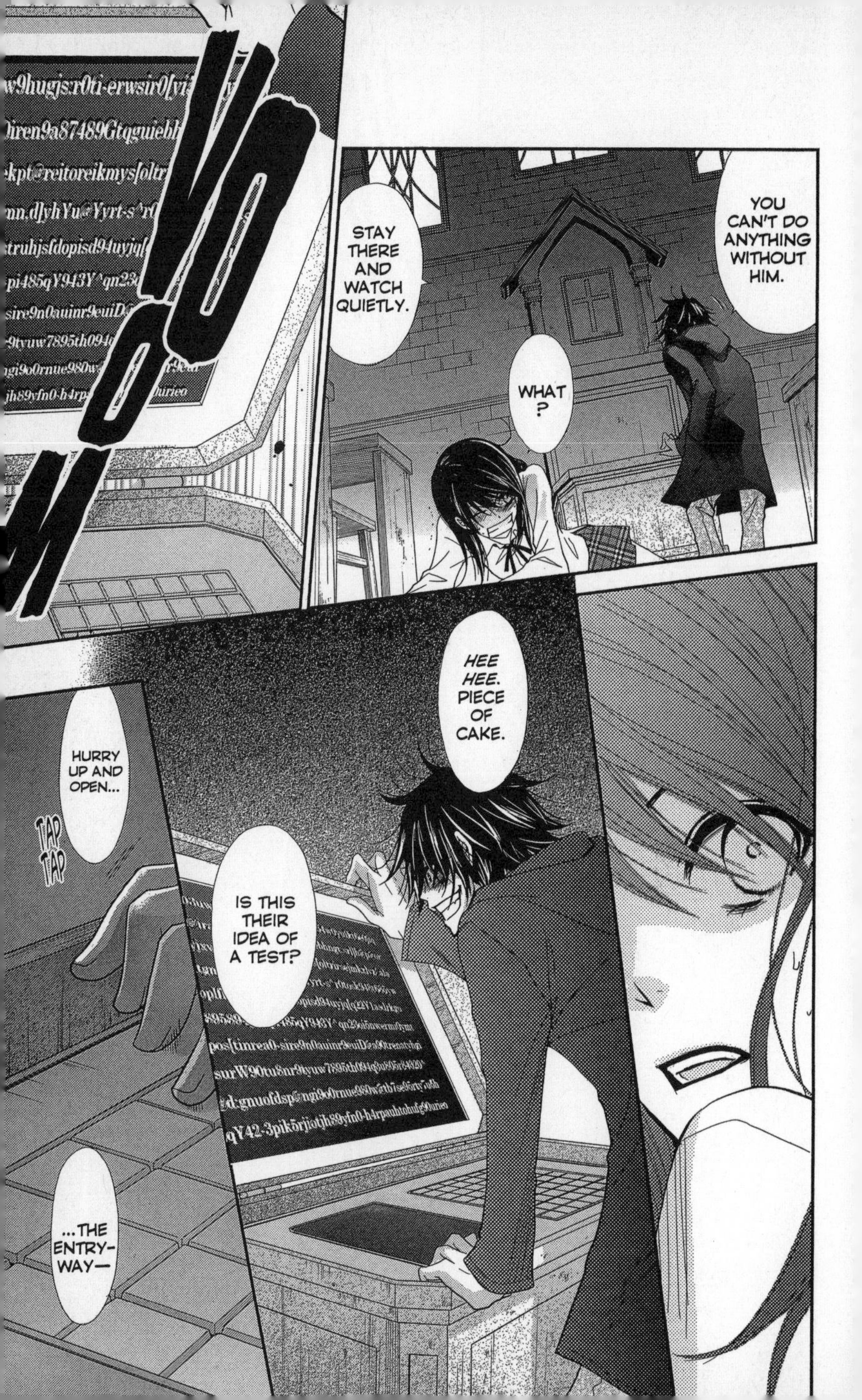
YOU CAN'T DO ANYTHING WITHOUT HIM.
STAY THERE AND WATCH QUIETLY.
WHAT?
HEE HEE. PIECE OF CAKE.
IS THIS THEIR IDEA OF A TEST?
HURRY UP AND OPEN...
TAP TAP
...THE ENTRY-WAY—

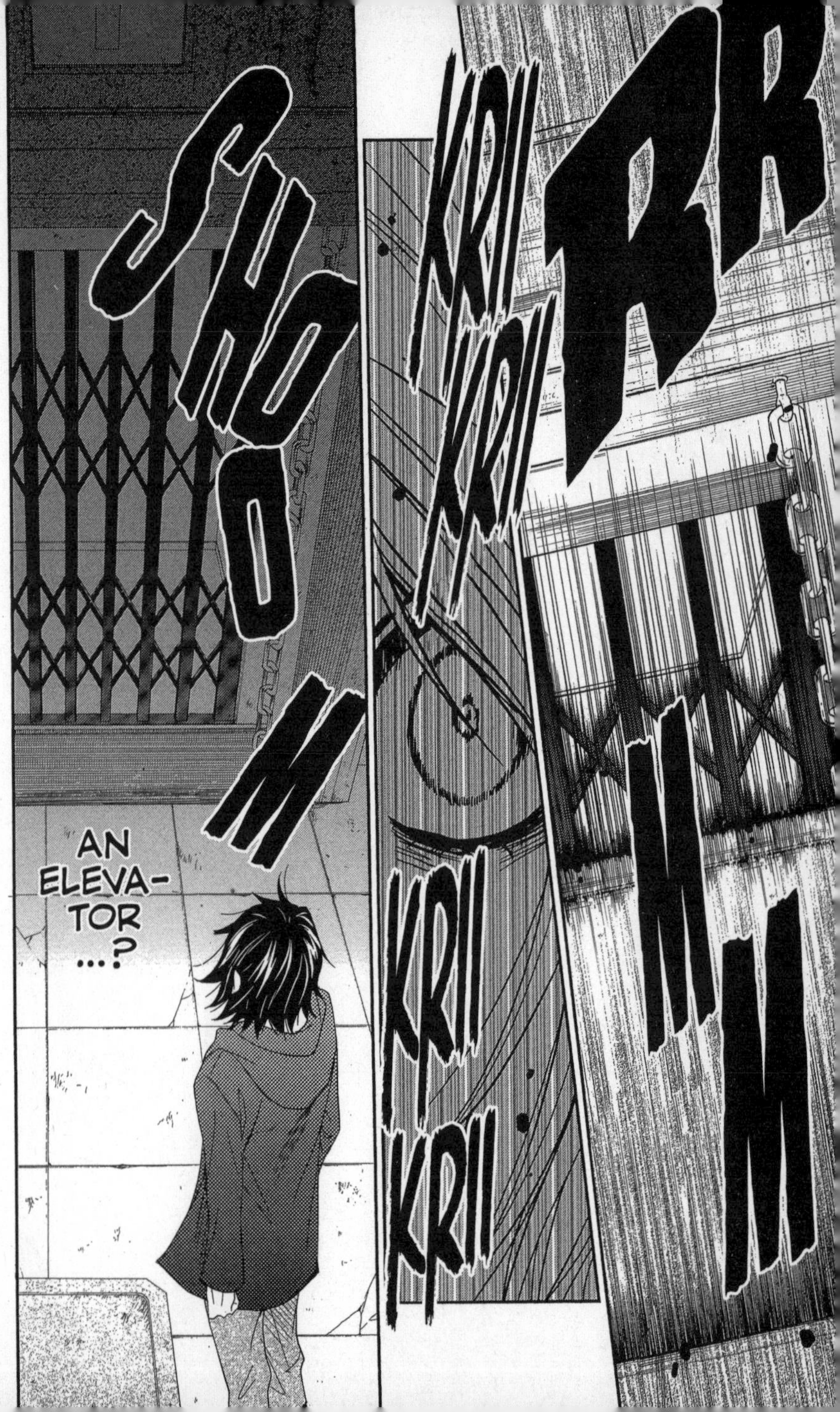
TRMM
KRII KRII KRII
KRII KRII
SHOOM
AN ELEVA-TOR...?

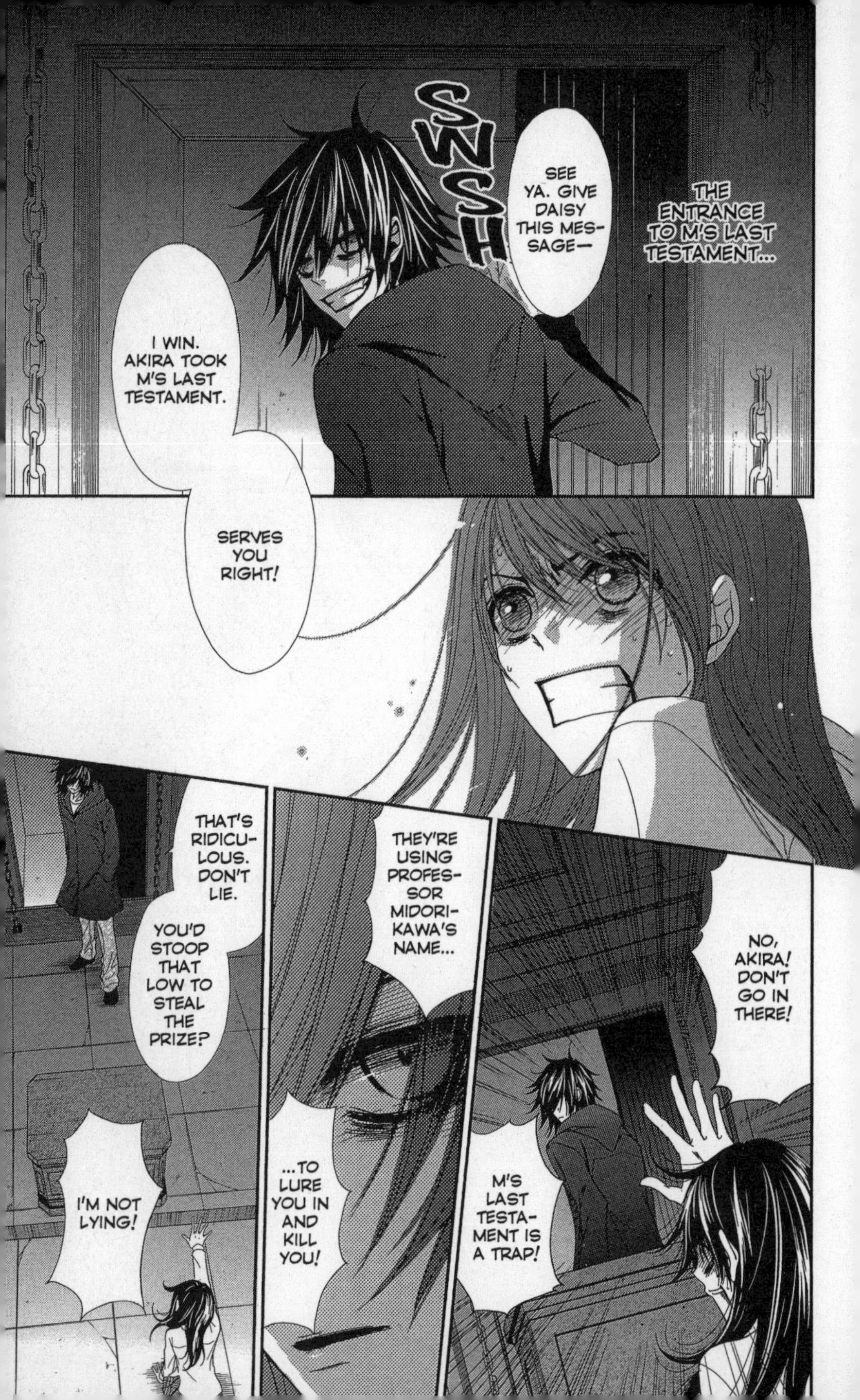
THE ENTRANCE TO M'S LAST TESTAMENT...
SWSH
SEE YA. GIVE DAISY THIS MES-SAGE—
I WIN. AKIRA TOOK M'S LAST TESTAMENT.
SERVES YOU RIGHT!
NO, AKIRA! DON'T GO IN THERE!
M'S LAST TESTA-MENT IS A TRAP!
THEY'RE USING PROFES-SOR MIDORI-KAWA'S NAME...
...TO LURE YOU IN AND KILL YOU!
THAT'S RIDICU-LOUS. DON'T LIE.
YOU'D STOOP THAT LOW TO STEAL THE PRIZE?
I'M NOT LYING!

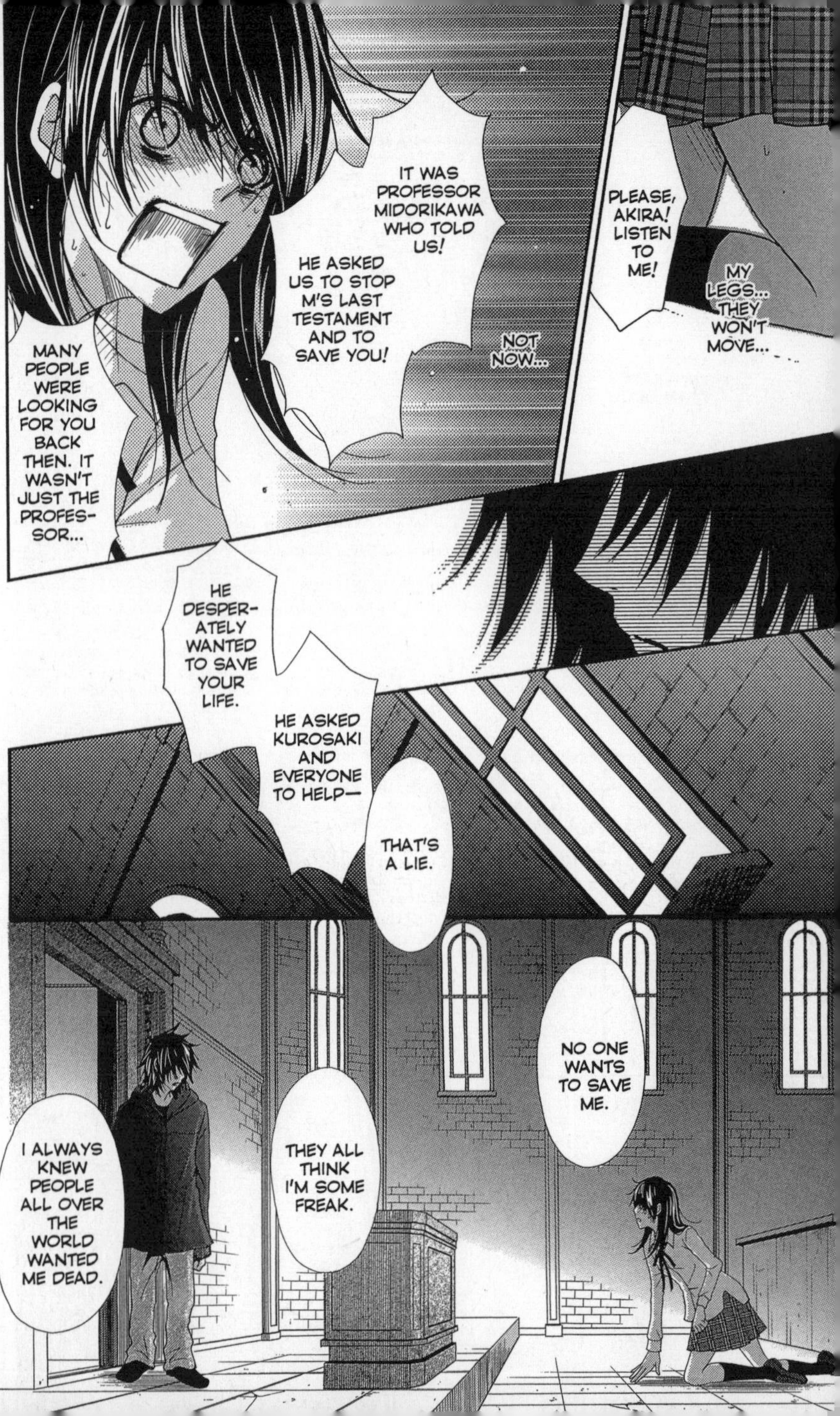
PLEASE, AKIRA! LISTEN TO ME!
MY LEGS... THEY WON'T MOVE...
IT WAS PROFESSOR MIDORIKAWA WHO TOLD US!
HE ASKED US TO STOP M'S LAST TESTAMENT AND TO SAVE YOU!
NOT NOW...
MANY PEOPLE WERE LOOKING FOR YOU BACK THEN. IT WASN'T JUST THE PROFES-SOR...
HE DESPER-ATELY WANTED TO SAVE YOUR LIFE.
HE ASKED KUROSAKI AND EVERYONE TO HELP—
THAT'S A LIE.
NO ONE WANTS TO SAVE ME.
THEY ALL THINK I'M SOME FREAK.
I ALWAYS KNEW PEOPLE ALL OVER THE WORLD WANTED ME DEAD.

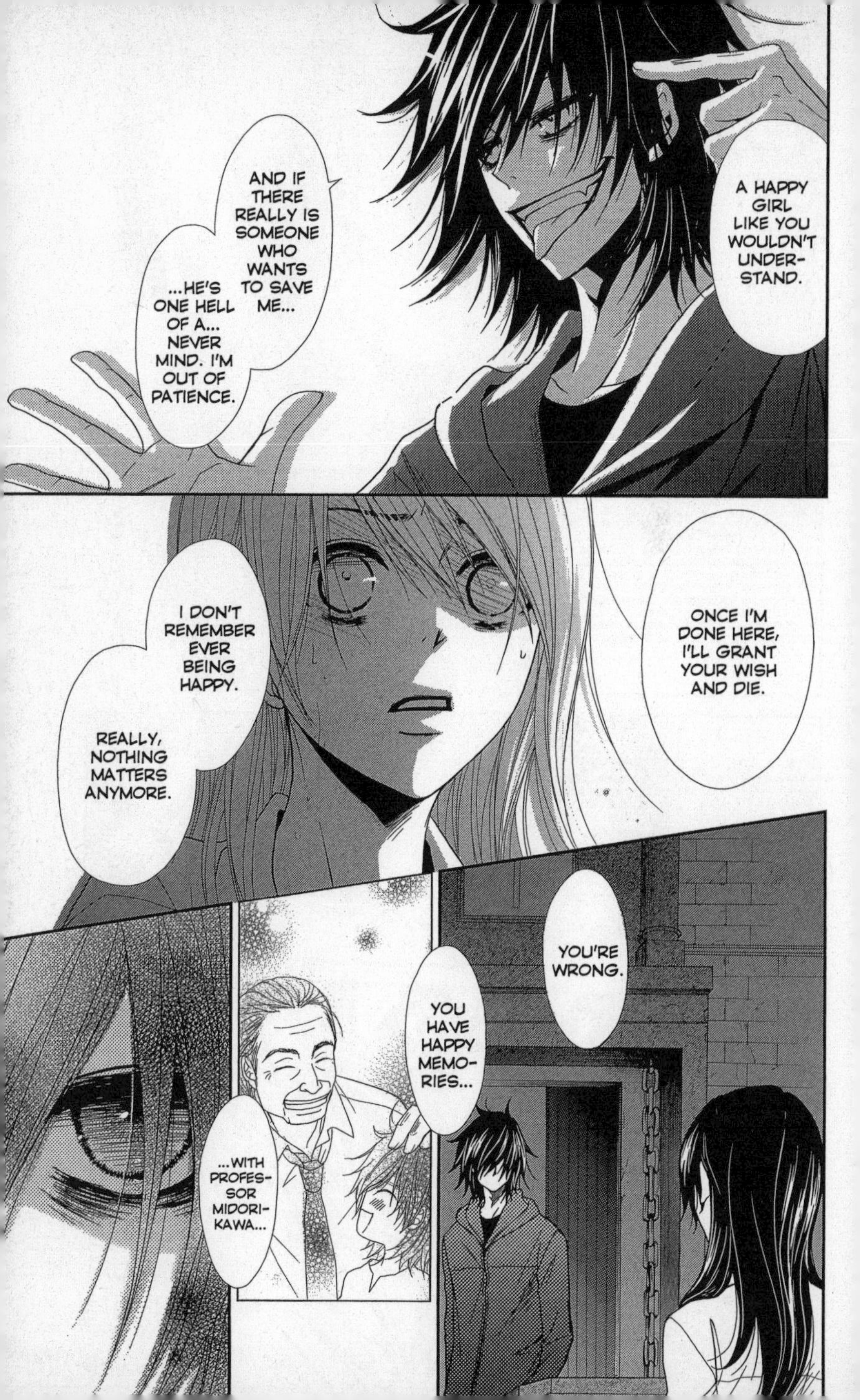
A HAPPY GIRL LIKE YOU WOULDN'T UNDER-STAND.
AND IF THERE REALLY IS SOMEONE WHO WANTS TO SAVE ME...
...HE'S ONE HELL OF A... NEVER MIND. I'M OUT OF PATIENCE.
ONCE I'M DONE HERE, I'LL GRANT YOUR WISH AND DIE.
I DON'T REMEMBER EVER BEING HAPPY.
REALLY, NOTHING MATTERS ANYMORE.
YOU'RE WRONG.
YOU HAVE HAPPY MEMO-RIES...
...WITH PROFES-SOR MIDORI-KAWA...

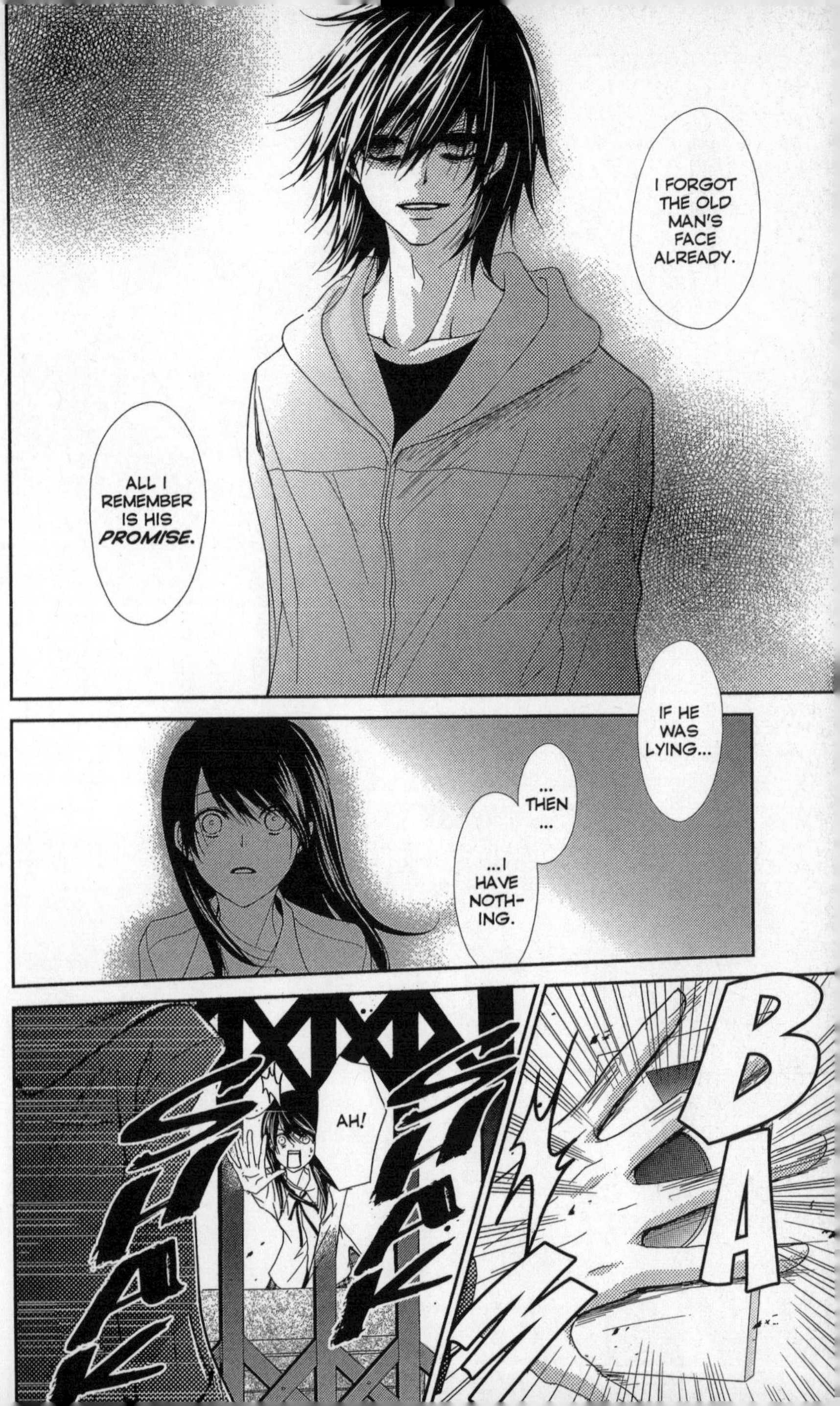
I FORGOT THE OLD MAN'S FACE ALREADY.
ALL I REMEMBER IS HIS *PROMISE*.
IF HE WAS LYING...
...THEN...
...I HAVE NOTHING.
BAM
AH!

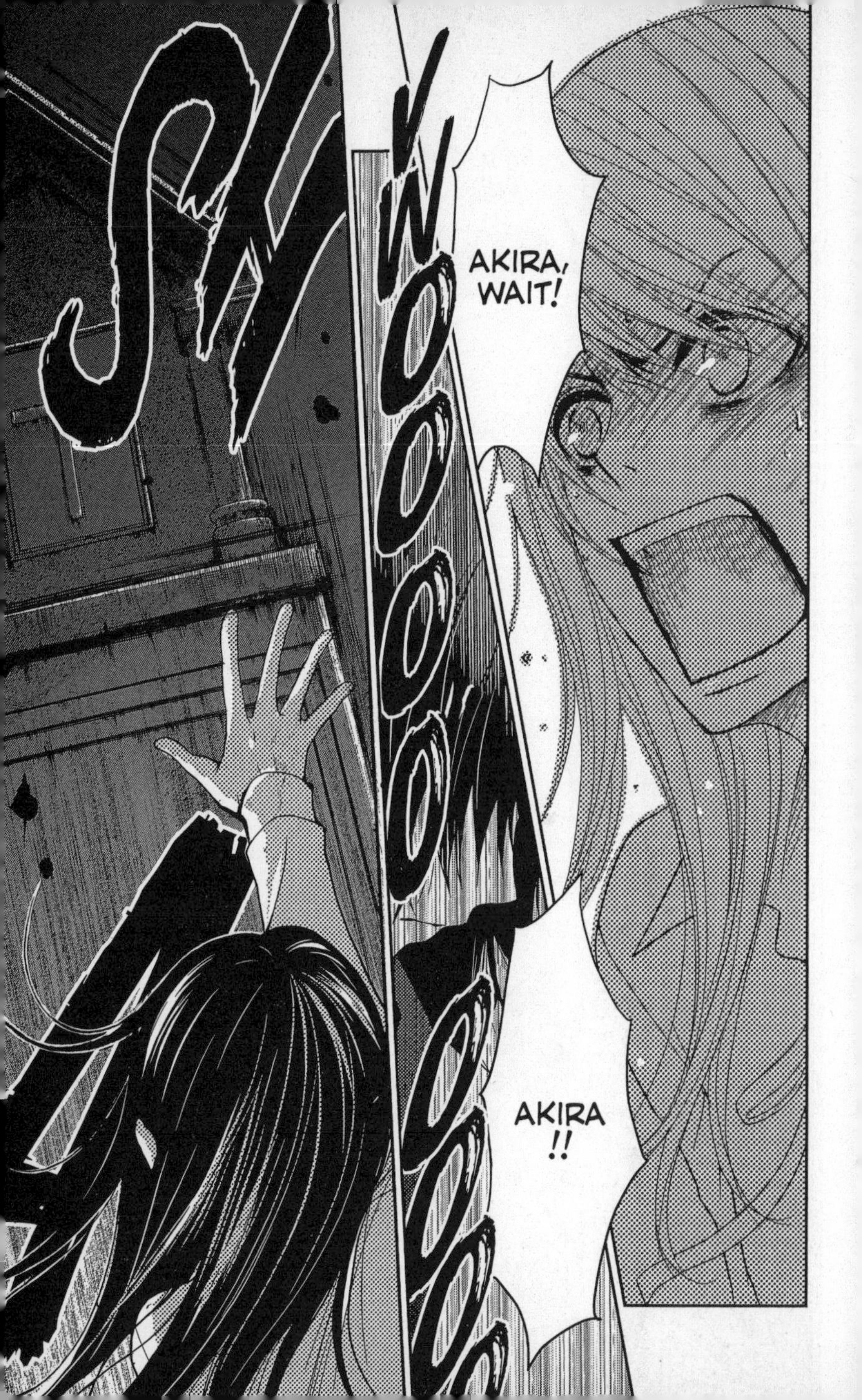
AKIRA, WAIT!
AKIRA !!

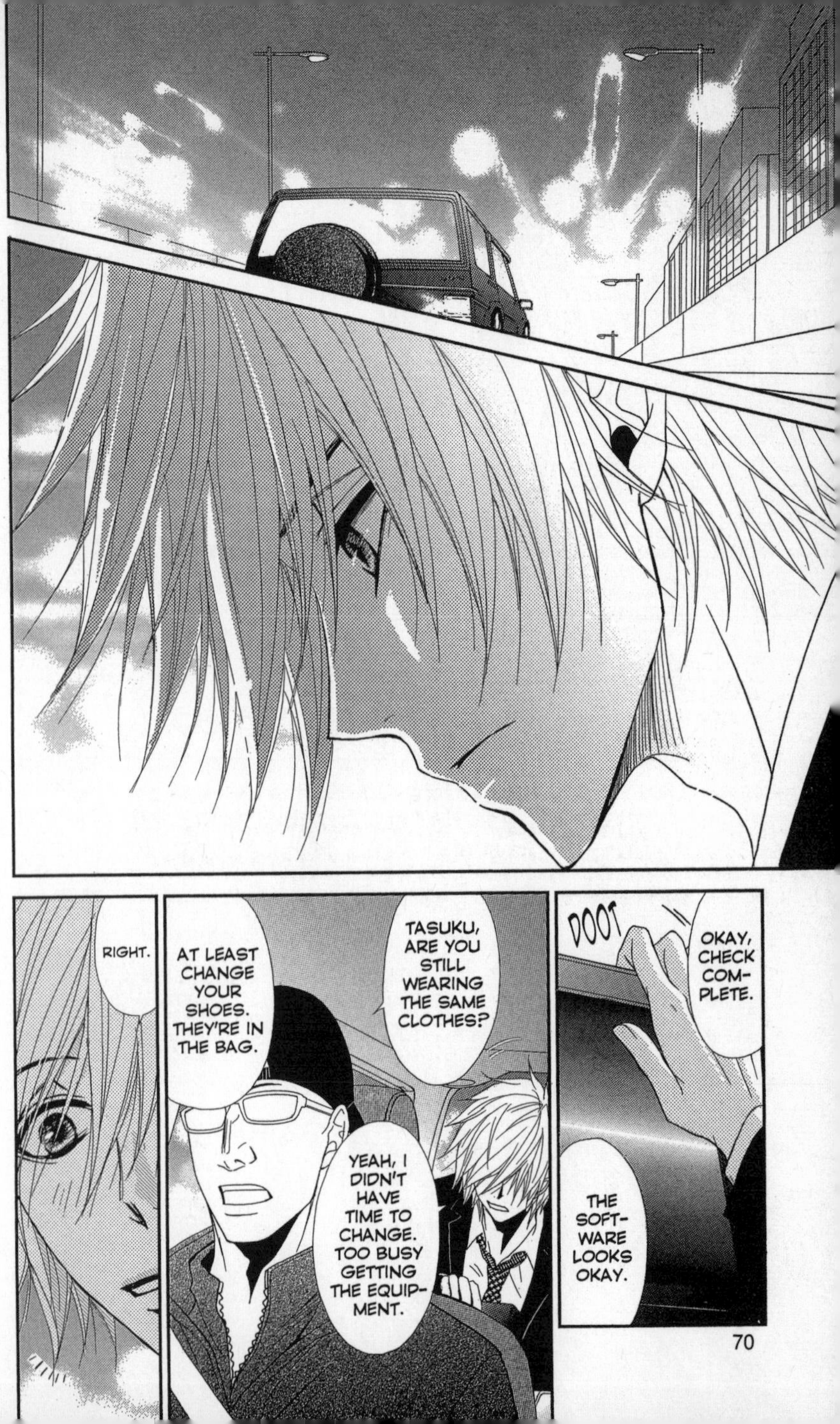
DOOT
OKAY, CHECK COM-PLETE.
THE SOFT-WARE LOOKS OKAY.
TASUKU, ARE YOU STILL WEARING THE SAME CLOTHES?
YEAH, I DIDN'T HAVE TIME TO CHANGE. TOO BUSY GETTING THE EQUIP-MENT.
AT LEAST CHANGE YOUR SHOES. THEY'RE IN THE BAG.
RIGHT.

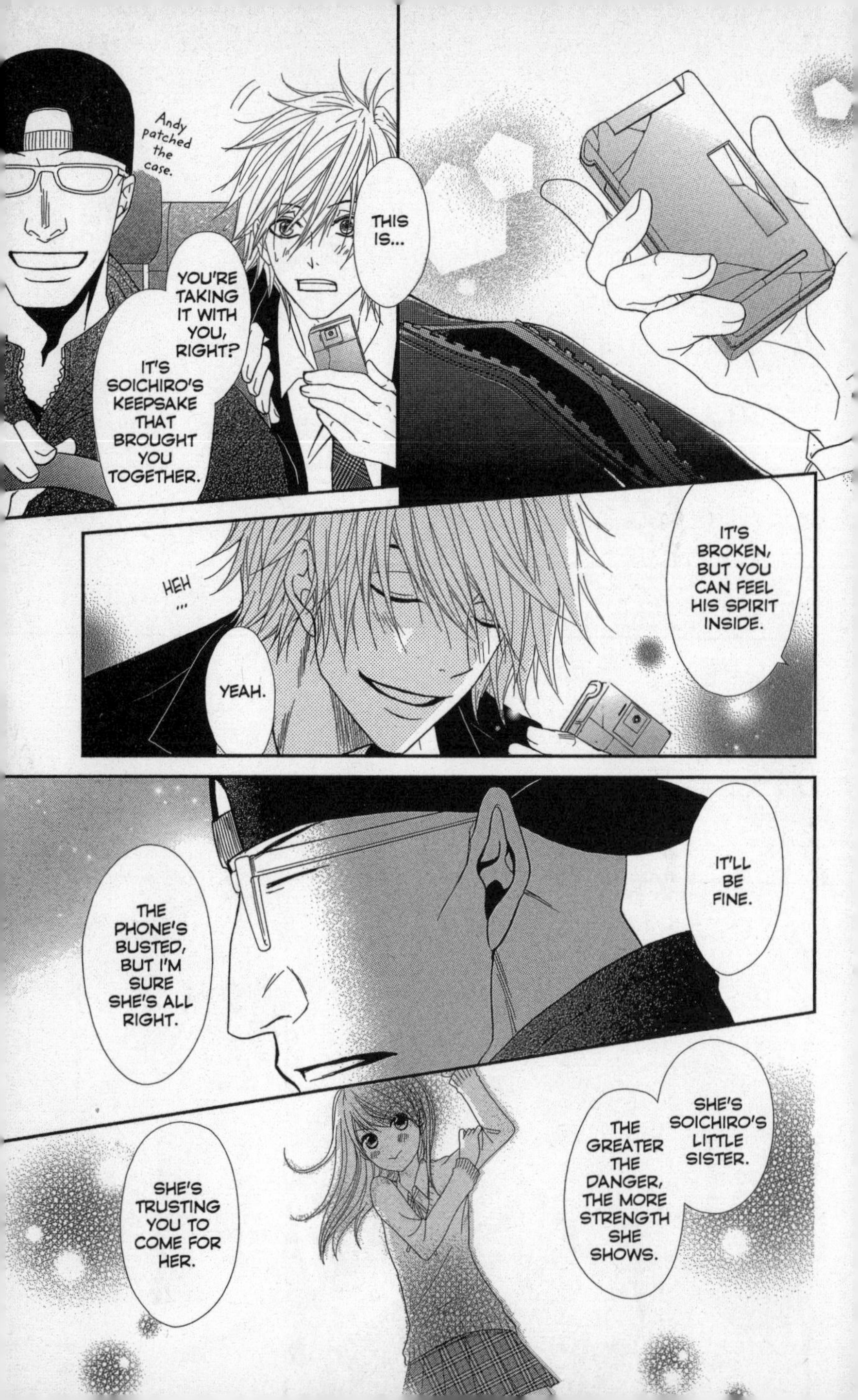
THIS IS...
Andy patched the case.
YOU'RE TAKING IT WITH YOU, RIGHT?
IT'S SOICHIRO'S KEEPSAKE THAT BROUGHT YOU TOGETHER.
IT'S BROKEN, BUT YOU CAN FEEL HIS SPIRIT INSIDE.
HEH...
YEAH.
IT'LL BE FINE.
THE PHONE'S BUSTED, BUT I'M SURE SHE'S ALL RIGHT.
SHE'S SOICHIRO'S LITTLE SISTER.
THE GREATER THE DANGER, THE MORE STRENGTH SHE SHOWS.
SHE'S TRUSTING YOU TO COME FOR HER.

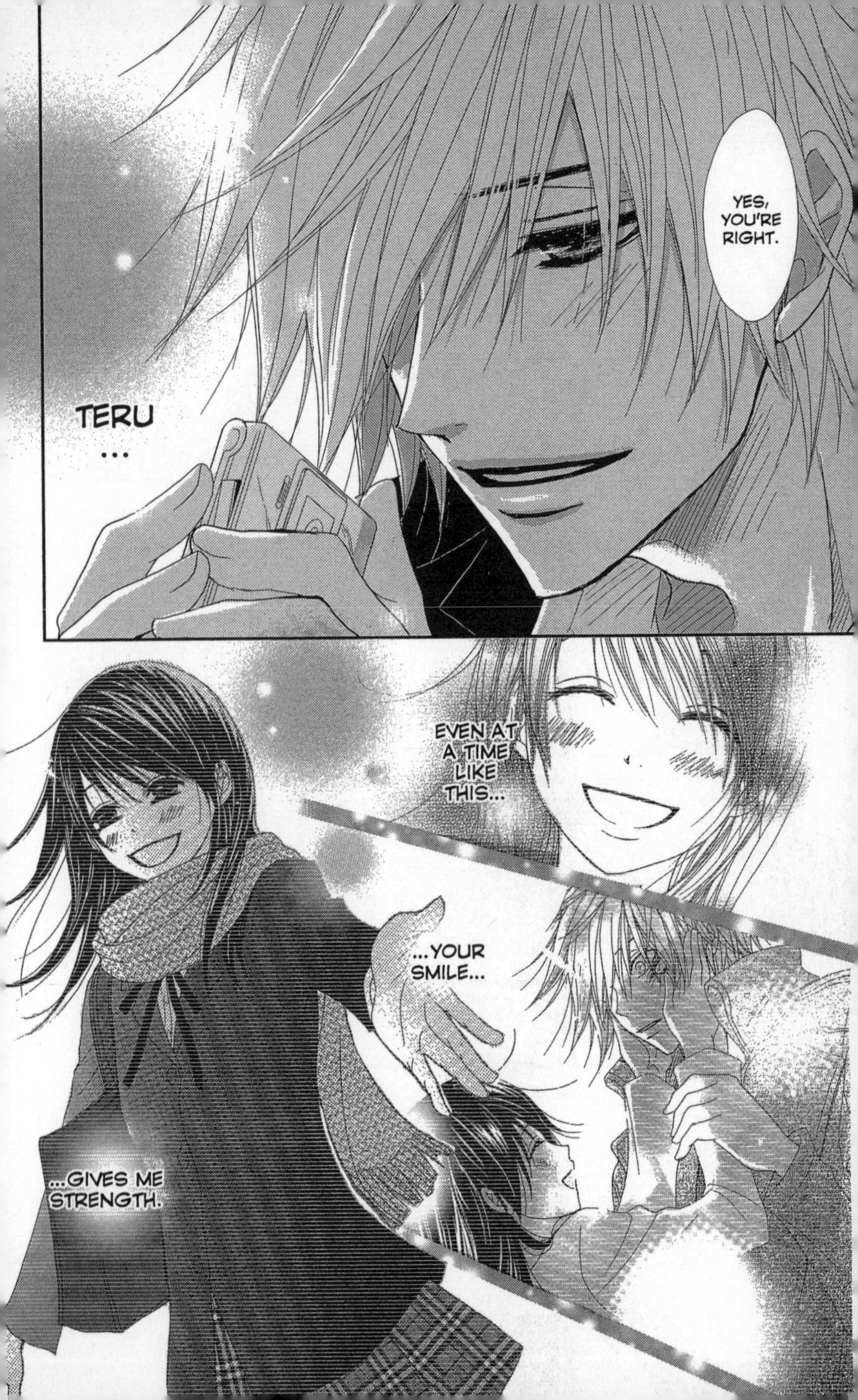
YES, YOU'RE RIGHT.
TERU ...
EVEN AT A TIME LIKE THIS...
...YOUR SMILE...
...GIVES ME STRENGTH.

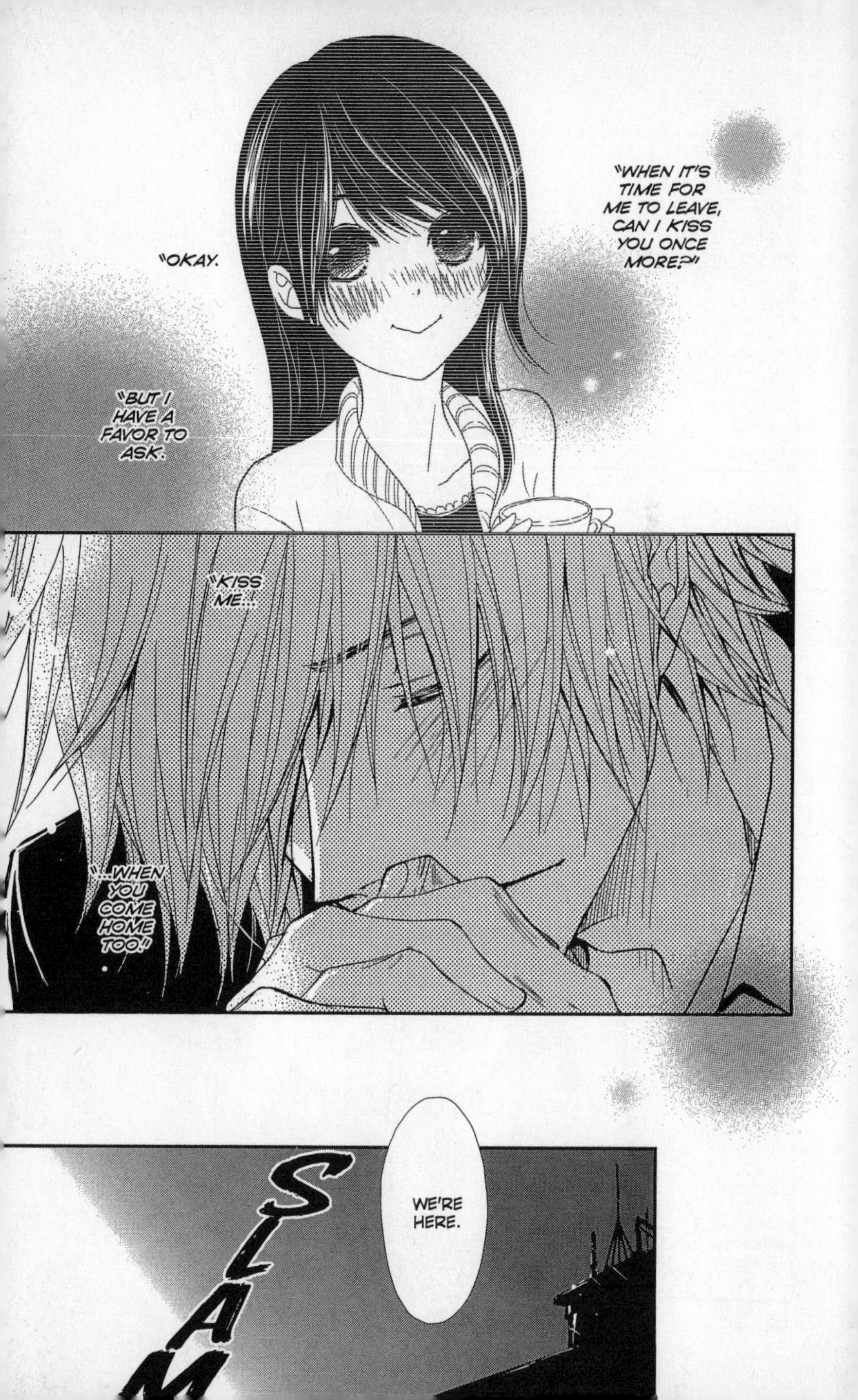
"WHEN IT'S TIME FOR ME TO LEAVE, CAN I KISS YOU ONCE MORE?"
"OKAY.
"BUT I HAVE A FAVOR TO ASK.
"KISS ME...
"...WHEN YOU COME HOME TOO."
WE'RE HERE.
SLAM

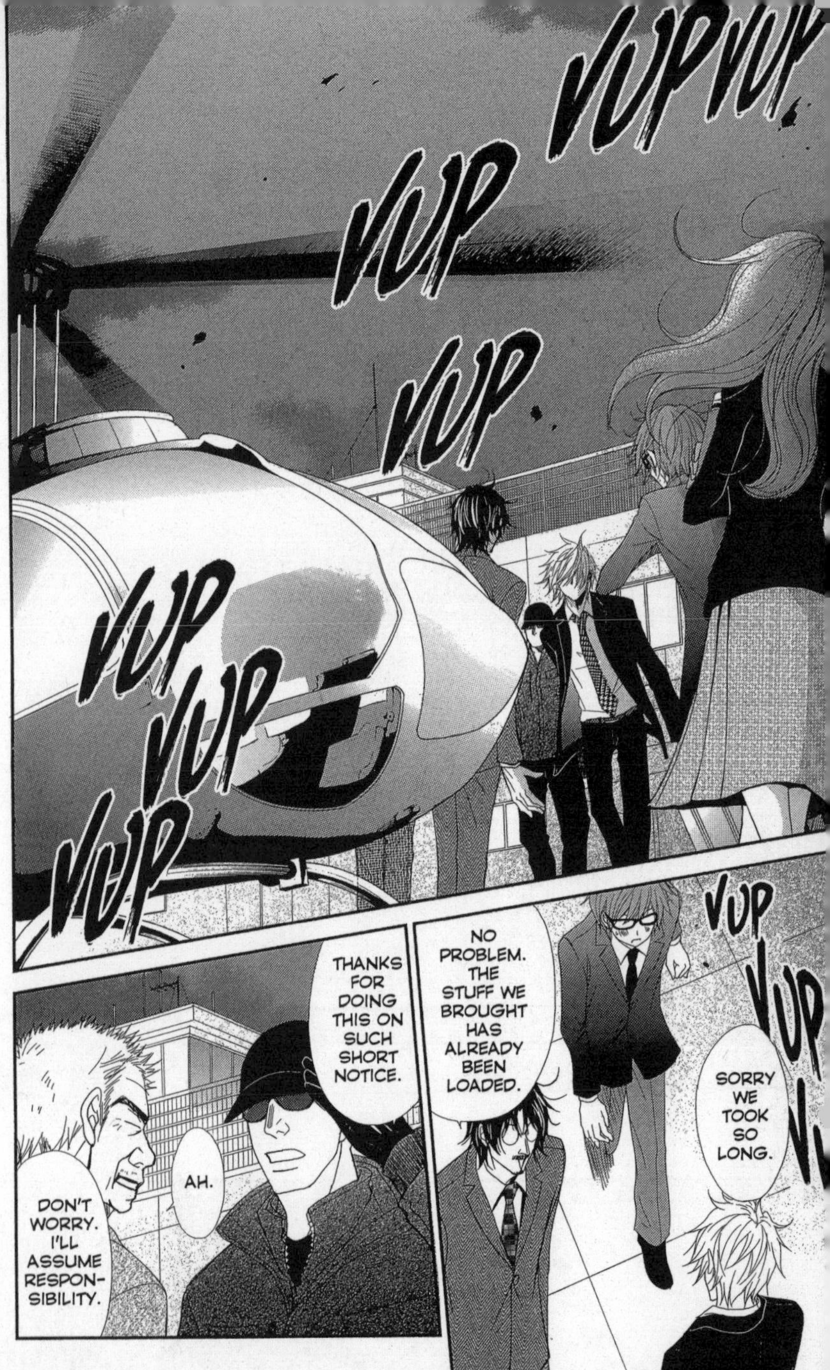
VUP VUP
VUP
VUP
VUP VUP VUP
VUP VUP VU
SORRY WE TOOK SO LONG.
NO PROBLEM. THE STUFF WE BROUGHT HAS ALREADY BEEN LOADED.
THANKS FOR DOING THIS ON SUCH SHORT NOTICE.
AH.
DON'T WORRY. I'LL ASSUME RESPON-SIBILITY.

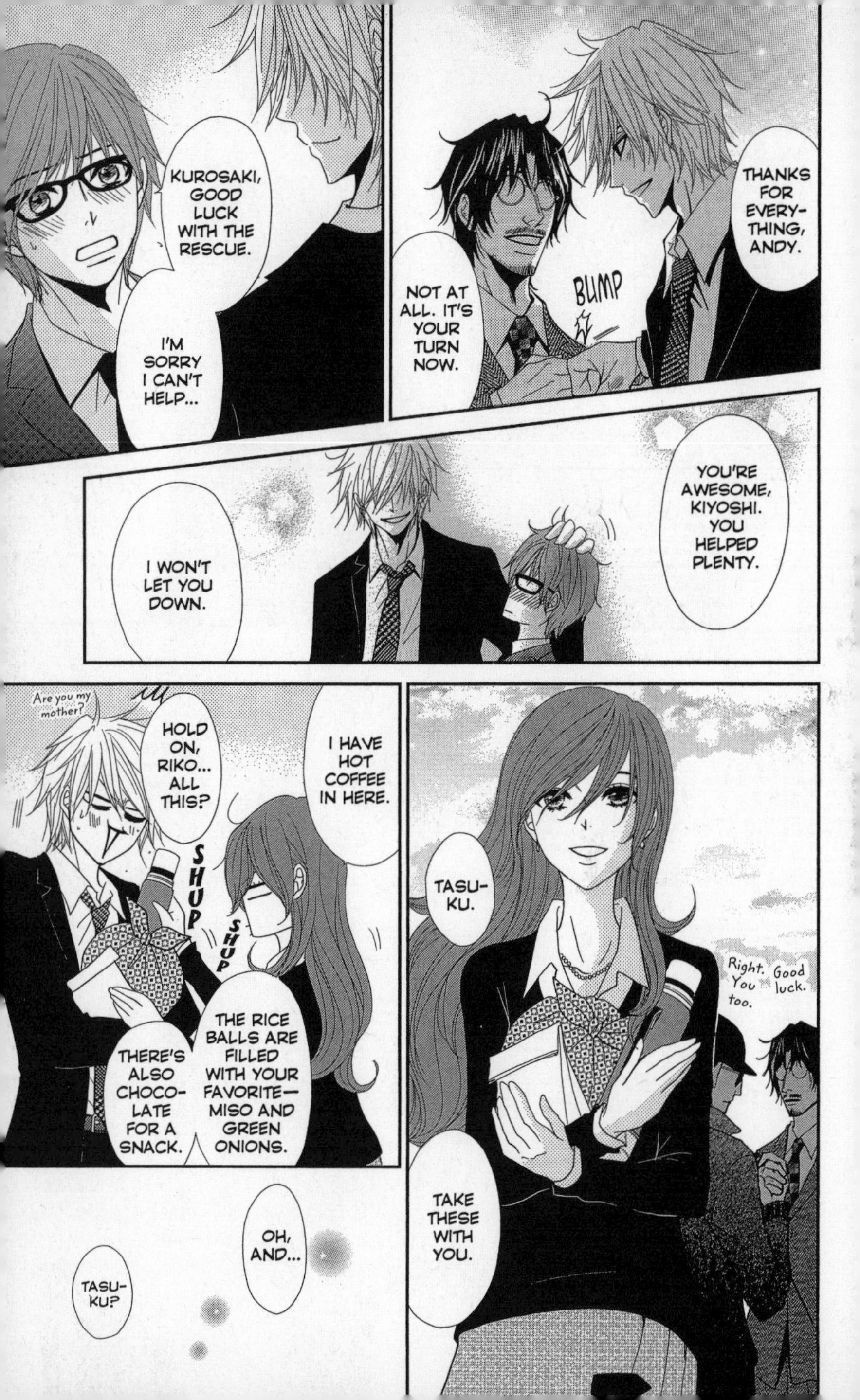
THANKS FOR EVERYTHING, ANDY.
NOT AT ALL. IT'S YOUR TURN NOW.
BUMP
KUROSAKI, GOOD LUCK WITH THE RESCUE.
I'M SORRY I CAN'T HELP...
YOU'RE AWESOME, KIYOSHI. YOU HELPED PLENTY.
I WON'T LET YOU DOWN.
TASUKU.
Right. Good luck. You too.
TAKE THESE WITH YOU.
I HAVE HOT COFFEE IN HERE.
HOLD ON, RIKO... ALL THIS?
Are you my mother?
SHUP
SHUP
THE RICE BALLS ARE FILLED WITH YOUR FAVORITE—MISO AND GREEN ONIONS.
THERE'S ALSO CHOCOLATE FOR A SNACK.
OH, AND...
TASUKU?

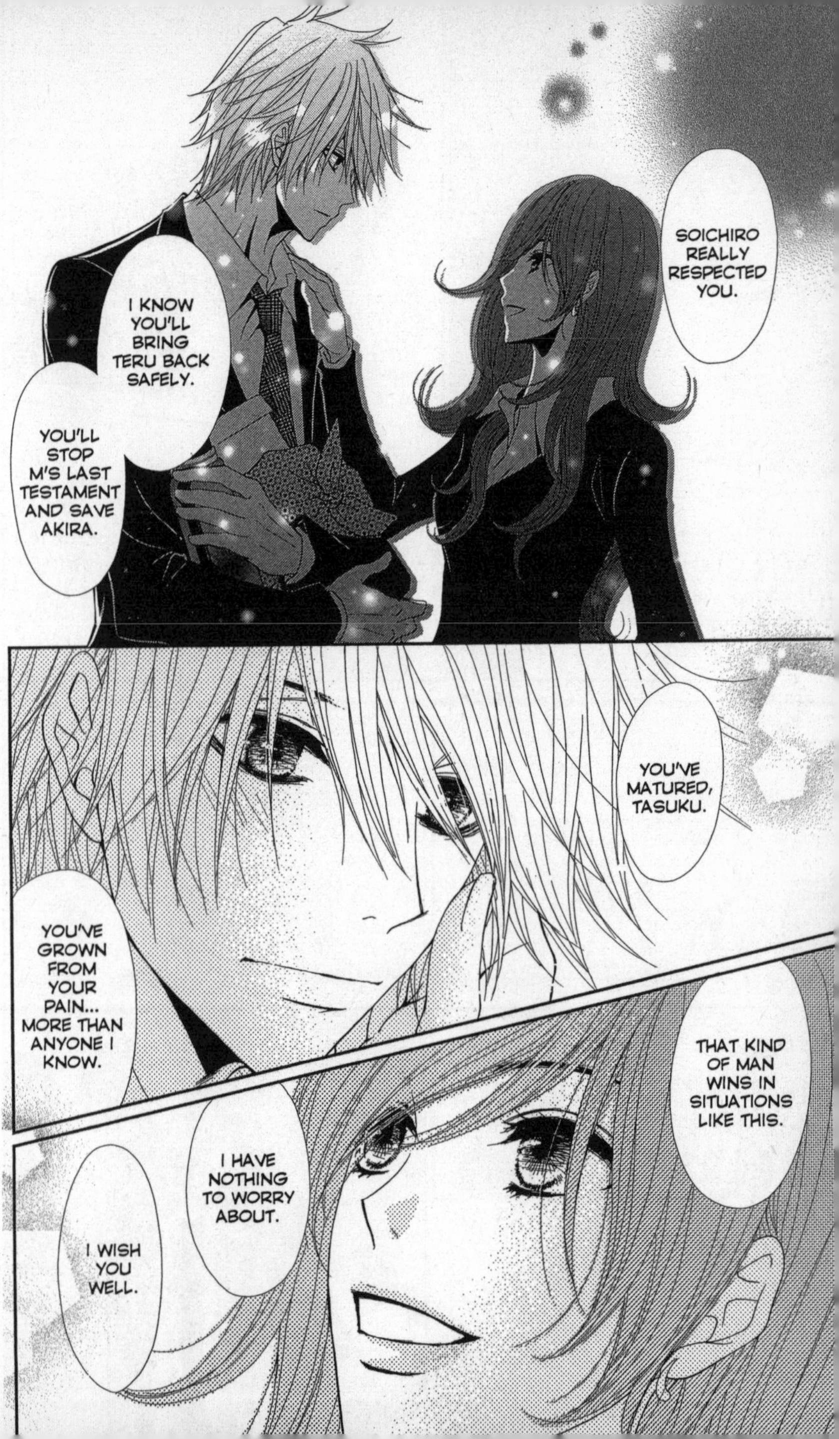
SOICHIRO REALLY RESPECTED YOU.
I KNOW YOU'LL BRING TERU BACK SAFELY.
YOU'LL STOP M'S LAST TESTAMENT AND SAVE AKIRA.
YOU'VE MATURED, TASUKU.
YOU'VE GROWN FROM YOUR PAIN... MORE THAN ANYONE I KNOW.
THAT KIND OF MAN WINS IN SITUATIONS LIKE THIS.
I HAVE NOTHING TO WORRY ABOUT.
I WISH YOU WELL.

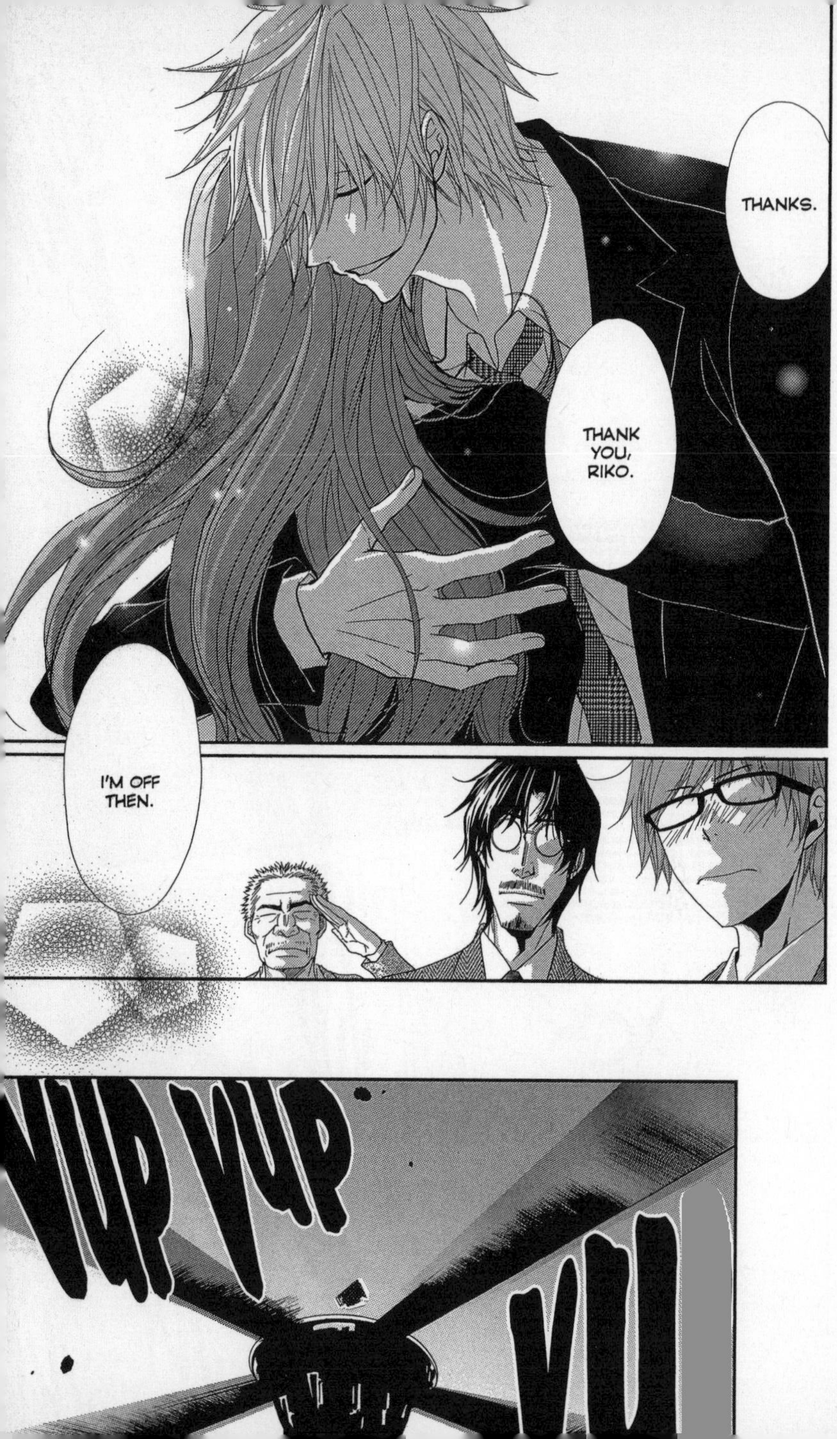
THANKS.
THANK YOU, RIKO.
I'M OFF THEN.
VUP VUP
VU

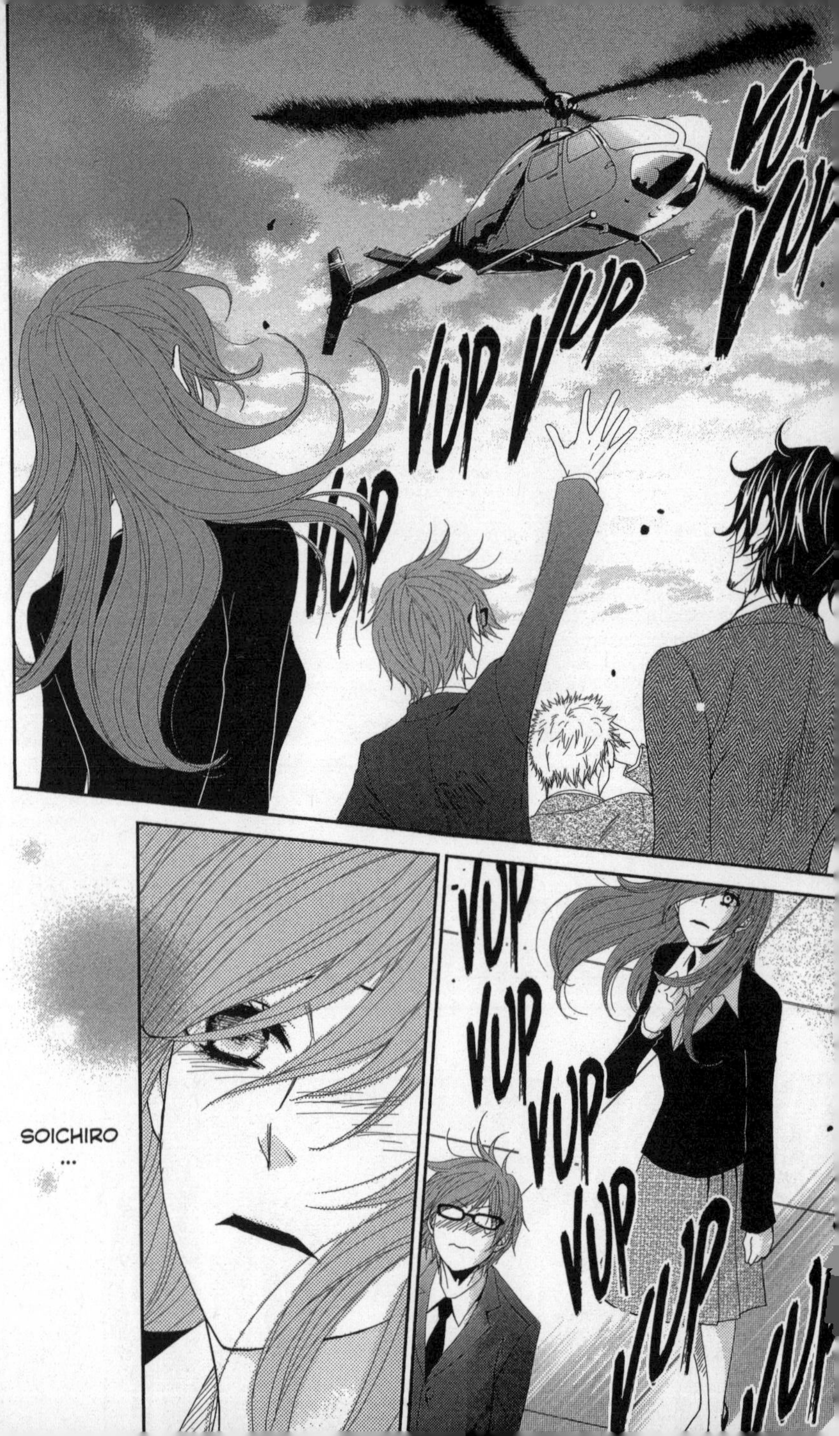

VOP VUP
VUP VUP VUP VUP
VUP VUP VUP VUP VUP VUP
SOICHIRO
...

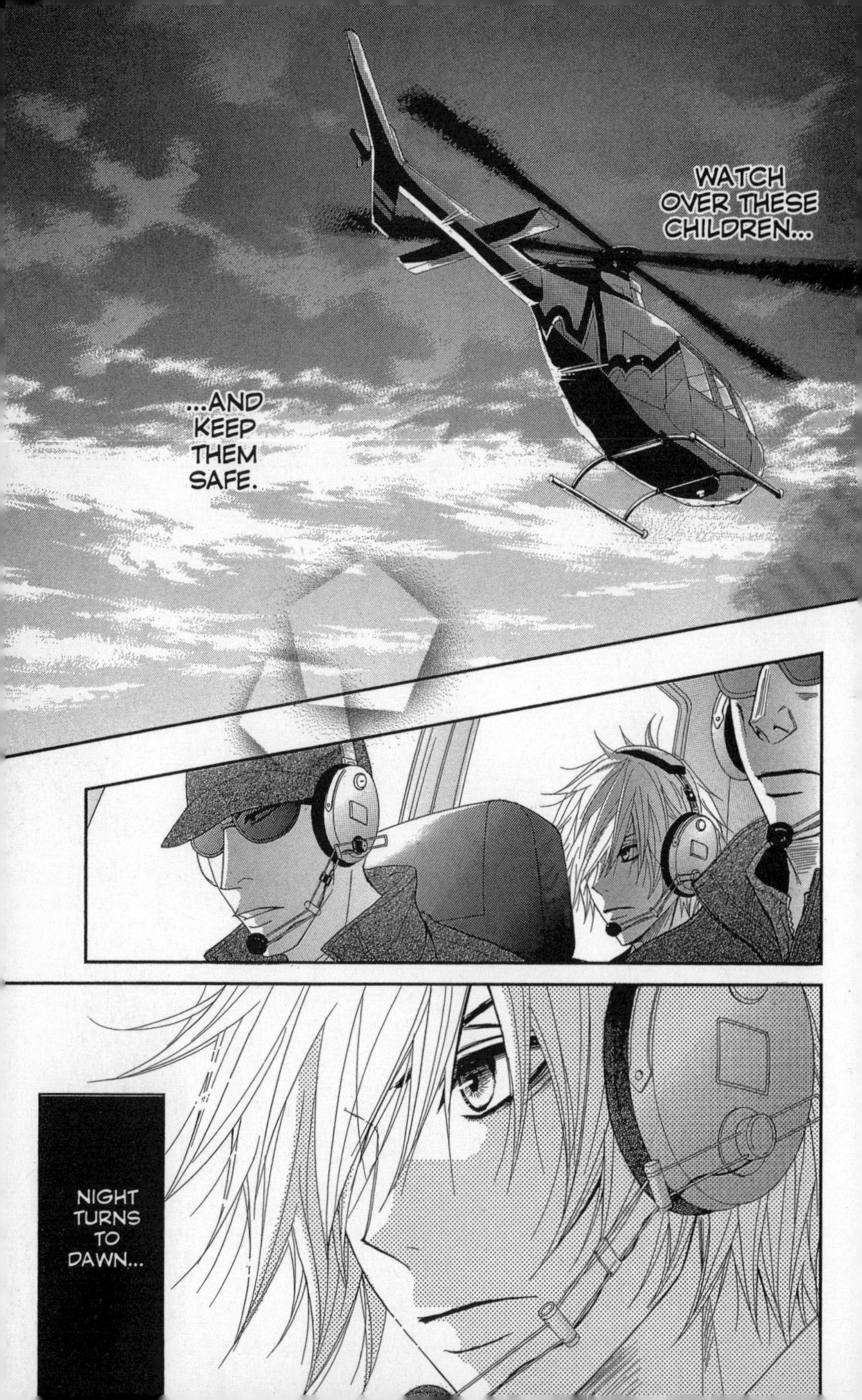
WATCH OVER THESE CHILDREN...
...AND KEEP THEM SAFE.
NIGHT TURNS TO DAWN...

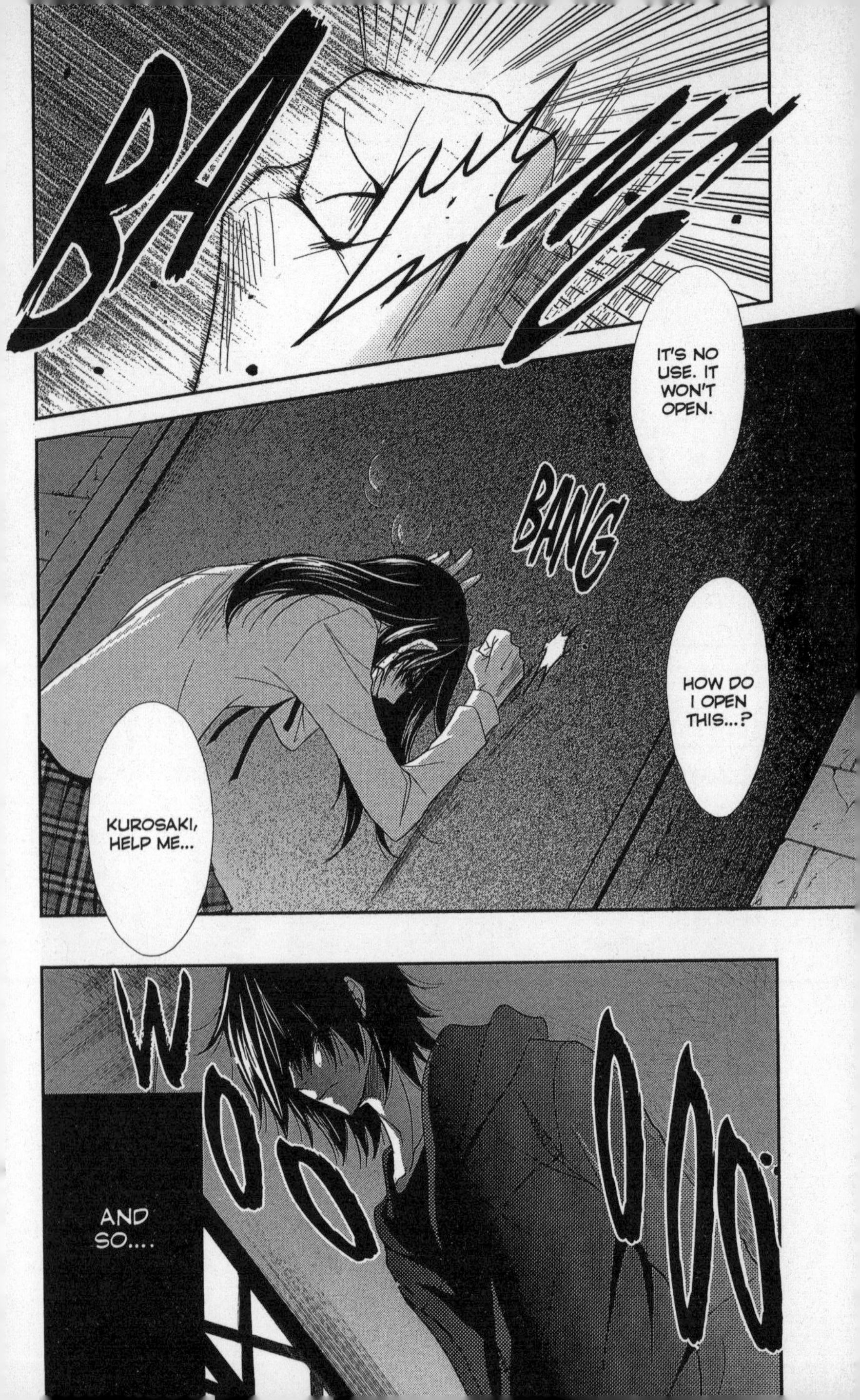
BAM
IT'S NO USE. IT WON'T OPEN.
BANG
HOW DO I OPEN THIS...?
KUROSAKI, HELP ME...
WOOOOOO
AND SO....

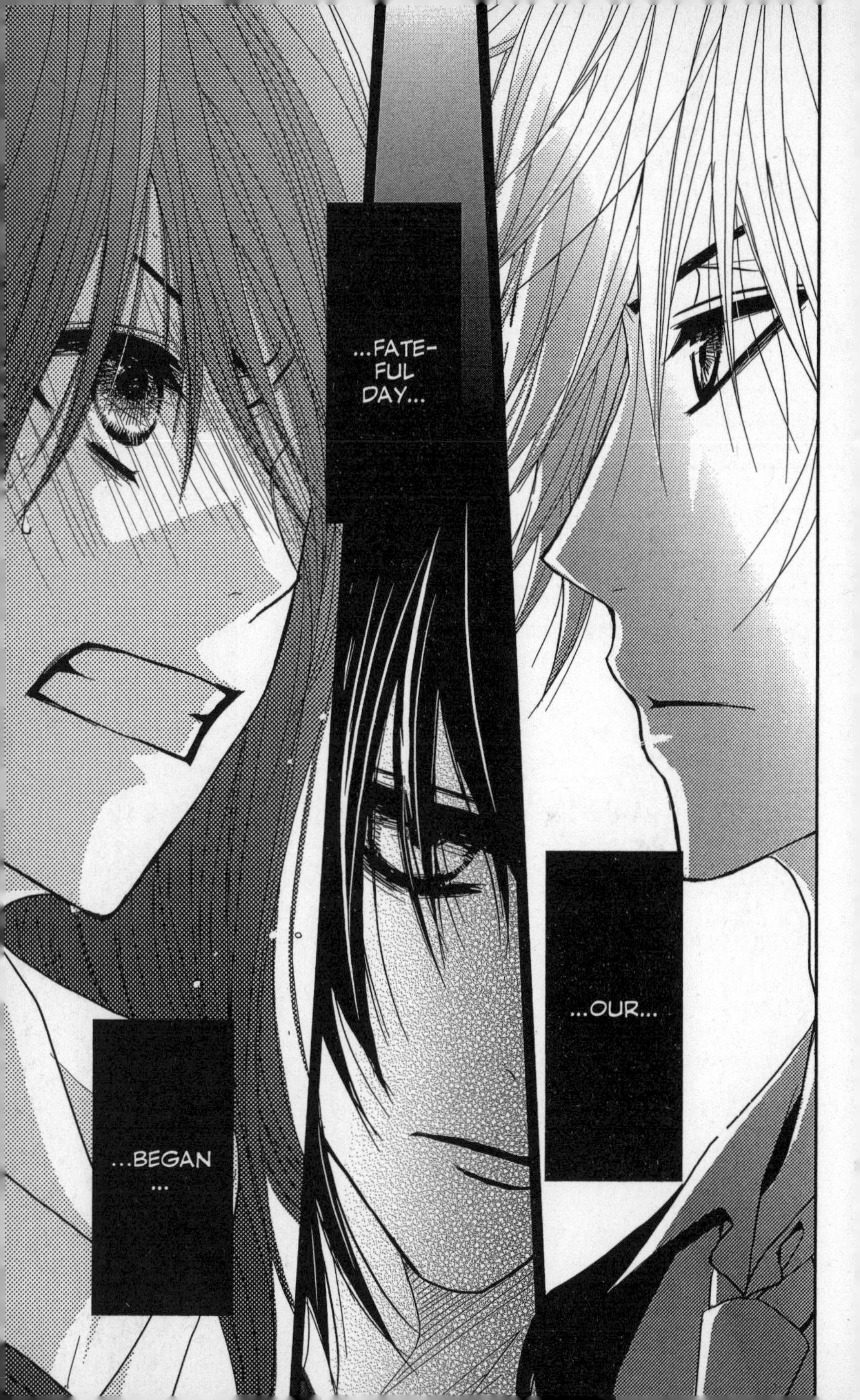
...OUR...
...FATE-FUL DAY...
...BEGAN ...

DENGEKI DAISY
QUESTION CORNER

RELOCATED → # BALDLY ASK!!! ④

IN VOLUME 9, CHAPTER 44, WHEN KUROSAKI MESSAGES TERU TO ASK IF SHE WANTED VANILLA OR STRAWBERRY ICE CREAM, WHICH DID TERU ULTIMATELY CHOOSE?
IT BOTHERS ME SO MUCH I'M ONLY ABLE TO GET EIGHT HOURS OF SLEEP EVERY NIGHT.

(DREAMY PANDA, YAMANASHI PREFECTURE)

HMM... EIGHT HOURS? I SLEPT 13 HOURS LAST NIGHT. (SORRY. IT WAS THE NIGHT AFTER MY DEADLINE.)
I'VE BEEN ASKED THIS QUESTION MANY TIMES ON MANY OCCASIONS. I MAY HAVE ALREADY ANSWERED THIS SOMEWHERE, BUT I BELIEVE TERU CHOSE STRAWBERRY. (I THINK EITHER STRAWBERRY OR GREEN TEA MATCHES TERU.)

WHILE TERU IS HAVING HER ICE CREAM, KUROSAKI TAKES A BITE OUT OF HER SPOON FROM THE SIDE. ANGRILY, TERU WOULD TELL HIM, "WHAT'D YOU DO THAT FOR?! GO BALD!" TO WHICH KUROSAKI WOULD SAY, "OKAY, OKAY. I'M SORRY." AND GIVE TERU SOME OF HIS VANILLA ICE CREAM. THEN TERU WOULD SAY, "IT'S SO GOOD," AND KUROSAKI WOULD BREAK INTO A BIG SMILE... IT'S TOO MUCH...

THAT'S ALL FOR THIS TIME!! "BALDLY ASK!!!" WILL END IN THE NEXT VOLUME! PLEASE STAY WITH US UNTIL THE VERY END!!

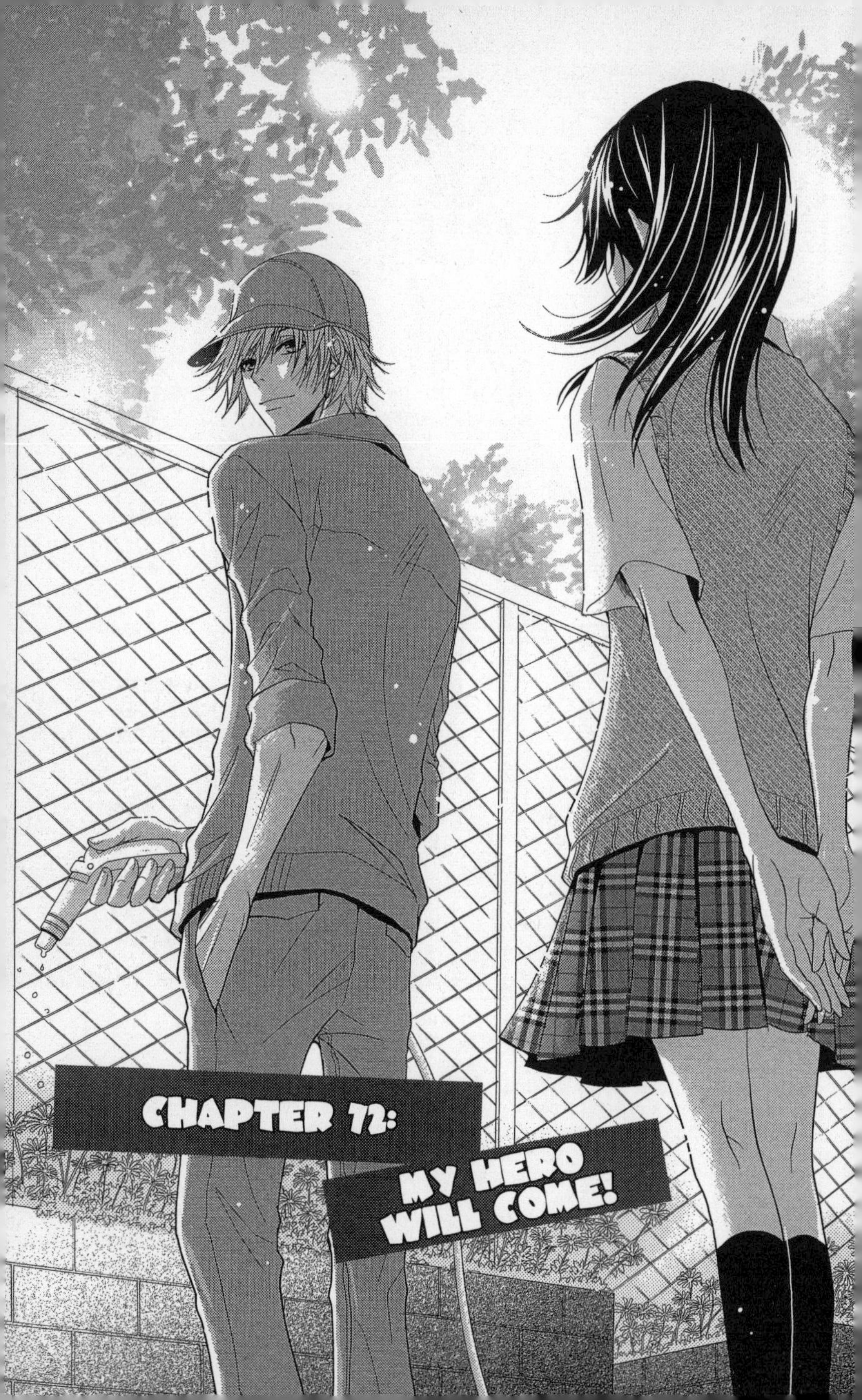
CHAPTER 72:
MY HERO WILL COME!

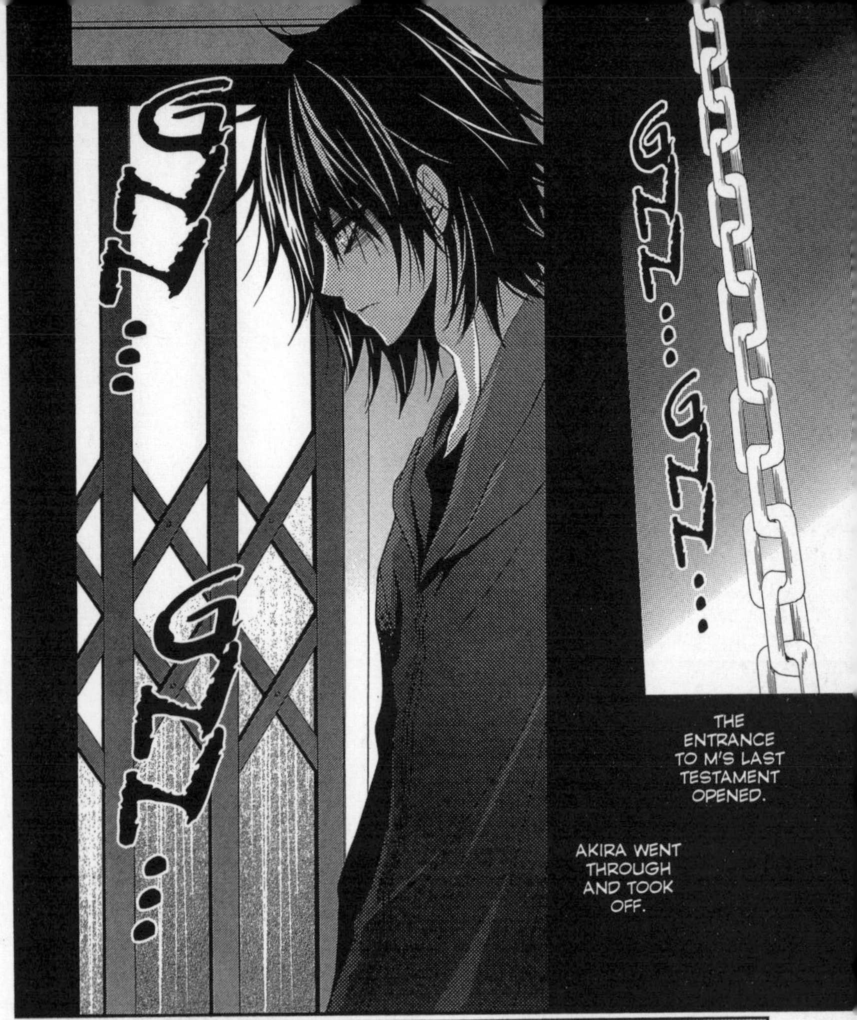
GIII... GIII...
THE ENTRANCE TO M'S LAST TESTAMENT OPENED.
AKIRA WENT THROUGH AND TOOK OFF.
GIII... GIII...

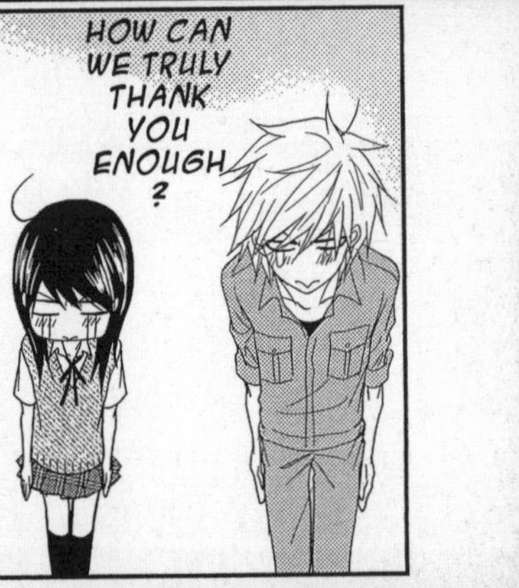
HOW CAN WE TRULY THANK YOU ENOUGH?

BEFORE WE BEGAN, I APOLOGIZED TO MY ASSISTANTS. "WE'RE DOING HELICOPTERS THIS MONTH. I'M SO SORRY." IN ADDITION TO THE HELICOPTER, THERE WAS A CHAPEL, A CORNICE ELEVATOR, AND A JUNGLE. I REALLY PUT MY ASSISTANTS THROUGH A LOT IN CHAPTER 71. (THEN AGAIN, I ALSO PUT THEM THROUGH A LOT WITH THE YACHT PARTY AND AMUSEMENT PARK CHAPTERS, TOO.)

I AM SLOW AT COMING UP WITH STORYBOARDS AND DRAWING PEOPLE. THESE PEOPLE SUPPORT ME BOTH IN THE TECHNICAL AND EMOTIONAL ASPECTS, AND THEY MAKE THE WORKPLACE A FUN PLACE TO BE. TO O-SAN, J-SAN, M-SAN, T-SAN, P-SAN, Y-SAN, L-SAN, AND SO MANY OTHERS, THANK YOU ALL SO VERY MUCH!!!!!

I COULDN'T STOP HIM...
IT WON'T OPEN. AGH...
KURO-SAKI, HELP ME...
AKIRA EASILY DECI-PHERED THE CODE...
...THAT OPENED THE EN-TRANCE.
VRR...
THERE'S NO WAY I COULD DECIPHER IT.
THERE WAS NOTHING I COULD DO.

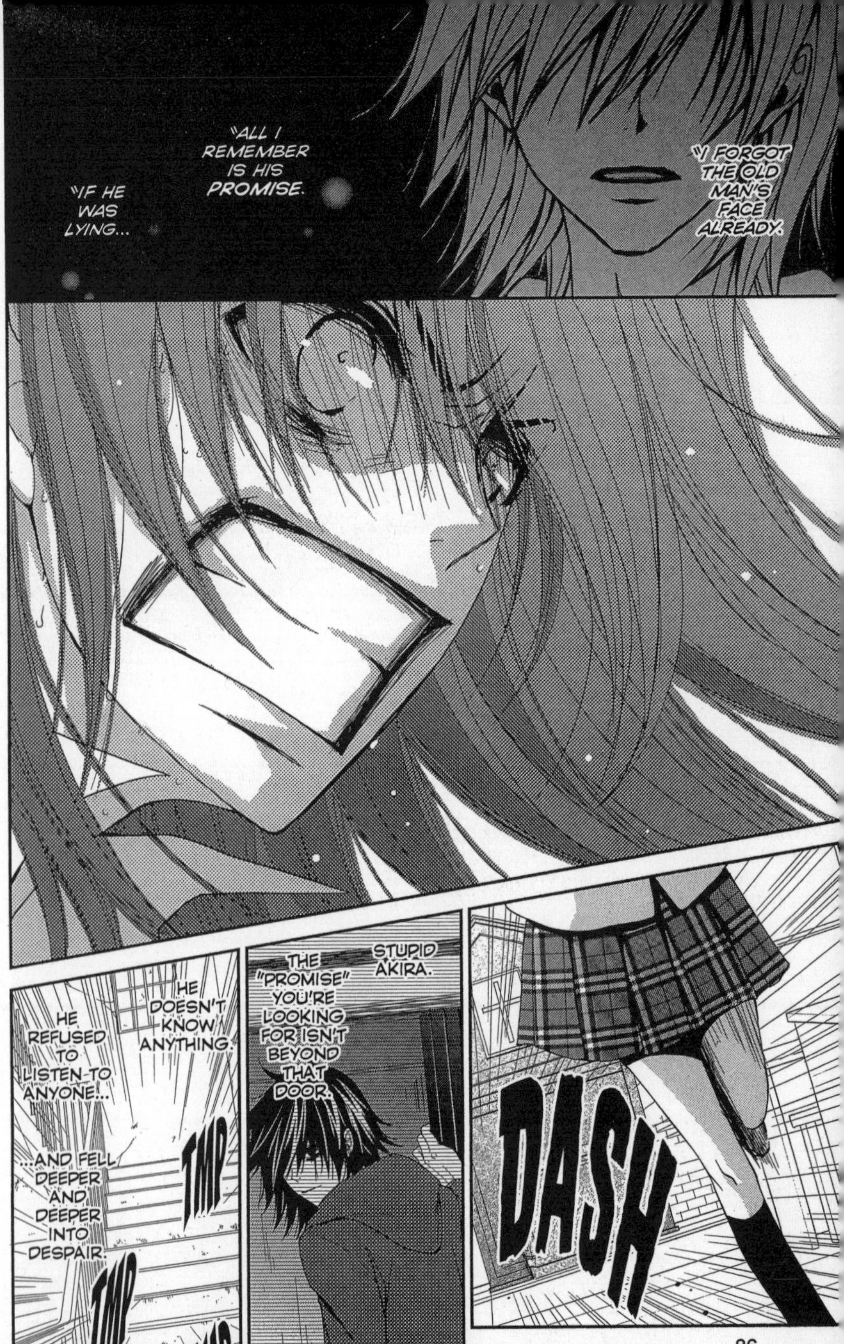

“I FORGOT THE OLD MAN'S FACE ALREADY.
“ALL I REMEMBER IS HIS PROMISE.
“IF HE WAS LYING...
DASH
STUPID AKIRA.
THE "PROMISE" YOU'RE LOOKING FOR ISN'T BEYOND THAT DOOR.
HE DOESN'T KNOW ANYTHING.
HE REFUSED TO LISTEN TO ANYONE...
...AND FELL DEEPER AND DEEPER INTO DESPAIR.
TMP
TMP
TMP

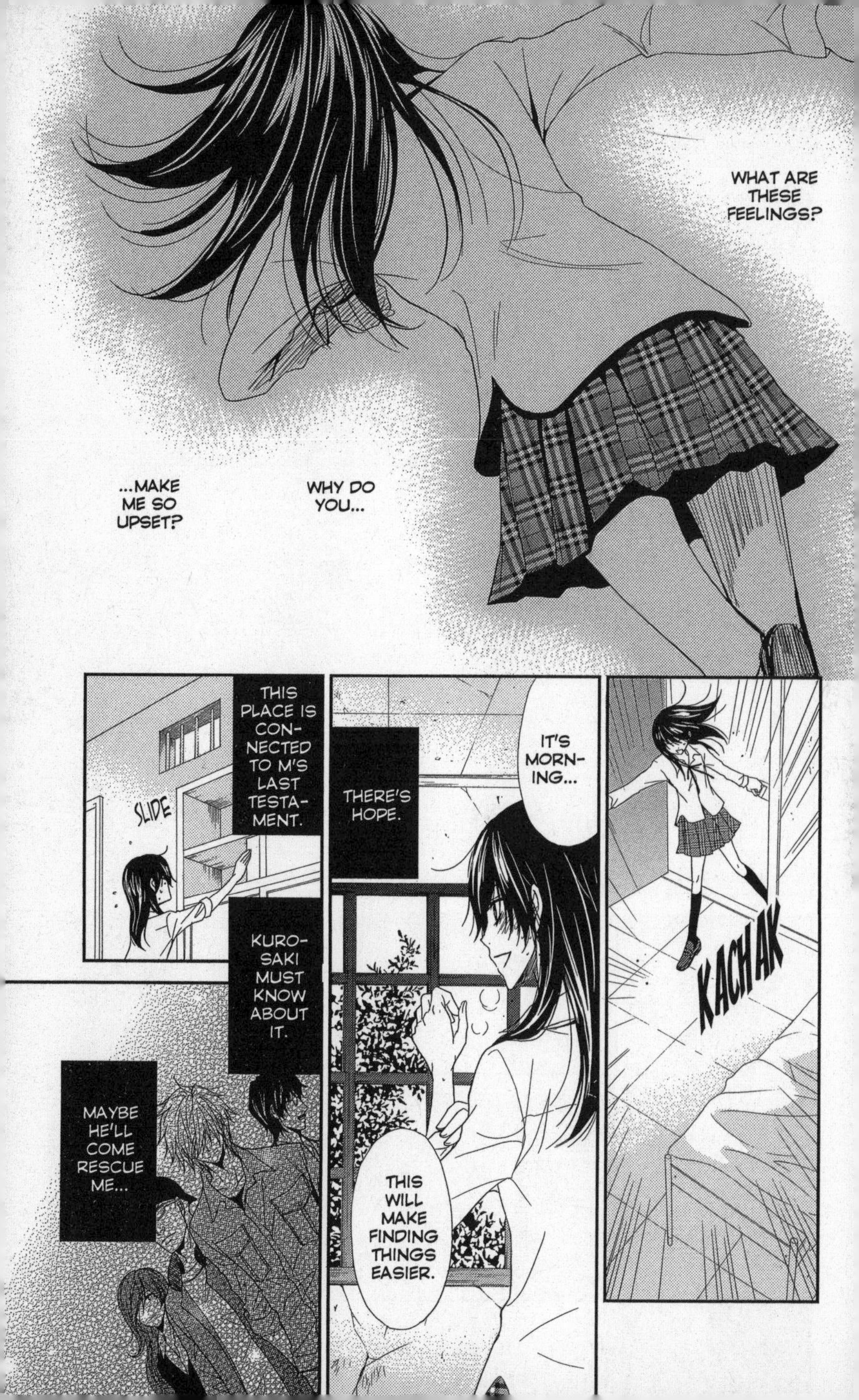
WHAT ARE THESE FEELINGS?
WHY DO YOU...
...MAKE ME SO UPSET?
KACHAK
IT'S MORN-ING...
THERE'S HOPE.
THIS WILL MAKE FINDING THINGS EASIER.
THIS PLACE IS CON-NECTED TO M'S LAST TESTA-MENT.
SLIDE
KURO-SAKI MUST KNOW ABOUT IT.
MAYBE HE'LL COME RESCUE ME...

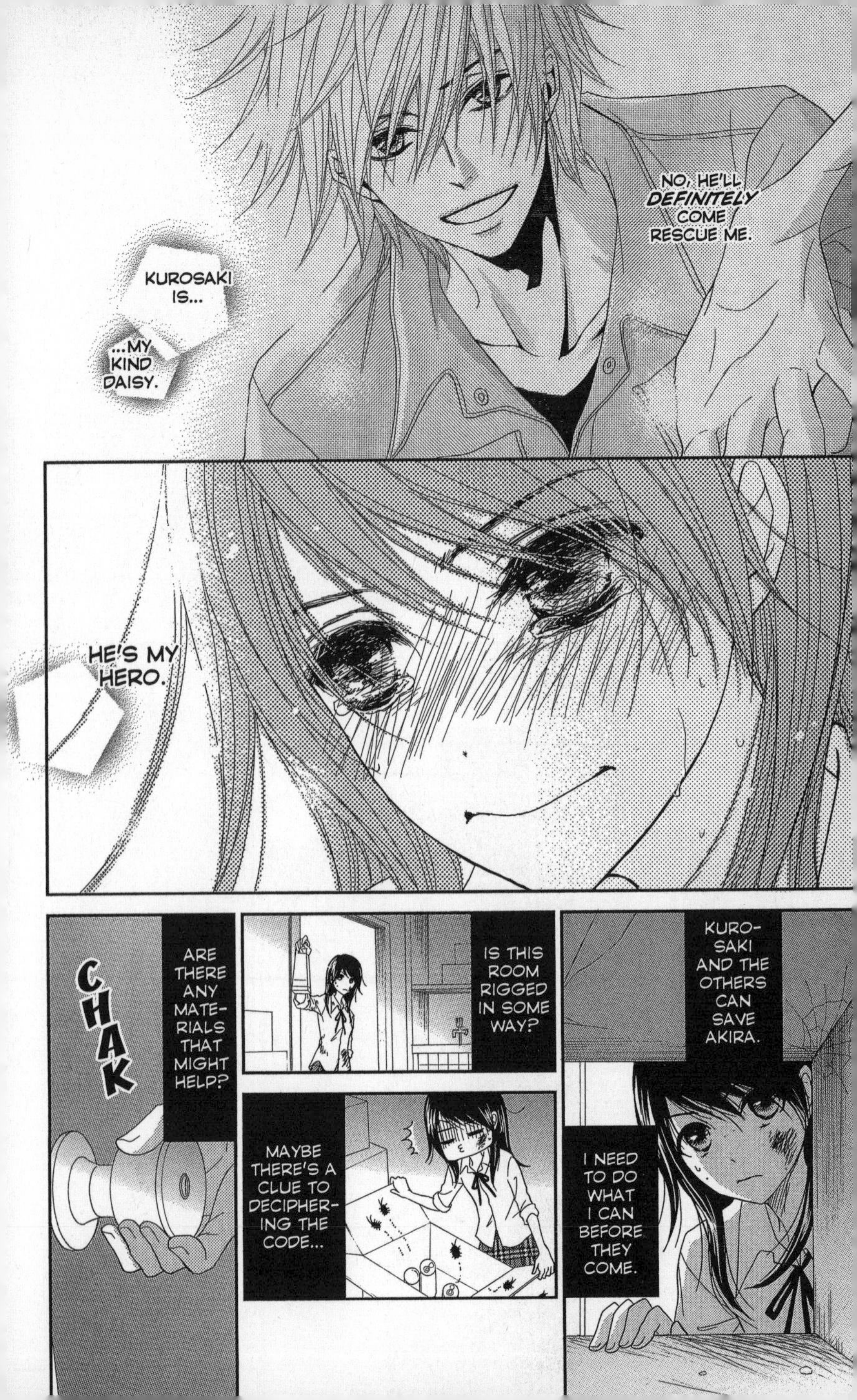
NO, HE'LL *DEFINITELY* COME RESCUE ME.
KUROSAKI IS...
...MY KIND DAISY.
HE'S MY HERO.
KURO-SAKI AND THE OTHERS CAN SAVE AKIRA.
I NEED TO DO WHAT I CAN BEFORE THEY COME.
IS THIS ROOM RIGGED IN SOME WAY?
MAYBE THERE'S A CLUE TO DECIPHER-ING THE CODE...
ARE THERE ANY MATE-RIALS THAT MIGHT HELP?
CHAK

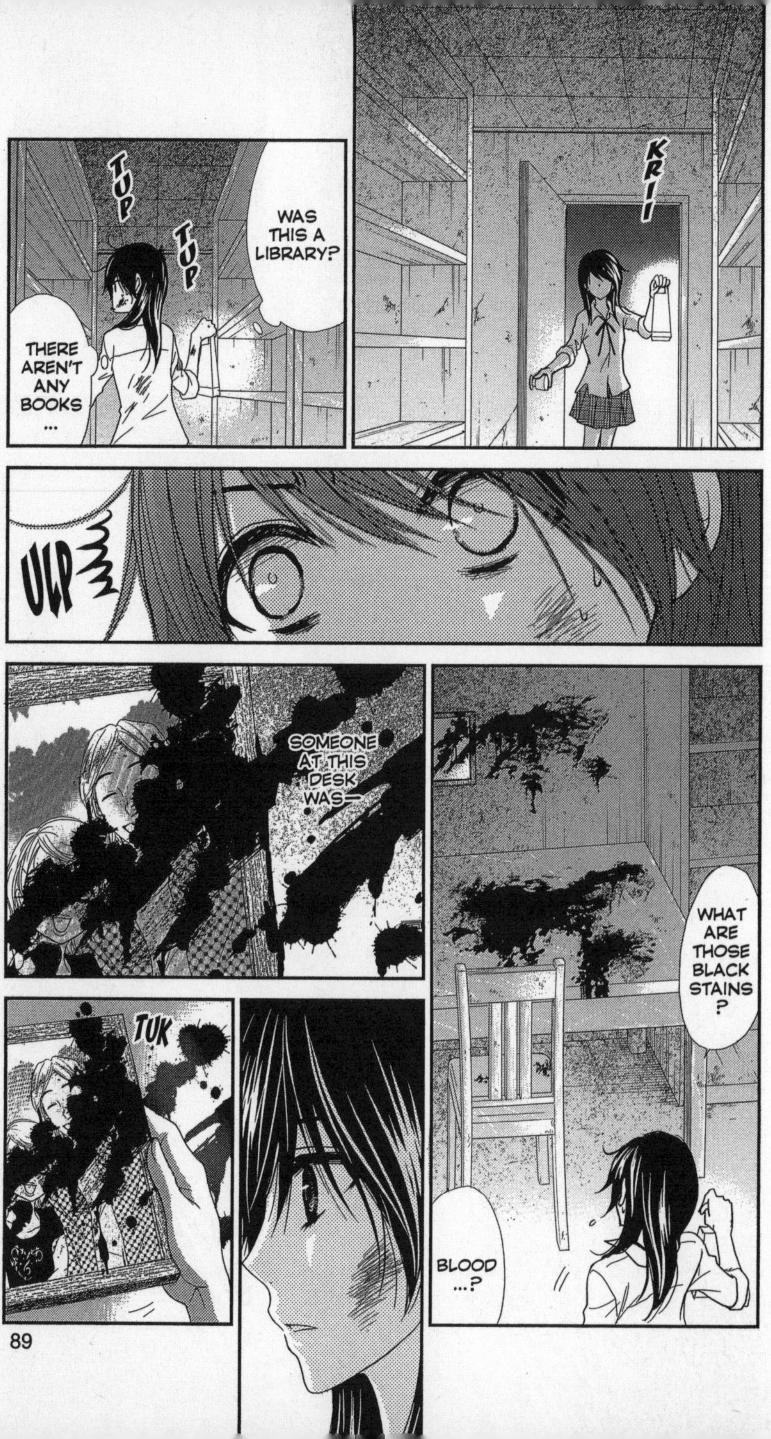
KRII
TUP TUP
WAS THIS A LIBRARY?
THERE AREN'T ANY BOOKS ...
ULP
WHAT ARE THOSE BLACK STAINS?
BLOOD ...?
SOMEONE AT THIS DESK WAS—
TUK

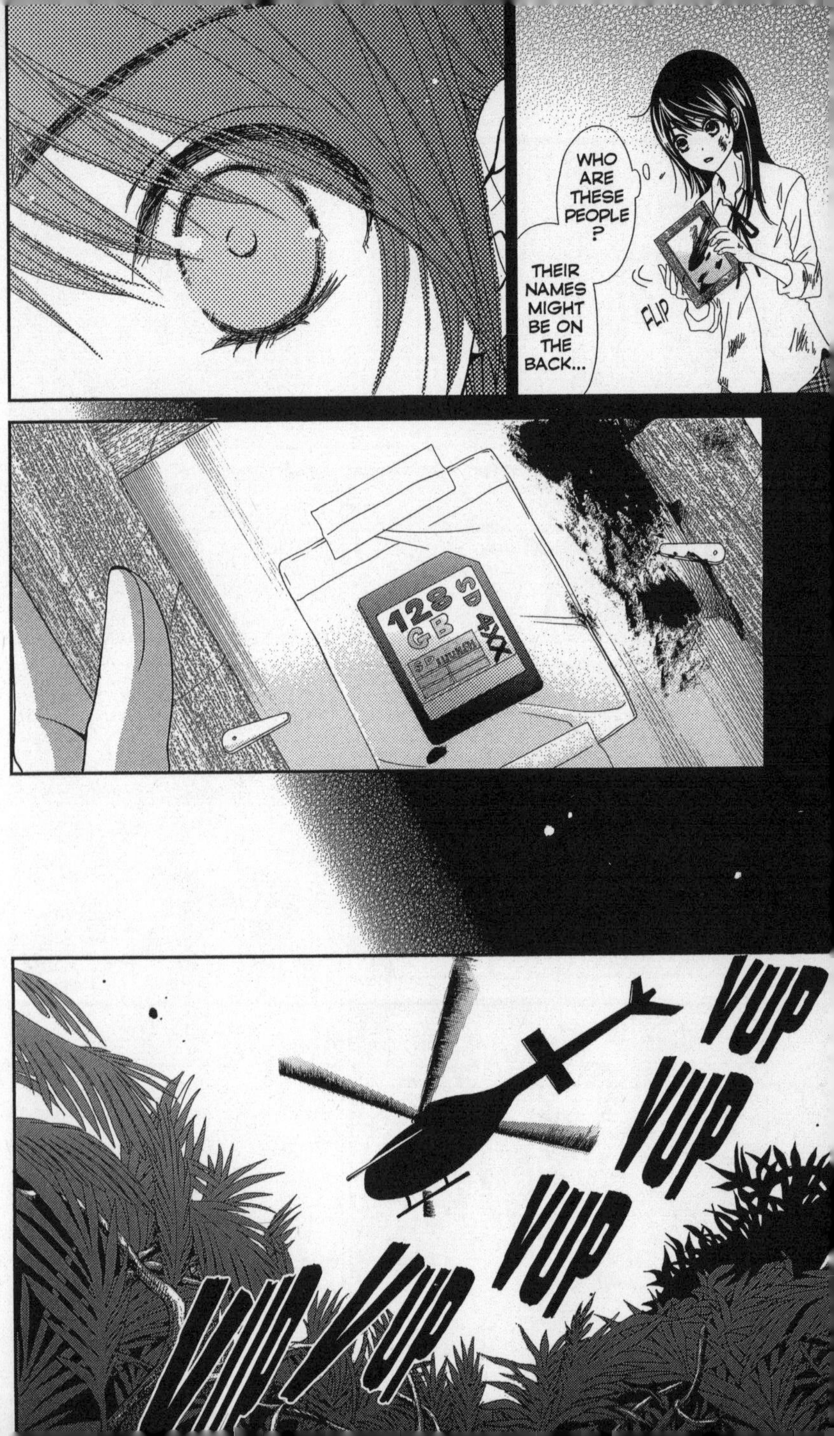
WHO ARE THESE PEOPLE?
THEIR NAMES MIGHT BE ON THE BACK...
FLIP
128 GB SD 4XX
VUP VUP VUP
VUP VUP

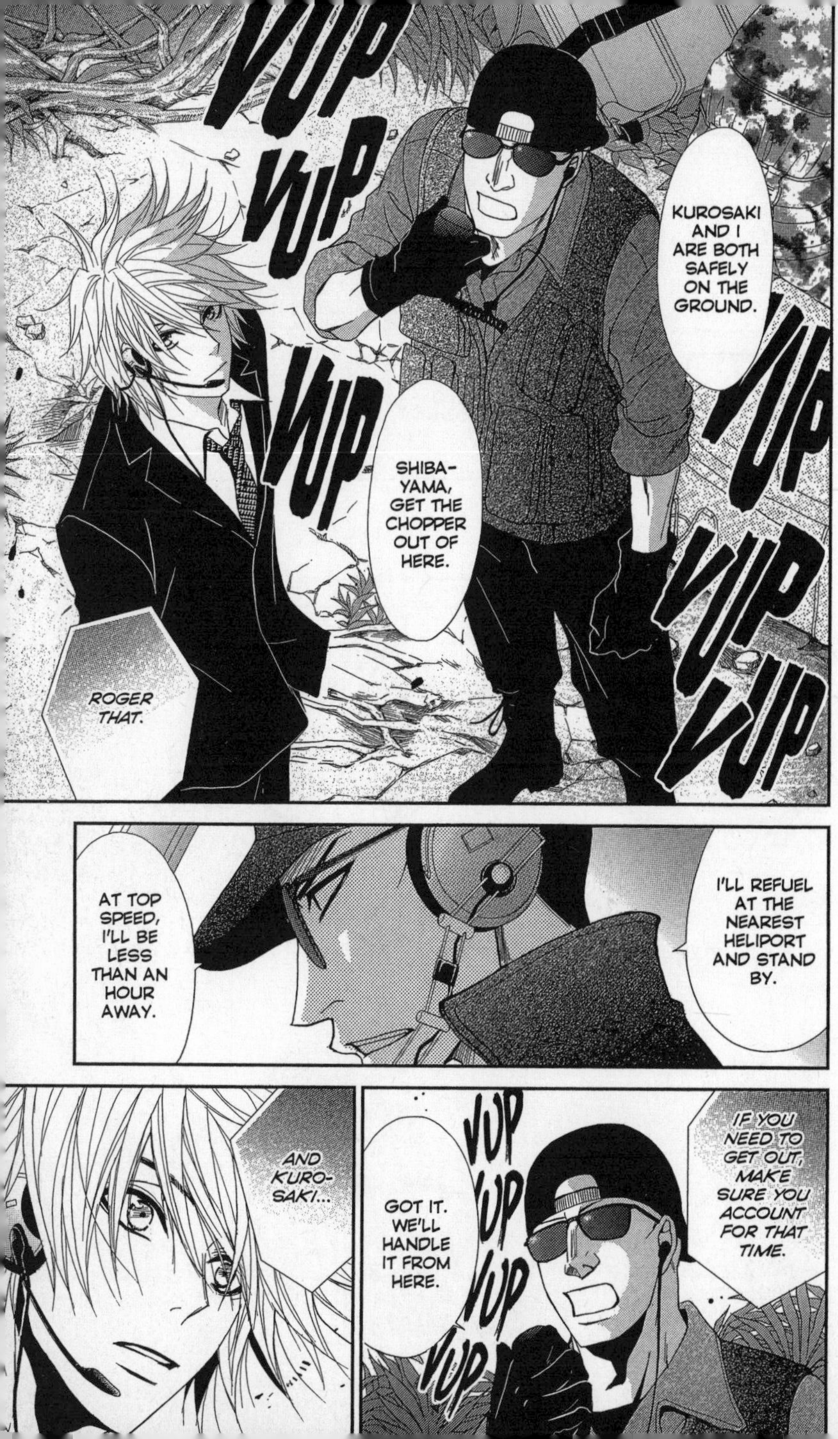
KUROSAKI AND I ARE BOTH SAFELY ON THE GROUND.
VUP VUP VUP VUP
VUP VUP VUP
SHIBA-YAMA, GET THE CHOPPER OUT OF HERE.
ROGER THAT.
I'LL REFUEL AT THE NEAREST HELIPORT AND STAND BY.
AT TOP SPEED, I'LL BE LESS THAN AN HOUR AWAY.
IF YOU NEED TO GET OUT, MAKE SURE YOU ACCOUNT FOR THAT TIME.
VUP VUP VUP VUP
GOT IT. WE'LL HANDLE IT FROM HERE.
AND KURO-SAKI...

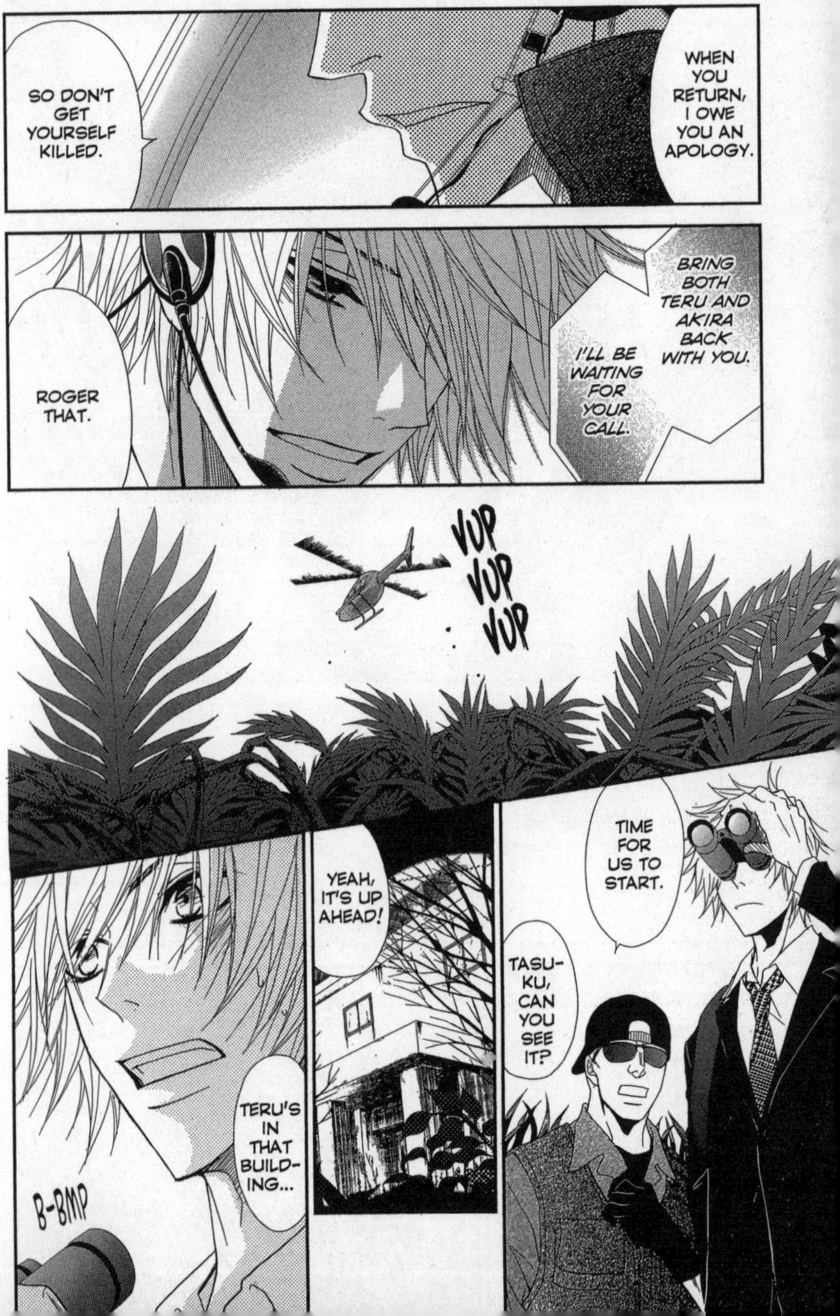
WHEN YOU RETURN, I OWE YOU AN APOLOGY.
SO DON'T GET YOURSELF KILLED.
BRING BOTH TERU AND AKIRA BACK WITH YOU.
I'LL BE WAITING FOR YOUR CALL.
ROGER THAT.
VUP VUP VUP
TIME FOR US TO START.
TASU-KU, CAN YOU SEE IT?
YEAH, IT'S UP AHEAD!
TERU'S IN THAT BUILD-ING...
B-BMP

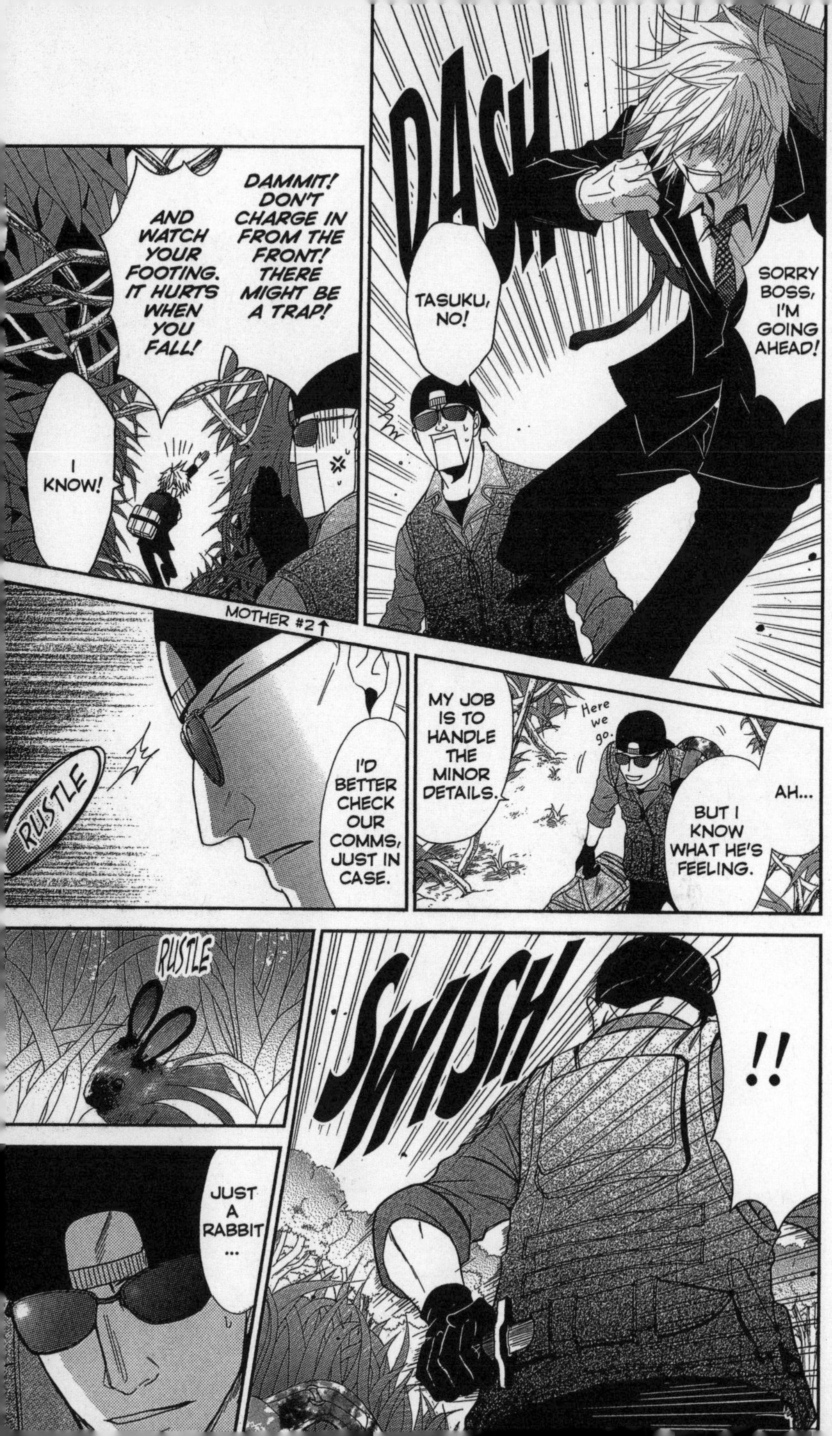
SORRY BOSS, I'M GOING AHEAD!
DASH
TASUKU, NO!
DAMMIT! DON'T CHARGE IN FROM THE FRONT! THERE MIGHT BE A TRAP!
AND WATCH YOUR FOOTING. IT HURTS WHEN YOU FALL!
I KNOW!
MOTHER #2↑
AH...
BUT I KNOW WHAT HE'S FEELING.
Here we go.
MY JOB IS TO HANDLE THE MINOR DETAILS.
I'D BETTER CHECK OUR COMMS, JUST IN CASE.
RUSTLE
SWISH
!!
RUSTLE
JUST A RABBIT ...

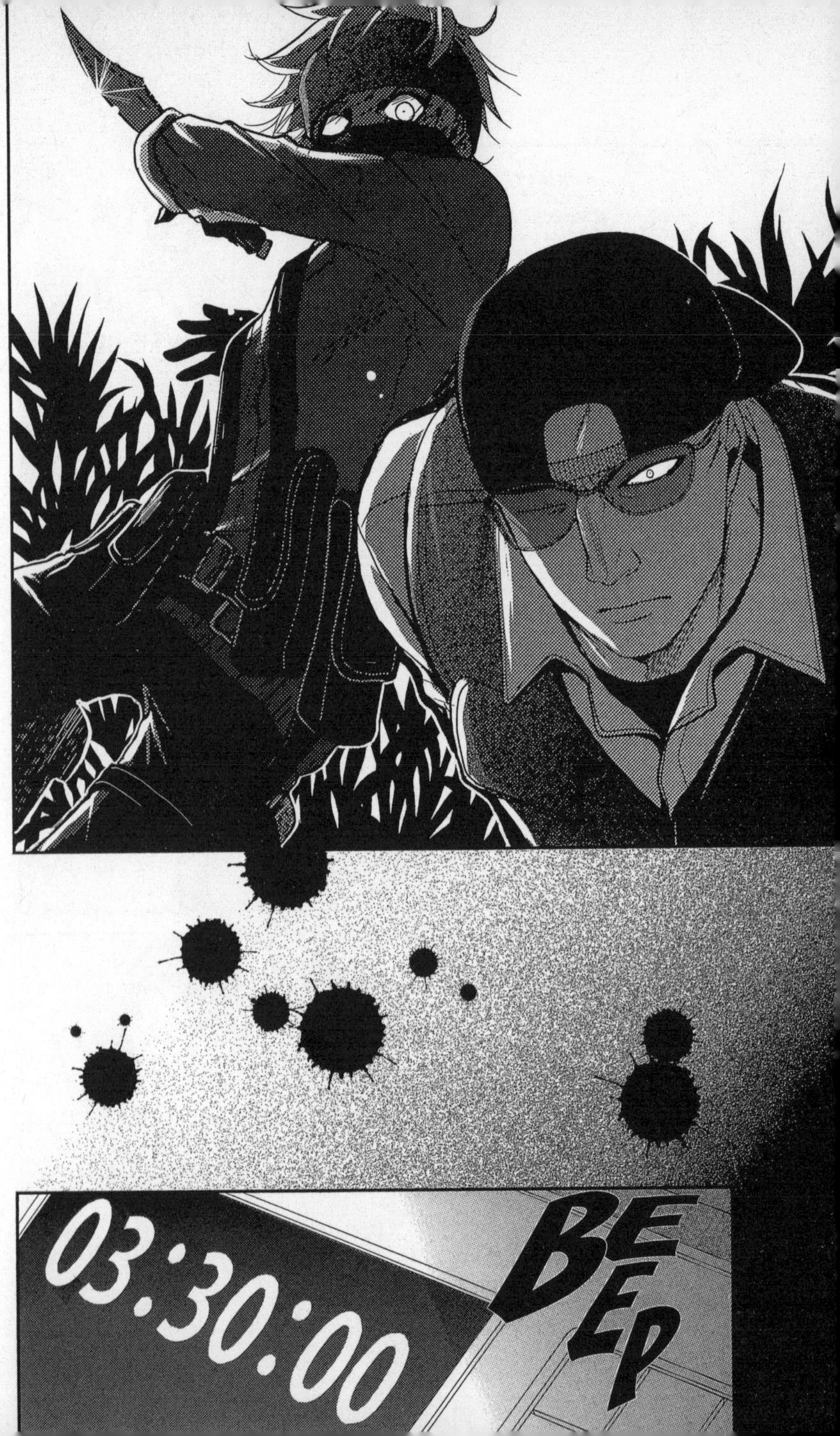
03:30:00
BEEP

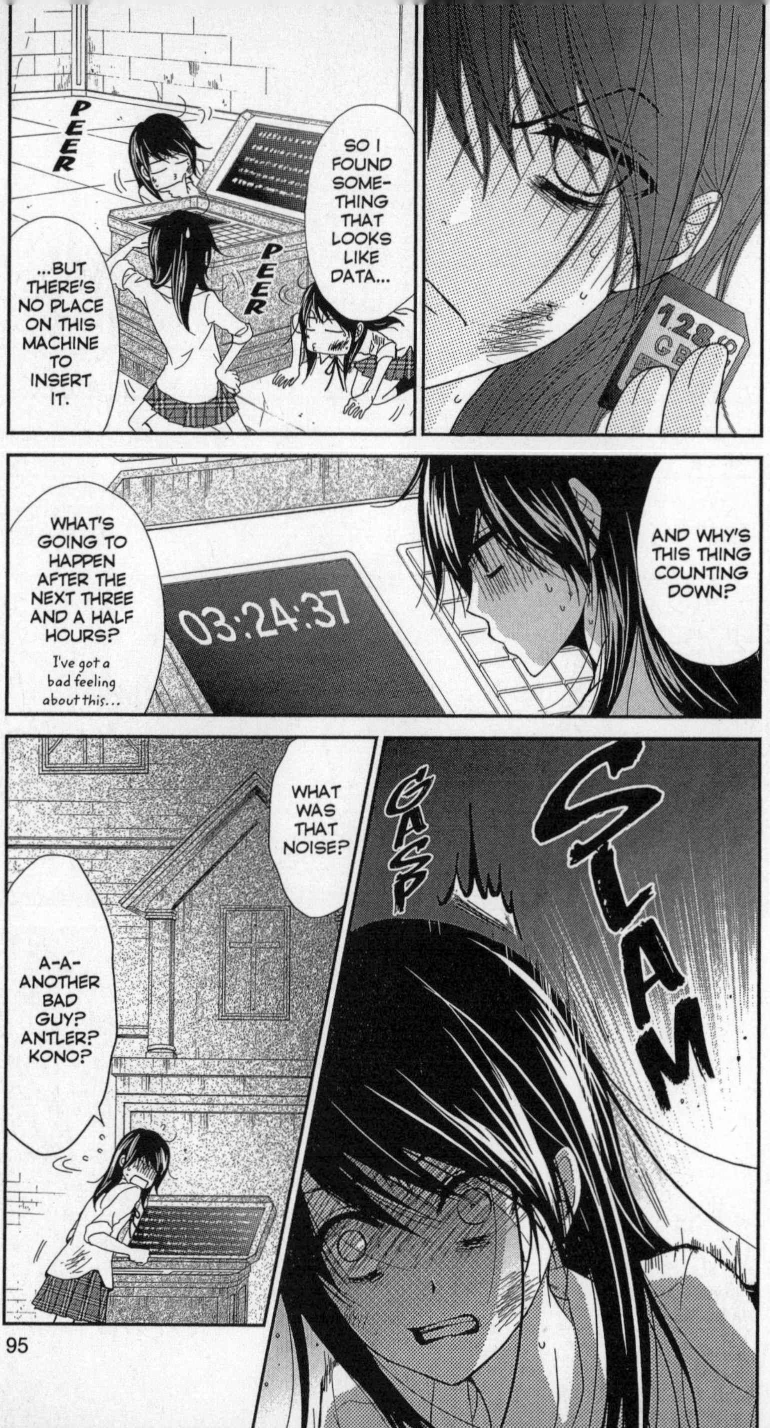
SO I FOUND SOME-THING THAT LOOKS LIKE DATA...
PEER
PEER
...BUT THERE'S NO PLACE ON THIS MACHINE TO INSERT IT.
AND WHY'S THIS THING COUNTING DOWN?
03:24:37
WHAT'S GOING TO HAPPEN AFTER THE NEXT THREE AND A HALF HOURS?
I've got a bad feeling about this...
SLAM
GASP
WHAT WAS THAT NOISE?
A-A-ANOTHER BAD GUY? ANTLER? KONO?

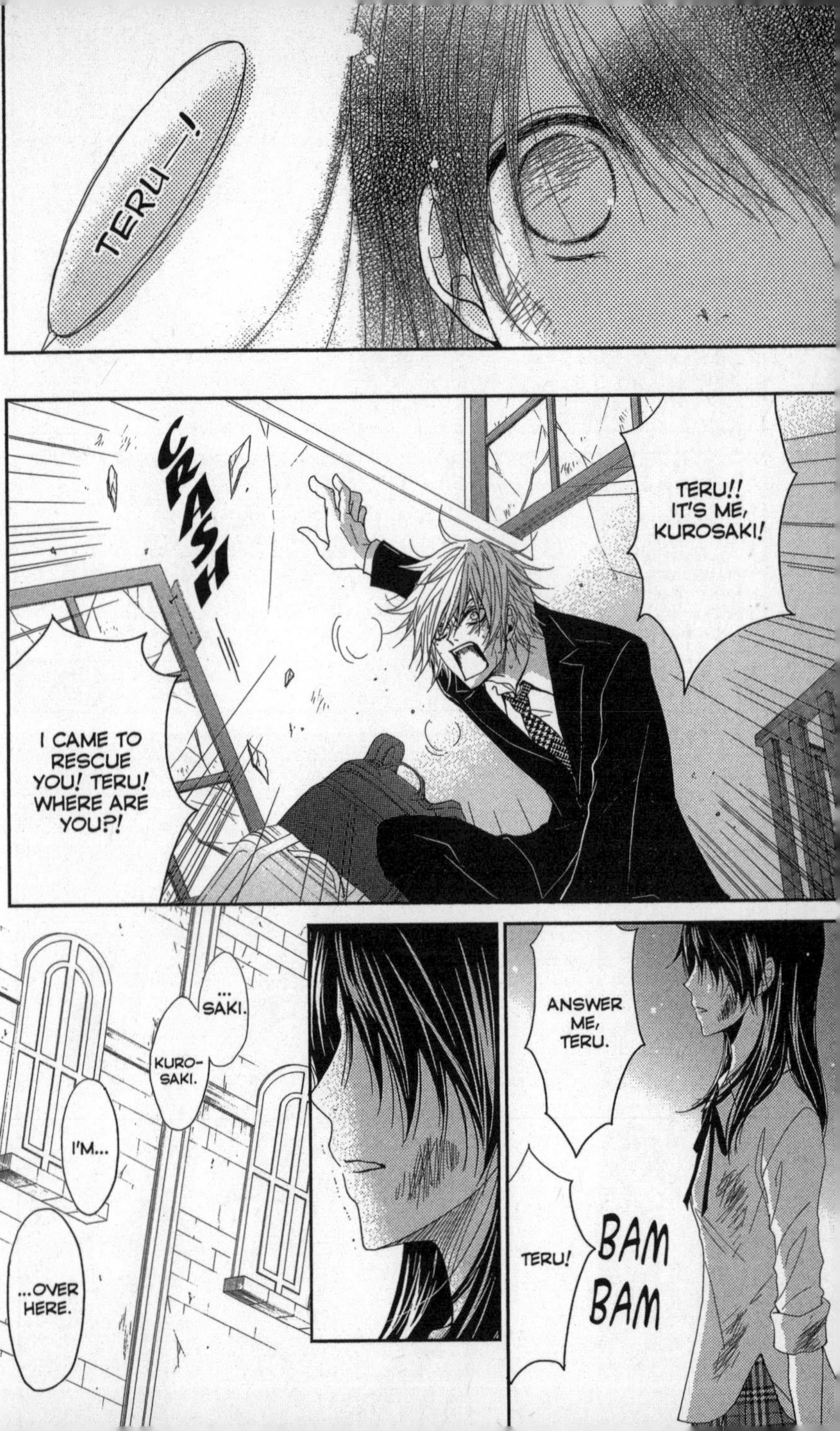
TERU—!
TERU!! IT'S ME, KUROSAKI!
CRASH
I CAME TO RESCUE YOU! TERU! WHERE ARE YOU?!
ANSWER ME, TERU.
BAM BAM
TERU!
...SAKI.
KURO-SAKI.
I'M...
...OVER HERE.

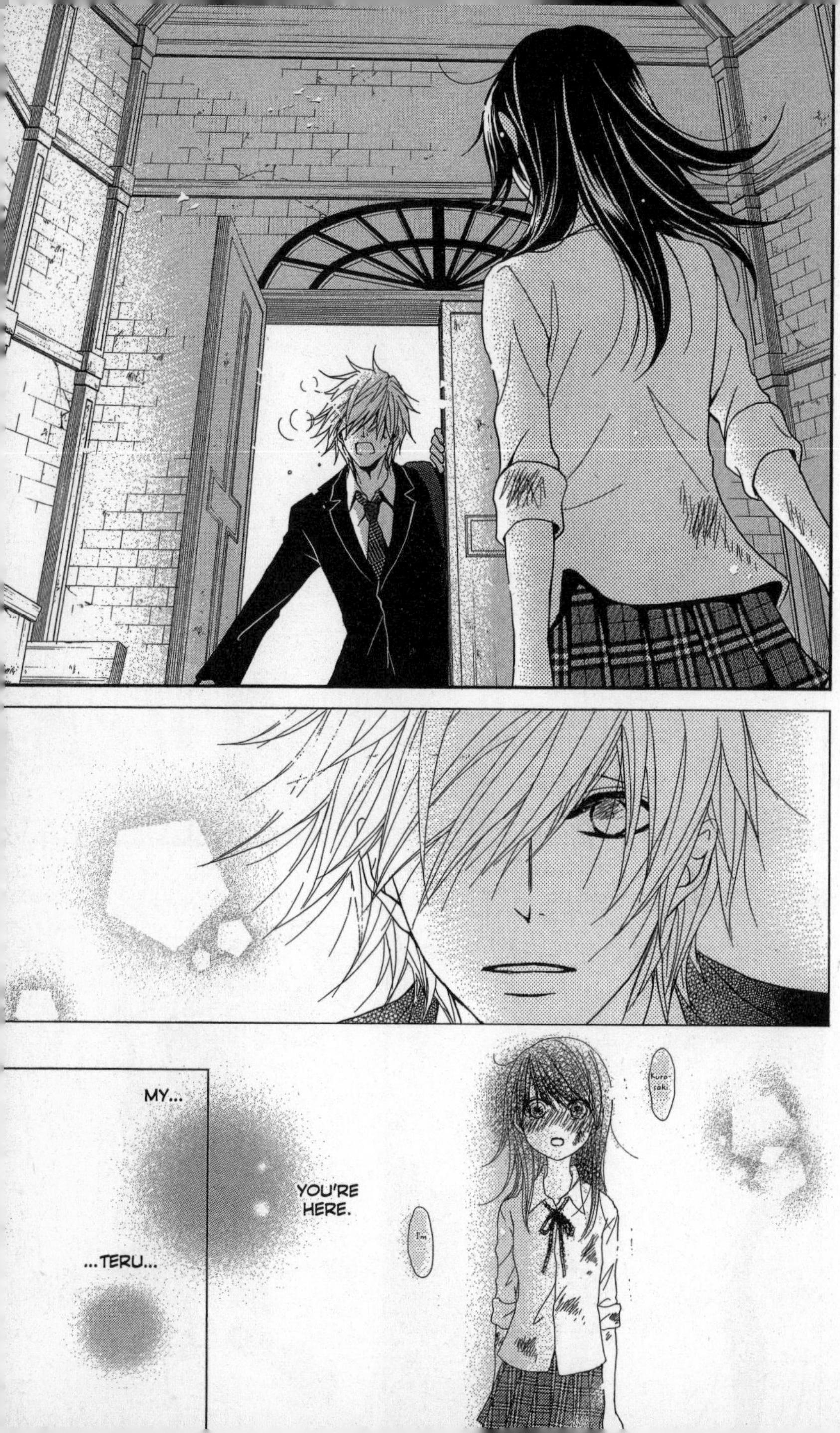
Kuro-saki.
YOU'RE HERE.
I'm
MY...
...TERU...

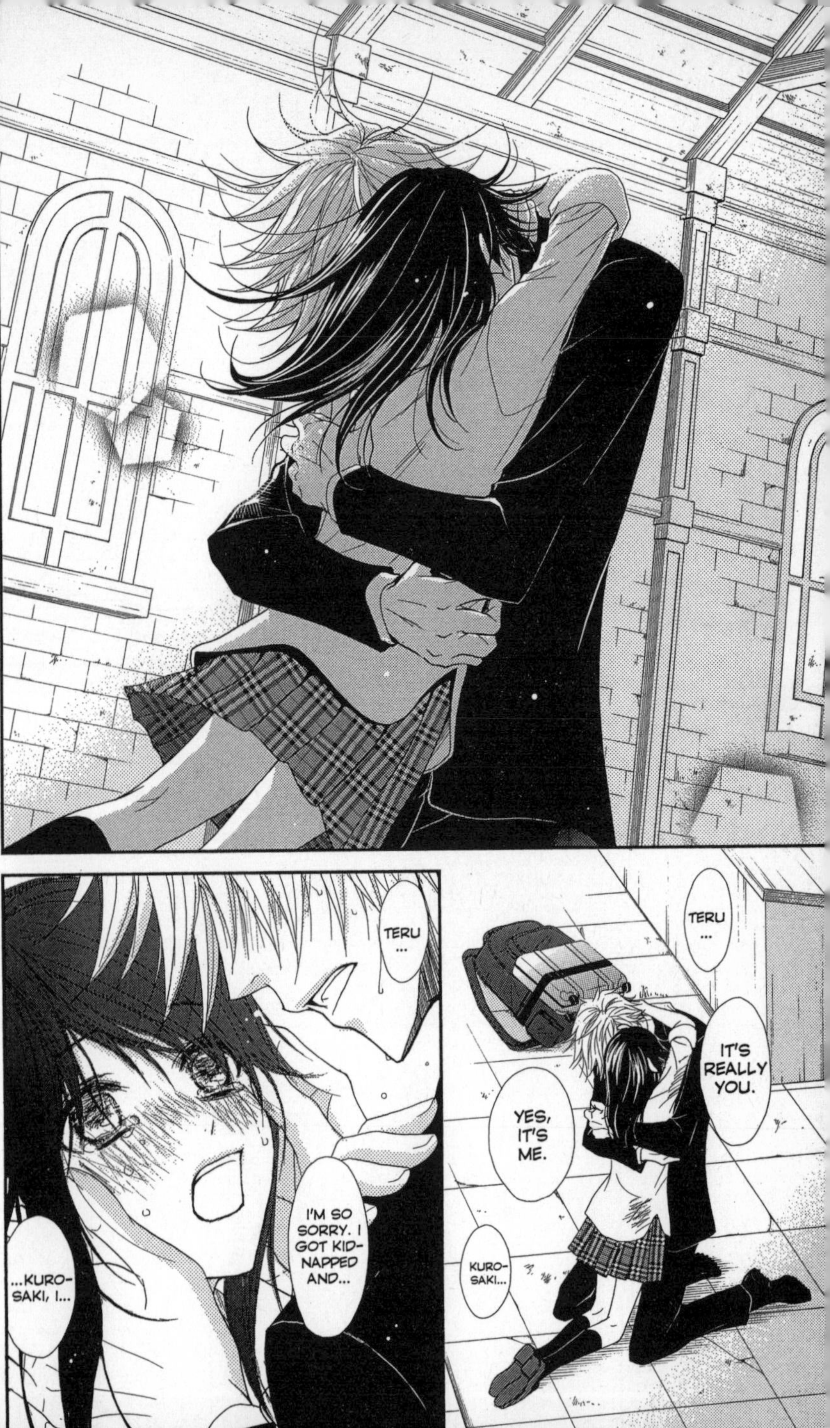
TERU ...
IT'S REALLY YOU.
YES, IT'S ME.
KURO-SAKI...
TERU ...
I'M SO SORRY. I GOT KID-NAPPED AND...
...KURO-SAKI, I...

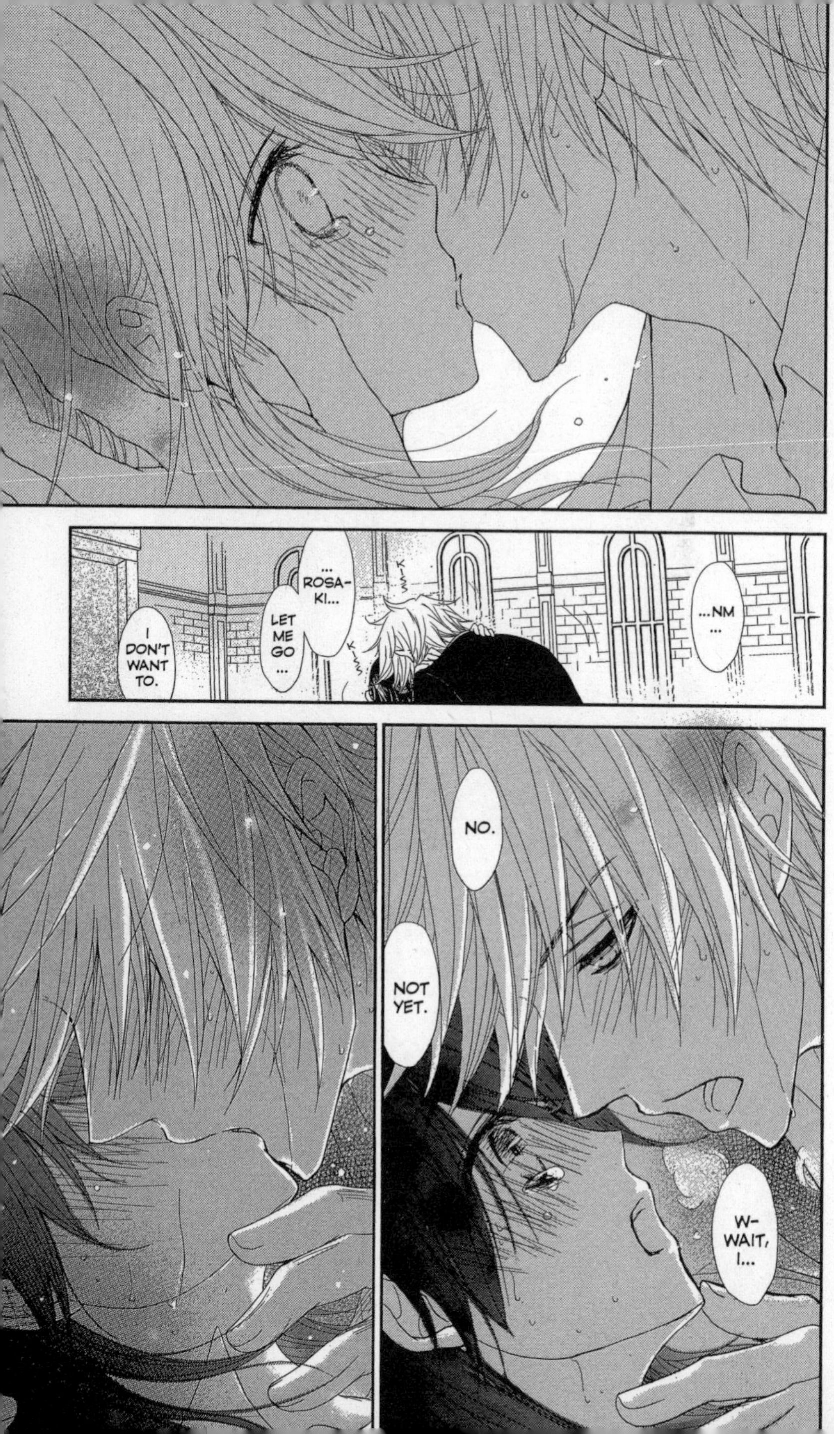
...NM ...
KISS
KISS
... ROSAKI...
LET ME GO ...
I DON'T WANT TO.
NO.
NOT YET.
W-WAIT, I...

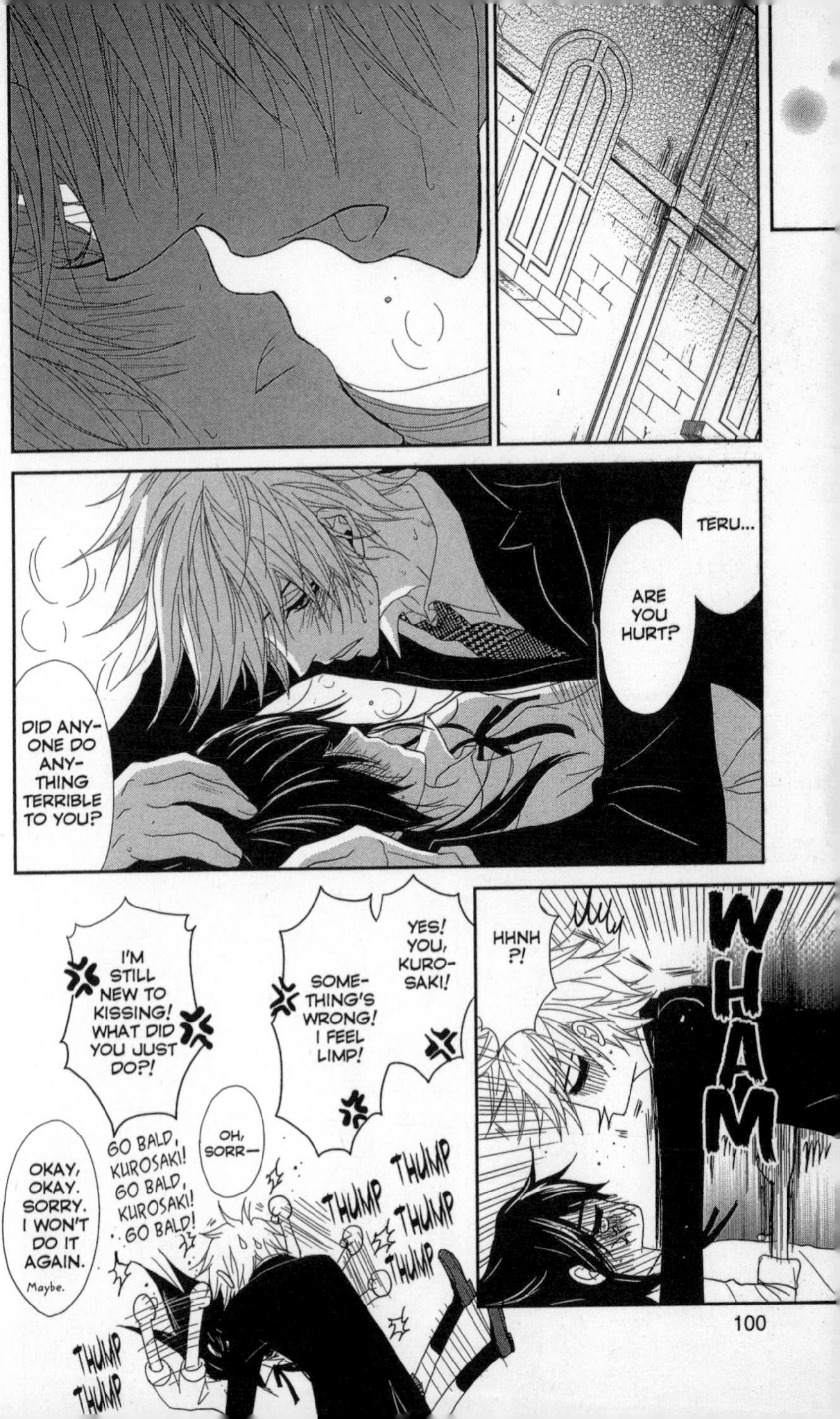
TERU...
ARE YOU HURT?
DID ANY-ONE DO ANY-THING TERRIBLE TO YOU?
WHAM
HHNH ?!
YES! YOU, KURO-SAKI!
SOME-THING'S WRONG! I FEEL LIMP!
I'M STILL NEW TO KISSING! WHAT DID YOU JUST DO?!
OH, SORR—
THUMP THUMP
THUMP THUMP
THUMP
GO BALD, KUROSAKI! GO BALD, KUROSAKI! GO BALD!
OKAY, OKAY. SORRY. I WON'T DO IT AGAIN.
Maybe.
THUMP THUMP

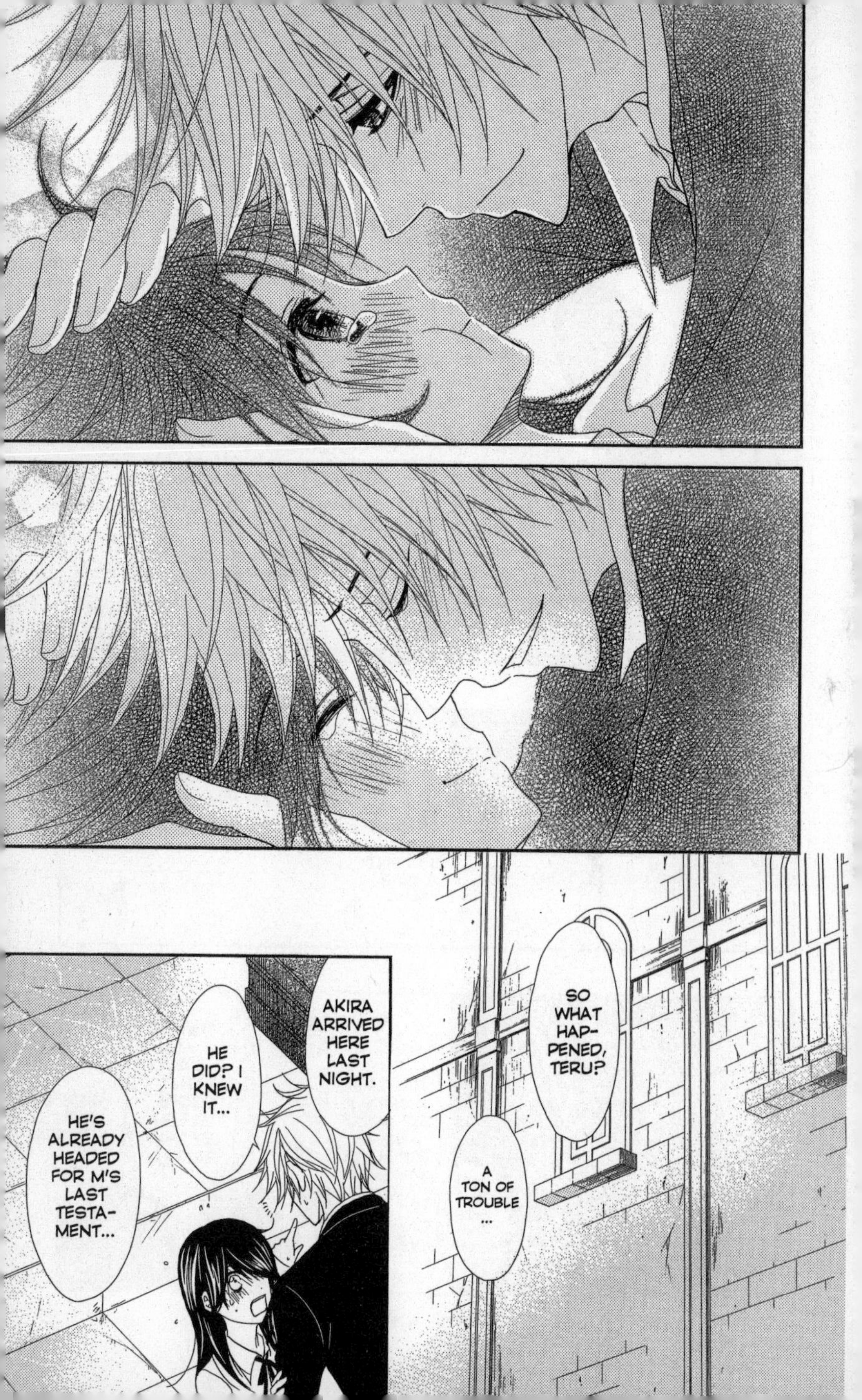
SO WHAT HAP-PENED, TERU?
A TON OF TROUBLE ...
AKIRA ARRIVED HERE LAST NIGHT.
HE DID? I KNEW IT...
HE'S ALREADY HEADED FOR M'S LAST TESTA-MENT...

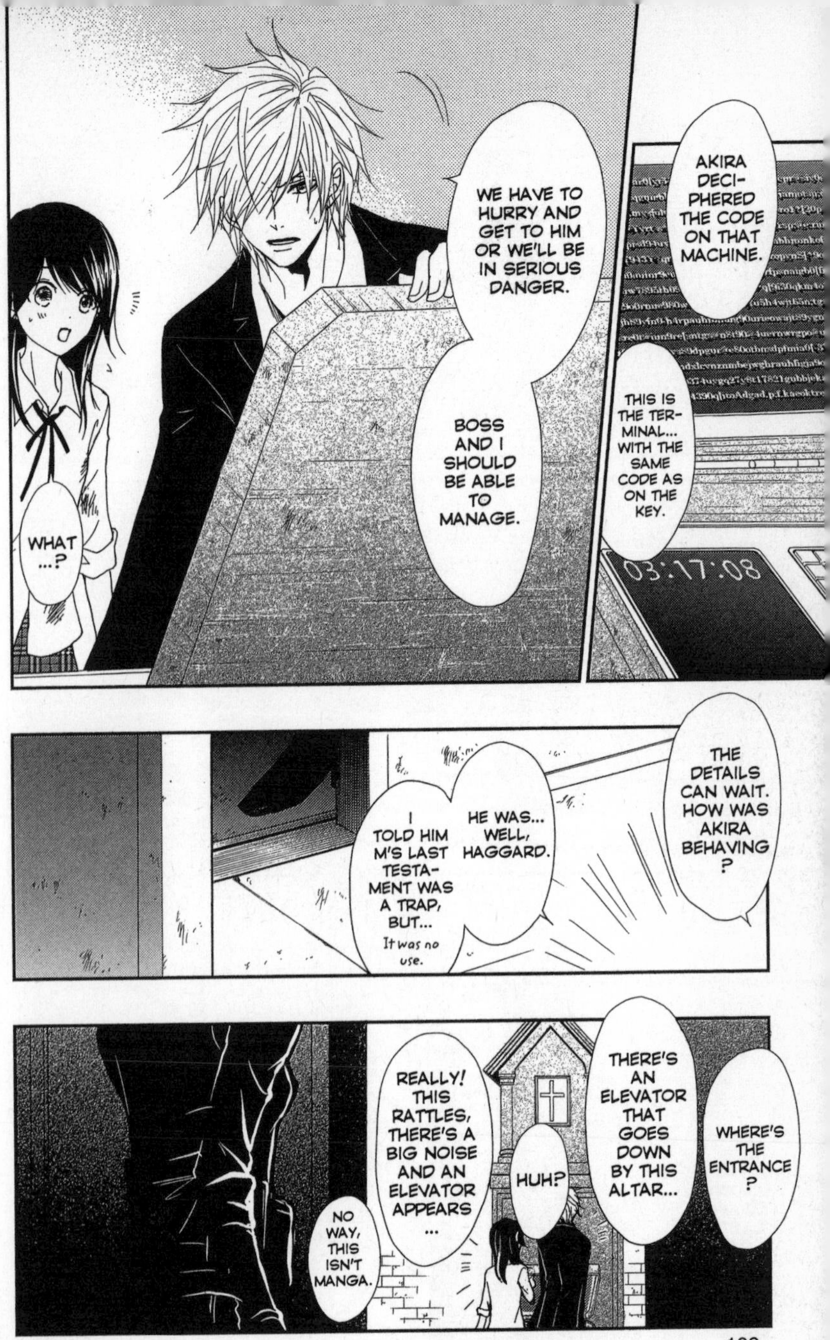
AKIRA DECIPHERED THE CODE ON THAT MACHINE.
THIS IS THE TERMINAL... WITH THE SAME CODE AS ON THE KEY.
03:17:08
WE HAVE TO HURRY AND GET TO HIM OR WE'LL BE IN SERIOUS DANGER.
BOSS AND I SHOULD BE ABLE TO MANAGE.
WHAT...?
THE DETAILS CAN WAIT. HOW WAS AKIRA BEHAVING?
HE WAS... WELL, HAGGARD.
I TOLD HIM M'S LAST TESTAMENT WAS A TRAP, BUT...
It was no use.
WHERE'S THE ENTRANCE?
THERE'S AN ELEVATOR THAT GOES DOWN BY THIS ALTAR...
HUH?
REALLY! THIS RATTLES, THERE'S A BIG NOISE AND AN ELEVATOR APPEARS...
NO WAY, THIS ISN'T MANGA.

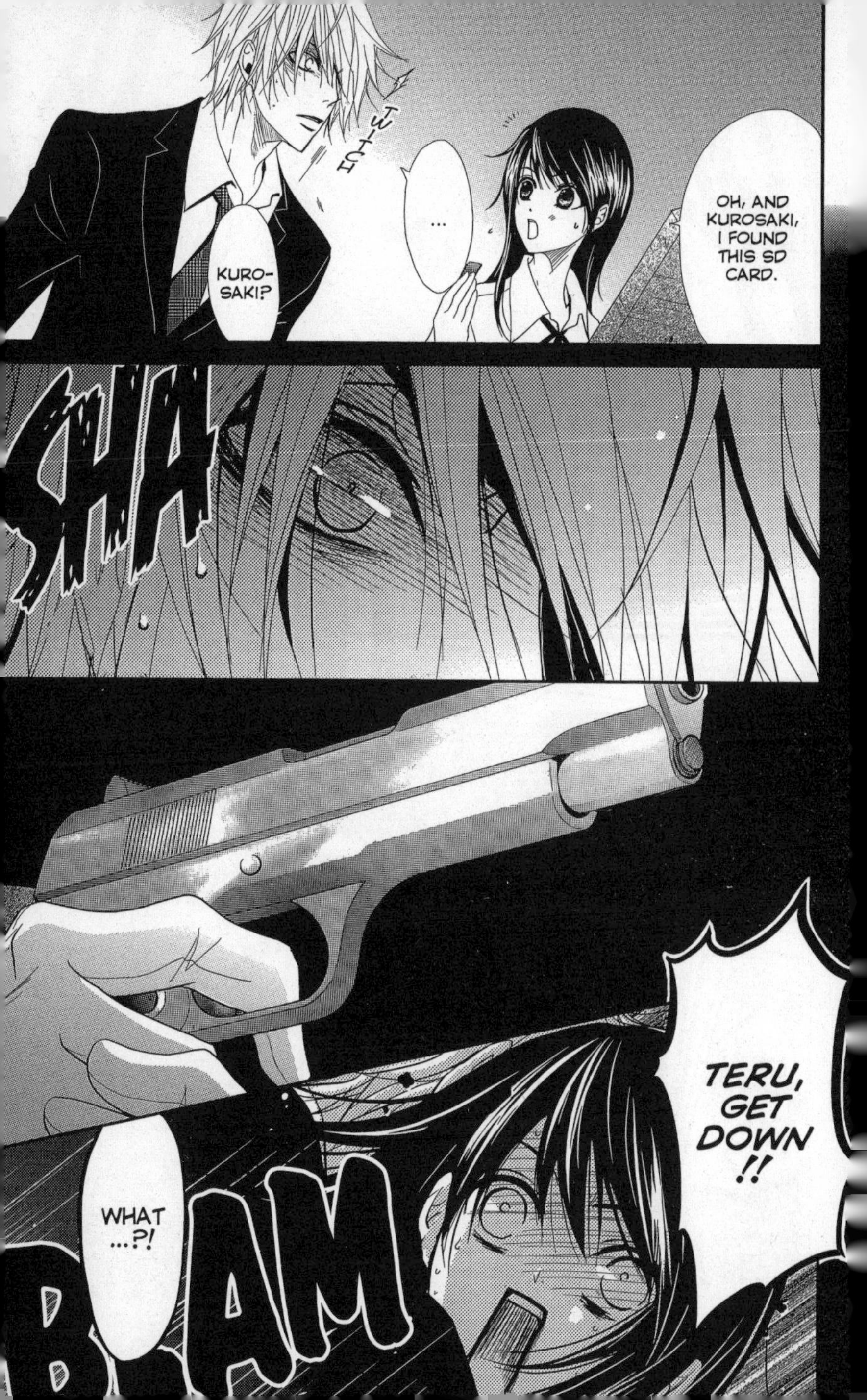
OH, AND KUROSAKI, I FOUND THIS SD CARD.
...
TWITCH
KURO-SAKI!?
SHA
TERU, GET DOWN!!
WHAT ...?!
BAM

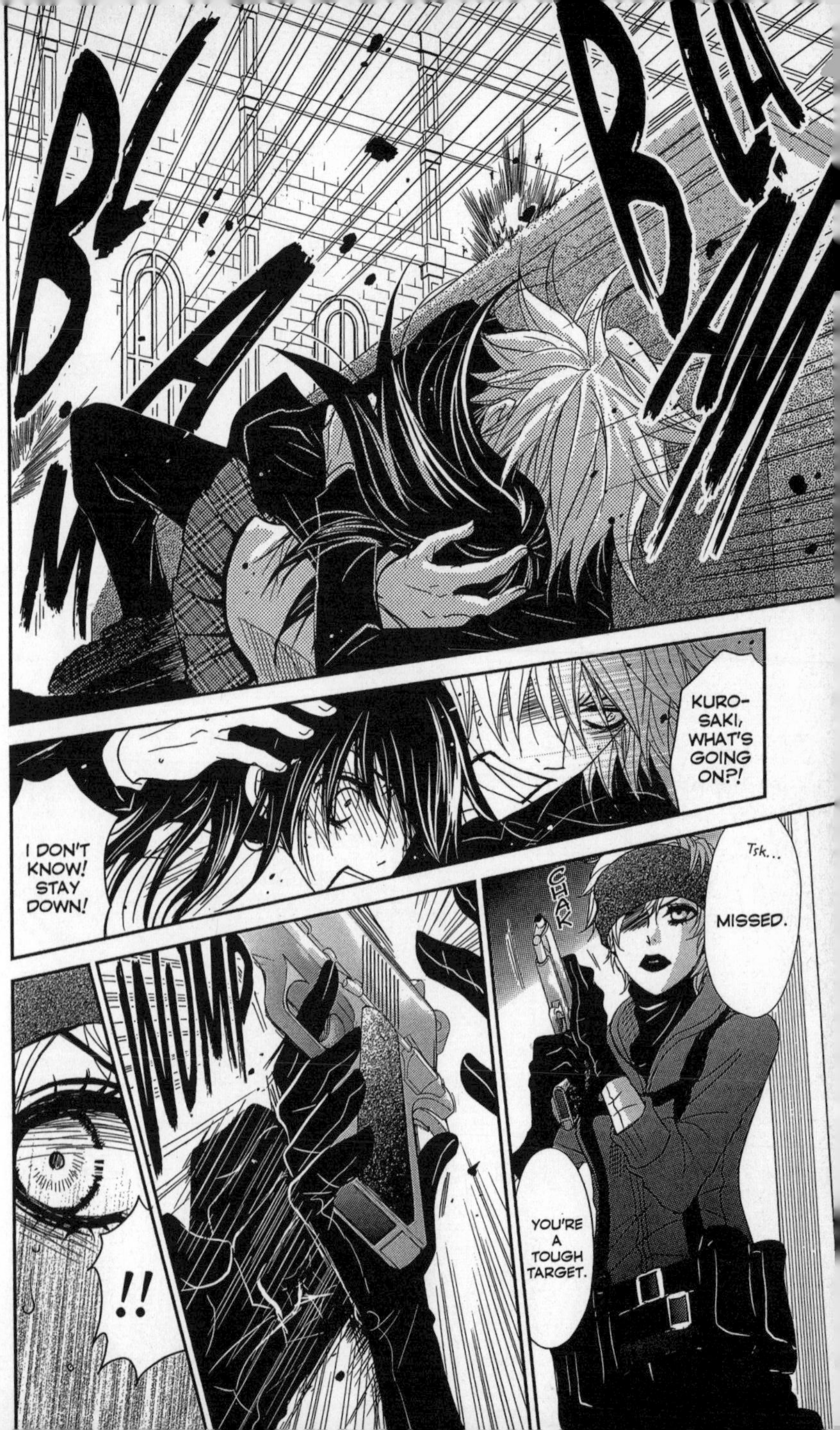
BLAM
BLAM
KURO-SAKI, WHAT'S GOING ON?!
I DON'T KNOW! STAY DOWN!
Tsk...
CHAK
MISSED.
YOU'RE A TOUGH TARGET.
WUMP
!!

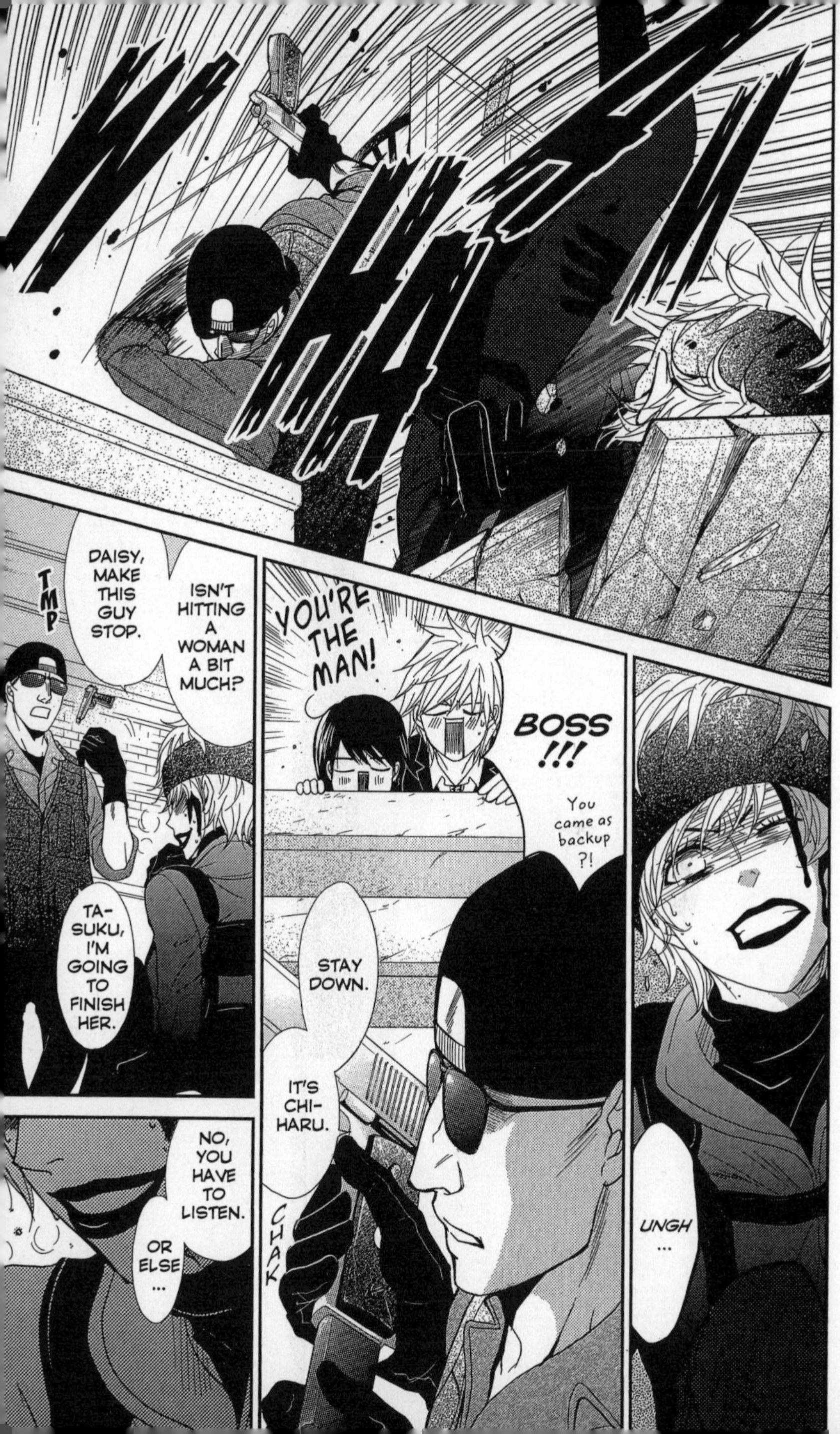
BOSS!!!
You came as backup?!
UNGH...
YOU'RE THE MAN!
STAY DOWN.
IT'S CHI-HARU.
CHAK
ISN'T HITTING A WOMAN A BIT MUCH?
DAISY, MAKE THIS GUY STOP.
TMP
TA-SUKU, I'M GOING TO FINISH HER.
NO, YOU HAVE TO LISTEN.
OR ELSE...

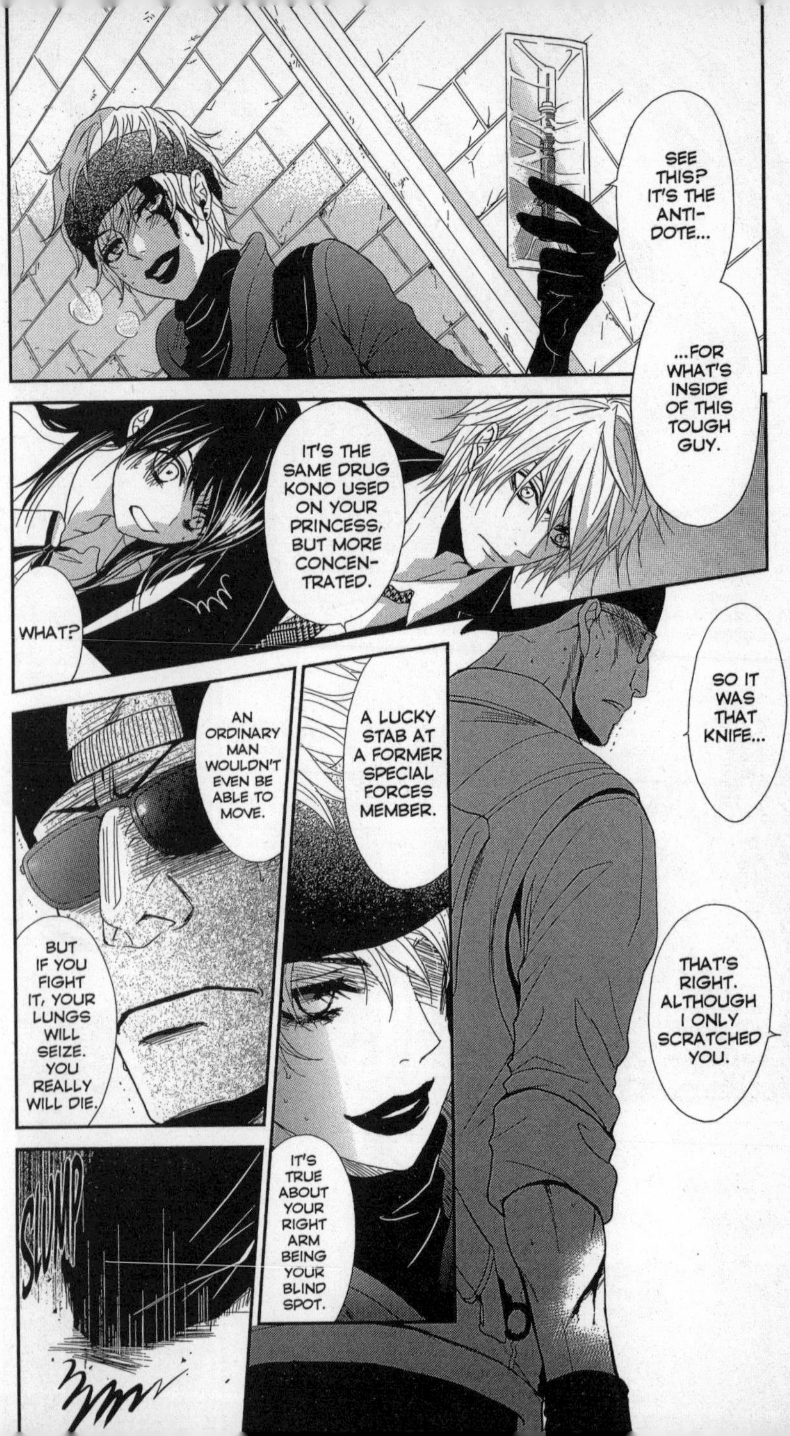
SEE THIS? IT'S THE ANTI-DOTE...
...FOR WHAT'S INSIDE OF THIS TOUGH GUY.
IT'S THE SAME DRUG KONO USED ON YOUR PRINCESS, BUT MORE CONCEN-TRATED.
WHAT?
SO IT WAS THAT KNIFE...
A LUCKY STAB AT A FORMER SPECIAL FORCES MEMBER.
AN ORDINARY MAN WOULDN'T EVEN BE ABLE TO MOVE.
THAT'S RIGHT. ALTHOUGH I ONLY SCRATCHED YOU.
BUT IF YOU FIGHT IT, YOUR LUNGS WILL SEIZE. YOU REALLY WILL DIE.
IT'S TRUE ABOUT YOUR RIGHT ARM BEING YOUR BLIND SPOT.
SLUMP

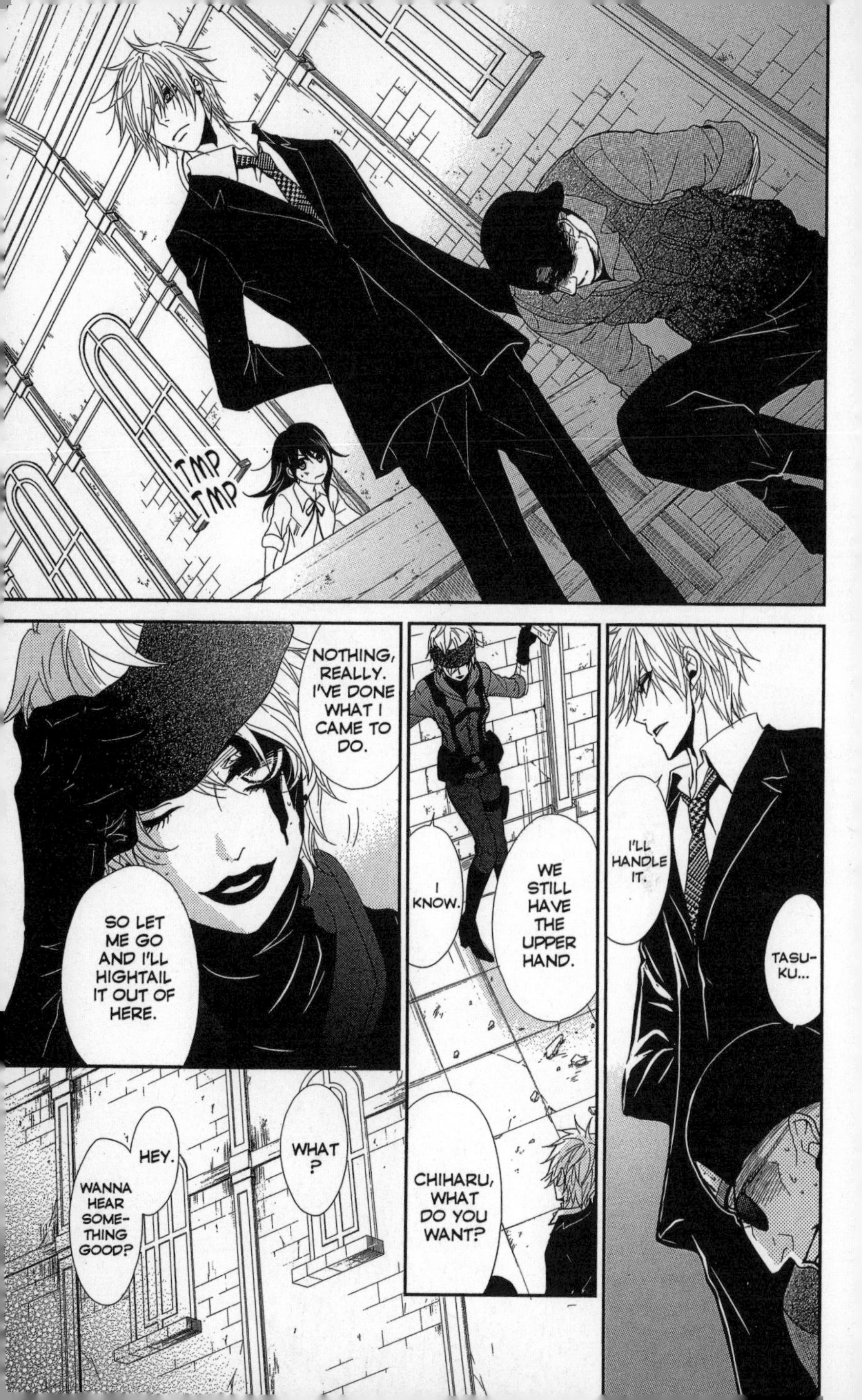
TMP TMP
TASU-KU...
I'LL HANDLE IT.
WE STILL HAVE THE UPPER HAND.
I KNOW.
CHIHARU, WHAT DO YOU WANT?
NOTHING, REALLY. I'VE DONE WHAT I CAME TO DO.
SO LET ME GO AND I'LL HIGHTAIL IT OUT OF HERE.
WHAT?
HEY.
WANNA HEAR SOME-THING GOOD?

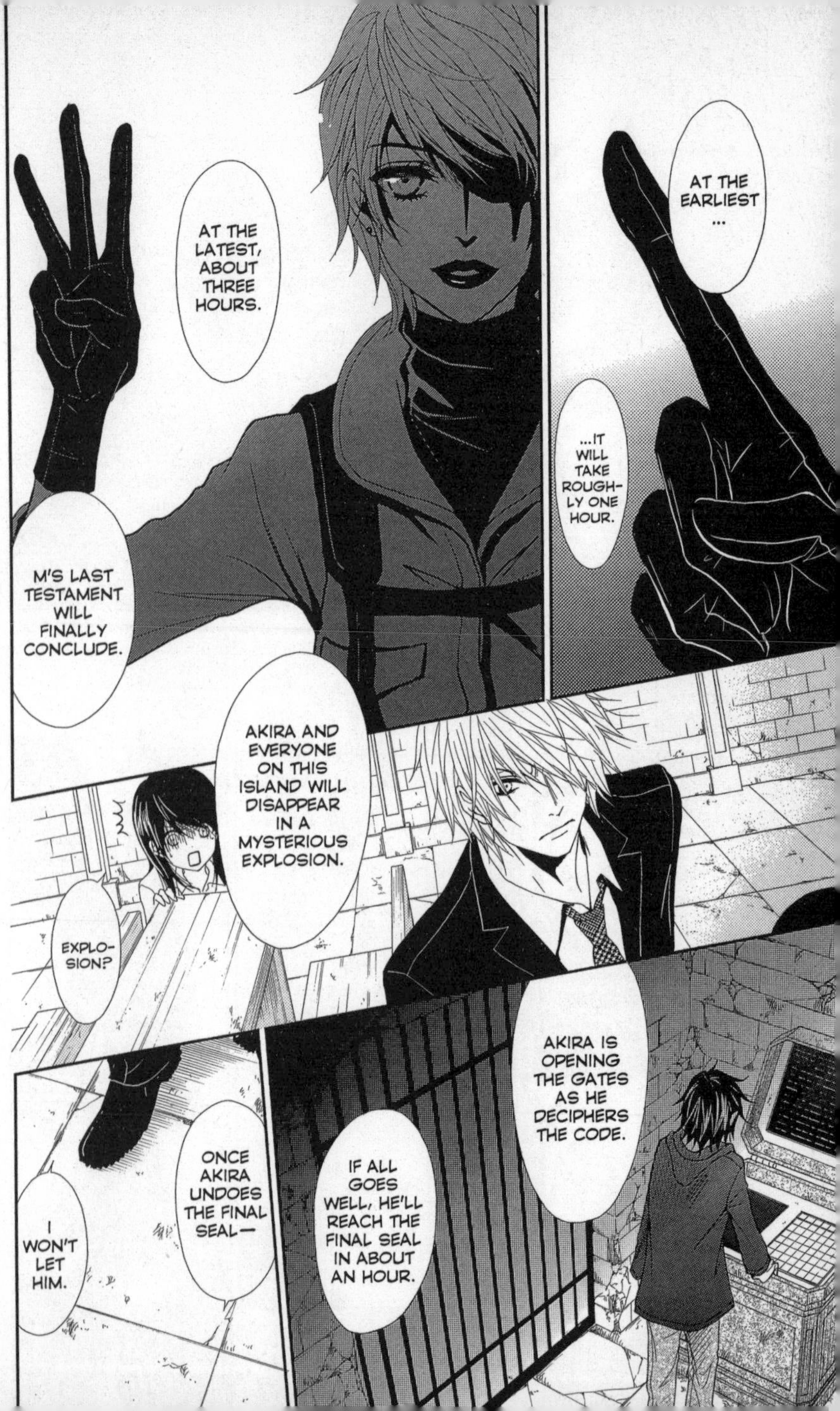
AT THE EARLIEST ...
...IT WILL TAKE ROUGHLY ONE HOUR.
AT THE LATEST, ABOUT THREE HOURS.
M'S LAST TESTAMENT WILL FINALLY CONCLUDE.
AKIRA AND EVERYONE ON THIS ISLAND WILL DISAPPEAR IN A MYSTERIOUS EXPLOSION.
EXPLOSION?
AKIRA IS OPENING THE GATES AS HE DECIPHERS THE CODE.
IF ALL GOES WELL, HE'LL REACH THE FINAL SEAL IN ABOUT AN HOUR.
ONCE AKIRA UNDOES THE FINAL SEAL—
I WON'T LET HIM.

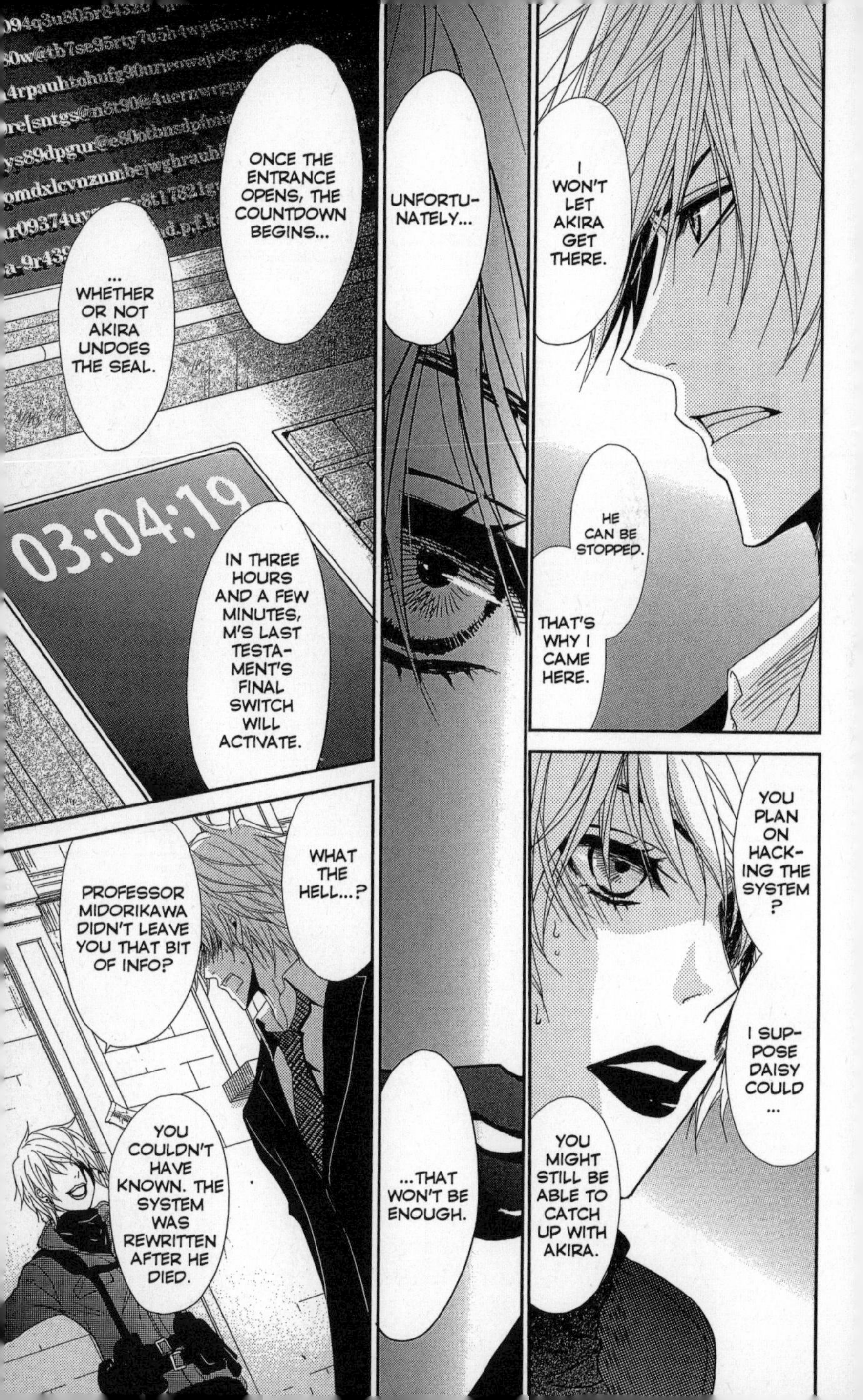
I WON'T LET AKIRA GET THERE.
HE CAN BE STOPPED.
THAT'S WHY I CAME HERE.
YOU PLAN ON HACKING THE SYSTEM?
I SUPPOSE DAISY COULD...
YOU MIGHT STILL BE ABLE TO CATCH UP WITH AKIRA.
UNFORTUNATELY...
...THAT WON'T BE ENOUGH.
ONCE THE ENTRANCE OPENS, THE COUNTDOWN BEGINS...
...WHETHER OR NOT AKIRA UNDOES THE SEAL.
03:04:19
IN THREE HOURS AND A FEW MINUTES, M'S LAST TESTAMENT'S FINAL SWITCH WILL ACTIVATE.
WHAT THE HELL...?
PROFESSOR MIDORIKAWA DIDN'T LEAVE YOU THAT BIT OF INFO?
YOU COULDN'T HAVE KNOWN. THE SYSTEM WAS REWRITTEN AFTER HE DIED.

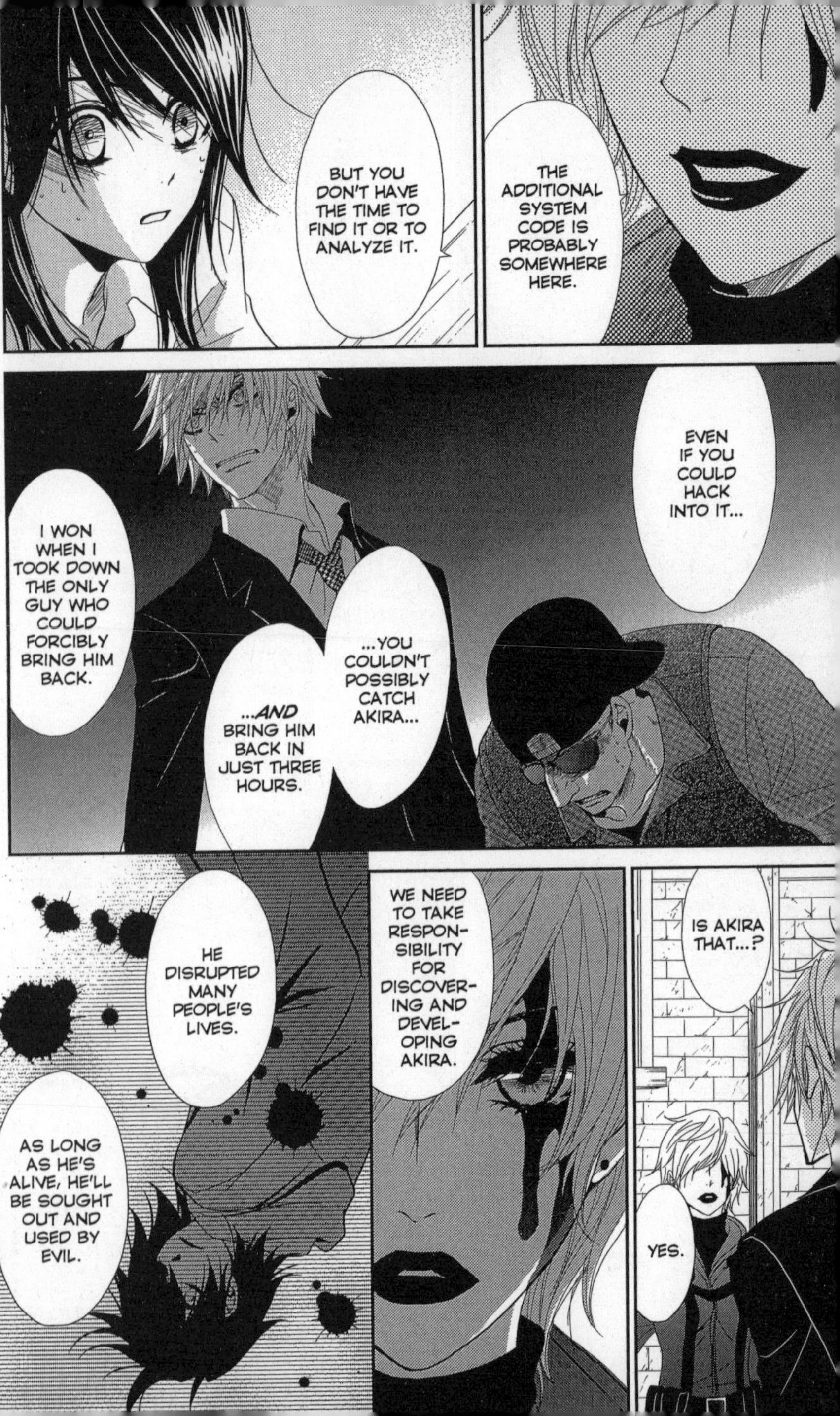
THE ADDITIONAL SYSTEM CODE IS PROBABLY SOMEWHERE HERE.
BUT YOU DON'T HAVE THE TIME TO FIND IT OR TO ANALYZE IT.
EVEN IF YOU COULD HACK INTO IT...
...YOU COULDN'T POSSIBLY CATCH AKIRA...
...*AND* BRING HIM BACK IN JUST THREE HOURS.
I WON WHEN I TOOK DOWN THE ONLY GUY WHO COULD FORCIBLY BRING HIM BACK.
IS AKIRA THAT...?
YES.
WE NEED TO TAKE RESPONSIBILITY FOR DISCOVERING AND DEVELOPING AKIRA.
HE DISRUPTED MANY PEOPLE'S LIVES.
AS LONG AS HE'S ALIVE, HE'LL BE SOUGHT OUT AND USED BY EVIL.

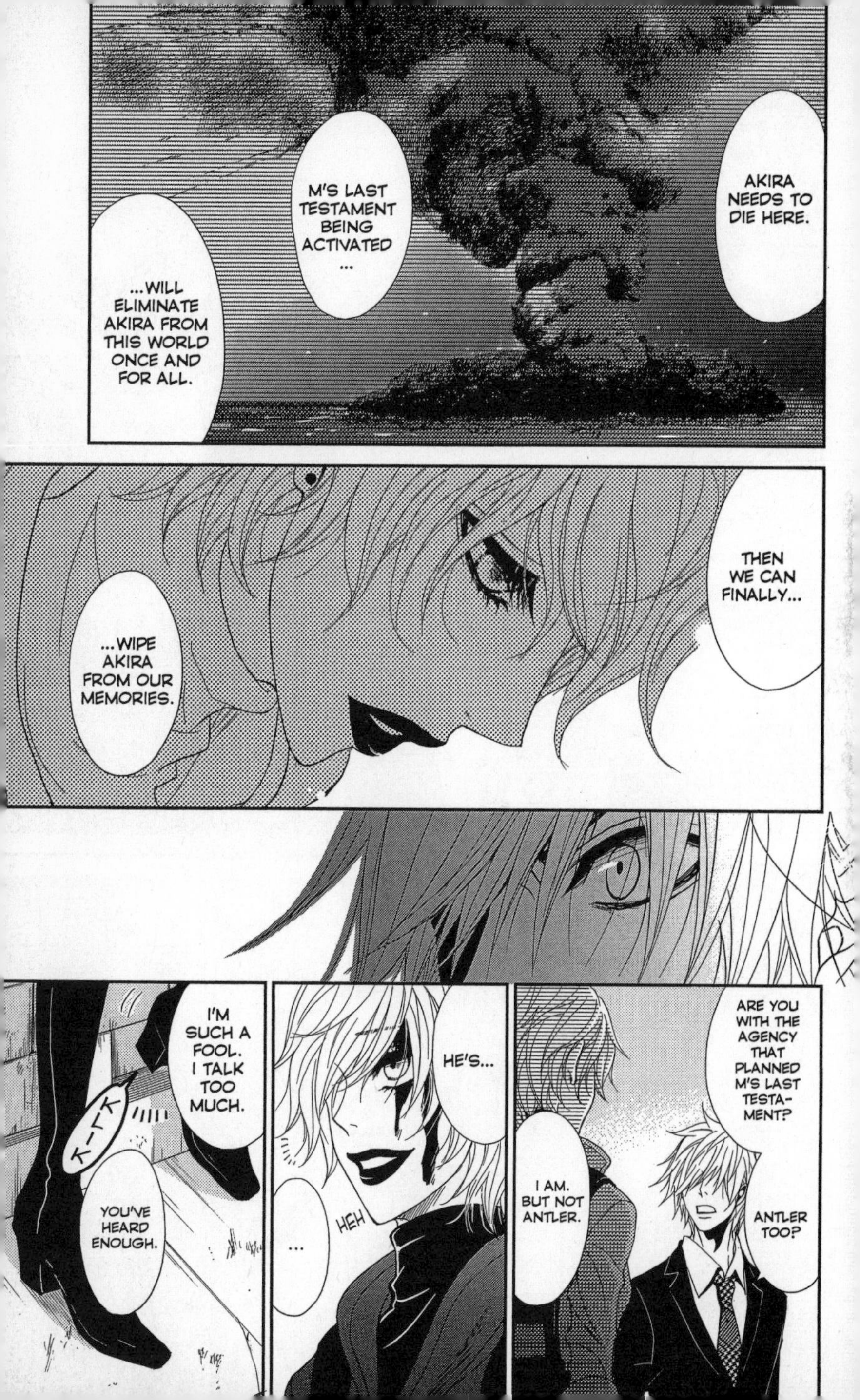
AKIRA NEEDS TO DIE HERE.
M'S LAST TESTAMENT BEING ACTIVATED ...
...WILL ELIMINATE AKIRA FROM THIS WORLD ONCE AND FOR ALL.
THEN WE CAN FINALLY...
...WIPE AKIRA FROM OUR MEMORIES.
ARE YOU WITH THE AGENCY THAT PLANNED M'S LAST TESTA-MENT?
ANTLER TOO?
I AM. BUT NOT ANTLER.
HE'S...
HEH
...
I'M SUCH A FOOL. I TALK TOO MUCH.
YOU'VE HEARD ENOUGH.

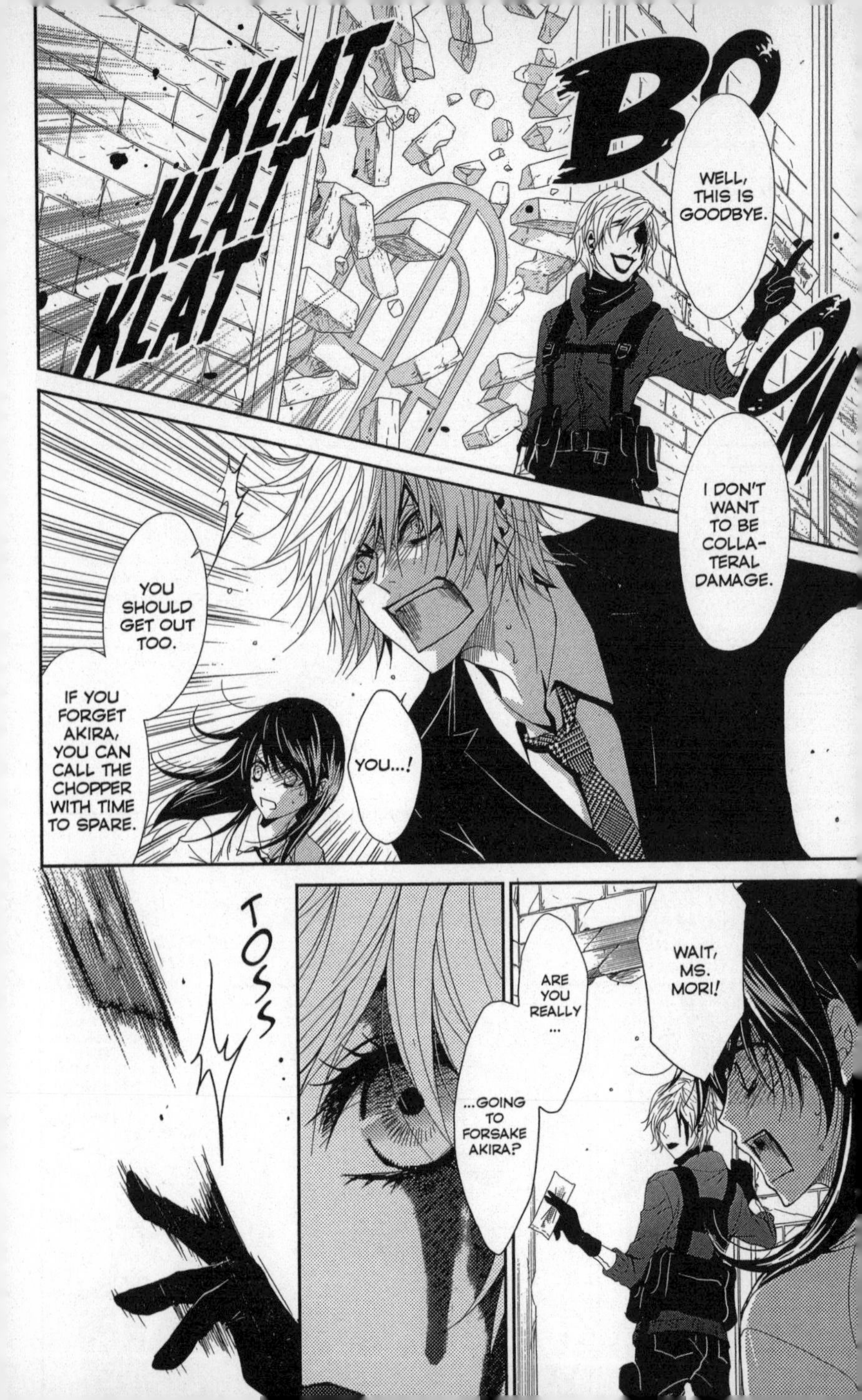
BOOM
WELL, THIS IS GOODBYE.
KLAT KLAT KLAT
I DON'T WANT TO BE COLLATERAL DAMAGE.
YOU...!
YOU SHOULD GET OUT TOO.
IF YOU FORGET AKIRA, YOU CAN CALL THE CHOPPER WITH TIME TO SPARE.
WAIT, MS. MORI!
ARE YOU REALLY ...
...GOING TO FORSAKE AKIRA?
TOSS

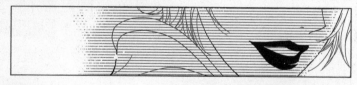

BEEP

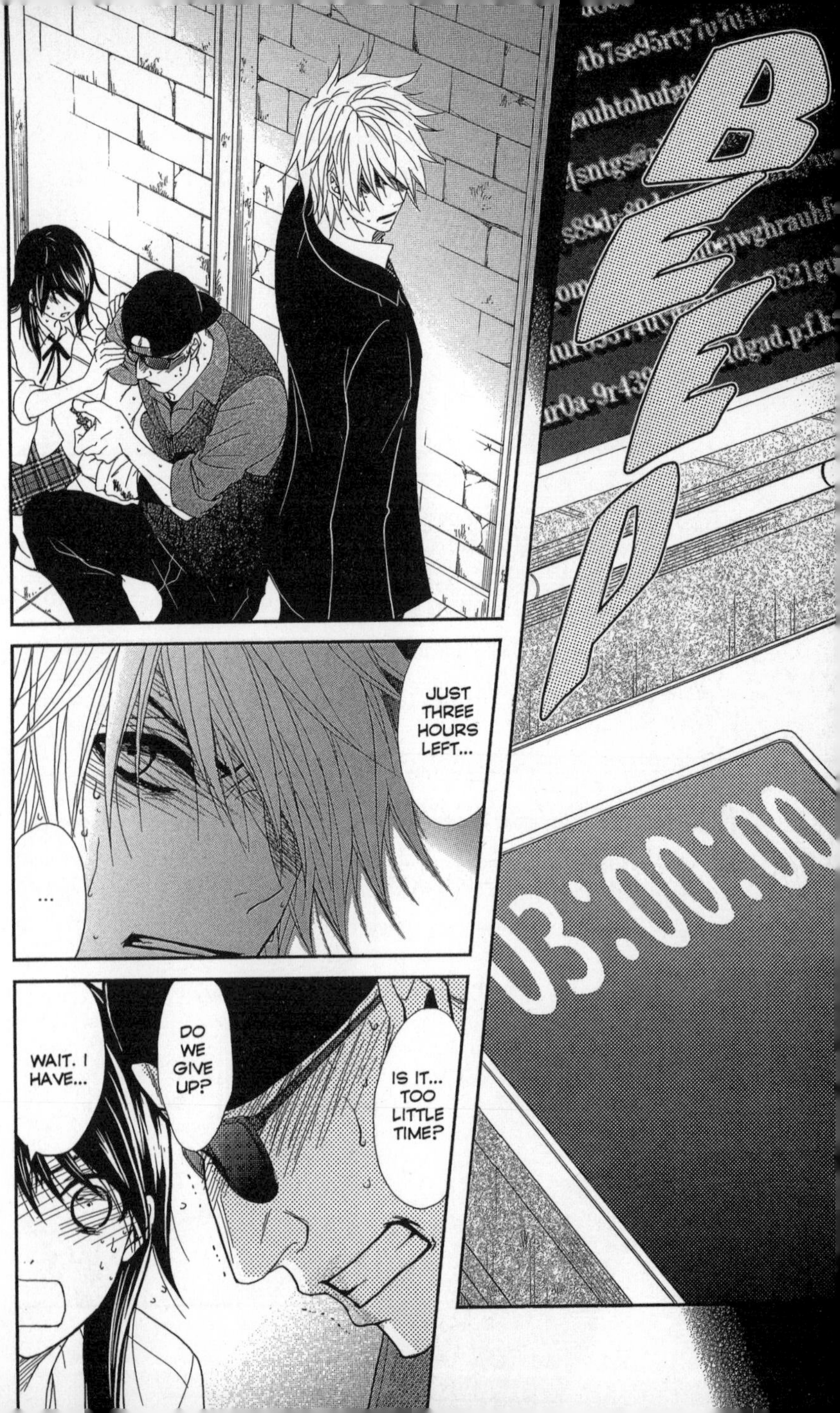
BEEP
03:00:00
JUST THREE HOURS LEFT...
...
IS IT... TOO LITTLE TIME?
DO WE GIVE UP?
WAIT. I HAVE...

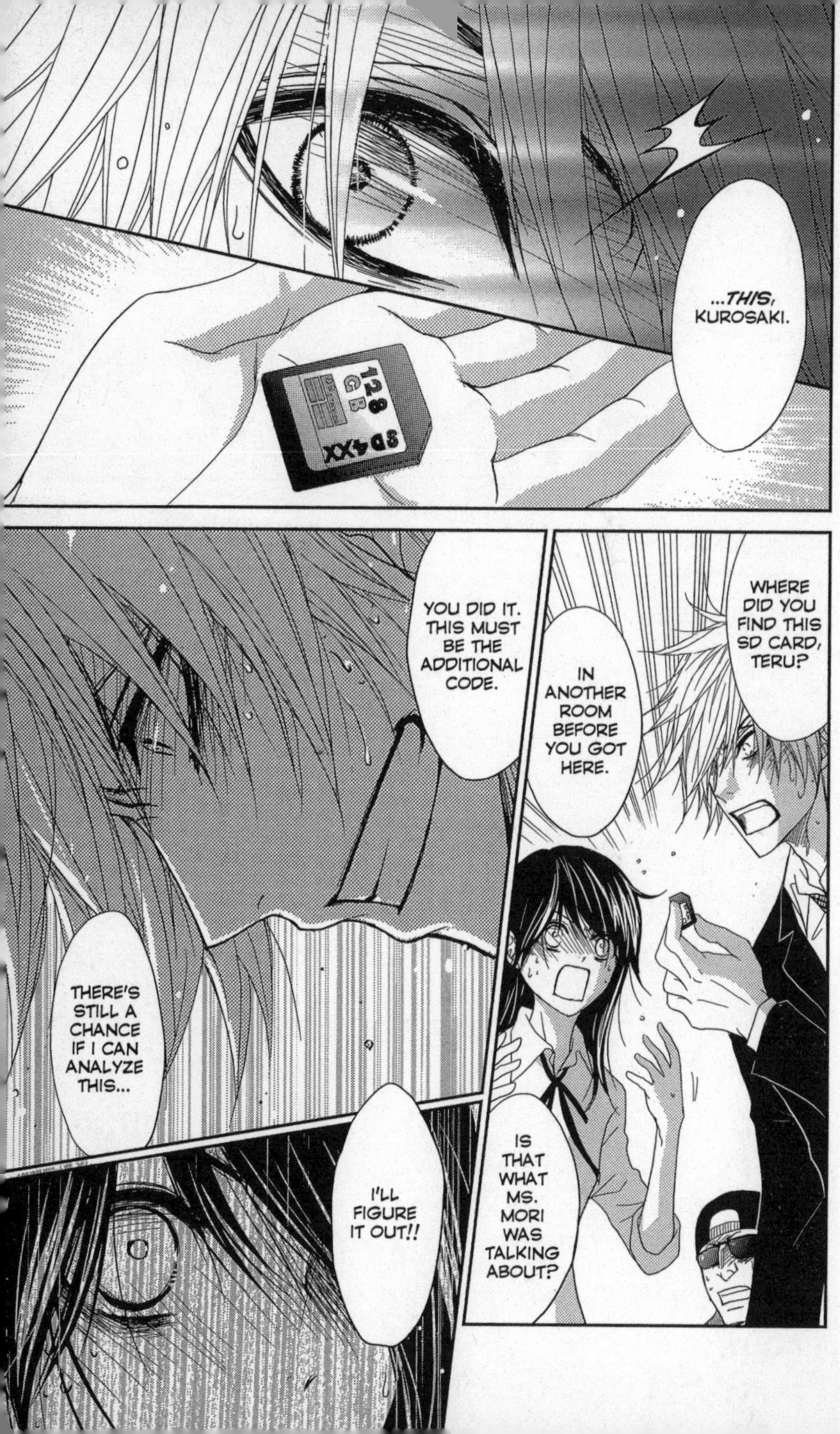
...THIS, KUROSAKI.
WHERE DID YOU FIND THIS SD CARD, TERU?
IN ANOTHER ROOM BEFORE YOU GOT HERE.
IS THAT WHAT MS. MORI WAS TALKING ABOUT?
YOU DID IT. THIS MUST BE THE ADDITIONAL CODE.
THERE'S STILL A CHANCE IF I CAN ANALYZE THIS...
I'LL FIGURE IT OUT!!

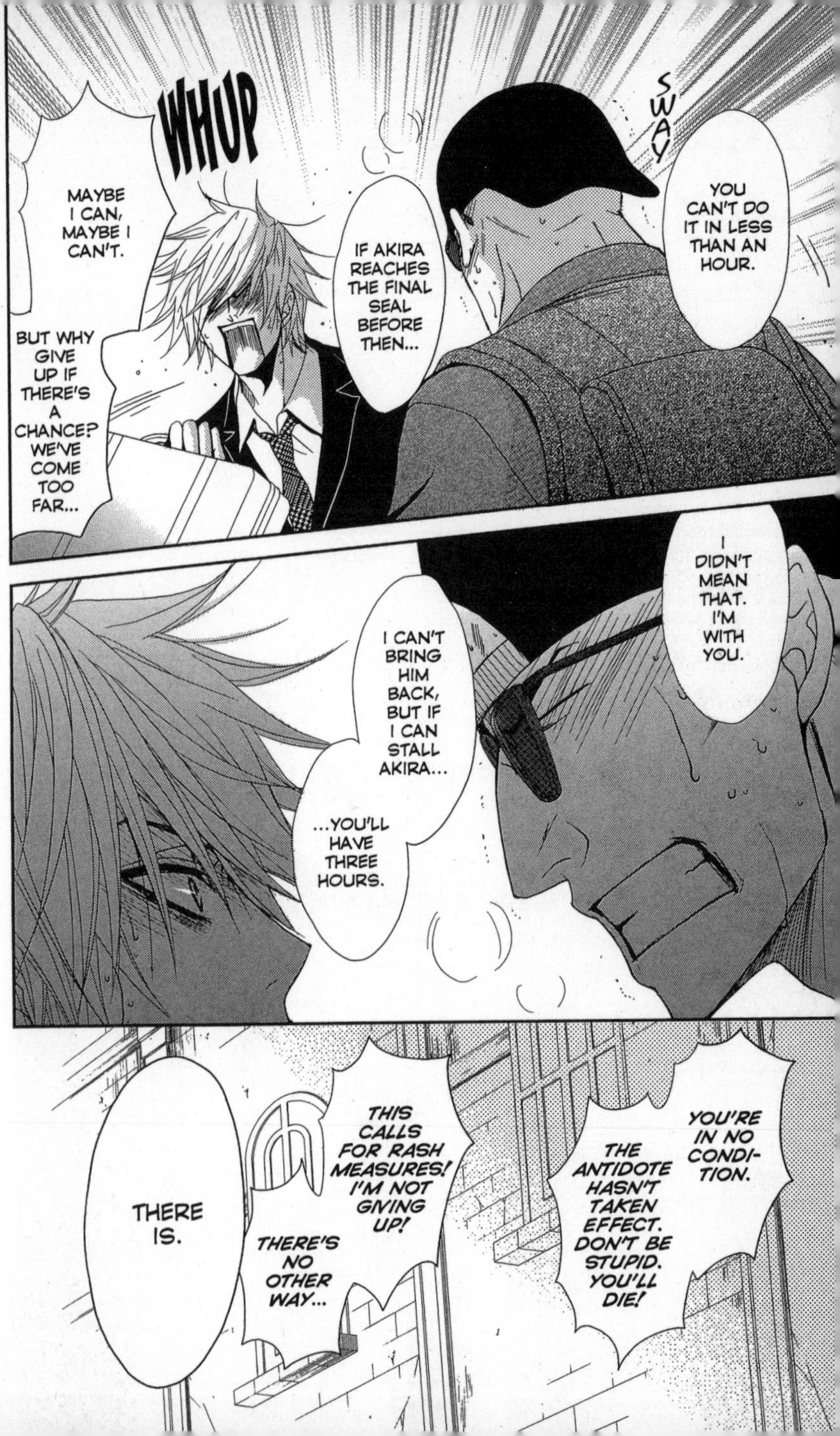
SWAY
YOU CAN'T DO IT IN LESS THAN AN HOUR.
IF AKIRA REACHES THE FINAL SEAL BEFORE THEN...
WHUP
MAYBE I CAN, MAYBE I CAN'T.
BUT WHY GIVE UP IF THERE'S A CHANCE? WE'VE COME TOO FAR...
I DIDN'T MEAN THAT. I'M WITH YOU.
I CAN'T BRING HIM BACK, BUT IF I CAN STALL AKIRA...
...YOU'LL HAVE THREE HOURS.
YOU'RE IN NO CONDITION.
THE ANTIDOTE HASN'T TAKEN EFFECT. DON'T BE STUPID. YOU'LL DIE!
THIS CALLS FOR RASH MEASURES! I'M NOT GIVING UP!
THERE'S NO OTHER WAY...
THERE IS.

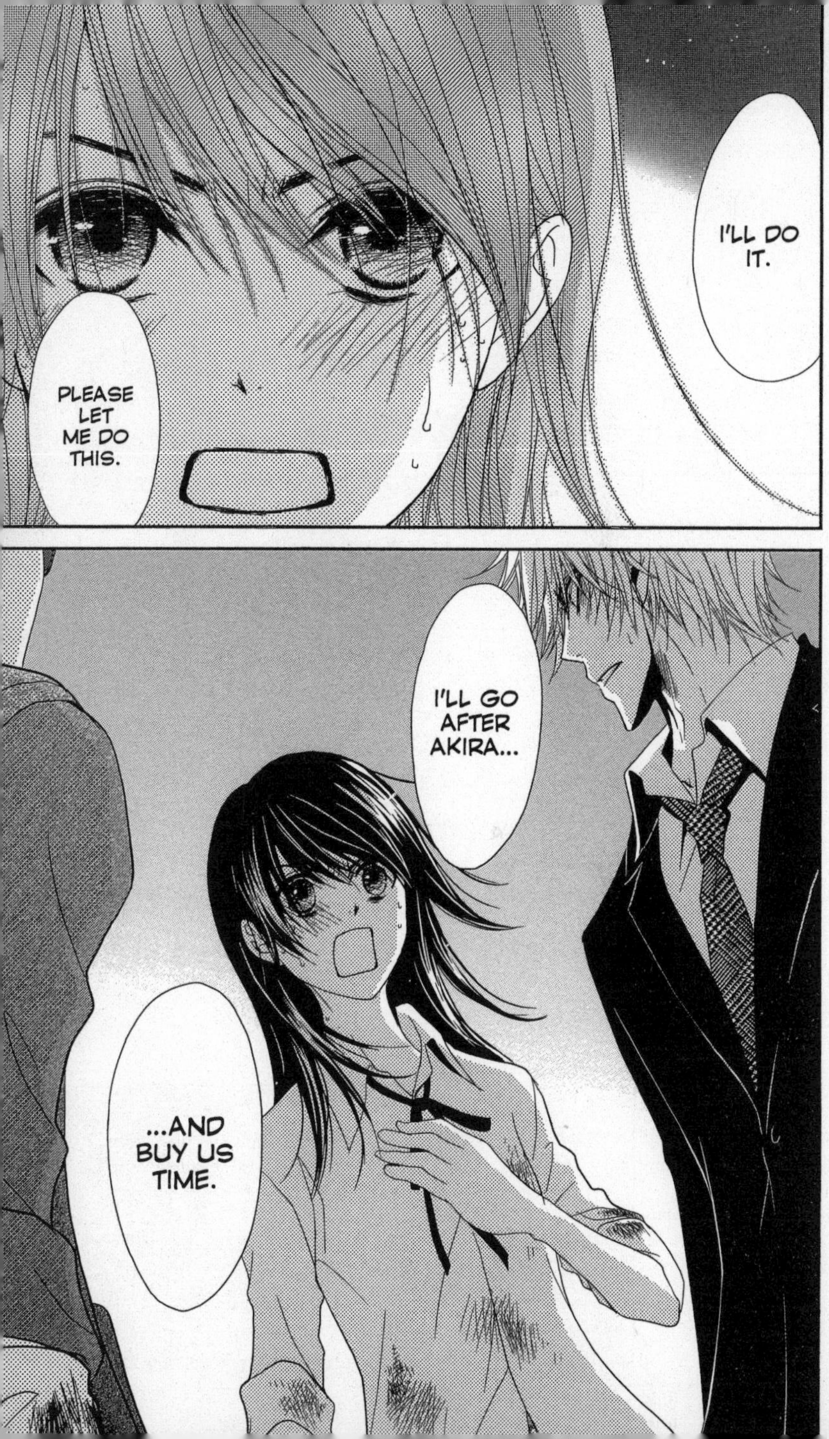
I'LL DO IT.
PLEASE LET ME DO THIS.
I'LL GO AFTER AKIRA...
...AND BUY US TIME.

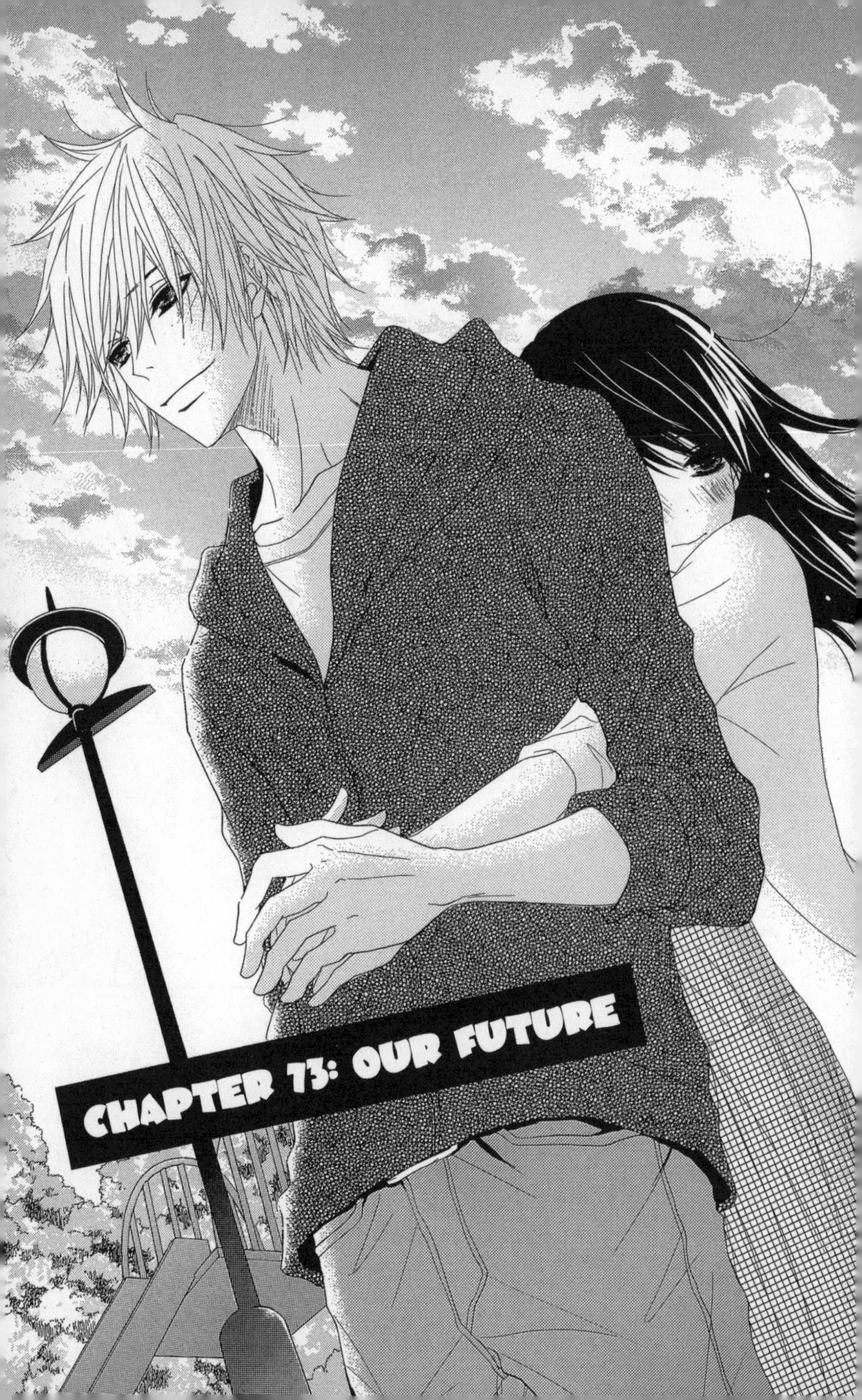
CHAPTER 13: OUR FUTURE

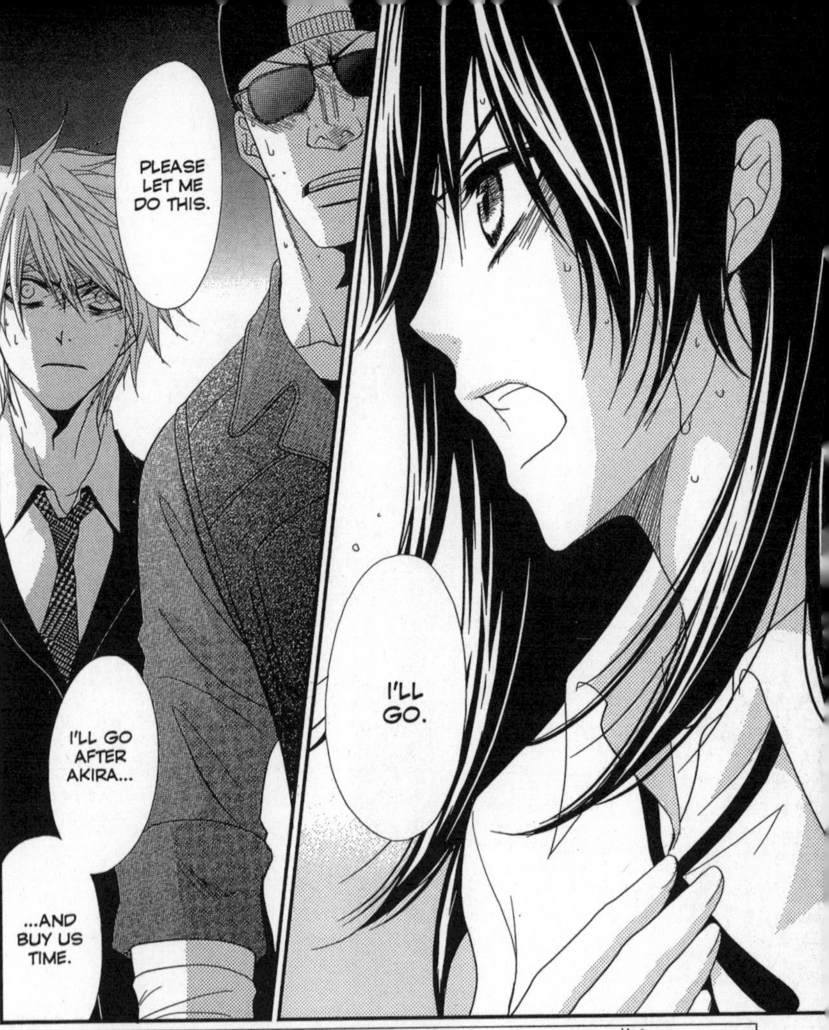
I'LL GO.
PLEASE LET ME DO THIS.
I'LL GO AFTER AKIRA...
...AND BUY US TIME.

THE PISTOL THAT CHIHARU IS USING WAS DRAWN BASED ON THE COLT COMBAT COMMANDER.

APPARENTLY, IT'S NO LONGER IN USE. I PROBABLY DIDN'T DO ENOUGH RESEARCH ON HOW IT'S HANDLED, SO MY DEPICTIONS MAY BE QUITE WRONG, BUT I HOPE YOU WILL FORGIVE ME.

MY REFERENCE WAS A MODEL GUN I STOLE FROM MY FATHER'S COLLECTION. SORRY, DAD. BUT, I THINK HE FORGIVES ME BECAUSE I GAVE HIM THE MODEL OF THE DILLINGER I USED AS A REFERENCE IN CHAPTER 49.

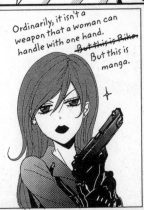

Ordinarily, it isn't a weapon that a woman can handle with one hand. ~~But this is Biko.~~ But this is manga.

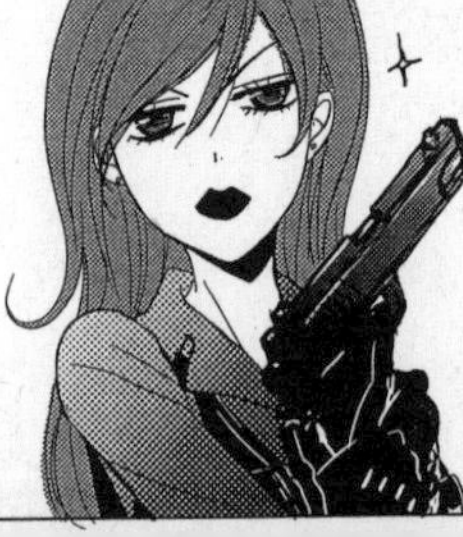

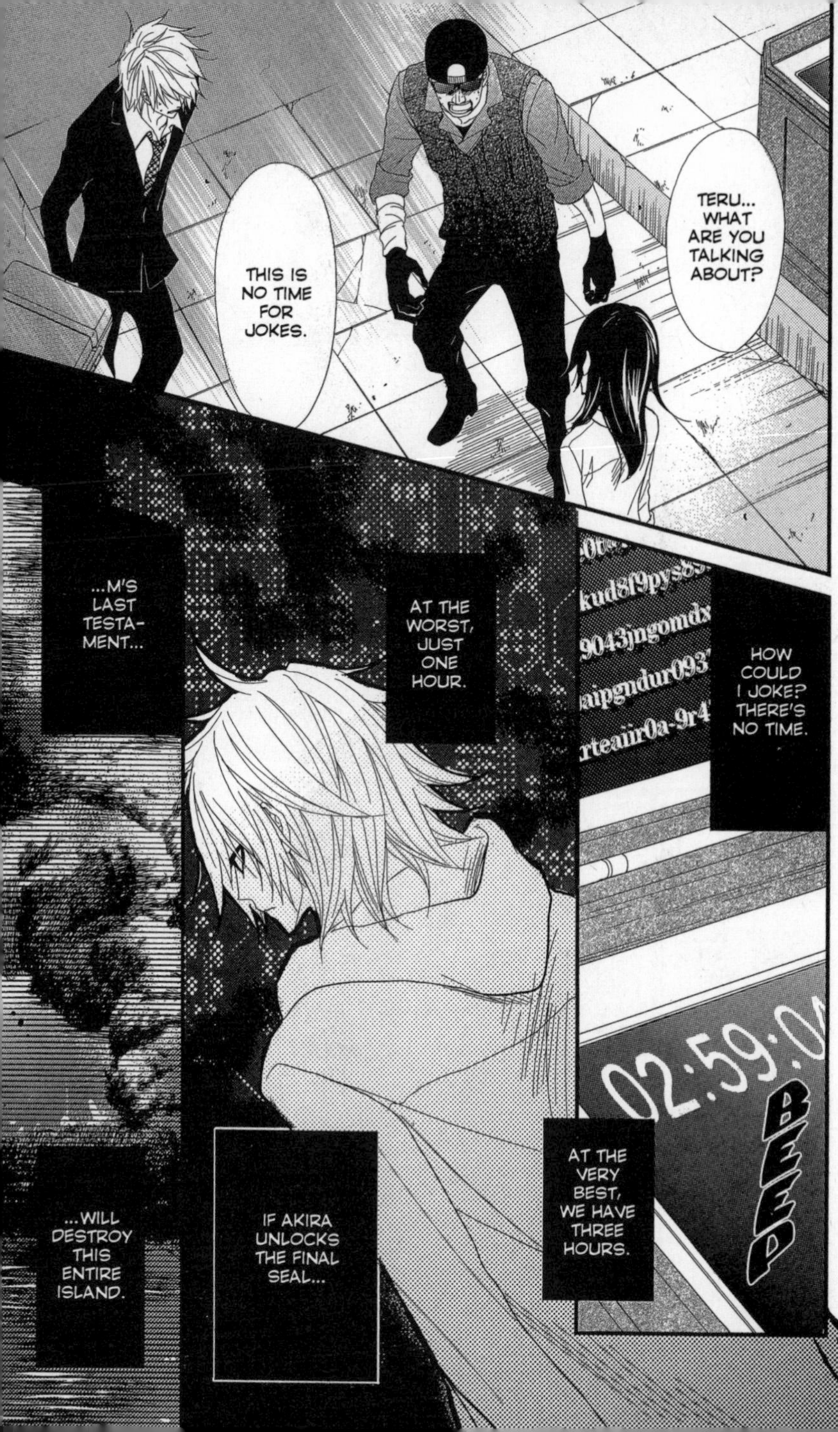
TERU... WHAT ARE YOU TALKING ABOUT?
THIS IS NO TIME FOR JOKES.
HOW COULD I JOKE? THERE'S NO TIME.
AT THE VERY BEST, WE HAVE THREE HOURS.
BEEP
AT THE WORST, JUST ONE HOUR.
IF AKIRA UNLOCKS THE FINAL SEAL...
...M'S LAST TESTAMENT...
...WILL DESTROY THIS ENTIRE ISLAND.

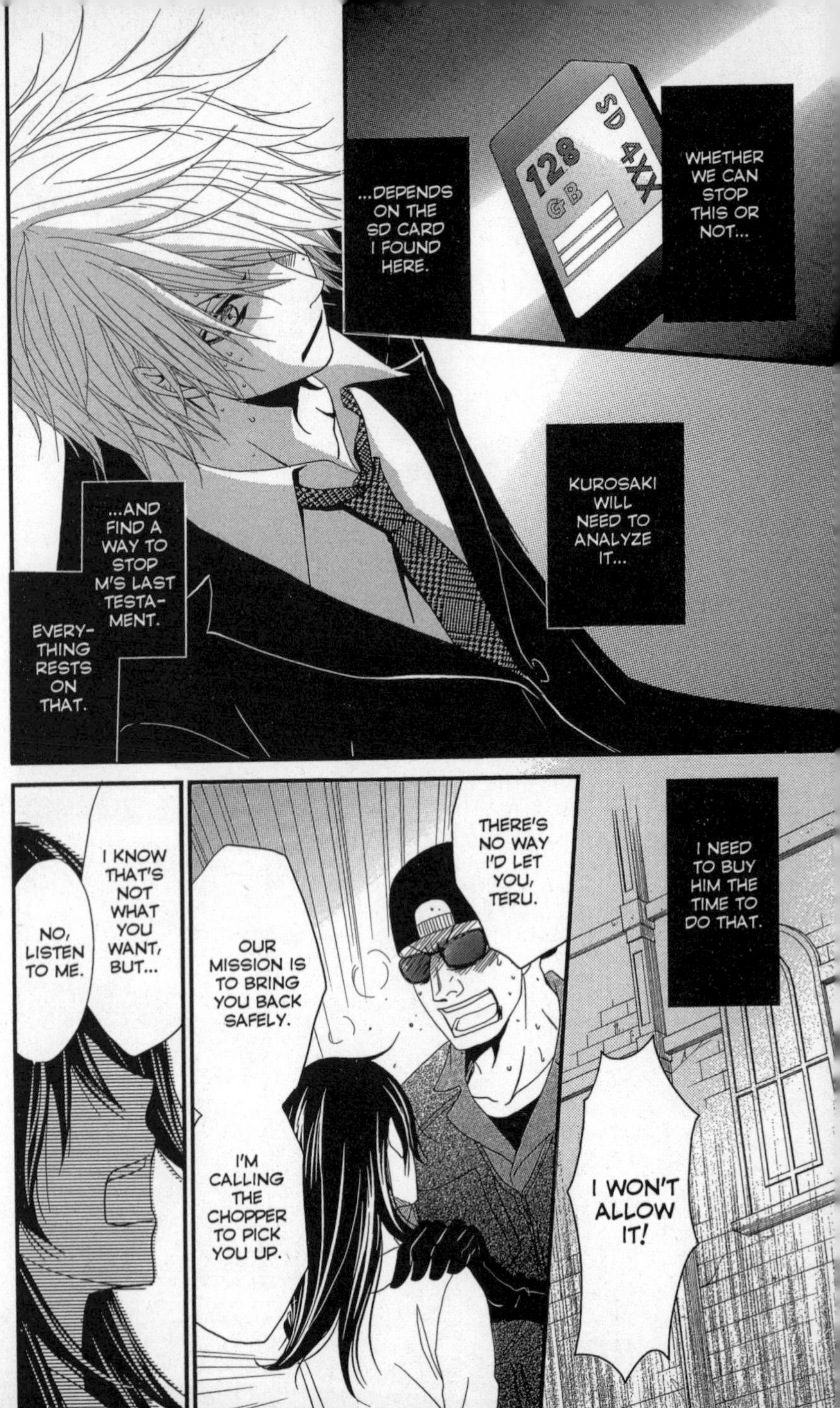
SD 4XX
128 GB
WHETHER WE CAN STOP THIS OR NOT...
...DEPENDS ON THE SD CARD I FOUND HERE.
KUROSAKI WILL NEED TO ANALYZE IT...
...AND FIND A WAY TO STOP M'S LAST TESTAMENT.
EVERYTHING RESTS ON THAT.
I NEED TO BUY HIM THE TIME TO DO THAT.
I WON'T ALLOW IT!
THERE'S NO WAY I'D LET YOU, TERU.
OUR MISSION IS TO BRING YOU BACK SAFELY.
I'M CALLING THE CHOPPER TO PICK YOU UP.
I KNOW THAT'S NOT WHAT YOU WANT, BUT...
NO, LISTEN TO ME.

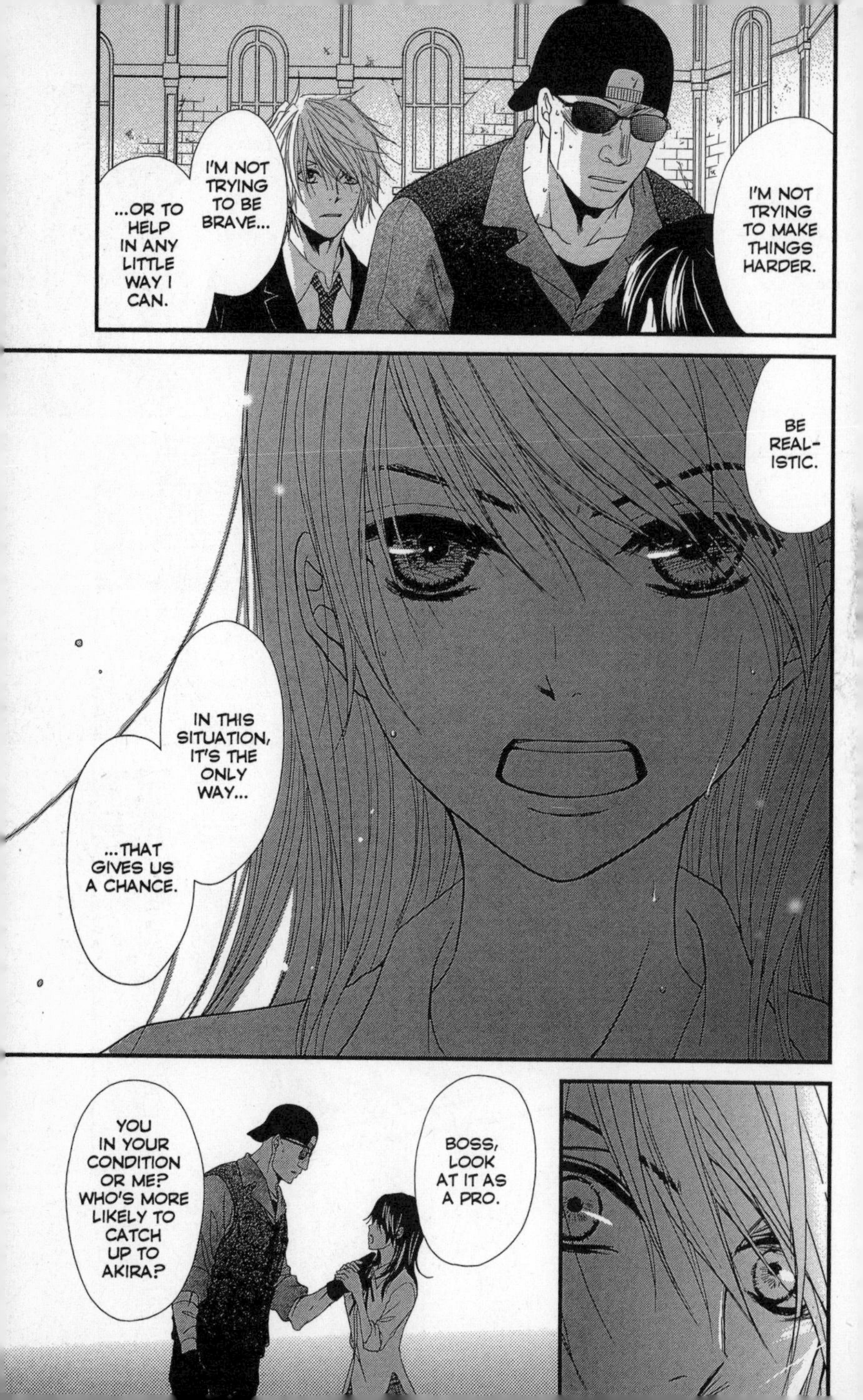
I'M NOT TRYING TO MAKE THINGS HARDER.
I'M NOT TRYING TO BE BRAVE...
...OR TO HELP IN ANY LITTLE WAY I CAN.
BE REAL-ISTIC.
IN THIS SITUATION, IT'S THE ONLY WAY...
...THAT GIVES US A CHANCE.
BOSS, LOOK AT IT AS A PRO.
YOU IN YOUR CONDITION OR ME? WHO'S MORE LIKELY TO CATCH UP TO AKIRA?

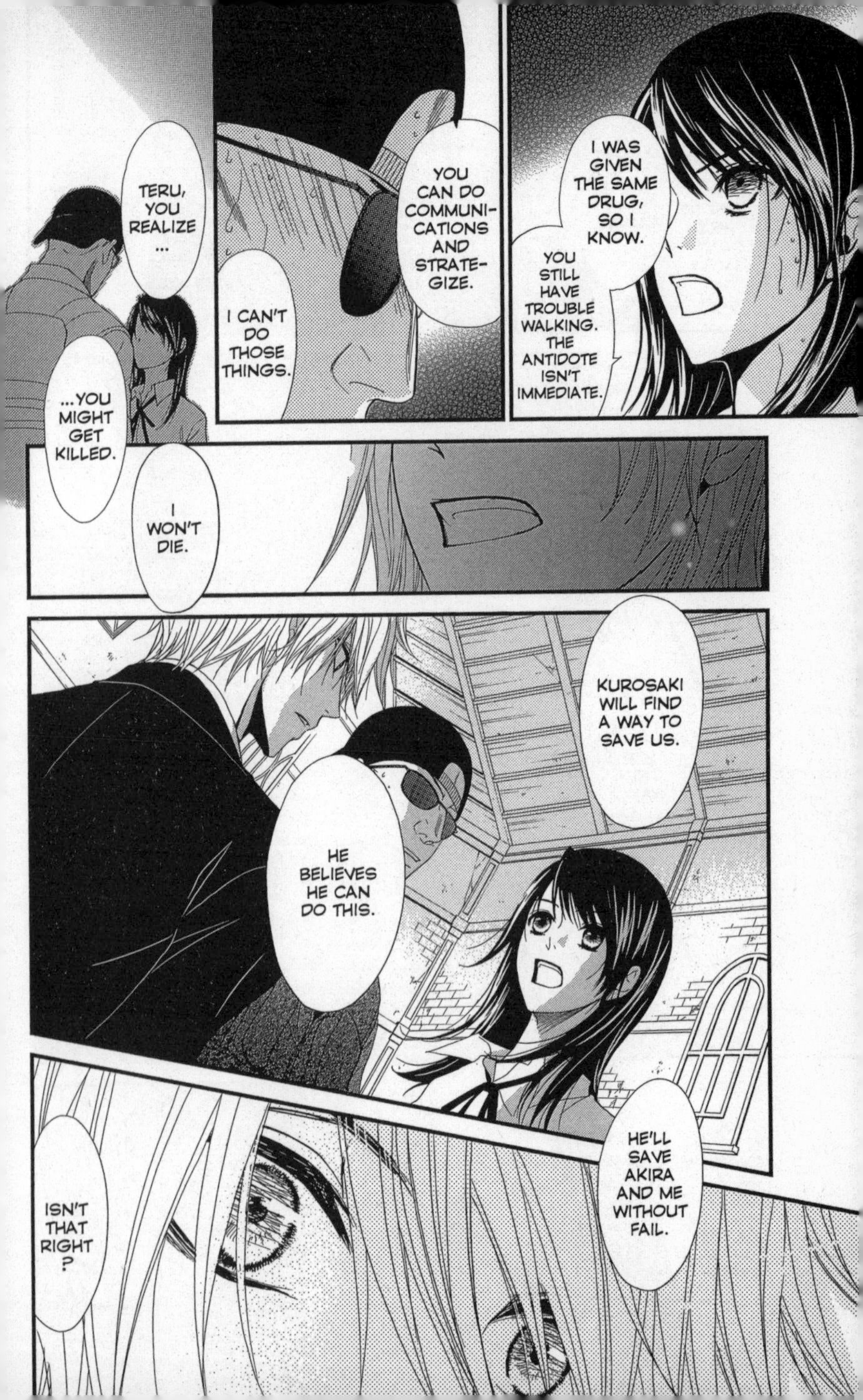
I WAS GIVEN THE SAME DRUG, SO I KNOW.
YOU STILL HAVE TROUBLE WALKING. THE ANTIDOTE ISN'T IMMEDIATE.
YOU CAN DO COMMUNICATIONS AND STRATEGIZE.
I CAN'T DO THOSE THINGS.
TERU, YOU REALIZE ...
...YOU MIGHT GET KILLED.
I WON'T DIE.
KUROSAKI WILL FIND A WAY TO SAVE US.
HE BELIEVES HE CAN DO THIS.
HE'LL SAVE AKIRA AND ME WITHOUT FAIL.
ISN'T THAT RIGHT?

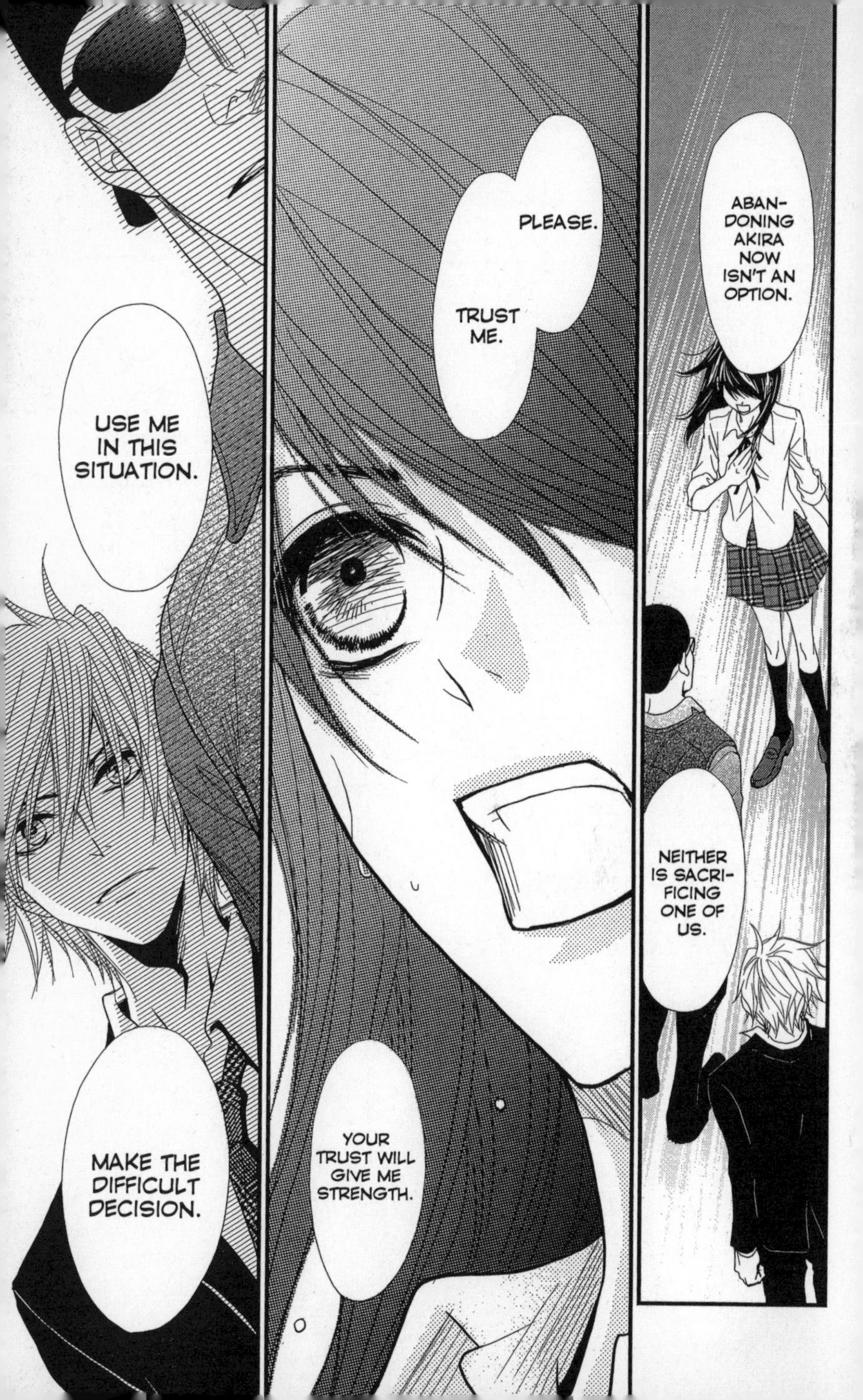
ABANDONING AKIRA NOW ISN'T AN OPTION.
NEITHER IS SACRIFICING ONE OF US.
PLEASE.
TRUST ME.
YOUR TRUST WILL GIVE ME STRENGTH.
USE ME IN THIS SITUATION.
MAKE THE DIFFICULT DECISION.

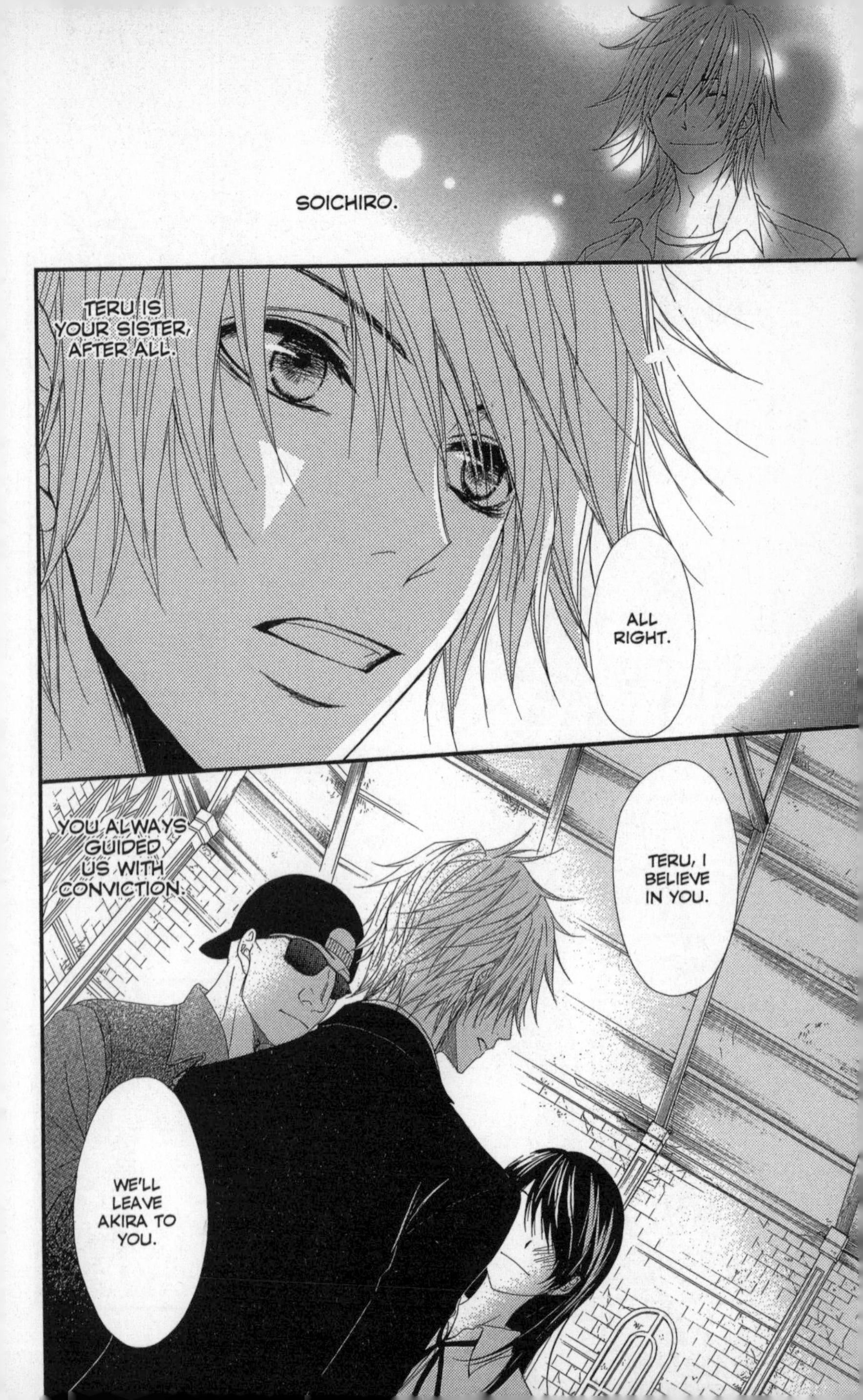
SOICHIRO.
TERU IS YOUR SISTER, AFTER ALL.
ALL RIGHT.
TERU, I BELIEVE IN YOU.
YOU ALWAYS GUIDED US WITH CONVICTION.
WE'LL LEAVE AKIRA TO YOU.

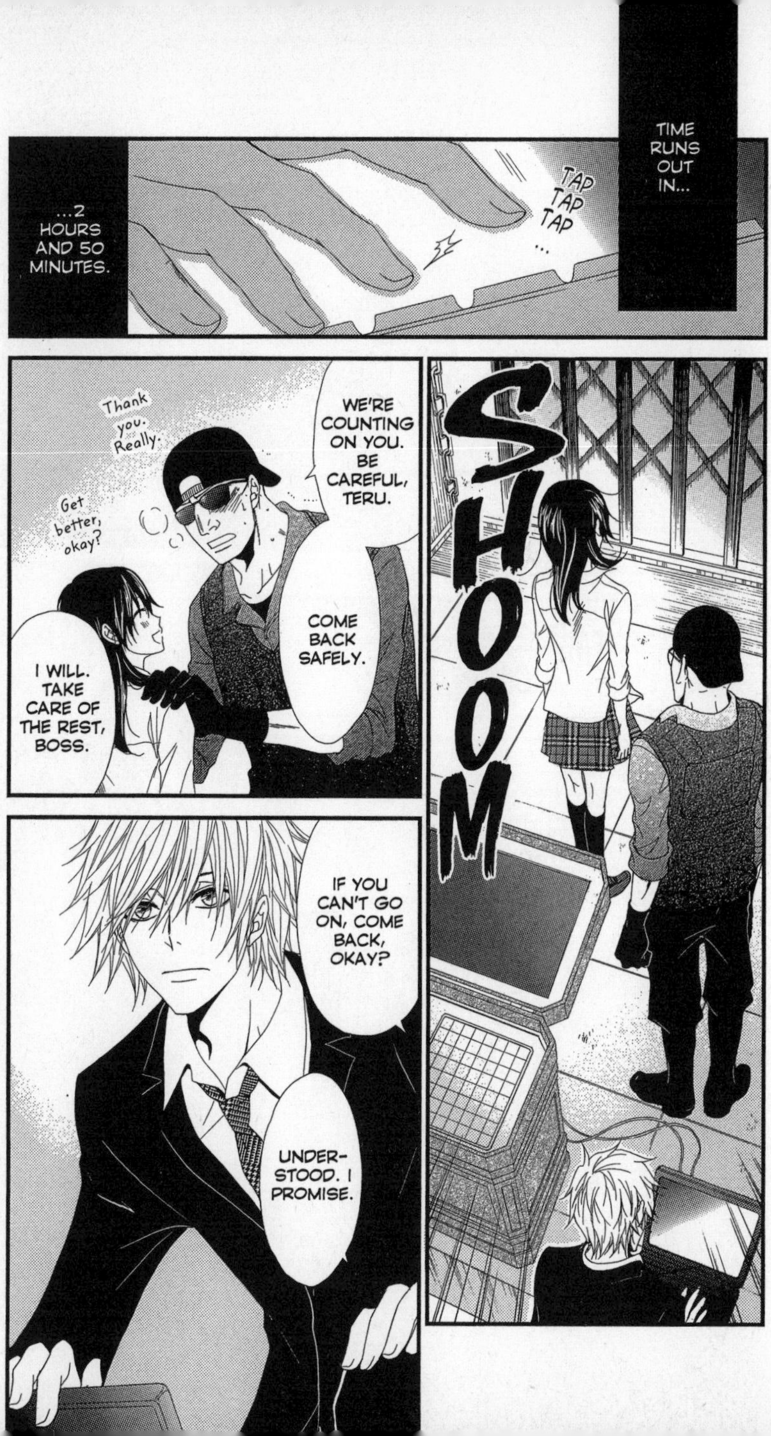
TIME RUNS OUT IN...
TAP TAP TAP ...
...2 HOURS AND 50 MINUTES.
SHOOM
WE'RE COUNTING ON YOU. BE CAREFUL, TERU.
Thank you. Really.
Get better, okay?
COME BACK SAFELY.
I WILL. TAKE CARE OF THE REST, BOSS.
IF YOU CAN'T GO ON, COME BACK, OKAY?
UNDER-STOOD. I PROMISE.

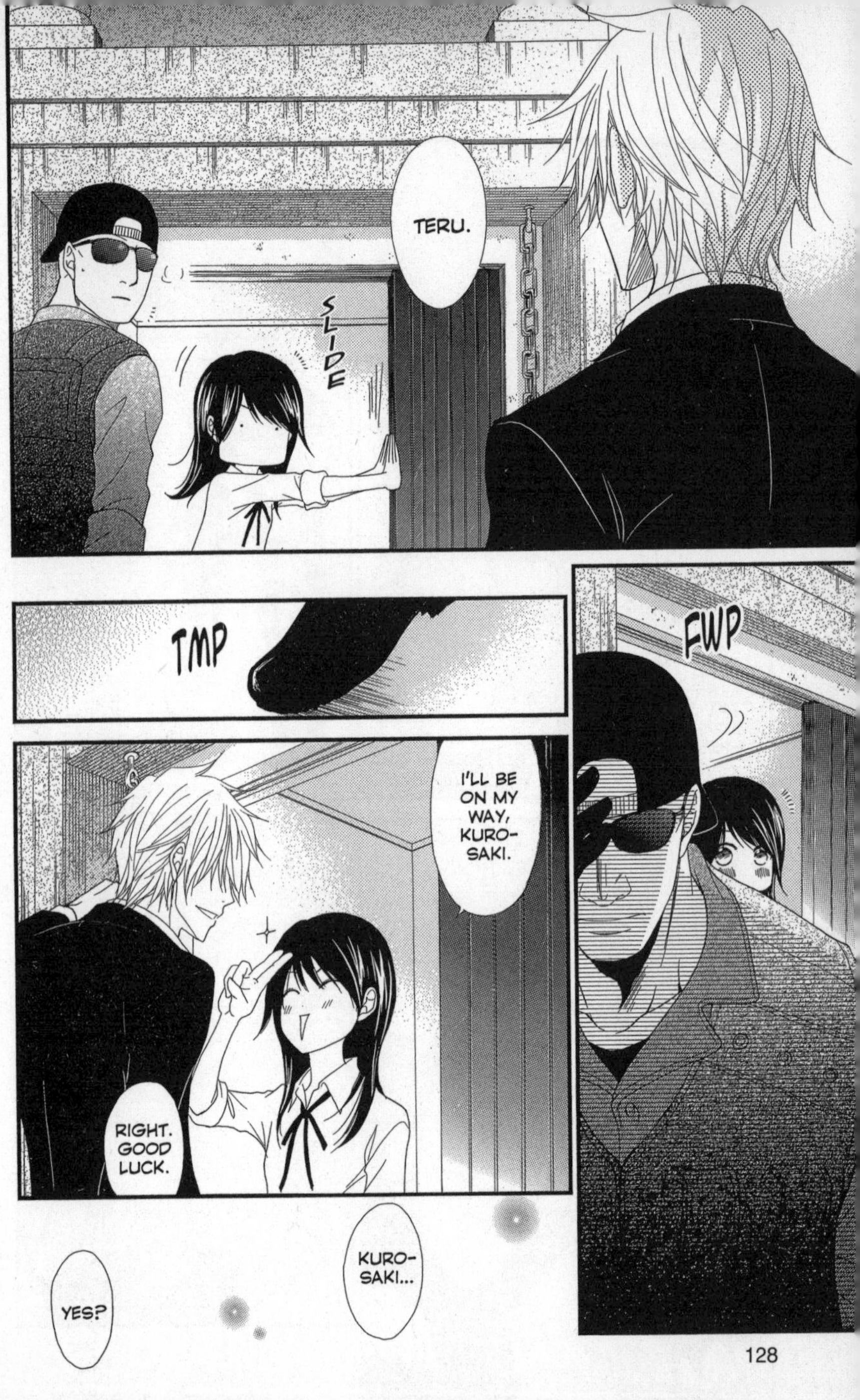
TERU.
SLIDE
FWP
TMP
I'LL BE ON MY WAY, KURO-SAKI.
RIGHT. GOOD LUCK.
KURO-SAKI...
YES?

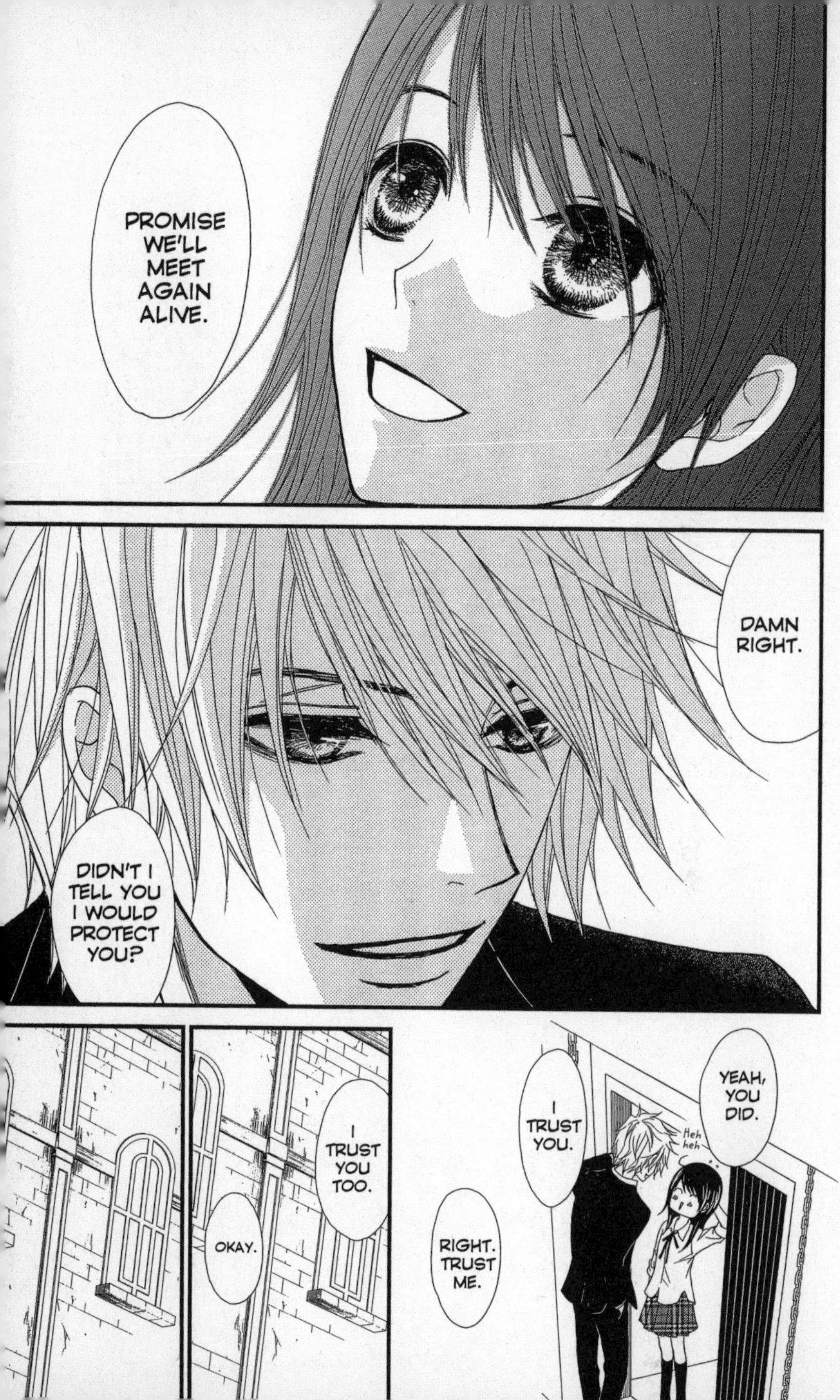
PROMISE WE'LL MEET AGAIN ALIVE.
DAMN RIGHT.
DIDN'T I TELL YOU I WOULD PROTECT YOU?
YEAH, YOU DID.
Heh heh
I TRUST YOU.
RIGHT. TRUST ME.
I TRUST YOU TOO.
OKAY.

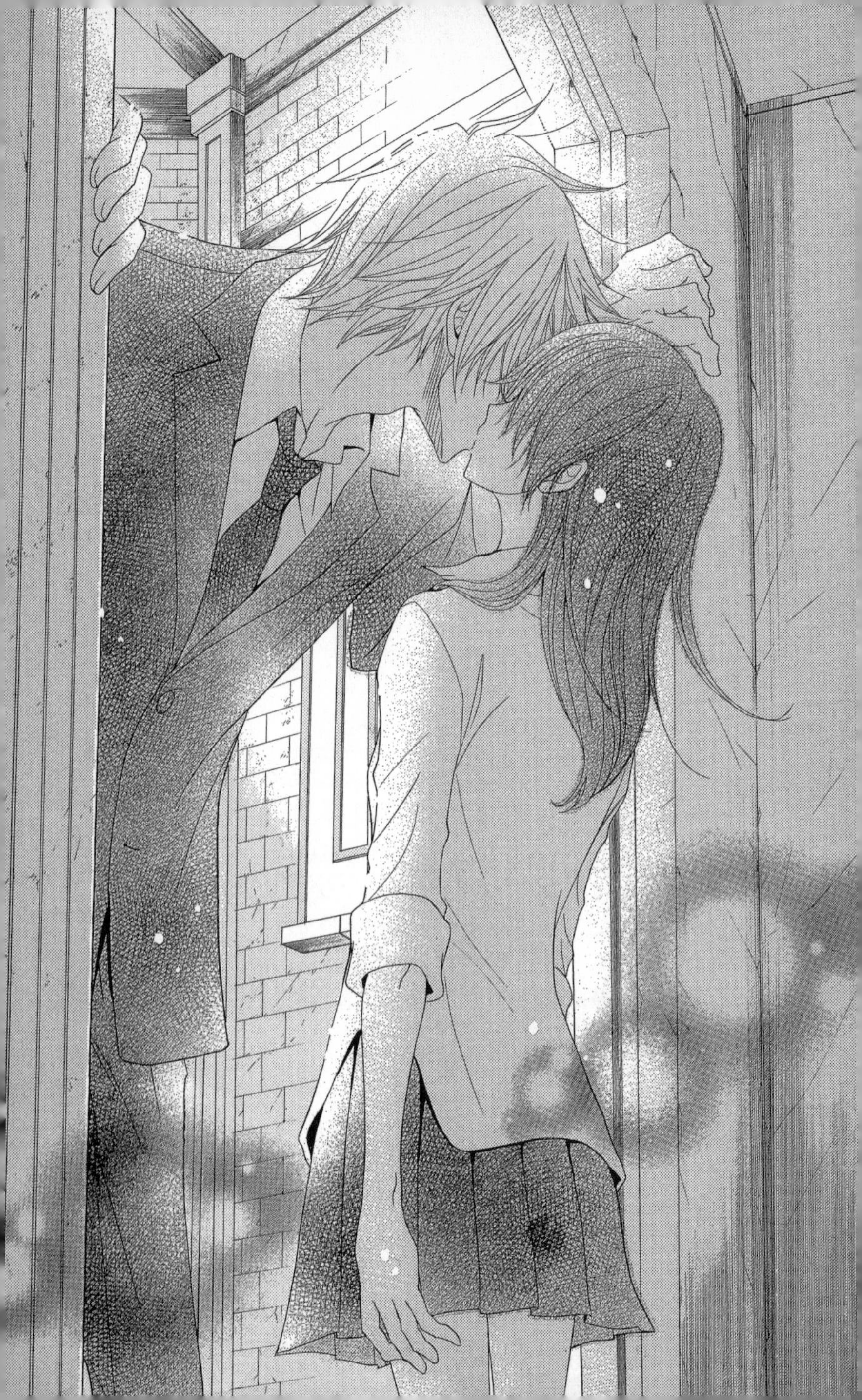

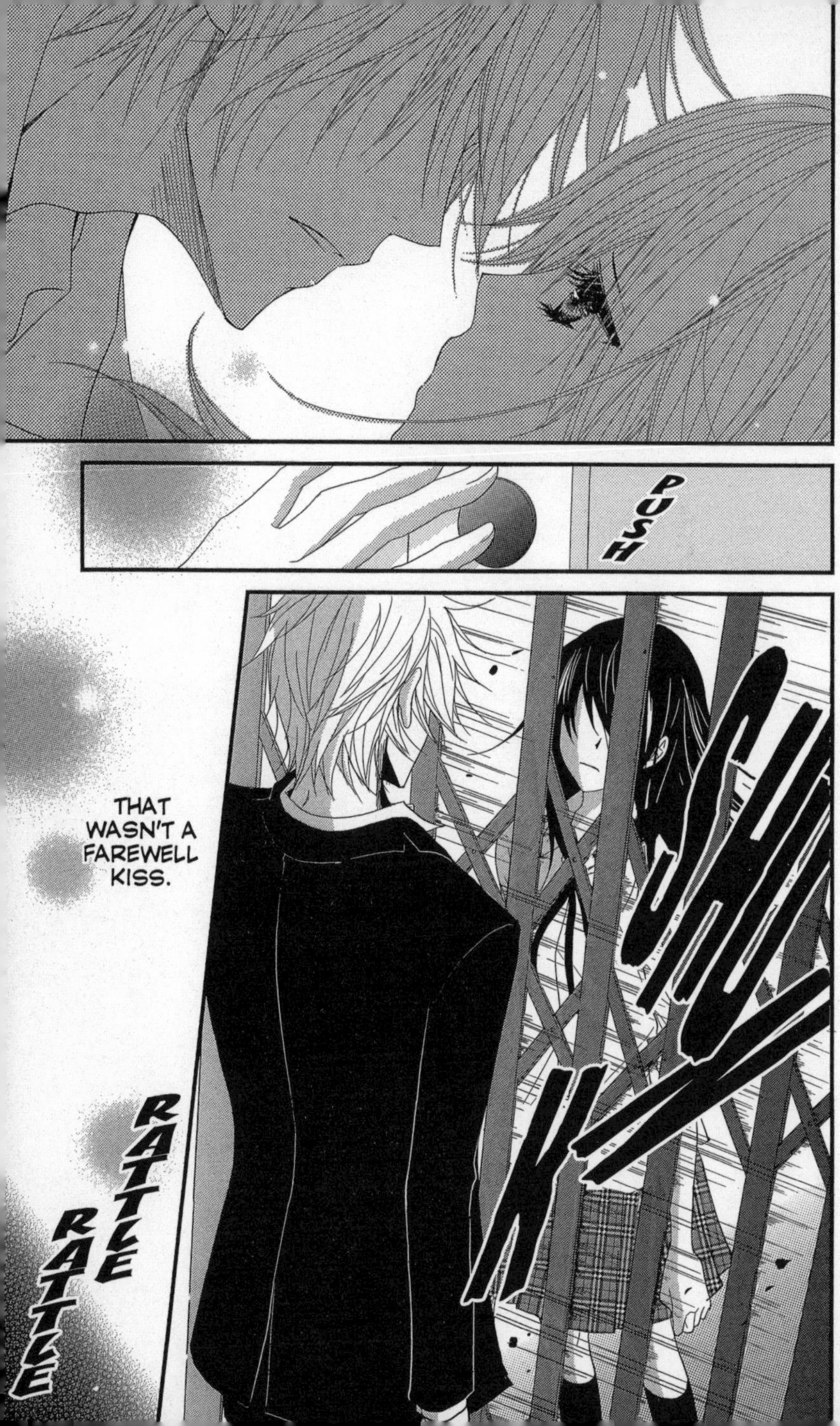
PUSH
THAT WASN'T A FAREWELL KISS.
RATTLE
RATTLE

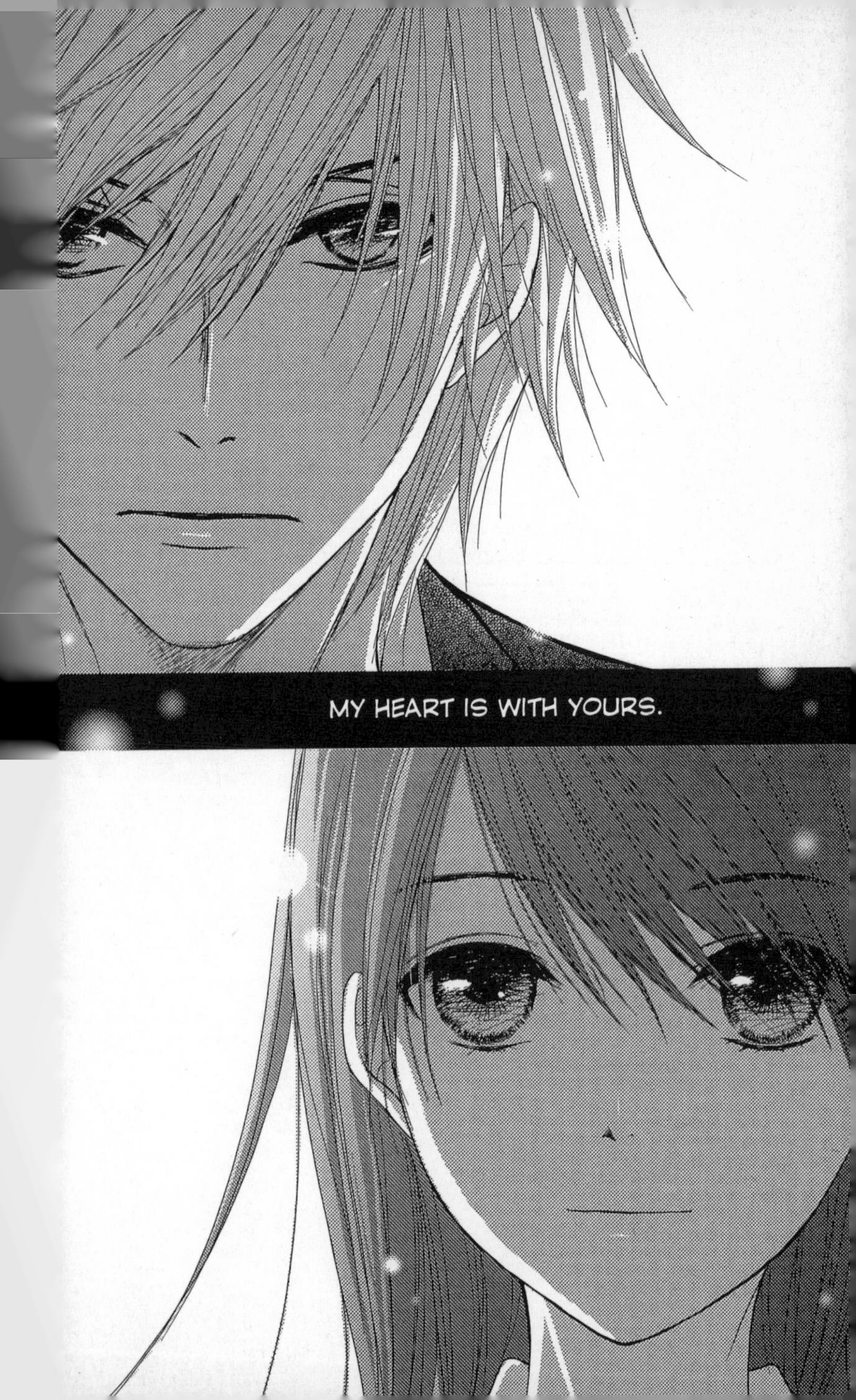
MY HEART IS WITH YOURS.

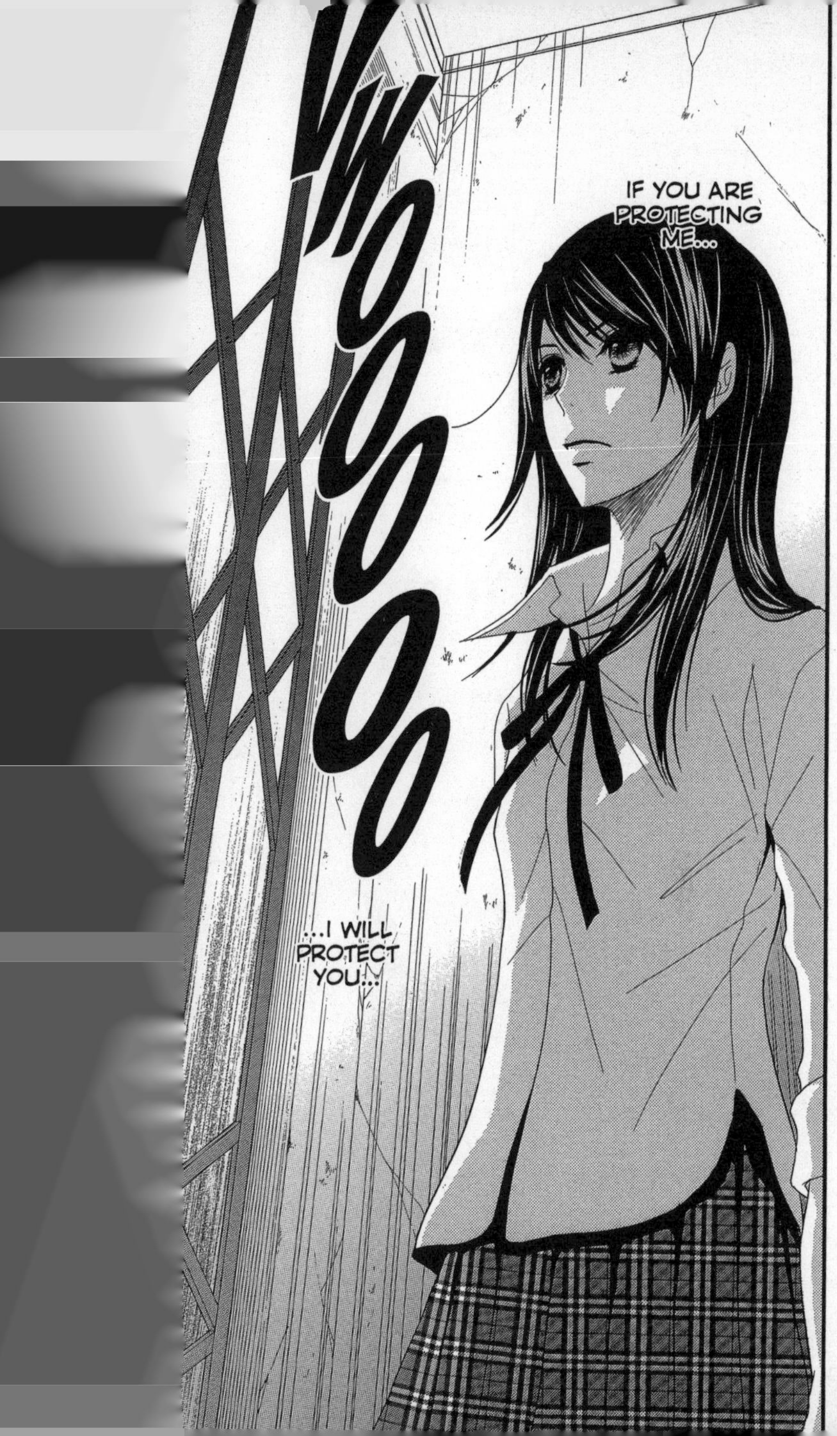
IF YOU ARE PROTECTING ME...
VWOOOOOOOO
...I WILL PROTECT YOU...

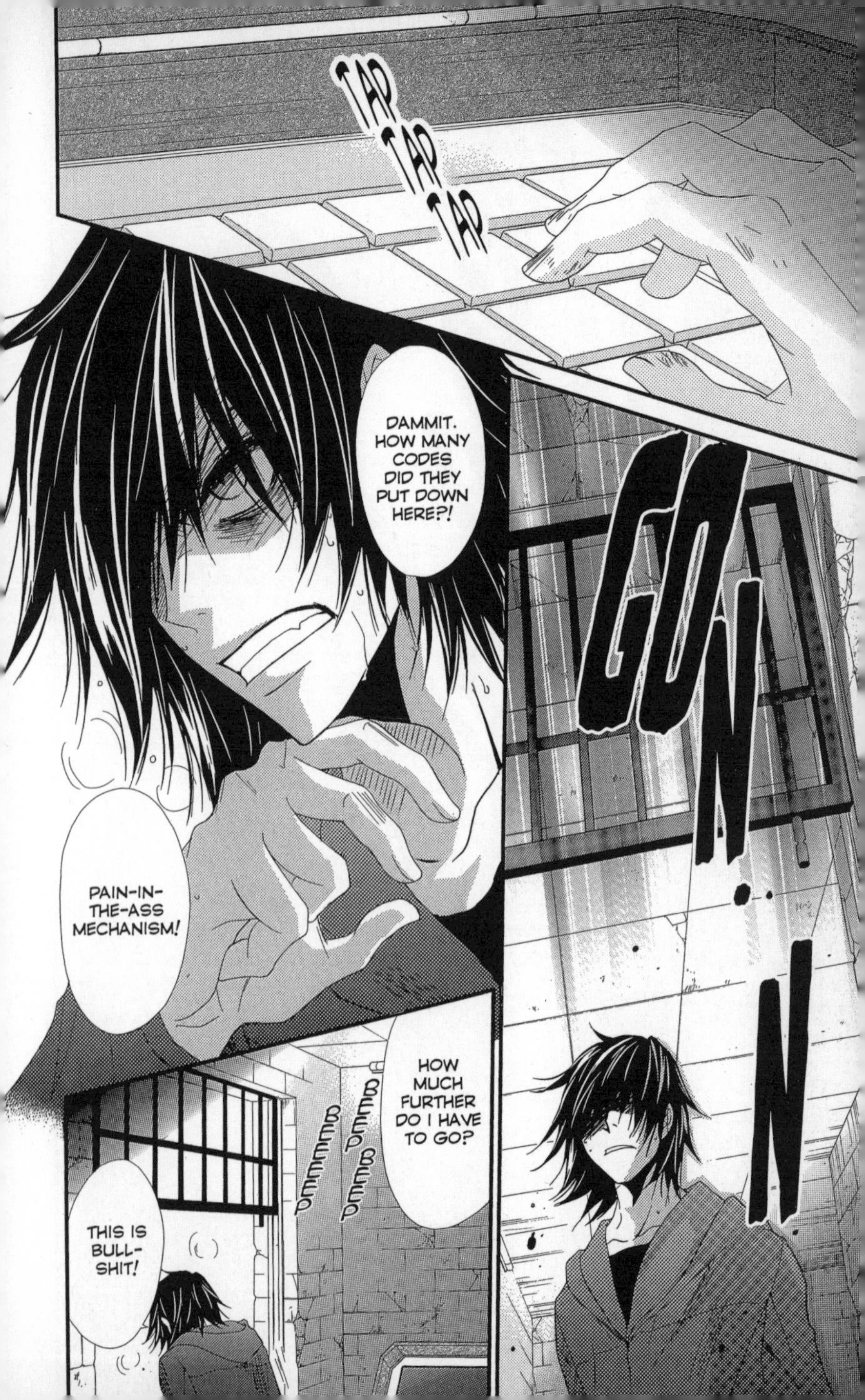
TAP TAP TAP
DAMMIT. HOW MANY CODES DID THEY PUT DOWN HERE?!
GON...N
PAIN-IN-THE-ASS MECHANISM!
HOW MUCH FURTHER DO I HAVE TO GO?
BEEP BEEP BEEEEP
THIS IS BULL-SHIT!

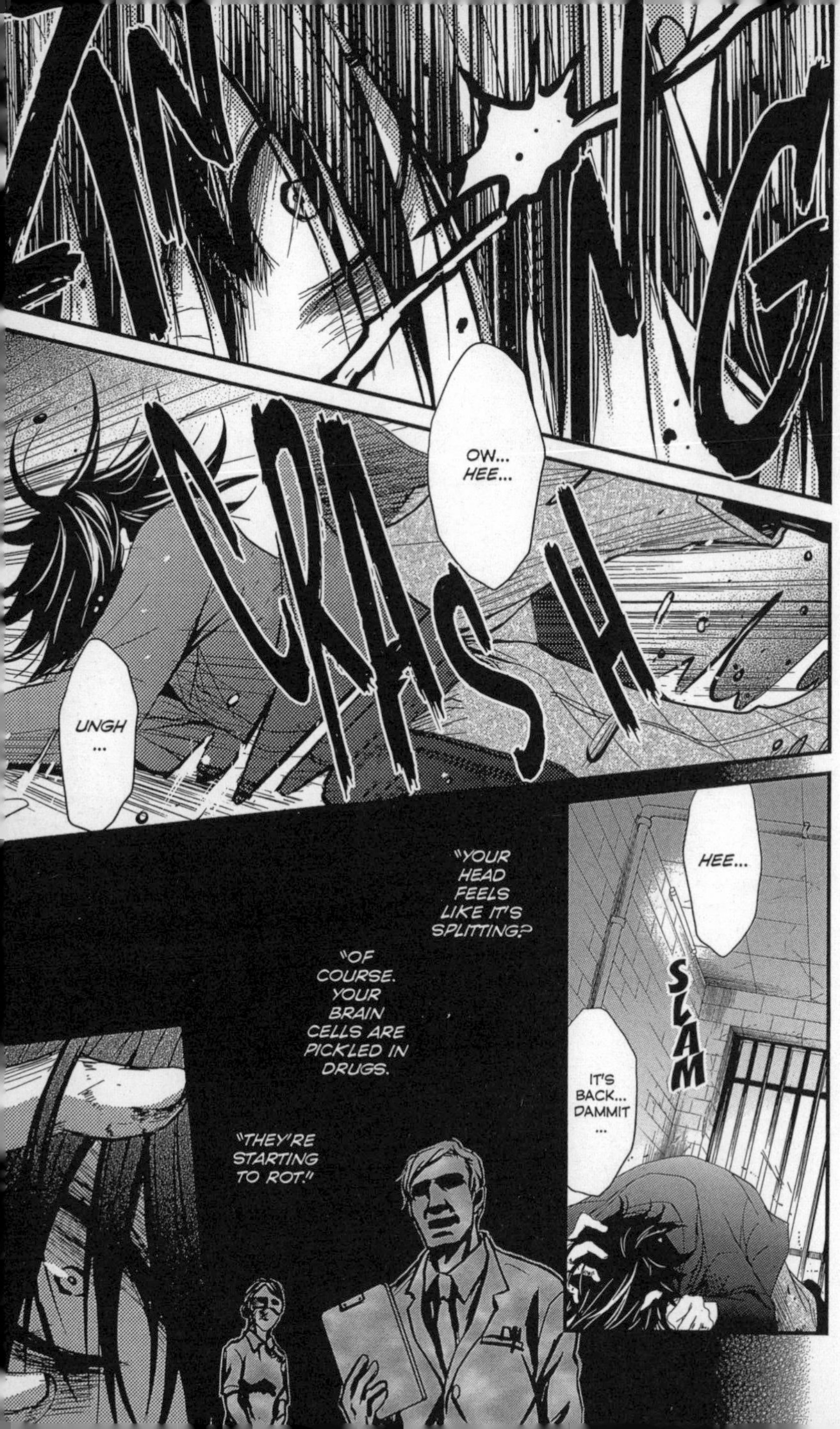
OW... HEE...
CRASH
UNGH ...
HEE...
SLAM
IT'S BACK... DAMMIT ...
"YOUR HEAD FEELS LIKE IT'S SPLITTING?
"OF COURSE. YOUR BRAIN CELLS ARE PICKLED IN DRUGS.
"THEY'RE STARTING TO ROT."

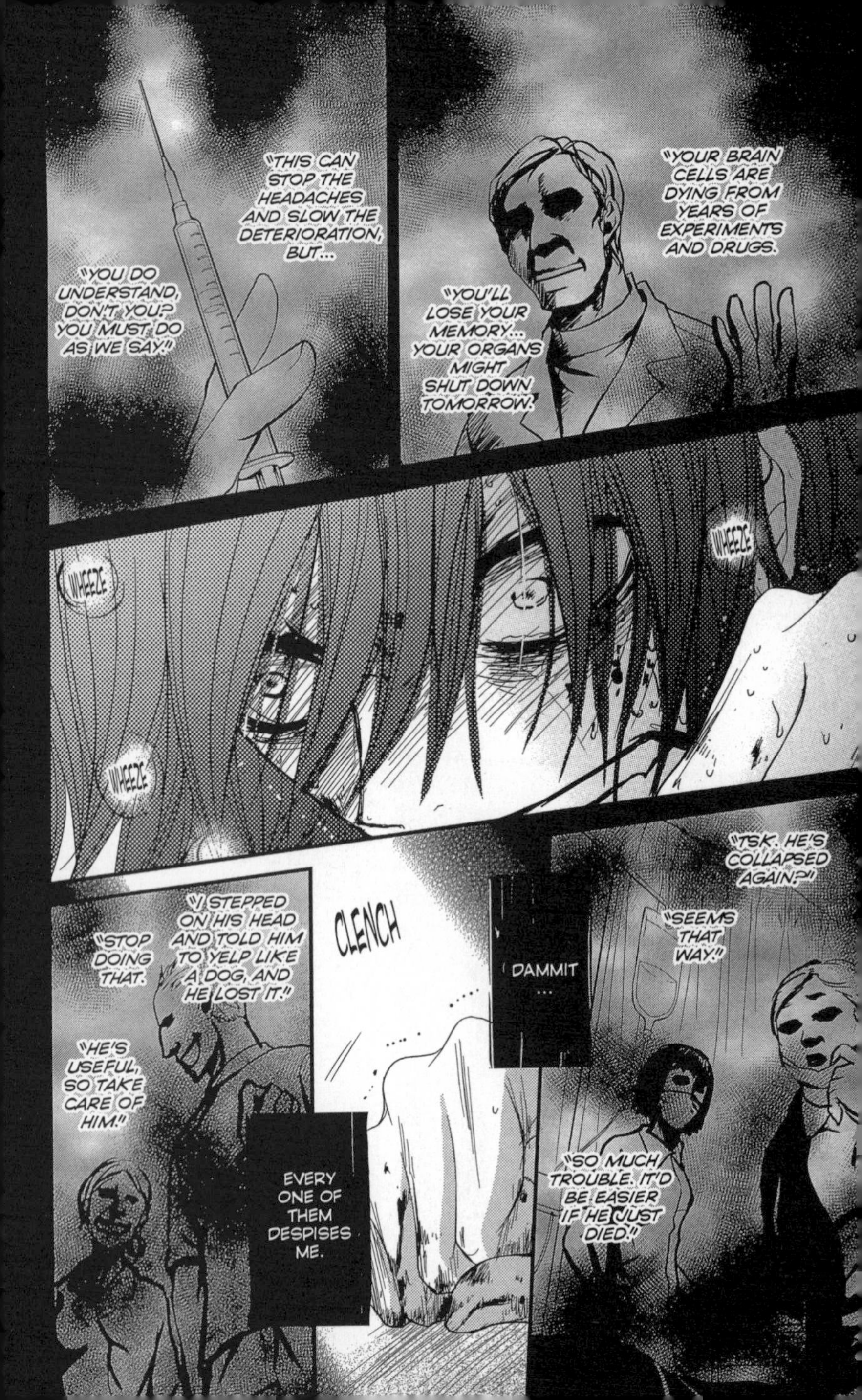
"YOUR BRAIN CELLS ARE DYING FROM YEARS OF EXPERIMENTS AND DRUGS.
"YOU'LL LOSE YOUR MEMORY... YOUR ORGANS MIGHT SHUT DOWN TOMORROW.
"THIS CAN STOP THE HEADACHES AND SLOW THE DETERIORATION, BUT...
"YOU DO UNDERSTAND, DON'T YOU? YOU MUST DO AS WE SAY."
WHEEZE
WHEEZE
WHEEZE
"TSK. HE'S COLLAPSED AGAIN?"
"SEEMS THAT WAY."
"SO MUCH TROUBLE. IT'D BE EASIER IF HE JUST DIED."
DAMMIT ...
CLENCH
EVERY ONE OF THEM DESPISES ME.
"I STEPPED ON HIS HEAD AND TOLD HIM TO YELP LIKE A DOG, AND HE LOST IT."
"STOP DOING THAT.
"HE'S USEFUL, SO TAKE CARE OF HIM."

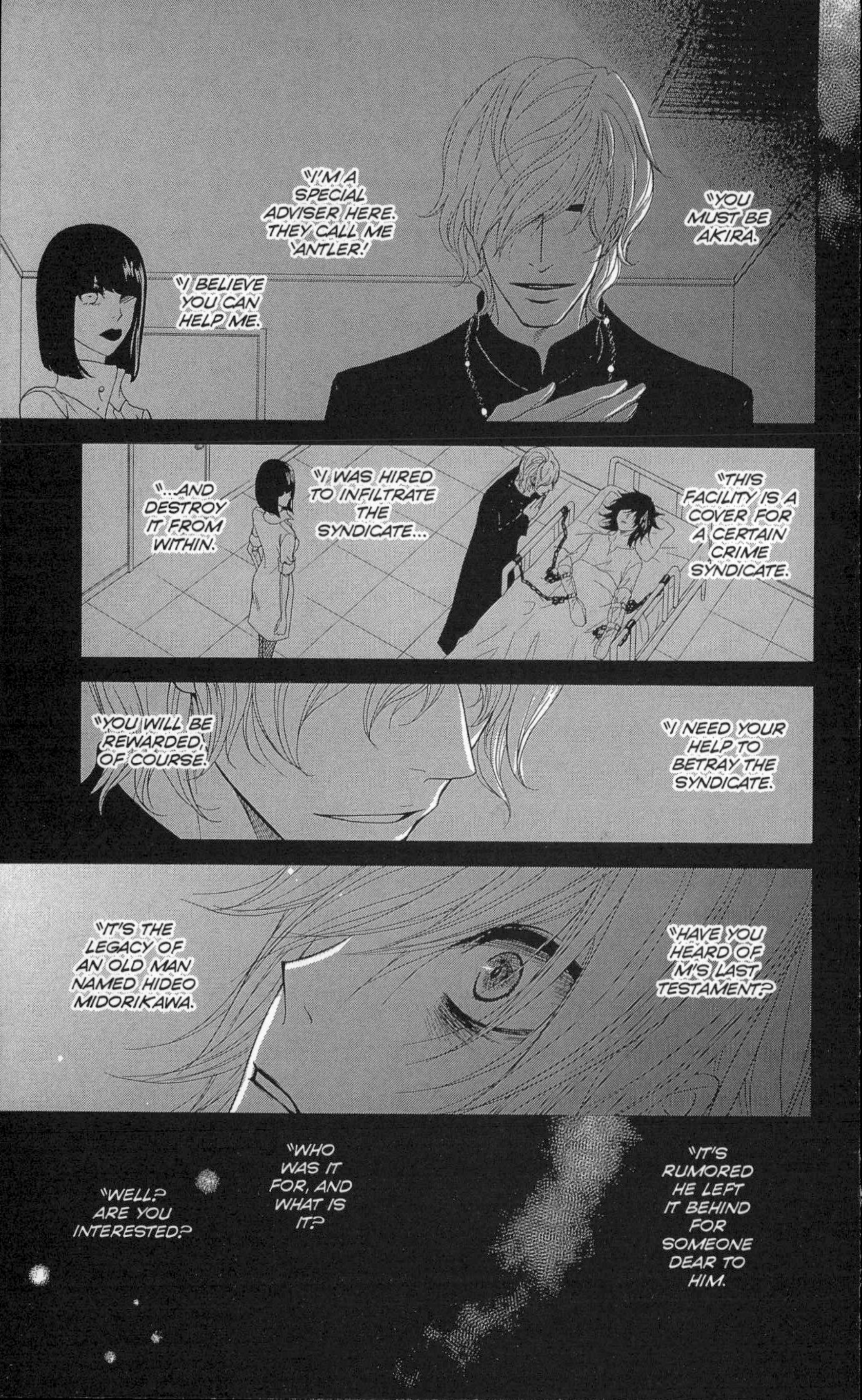
"YOU MUST BE AKIRA.
"I'M A SPECIAL ADVISER HERE. THEY CALL ME ANTLER.
"I BELIEVE YOU CAN HELP ME.
"THIS FACILITY IS A COVER FOR A CERTAIN CRIME SYNDICATE.
"I WAS HIRED TO INFILTRATE THE SYNDICATE...
"...AND DESTROY IT FROM WITHIN.
"I NEED YOUR HELP TO BETRAY THE SYNDICATE.
"YOU WILL BE REWARDED, OF COURSE.
"HAVE YOU HEARD OF M'S LAST TESTAMENT?
"IT'S THE LEGACY OF AN OLD MAN NAMED HIDEO MIDORIKAWA.
"IT'S RUMORED HE LEFT IT BEHIND FOR SOMEONE DEAR TO HIM.
"WHO WAS IT FOR, AND WHAT IS IT?
"WELL? ARE YOU INTERESTED?

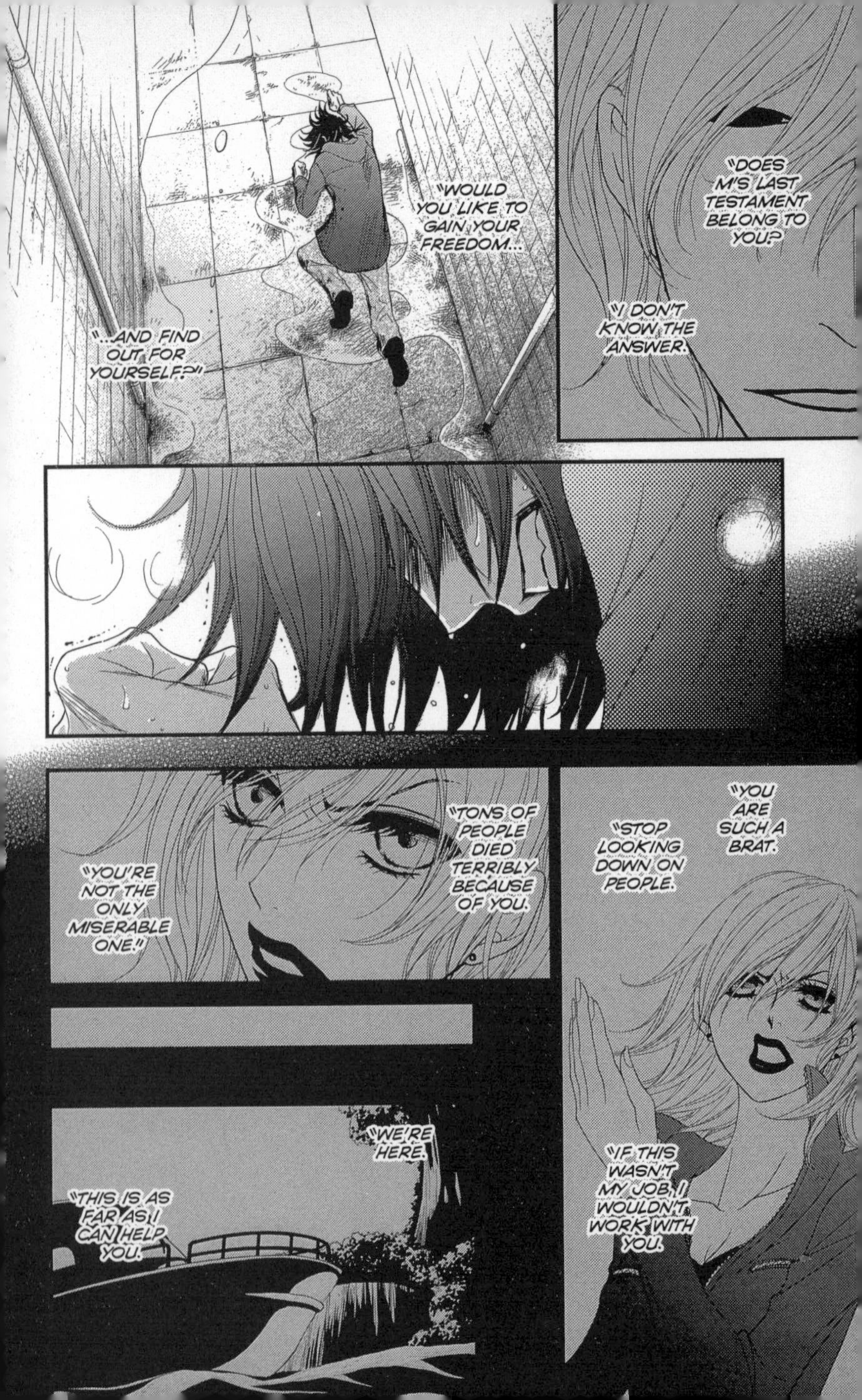
"DOES M'S LAST TESTAMENT BELONG TO YOU?
"I DON'T KNOW THE ANSWER.
"WOULD YOU LIKE TO GAIN YOUR FREEDOM...
"...AND FIND OUT FOR YOURSELF?"
"YOU ARE SUCH A BRAT.
"STOP LOOKING DOWN ON PEOPLE.
"IF THIS WASN'T MY JOB, I WOULDN'T WORK WITH YOU.
"TONS OF PEOPLE DIED TERRIBLY BECAUSE OF YOU.
"YOU'RE NOT THE ONLY MISERABLE ONE."
"WE'RE HERE.
"THIS IS AS FAR AS I CAN HELP YOU.

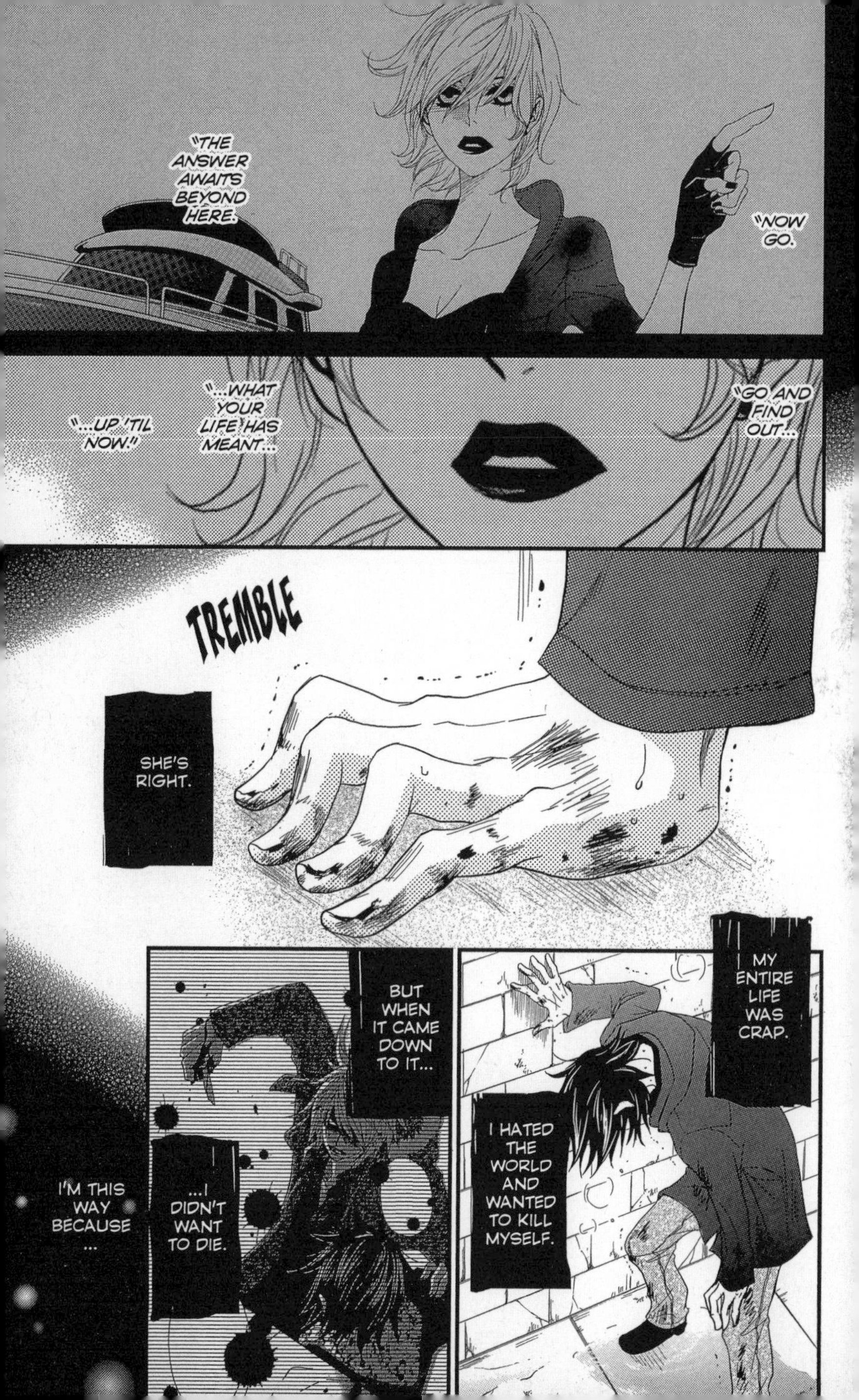

"THE ANSWER AWAITS BEYOND HERE.
"NOW GO.
"GO AND FIND OUT...
"...WHAT YOUR LIFE HAS MEANT...
"...UP 'TIL NOW."
TREMBLE
SHE'S RIGHT.
MY ENTIRE LIFE WAS CRAP.
I HATED THE WORLD AND WANTED TO KILL MYSELF.
BUT WHEN IT CAME DOWN TO IT...
...I DIDN'T WANT TO DIE.
I'M THIS WAY BECAUSE ...

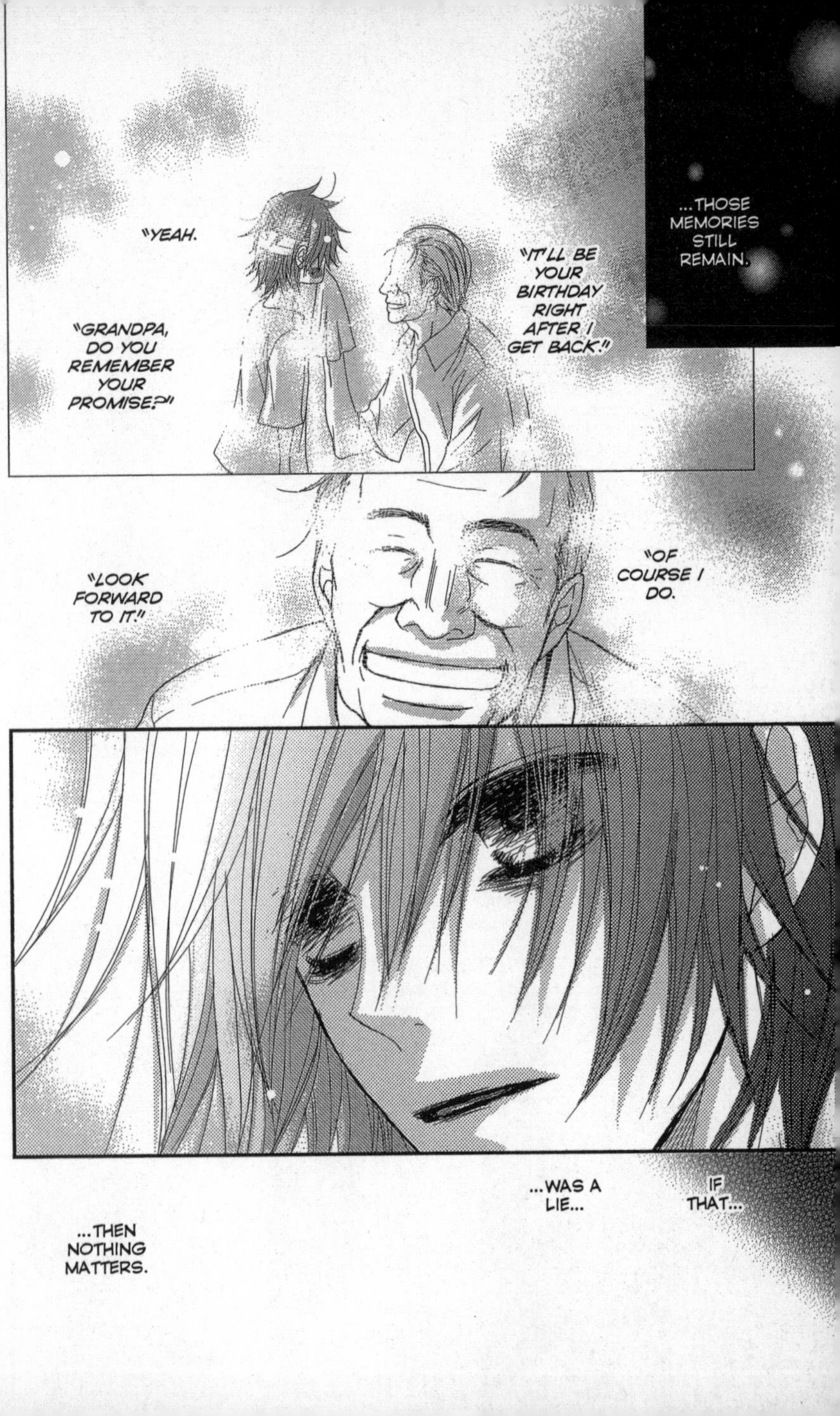
...THOSE MEMORIES STILL REMAIN.
"IT'LL BE YOUR BIRTHDAY RIGHT AFTER I GET BACK."
"YEAH.
"GRANDPA, DO YOU REMEMBER YOUR PROMISE?"
"OF COURSE I DO.
"LOOK FORWARD TO IT."
IF THAT...
...WAS A LIE...
...THEN NOTHING MATTERS.

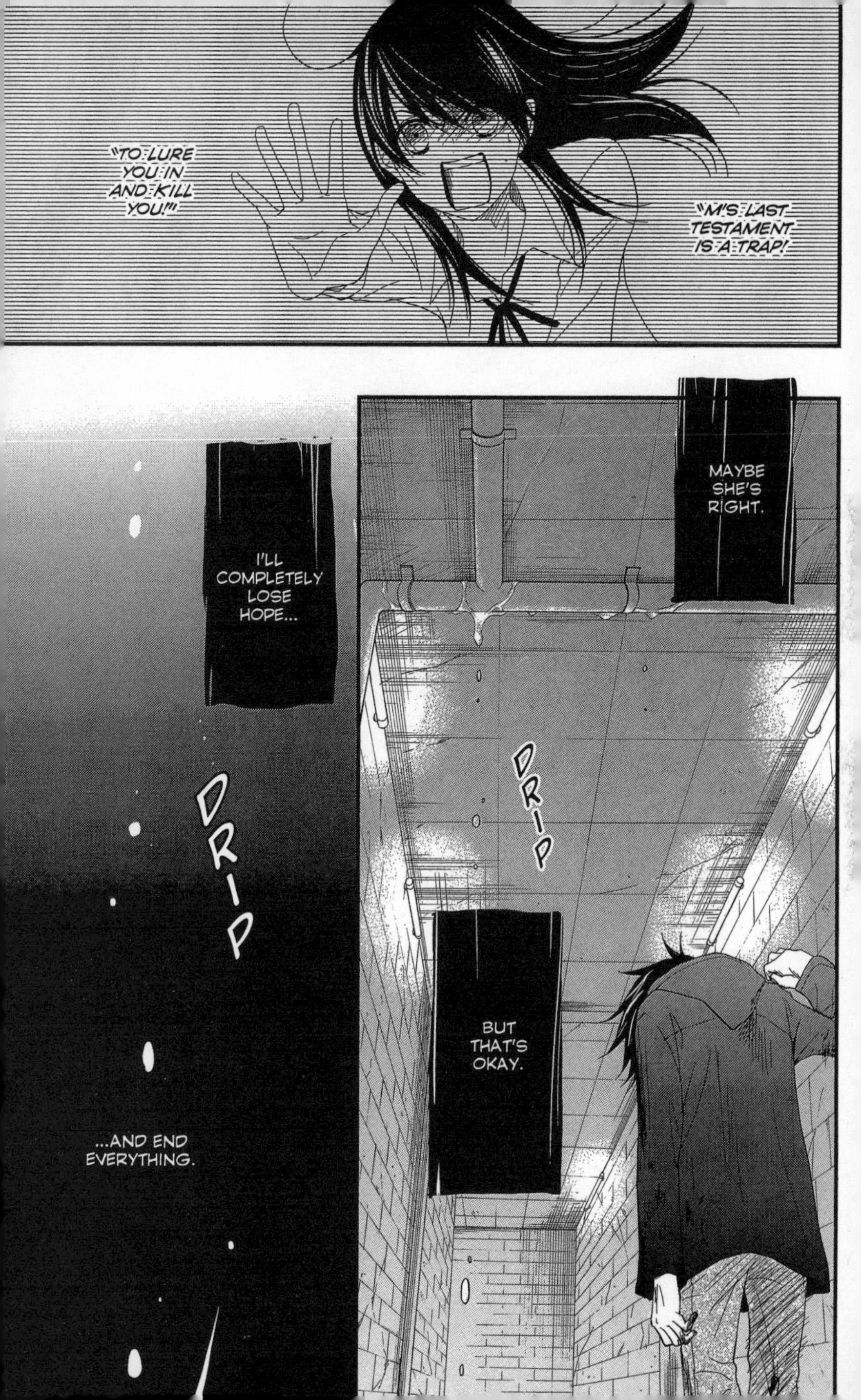
"M'S LAST TESTAMENT IS A TRAP!
"TO LURE YOU IN AND KILL YOU!"
MAYBE SHE'S RIGHT.
DRIP
BUT THAT'S OKAY.
I'LL COMPLETELY LOSE HOPE...
DRIP
...AND END EVERYTHING.

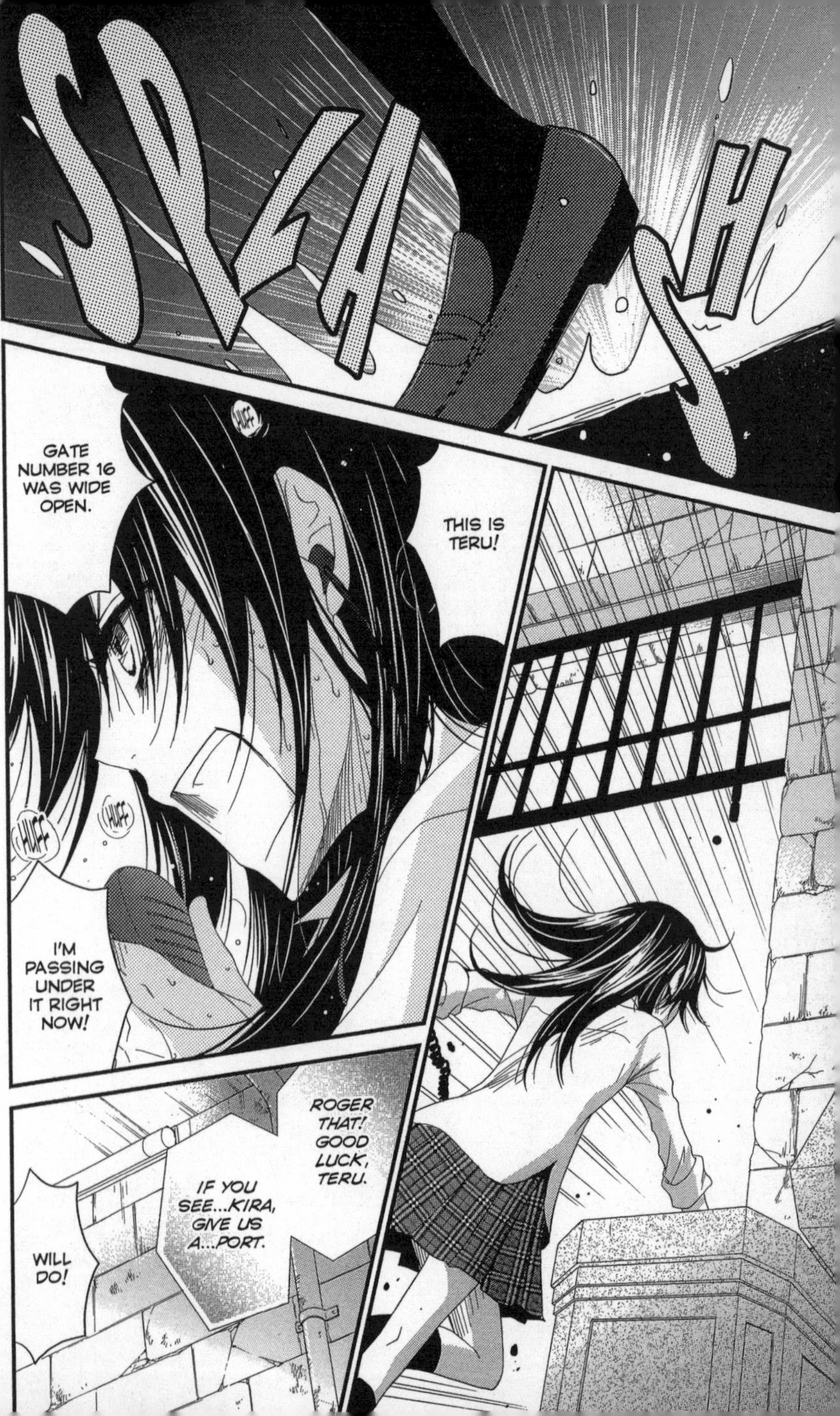
SPLASH
HUFF
THIS IS TERU!
GATE NUMBER 16 WAS WIDE OPEN.
HUFF
HUFF
I'M PASSING UNDER IT RIGHT NOW!
ROGER THAT! GOOD LUCK, TERU.
IF YOU SEE...KIRA, GIVE US A...PORT.
WILL DO!

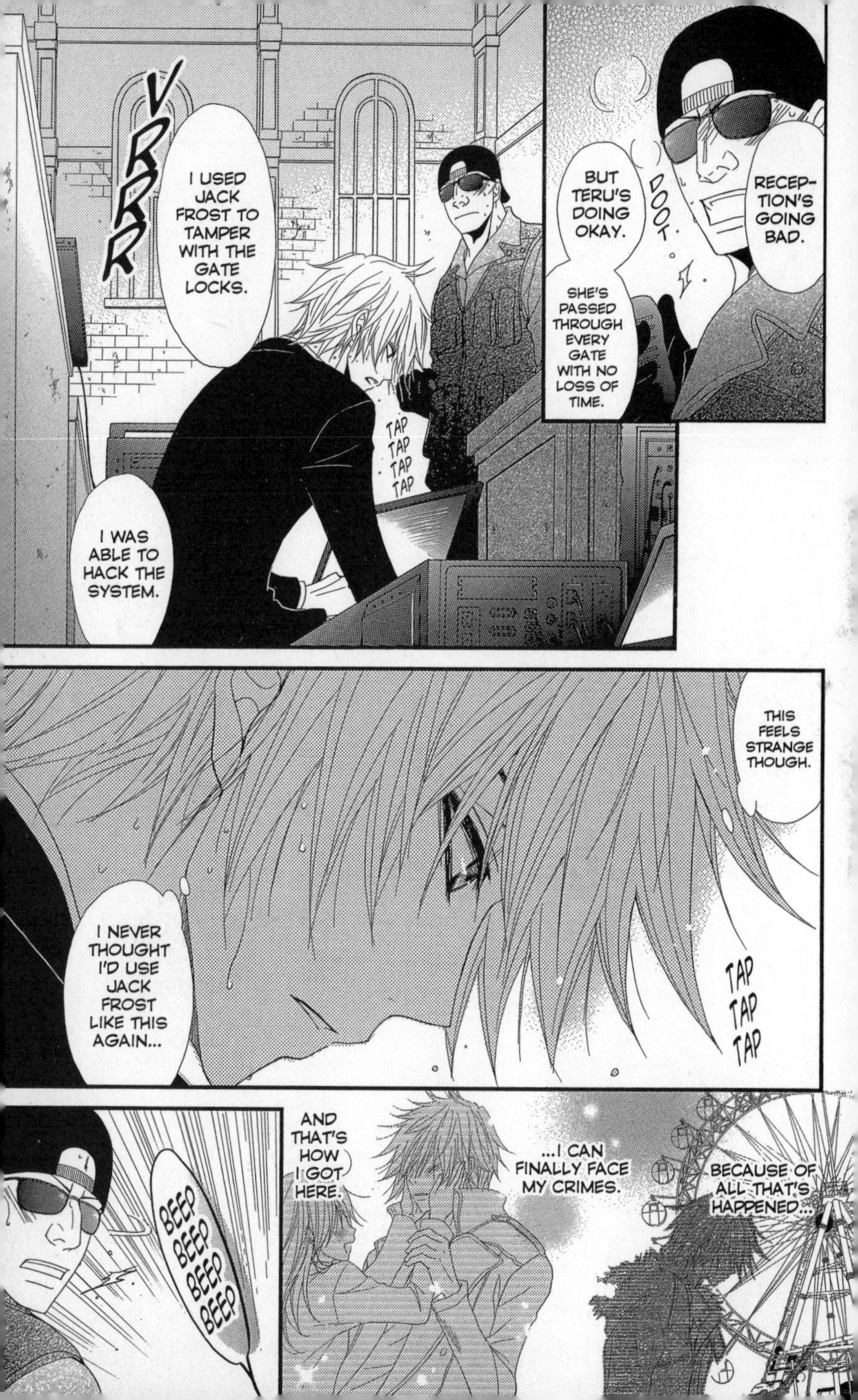
RECEPTION'S GOING BAD.
DOOT
BUT TERU'S DOING OKAY.
SHE'S PASSED THROUGH EVERY GATE WITH NO LOSS OF TIME.
VRRR
I USED JACK FROST TO TAMPER WITH THE GATE LOCKS.
TAP TAP TAP TAP
I WAS ABLE TO HACK THE SYSTEM.
THIS FEELS STRANGE THOUGH.
TAP TAP TAP
I NEVER THOUGHT I'D USE JACK FROST LIKE THIS AGAIN...
BECAUSE OF ALL THAT'S HAPPENED...
...I CAN FINALLY FACE MY CRIMES.
AND THAT'S HOW I GOT HERE.
BEEP BEEP BEEP BEEP

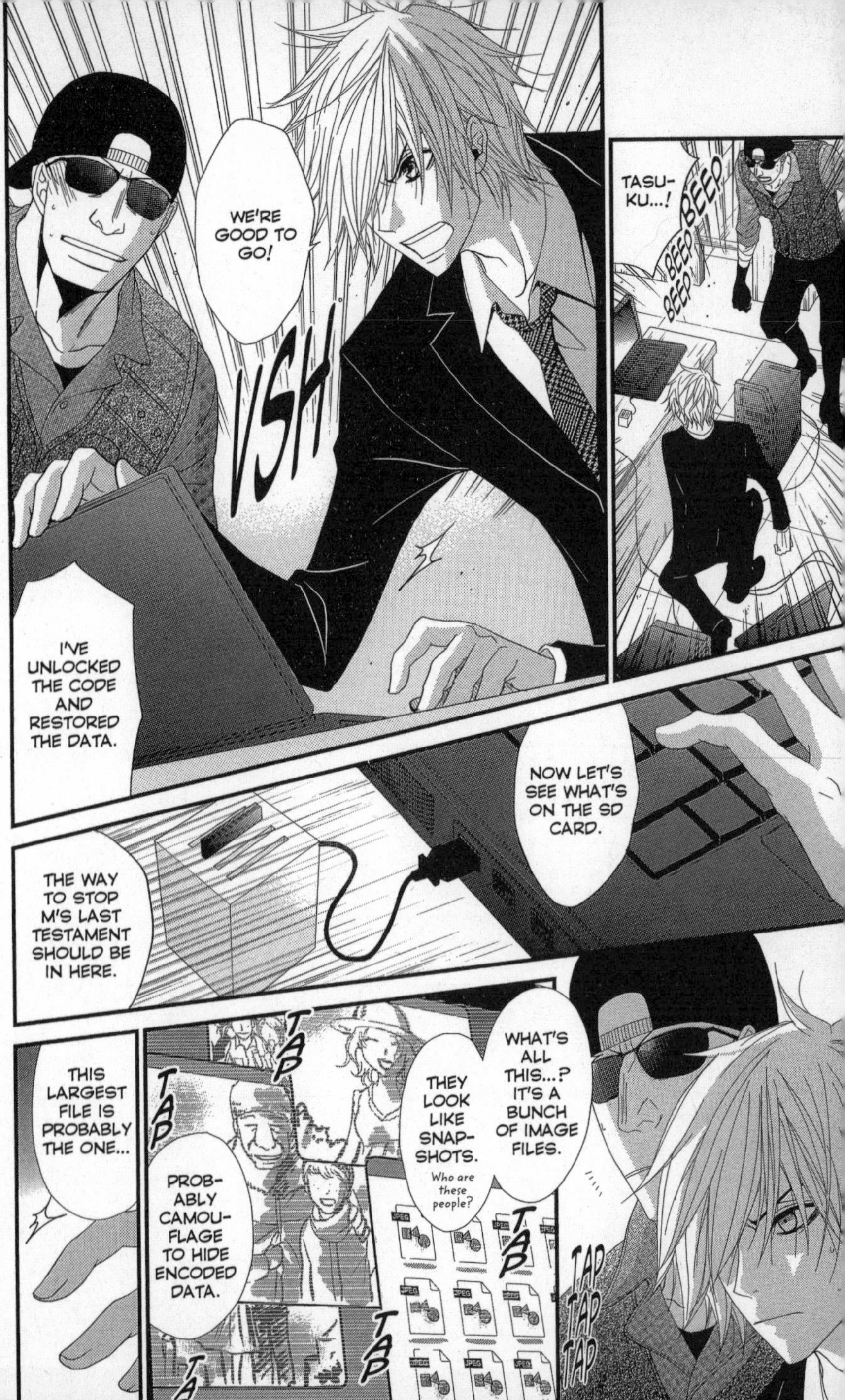
TASU-KU...!
BEEP BEEP BEEP BEEP
WE'RE GOOD TO GO!
VSH
I'VE UNLOCKED THE CODE AND RESTORED THE DATA.
NOW LET'S SEE WHAT'S ON THE SD CARD.
THE WAY TO STOP M'S LAST TESTAMENT SHOULD BE IN HERE.
WHAT'S ALL THIS...? IT'S A BUNCH OF IMAGE FILES.
TAP TAP TAP
THEY LOOK LIKE SNAP-SHOTS.
Who are these people?
TAP
TAP
TAP
PROB-ABLY CAMOU-FLAGE TO HIDE ENCODED DATA.
TAP
TAP
THIS LARGEST FILE IS PROBABLY THE ONE...

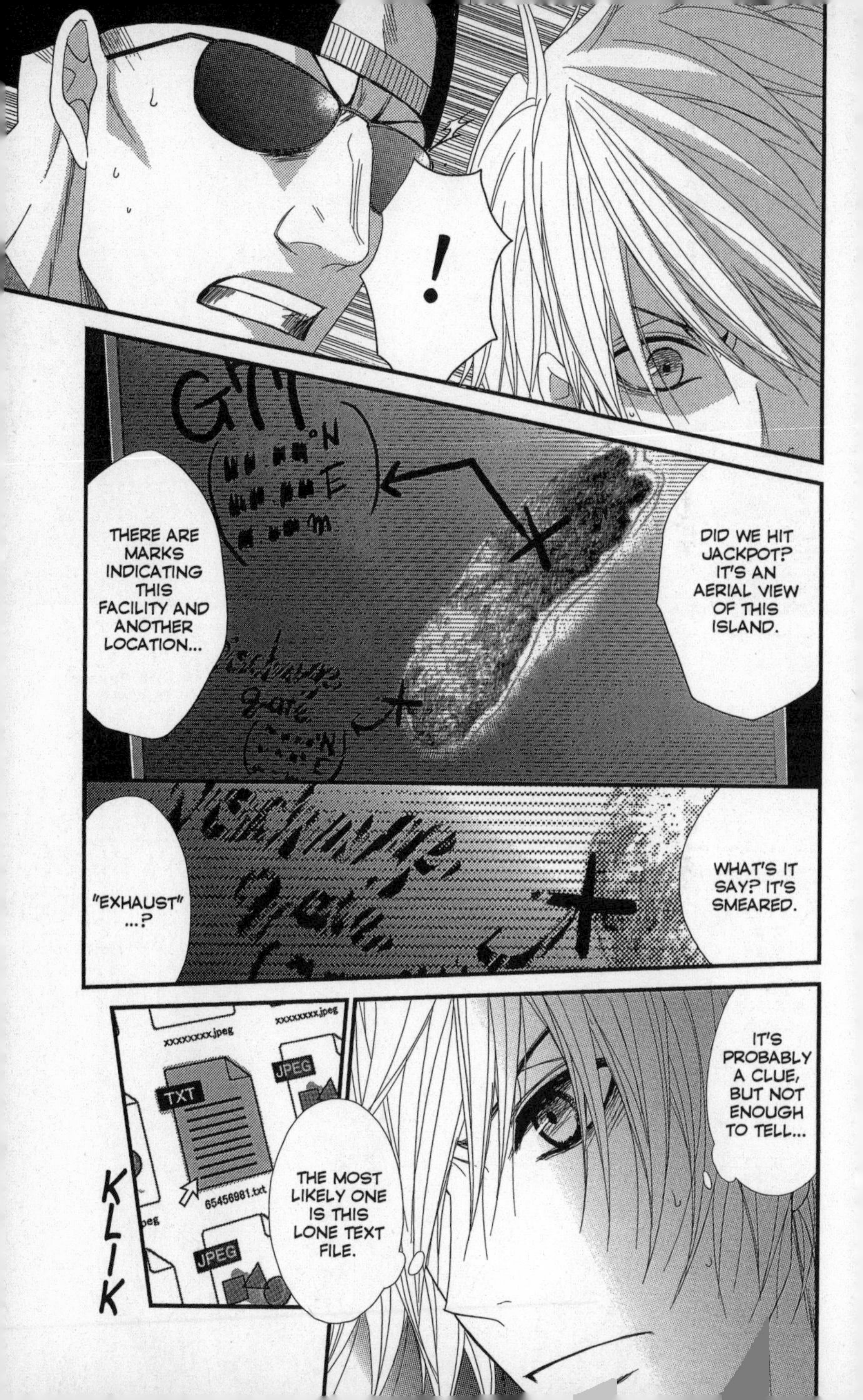
!
DID WE HIT JACKPOT? IT'S AN AERIAL VIEW OF THIS ISLAND.
THERE ARE MARKS INDICATING THIS FACILITY AND ANOTHER LOCATION...
WHAT'S IT SAY? IT'S SMEARED.
"EXHAUST" ...?
IT'S PROBABLY A CLUE, BUT NOT ENOUGH TO TELL...
THE MOST LIKELY ONE IS THIS LONE TEXT FILE.
xxxxxxxx.jpeg
xxxxxxxx.jpeg
JPEG
TXT
65456981.txt
JPEG
KLIK

3, xxxx
eek ago, I was officially appo
e the person in charge of "M
ay, I arrived at the place wh
as very hot. I felt reluctant, I

ember 24, xxxx
eived a card from "C" that s
rry Christmas!" I was rea
w she is persevering. s

28, xxxx
been almost a year nov
the system is starting t
almost complete, but I m

WHAT...?

THIS IS...

NO... IT'S NOT.

Sorry. I'm no good at English.

IS IT THE SOURCE CODE FOR M'S LAST TESTAMENT?

WHAT IS IT, TASUKU? WHAT'S IT SAY?

IT'S MORE THAN JUST SOURCE CODE.

the system completed
an order to dismantle
with anger.

ur agreement!
that this system could pro
now that it was ultimately
ow what to say.

IT TELLS WHY M'S LAST TESTAMENT'S SOURCE CODE WAS CHANGED.

, xxxx
uaded to continue m
ior has been worried
e must get rid of this
sake of humankind.

October 11, xxxx
I just got a call from "C."

...OF THE PERSON WHO CREATED THE M'S LAST TESTAMENT SYSTEM.

THIS IS A DIARY...

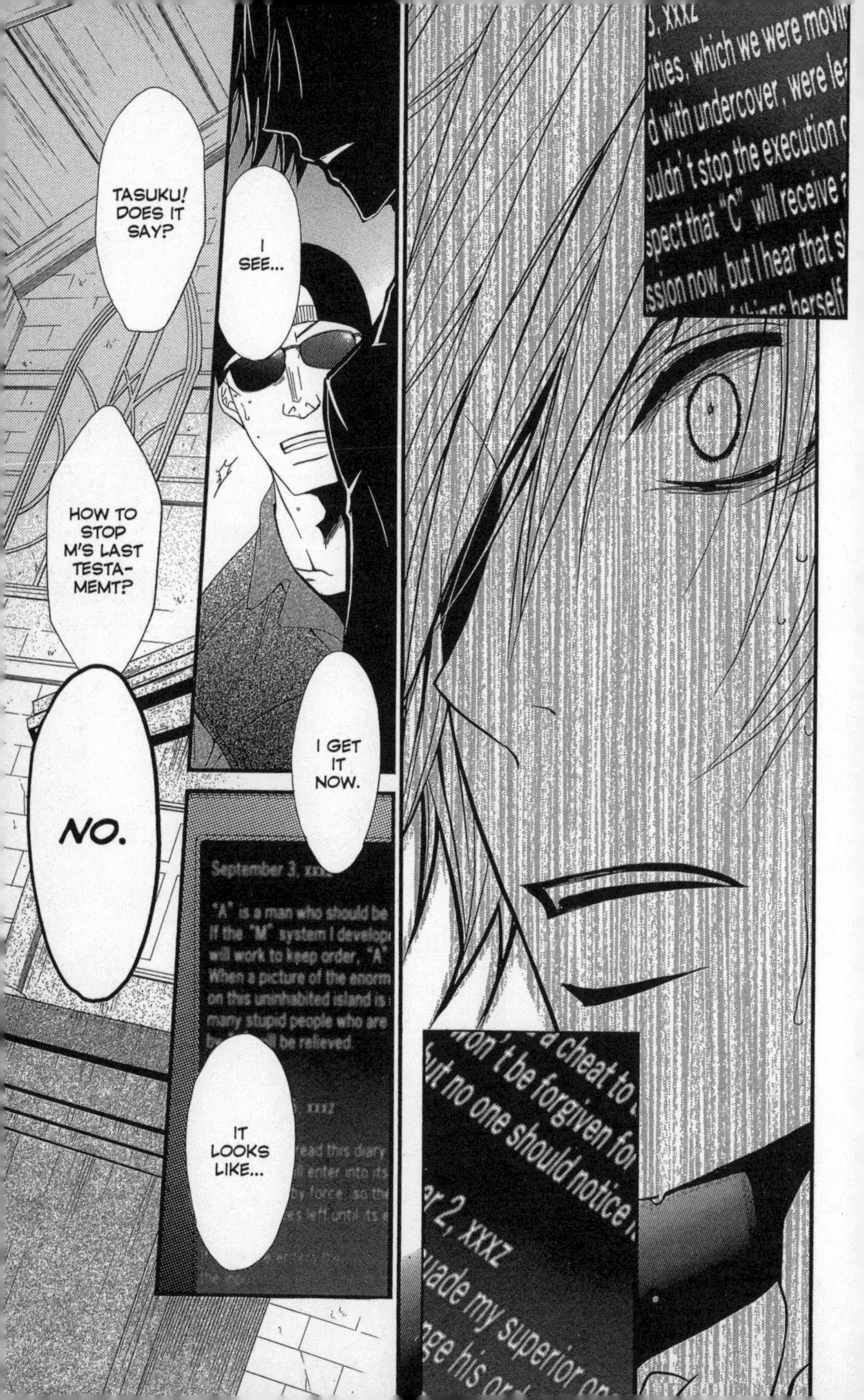
3, XXXZ
ities, which we were movi
d with undercover, were le
uldn't stop the execution
spect that "C" will receive
ssion now, but I hear that s
on't be forgiven fo
But no one should notice
er 2, XXXZ
uade my superior
I SEE...
September 3, xxxz
"A" is a man who should be
If the "M" system I develop
will work to keep order. "A"
When a picture of the enorm
on this uninhabited island is
many stupid people who are
I GET IT NOW.
IT LOOKS LIKE...
TASUKU! DOES IT SAY?
HOW TO STOP M'S LAST TESTA-MEMT?
NO.

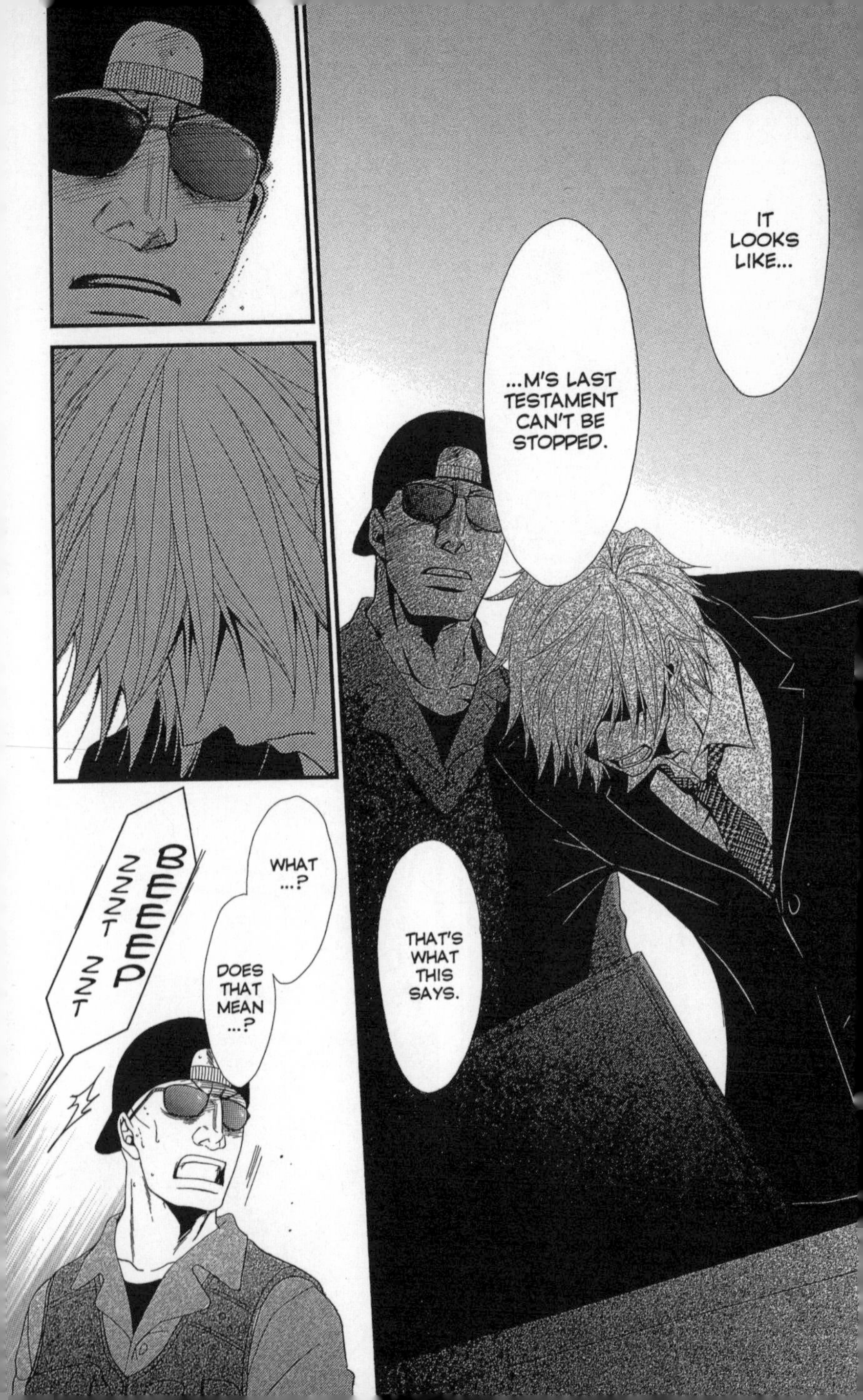
IT LOOKS LIKE...
...M'S LAST TESTAMENT CAN'T BE STOPPED.
THAT'S WHAT THIS SAYS.
WHAT ...?
DOES THAT MEAN ...?
BEEEEP
ZZZT ZZT

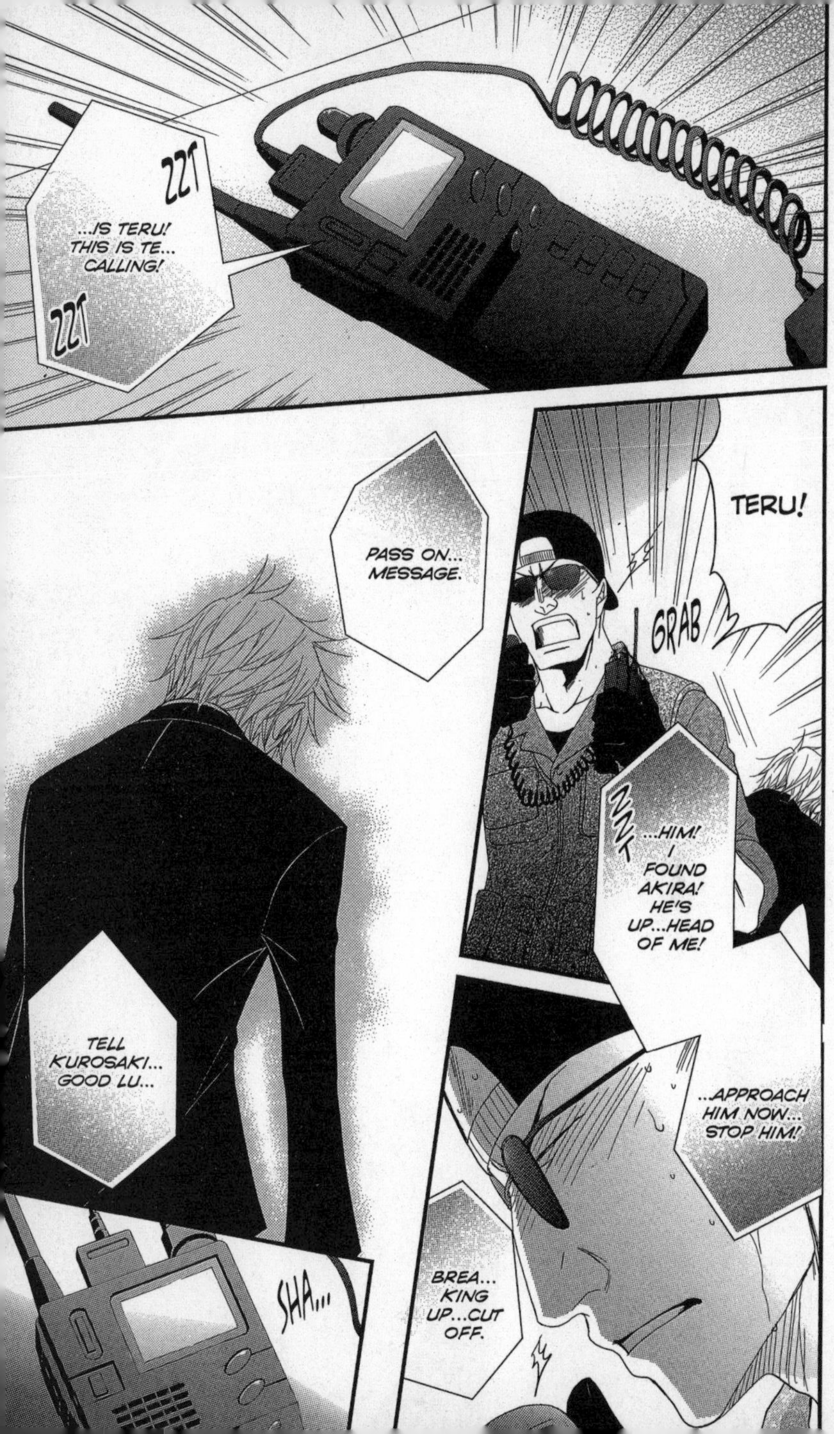
ZZT
...IS TERU! THIS IS TE... CALLING!
ZZT
TERU!
GRAB
NNK
...HIM! I FOUND AKIRA! HE'S UP...HEAD OF ME!
...APPROACH HIM NOW... STOP HIM!
BREA... KING UP...CUT OFF.
PASS ON... MESSAGE.
TELL KUROSAKI... GOOD LU...
SHA...

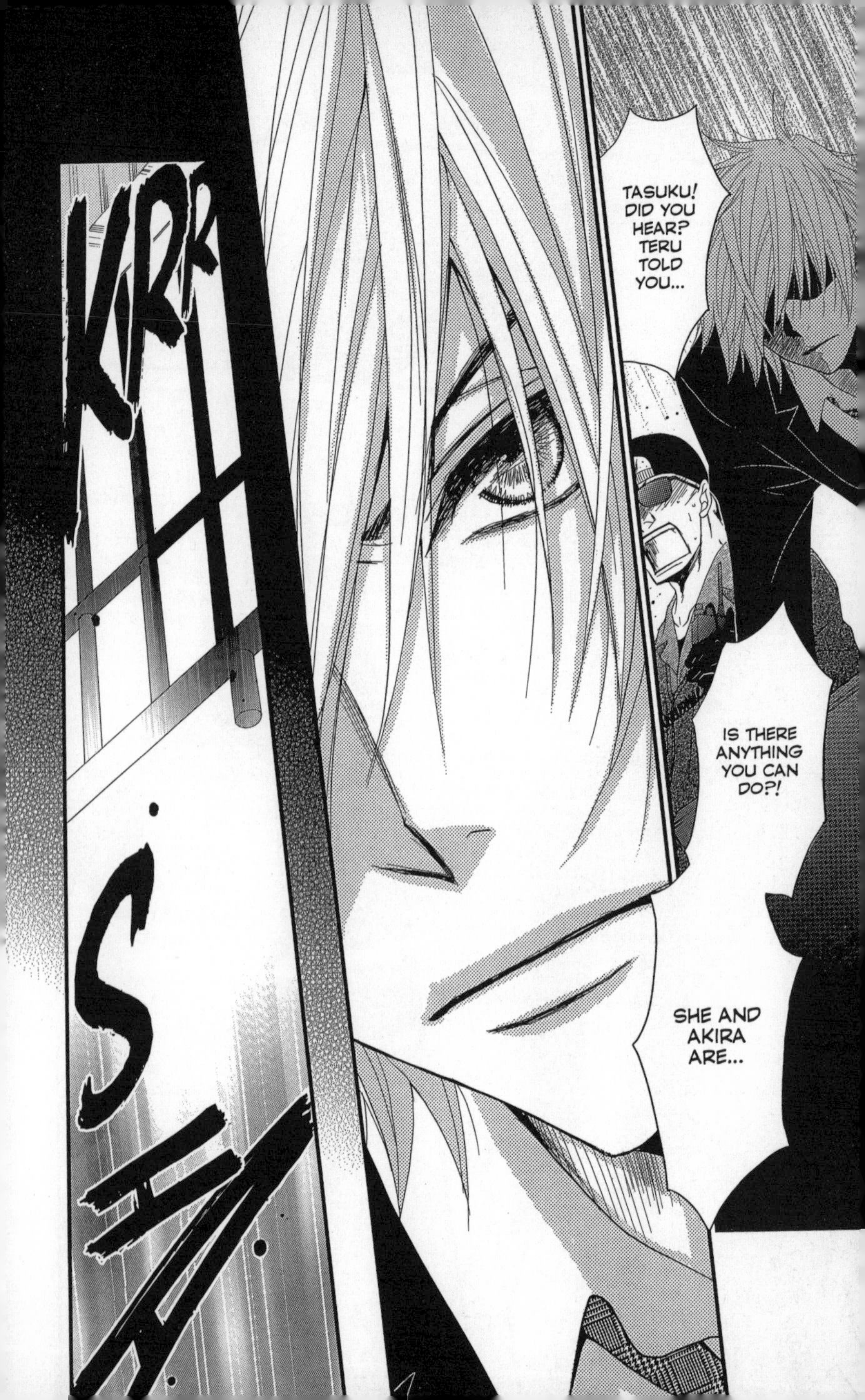
TASUKU! DID YOU HEAR? TERU TOLD YOU...
IS THERE ANYTHING YOU CAN DO?!
SHE AND AKIRA ARE...
KRR
SHA

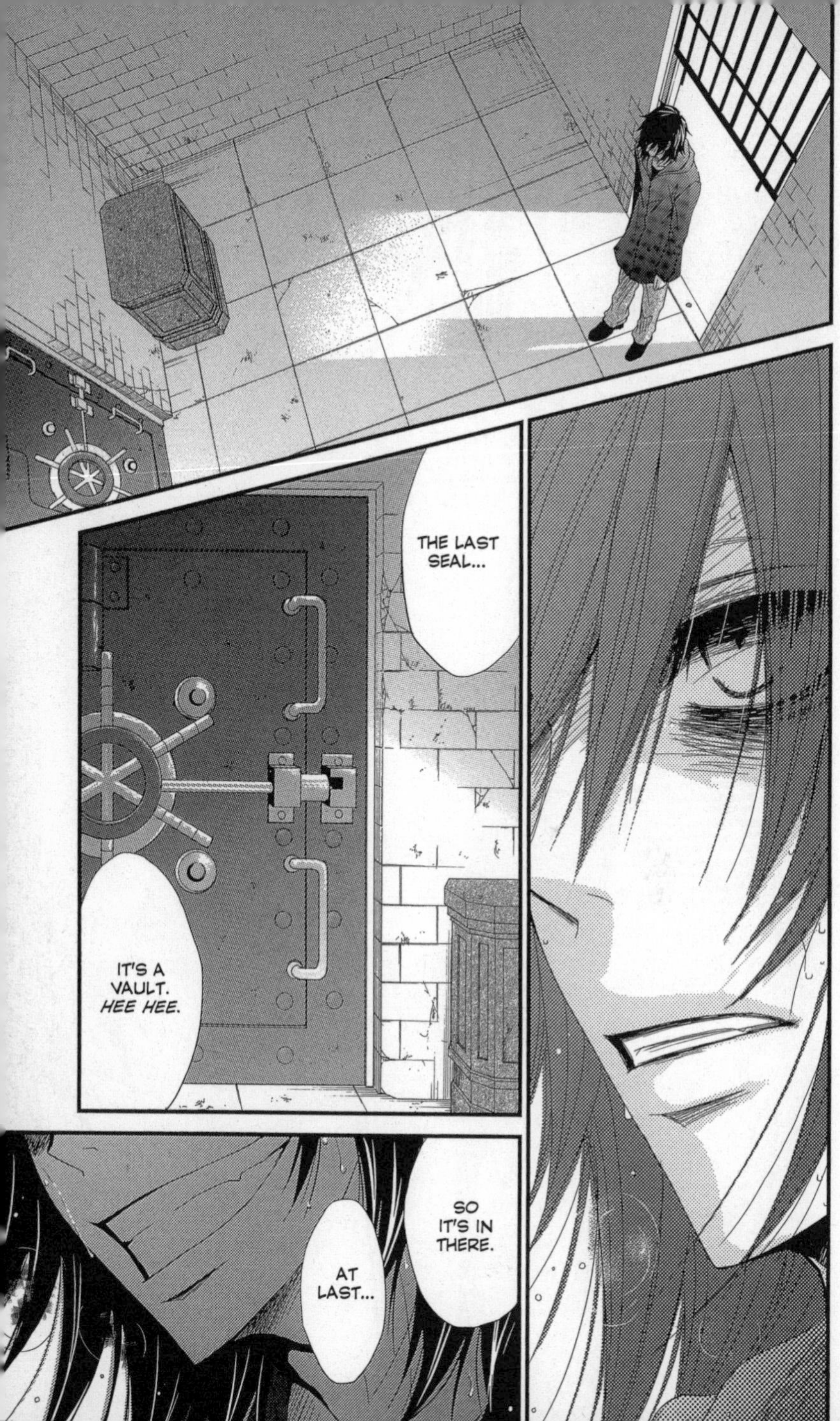
THE LAST SEAL...
IT'S A VAULT. *HEE HEE.*
SO IT'S IN THERE.
AT LAST...

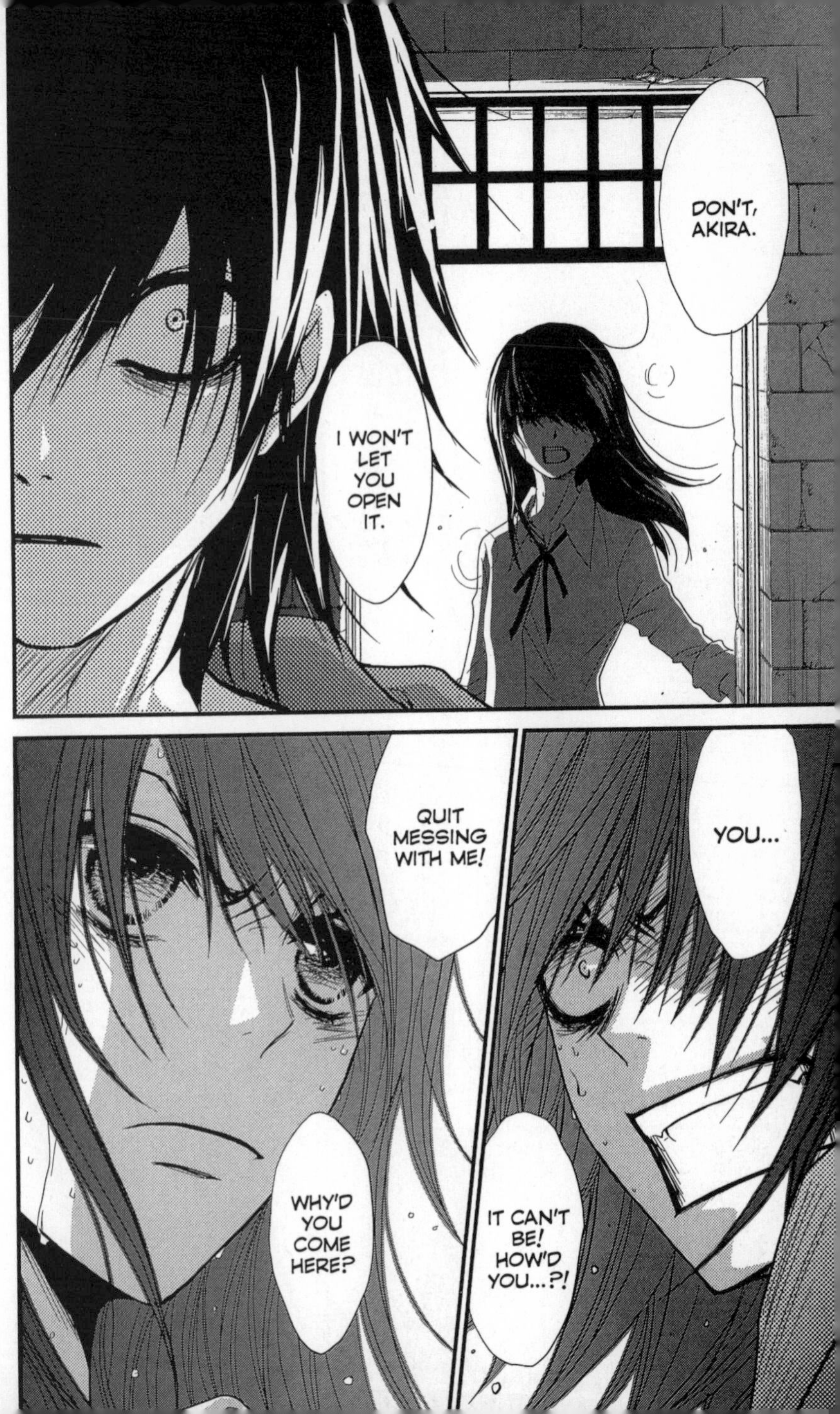
DON'T, AKIRA.
I WON'T LET YOU OPEN IT.
YOU...
IT CAN'T BE! HOW'D YOU...?!
QUIT MESSING WITH ME!
WHY'D YOU COME HERE?

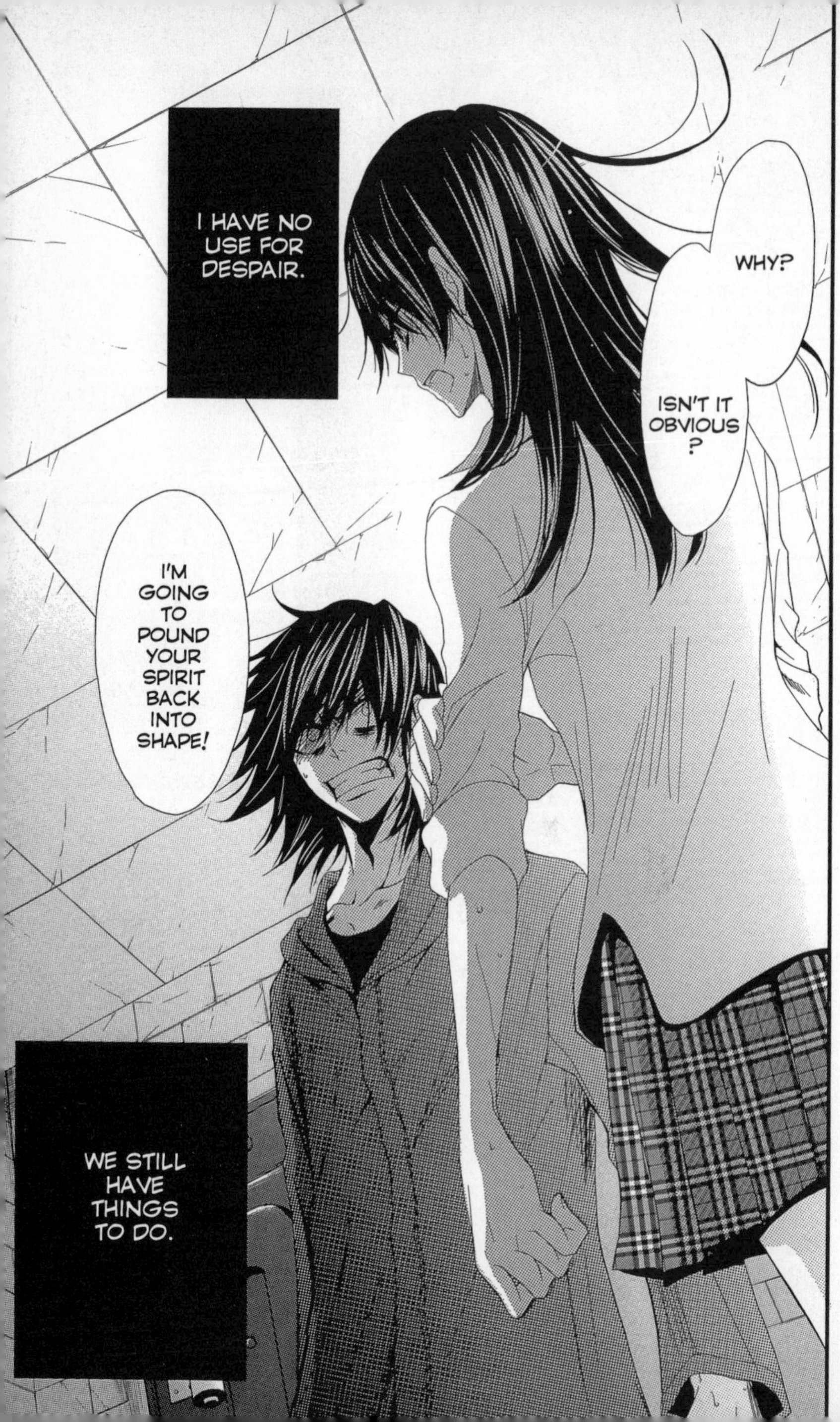
WHY?
ISN'T IT OBVIOUS?
I HAVE NO USE FOR DESPAIR.
I'M GOING TO POUND YOUR SPIRIT BACK INTO SHAPE!
WE STILL HAVE THINGS TO DO.

THE BEST ☆ OF ☆ THE SECRET SCHOOL CUSTODIAN OFFICE ♥

THE 10TH ONE OF THIS SUPER POPULAR SECTION ♥

THERE IS A *DENGEKI DAISY* FAN SEGMENT BOLDLY FEATURED IN *BETSUCOMI* THAT IS APTLY TITLED, "THE SECRET SCHOOL CUSTODIAN OFFICE ♥"!

WITH ARBITRARY EYES, WE EXAMINED ALL THE GREAT WORK FEATURED THERE AND PICKED THE "BEST" AMONG THEM THAT WE WANTED TO LEAVE FOR POSTERITY!

THE "BEST OF" FOR VOLUME 15 IS... "MEMORIAL [X] CROSSWORD"

ON THE EVE OF THE FINAL CHAPTER!!

MEMORIAL X CROSSWORD

THE CLUES WILL LEAD YOU TO THE KEYWORD!!

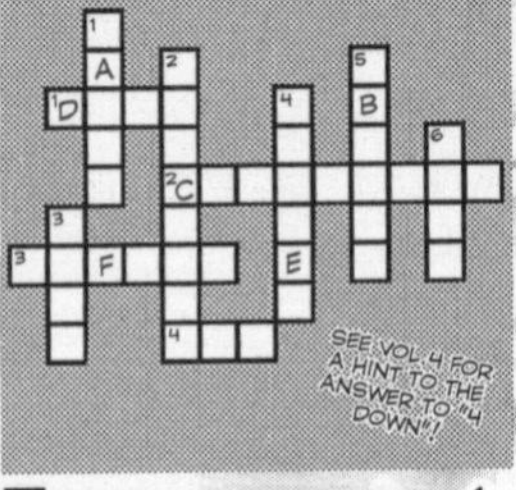

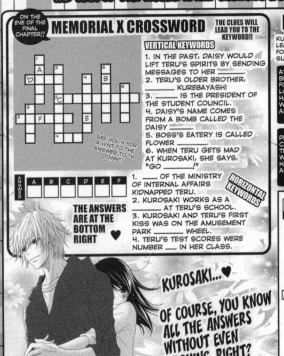

SEE VOL. 4 FOR A HINT TO THE ANSWER TO "4 DOWN"!

VERTICAL KEYWORDS

1. IN THE PAST, DAISY WOULD LIFT TERU'S SPIRITS BY SENDING MESSAGES TO HER ______.
2. TERU'S OLDER BROTHER, ______ KUREBAYASHI
3. ______ IS THE PRESIDENT OF THE STUDENT COUNCIL.
4. DAISY'S NAME COMES FROM A BOMB CALLED THE DAISY ______.
5. BOSS'S EATERY IS CALLED FLOWER ______.
6. WHEN TERU GETS MAD AT KUROSAKI, SHE SAYS, "GO ______!"

ANSWER	A	B	C	D	E	F

HORIZONTAL KEYWORDS

1. ___ OF THE MINISTRY OF INTERNAL AFFAIRS KIDNAPPED TERU.
2. KUROSAKI WORKS AS A ______ AT TERU'S SCHOOL.
3. KUROSAKI AND TERU'S FIRST KISS WAS ON THE AMUSEMENT PARK ______ WHEEL.
4. TERU'S TEST SCORES WERE NUMBER ___ IN HER CLASS.

THE ANSWERS ARE AT THE BOTTOM RIGHT ♥

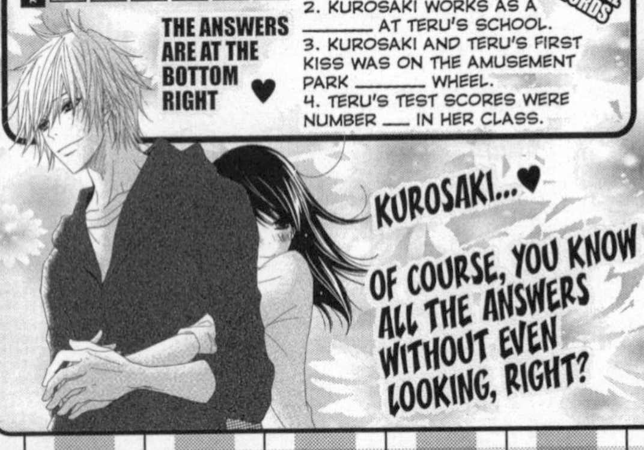

KUROSAKI...♥
OF COURSE, YOU KNOW ALL THE ANSWERS WITHOUT EVEN LOOKING, RIGHT?

MAIL CORNER!

KUROSAKI AND FRIENDS WILL BE LEAVING US SOON. WE'LL BE LOOKING FORWARD TO YOUR LETTERS OF SUPPORT UNTIL THE VERY END!

AT FIRST, I ROOTED FOR KUROSAKI, BUT NOW I'M HEAD OVER HEELS FOR AKIRA! I'M EXCITEDLY LOOKING FORWARD TO WHAT HAPPENS TO AKIRA! ALSO, I CAN'T WAIT TO SEE WHERE KUROSAKI AND TERU'S LOVE GOES!

-KYAHOTAN, MIYAZAKI PREFECTURE

PLEASE DON'T SAY IT'S THE FINAL CHAPTER! I WILL, HOWEVER, CRY TEARS AND FOLLOW YOU ALL THE WAY THROUGH! I PRAY THAT A HAPPY FUTURE AWAITS KUROSAKI AND TERU!

- RITA., TOCHIGI PREFECTUREE

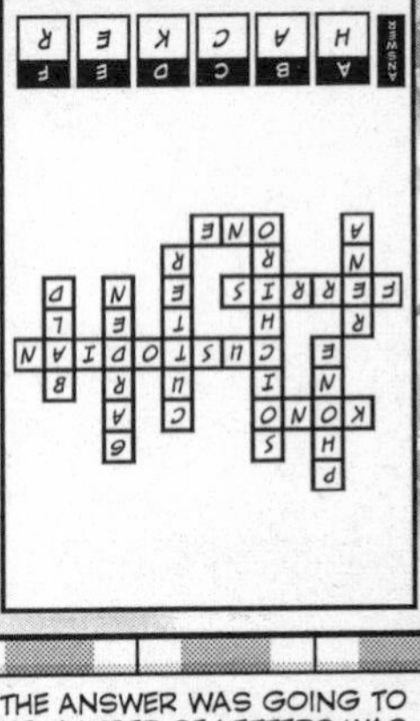

JUDGES' COMMENTS

- [FOR THE JAPANESE VERSION] I MADE UP MY MIND THAT THE ANSWER WAS GOING TO BE "GO BALD," BUT ONLY THE FIRST LETTER MATCHED. (THE NUMBER OF LETTERS WAS WRONG AS WELL.)

(HEAD JUDGE: KYOUSUKE MOTOMI)

- CROSSWORDS GET YOU SO EXCITED! KEEP ON TRYING AGAIN AND AGAIN WITH THE GRAPHIC NOVELS IN HAND! ♪

(JUDGE: *DAISY* EDITOR)

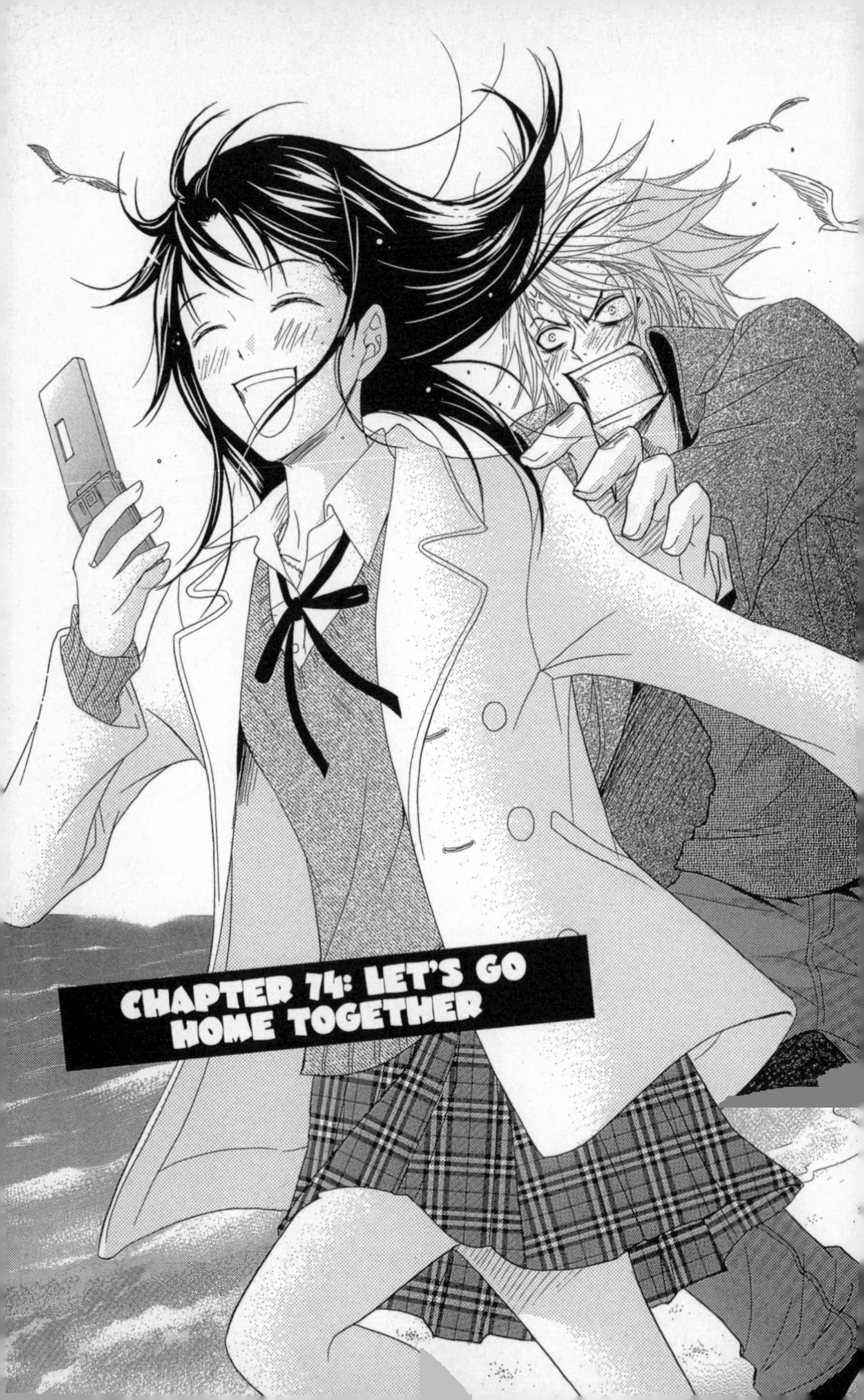
CHAPTER 74: LET'S GO HOME TOGETHER

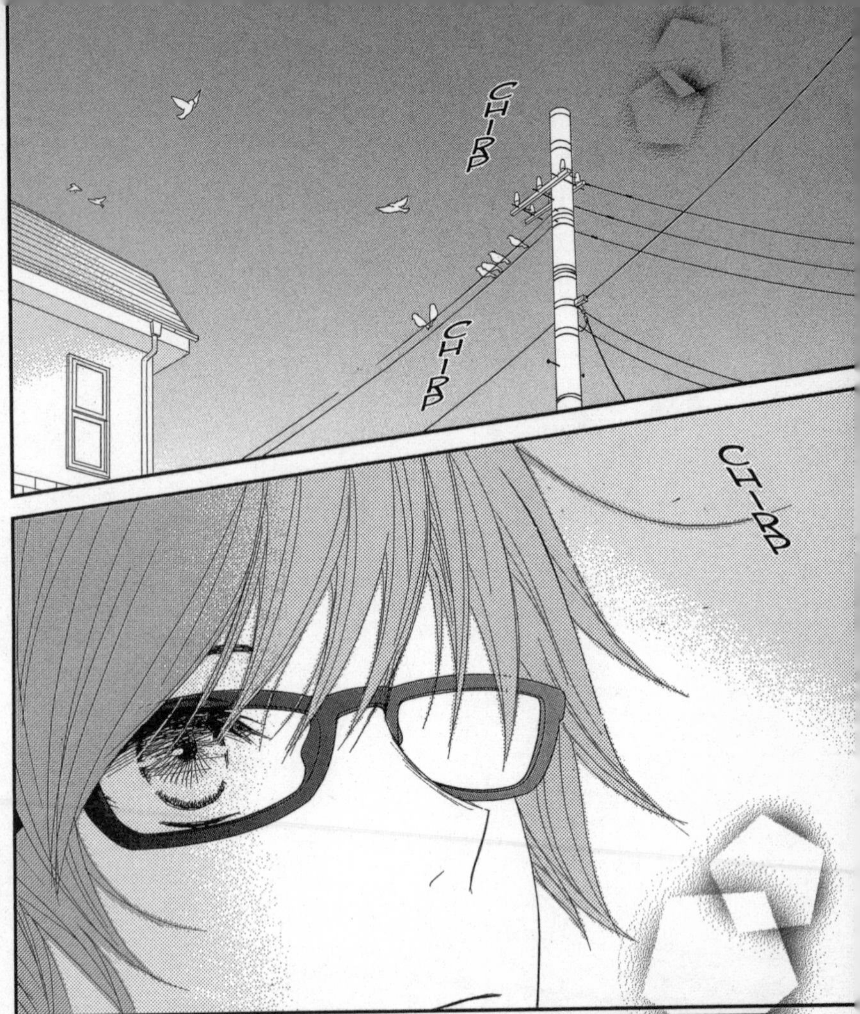
CHIRP
CHIRP
CHIRP

THE TITLE PAGES FOR CHAPTERS 72, 73 AND 74 ARE REMINISCENCES OF MEMORABLE PAST *DENGEKI DAISY* SCENES THAT I SNUCK IN AS THE FINAL CHAPTERS APPROACH, BUT THEY'RE PORTRAYED FROM A DIFFERENT PERSPECTIVE. THE TITLE PAGE FOR CHAPTER 72 IS A SCENE FROM CHAPTER ONE—"ARE YOU DAISY?" (KUROSAKI TURNS THE OPPOSITE WAY, HOWEVER. SORRY.) THE TITLE PAGE OF CHAPTER 73 IS THAT SCENE "DON'T IGNORE ME, GABE!" FROM THE END OF VOLUME 4, CHAPTER 17. AND THE TITLE PAGE FOR CHAPTER 74 IS A SCENE FROM VOLUME 9, CHAPTER 41 WHERE KUROSAKI CHASES TERU AS SHE TEASES HIM BY READING A MESSAGE FROM DAISY. DID ANYONE RECOGNIZE THEM ALL?

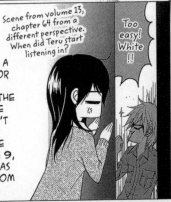

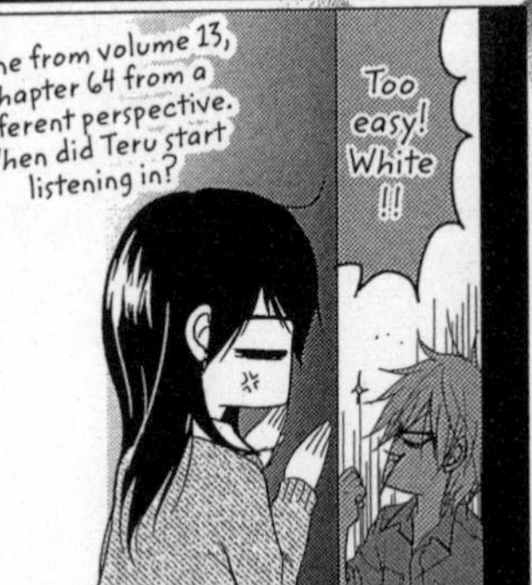
Scene from volume 13, chapter 64 from a different perspective. When did Teru start listening in?
Too easy! White !!

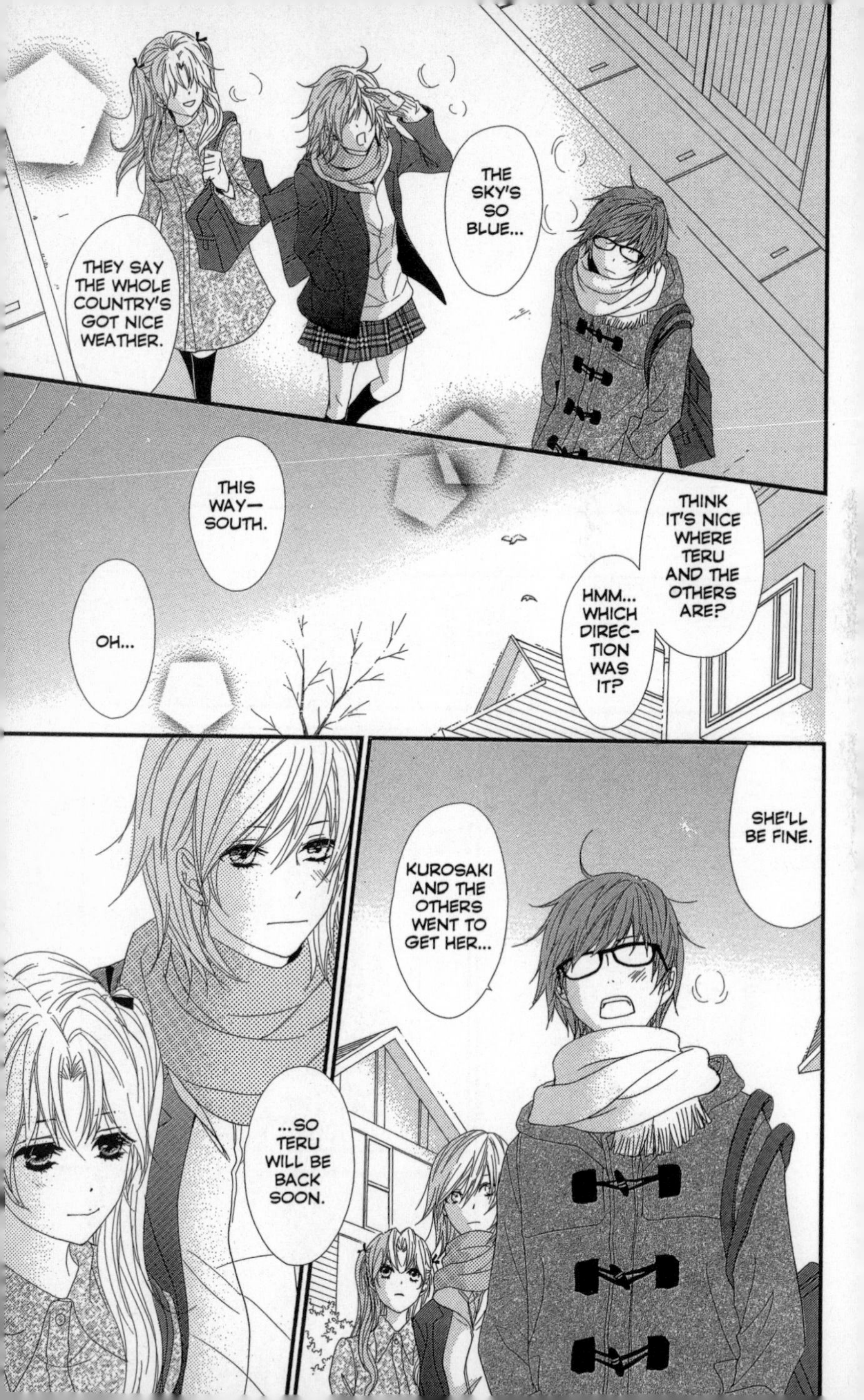
THE SKY'S SO BLUE...
THEY SAY THE WHOLE COUNTRY'S GOT NICE WEATHER.
THINK IT'S NICE WHERE TERU AND THE OTHERS ARE?
HMM... WHICH DIRECTION WAS IT?
THIS WAY—SOUTH.
OH...
SHE'LL BE FINE.
KUROSAKI AND THE OTHERS WENT TO GET HER...
...SO TERU WILL BE BACK SOON.

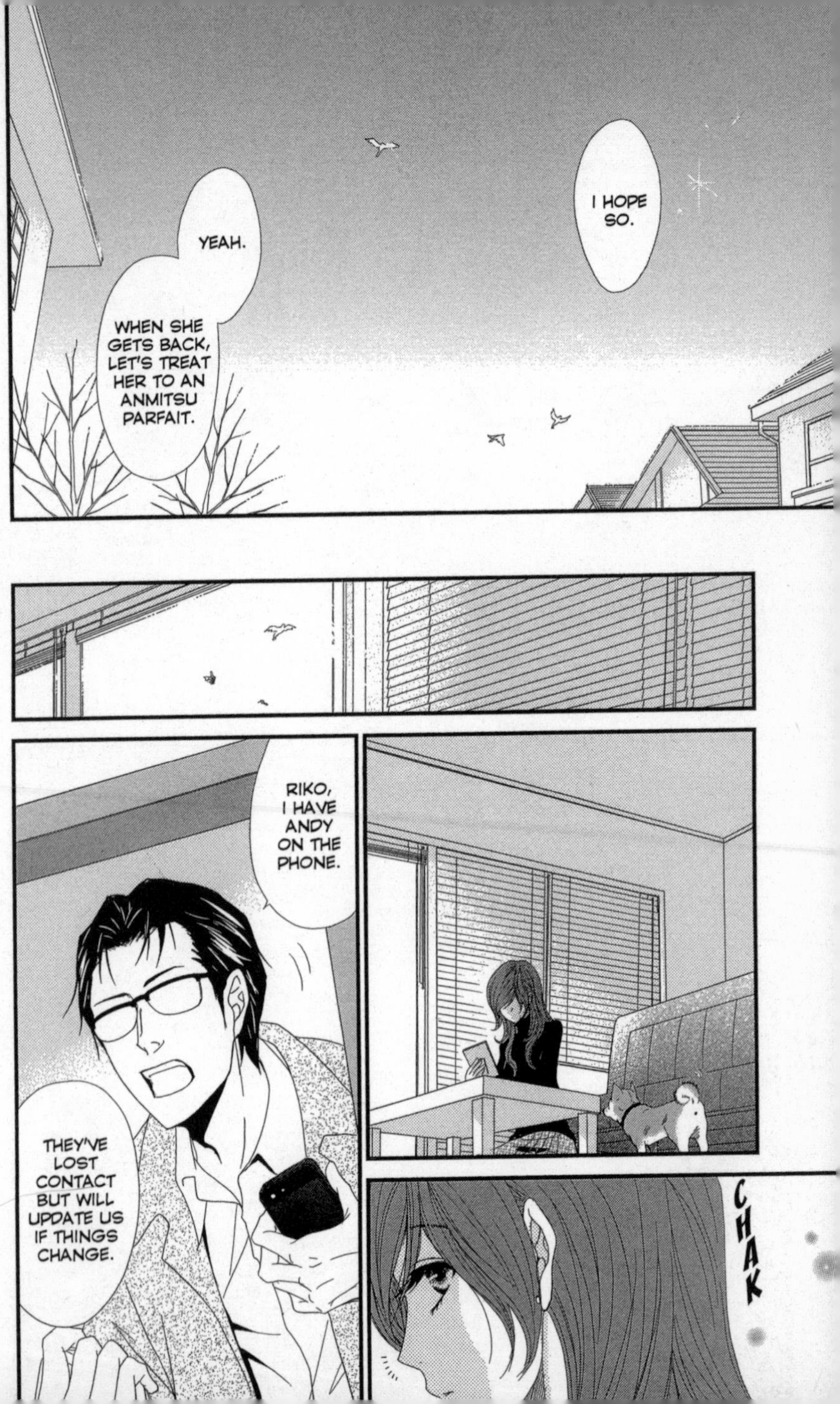
I HOPE SO.
YEAH.
WHEN SHE GETS BACK, LET'S TREAT HER TO AN ANMITSU PARFAIT.
CHAK
RIKO, I HAVE ANDY ON THE PHONE.
THEY'VE LOST CONTACT BUT WILL UPDATE US IF THINGS CHANGE.

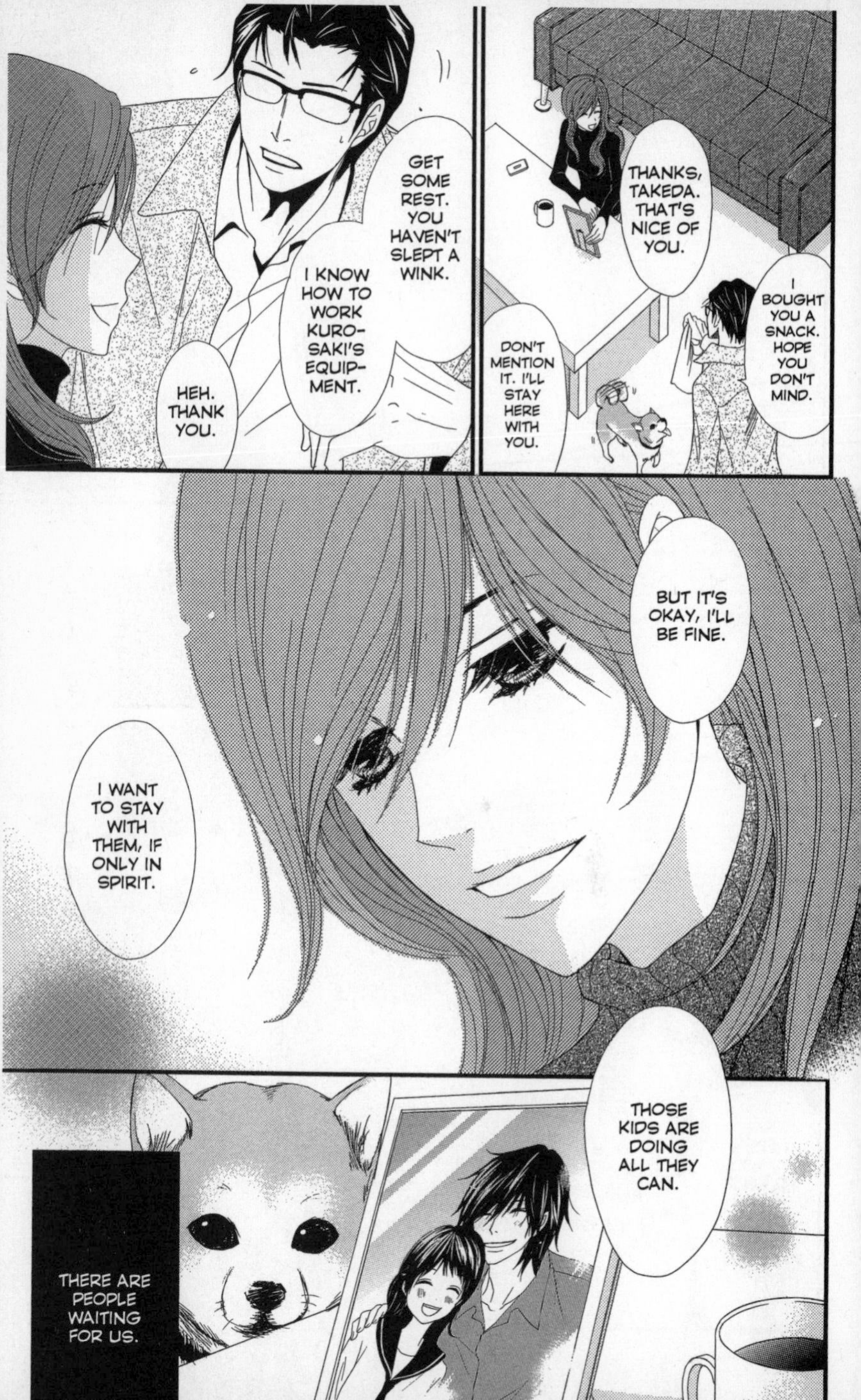
I BOUGHT YOU A SNACK. HOPE YOU DON'T MIND.
THANKS, TAKEDA. THAT'S NICE OF YOU.
DON'T MENTION IT. I'LL STAY HERE WITH YOU.
GET SOME REST. YOU HAVEN'T SLEPT A WINK.
I KNOW HOW TO WORK KURO-SAKI'S EQUIP-MENT.
HEH. THANK YOU.
BUT IT'S OKAY, I'LL BE FINE.
THOSE KIDS ARE DOING ALL THEY CAN.
I WANT TO STAY WITH THEM, IF ONLY IN SPIRIT.
THERE ARE PEOPLE WAITING FOR US.

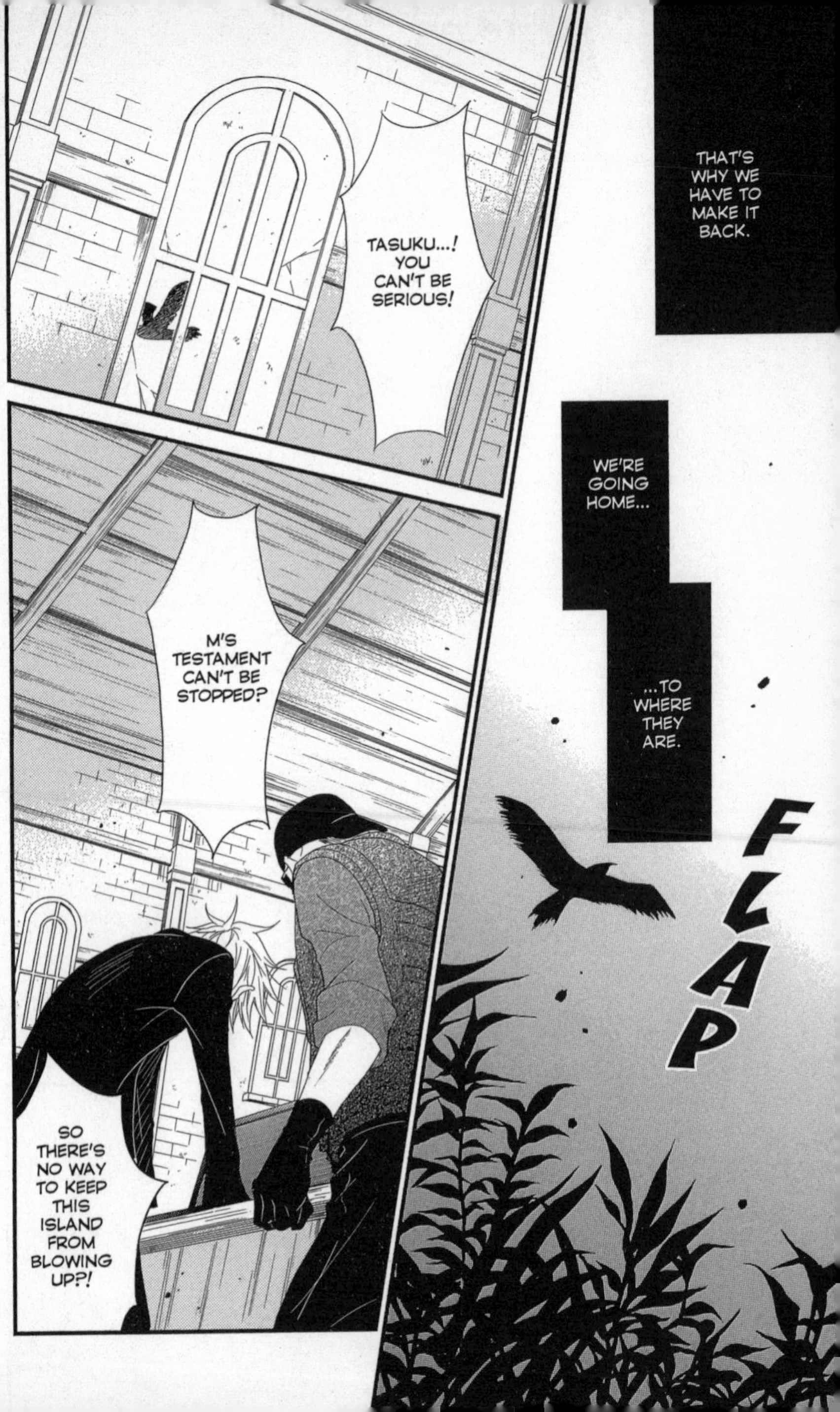
THAT'S WHY WE HAVE TO MAKE IT BACK.
WE'RE GOING HOME...
...TO WHERE THEY ARE.
FLAP
TASUKU...! YOU CAN'T BE SERIOUS!
M'S TESTAMENT CAN'T BE STOPPED?
SO THERE'S NO WAY TO KEEP THIS ISLAND FROM BLOWING UP?!

THIS ISLAND BLOWING UP WILL BE PROOF OF AKIRA'S DEATH...

...AND THAT WILL COMPLETE M'S LAST TESTAMENT.

THIS IS THE SYSTEM MANAGER'S DIARY.

NOTHING CAN STOP M'S LAST TESTAMENT ONCE IT'S ACTIVATED.

THAT'S WHAT IT SAYS.

uary 8. xxxz
ctivities, which we were moving
ndercover, were leaked by
uldn't stop the execution
ct that "C" will receive
on now, but I hear that s
ing care of things herse
orry I can't do

ne 7, xxxz
I haven't bee
I'm plotting

July 7, xxxz
I added a cl   at.
I won't be t
but no one

AKIRA AND TERU ARE...

BOSS.

THEN... THERE'S NOTHING MORE WE CAN DO?

I'M GOING AFTER TERU.

ARE YOU CRAZY?! AND BE THE LONE SURVIVOR?!

CALL THE CHOPPER AND GET YOURSELF OUT OF HERE.

I'M NOT THAT KIND OF GUY! I'M NOT LEAVING YOU.

BOSS!!

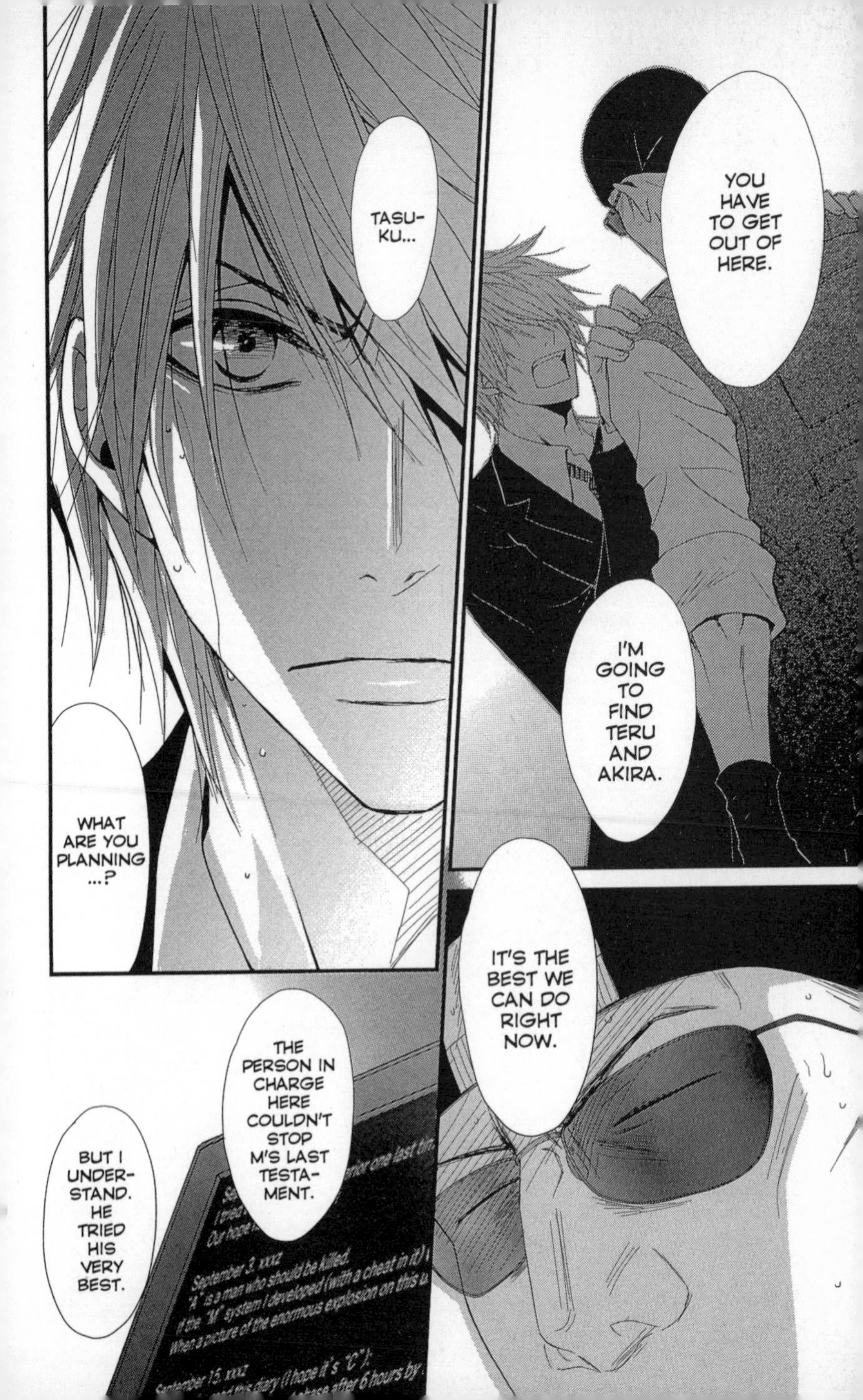
YOU HAVE TO GET OUT OF HERE.
I'M GOING TO FIND TERU AND AKIRA.
TASU-KU...
WHAT ARE YOU PLANNING ...?
IT'S THE BEST WE CAN DO RIGHT NOW.
THE PERSON IN CHARGE HERE COULDN'T STOP M'S LAST TESTA-MENT.
BUT I UNDER-STAND. HE TRIED HIS VERY BEST.

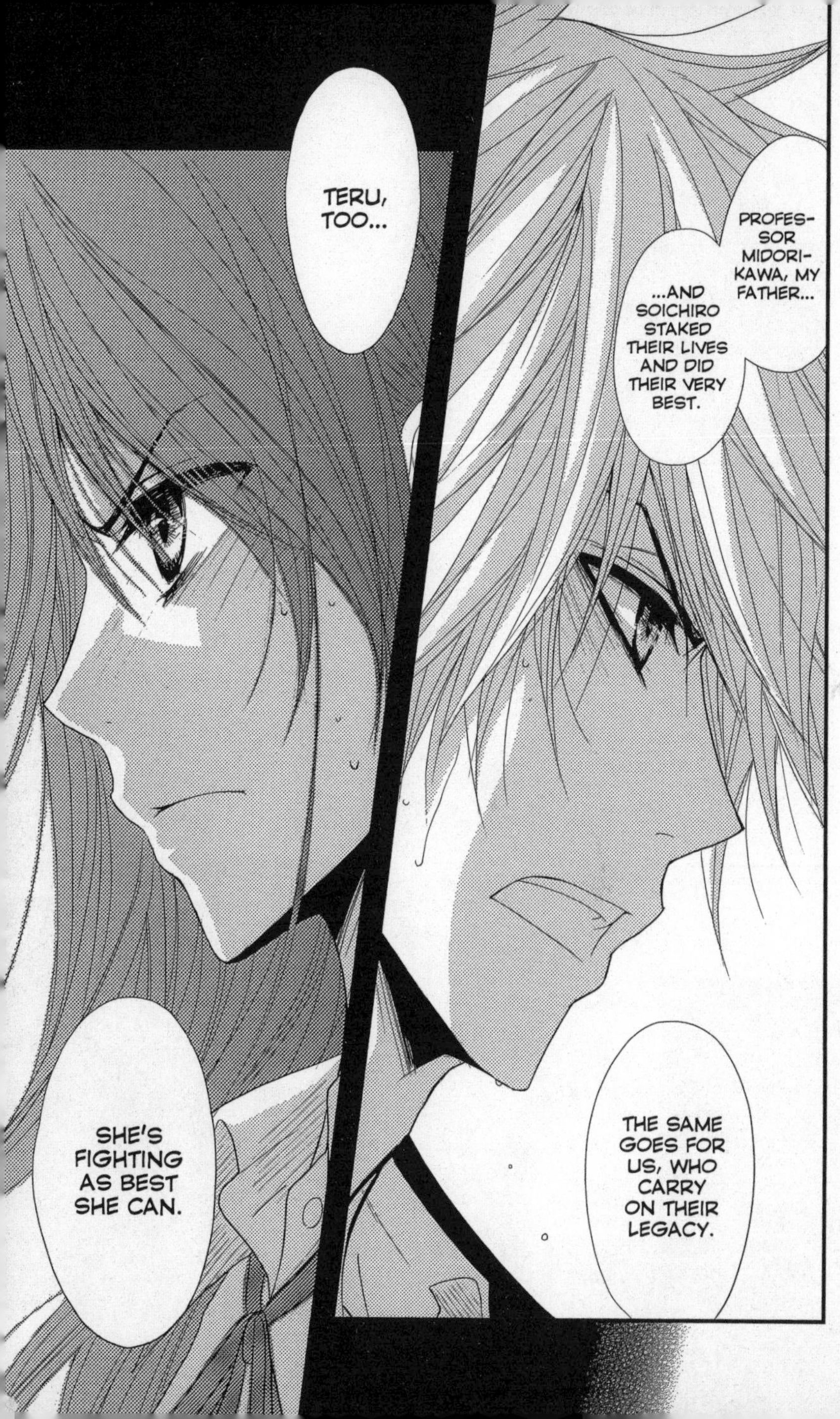
PROFES-
SOR
MIDORI-
KAWA, MY
FATHER...
...AND
SOICHIRO
STAKED
THEIR LIVES
AND DID
THEIR VERY
BEST.
THE SAME
GOES FOR
US, WHO
CARRY
ON THEIR
LEGACY.
TERU,
TOO...
SHE'S
FIGHTING
AS BEST
SHE CAN.

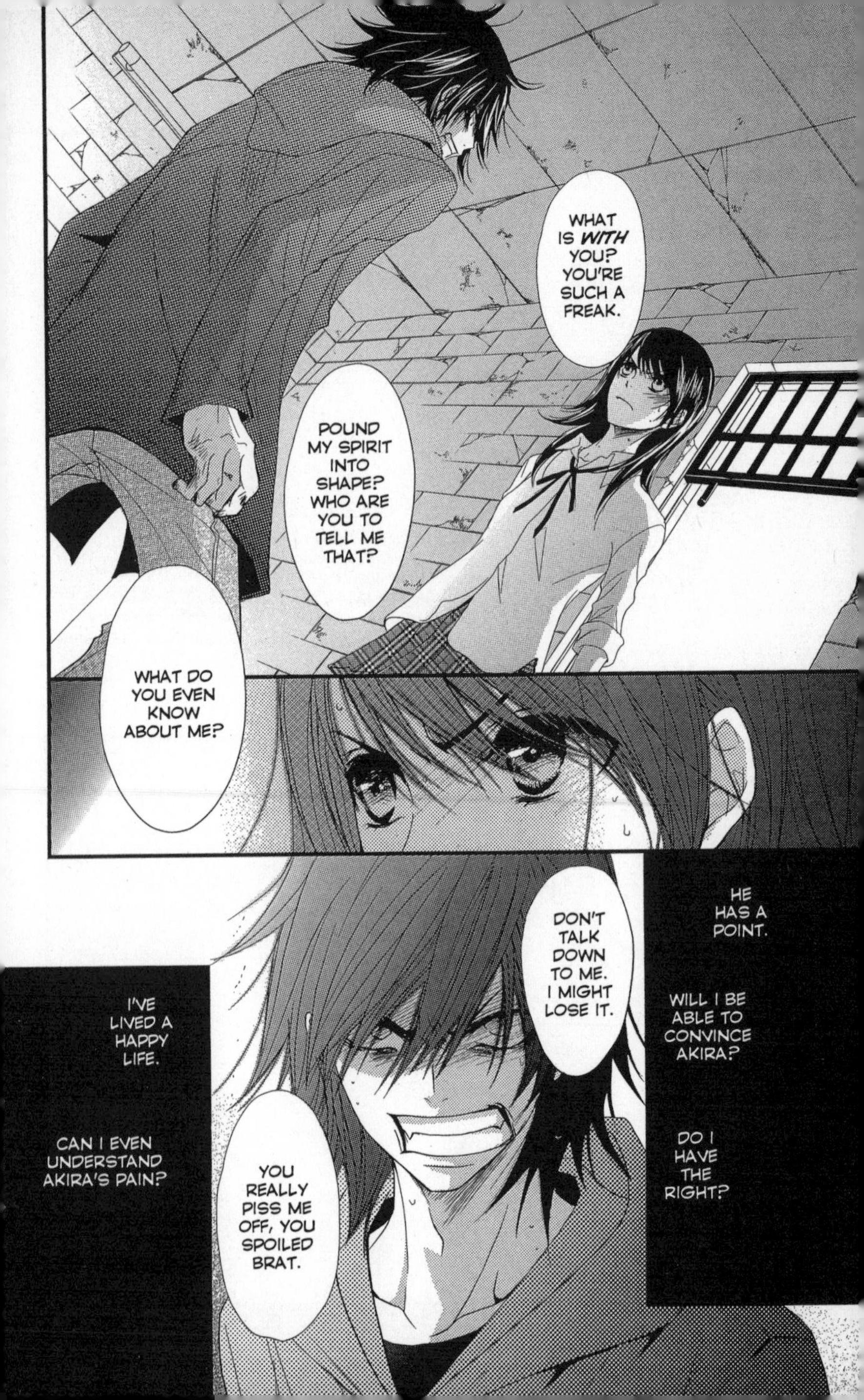
WHAT IS *WITH* YOU? YOU'RE SUCH A FREAK.
POUND MY SPIRIT INTO SHAPE? WHO ARE YOU TO TELL ME THAT?
WHAT DO YOU EVEN KNOW ABOUT ME?
HE HAS A POINT.
WILL I BE ABLE TO CONVINCE AKIRA?
DO I HAVE THE RIGHT?
DON'T TALK DOWN TO ME. I MIGHT LOSE IT.
YOU REALLY PISS ME OFF, YOU SPOILED BRAT.
I'VE LIVED A HAPPY LIFE.
CAN I EVEN UNDERSTAND AKIRA'S PAIN?

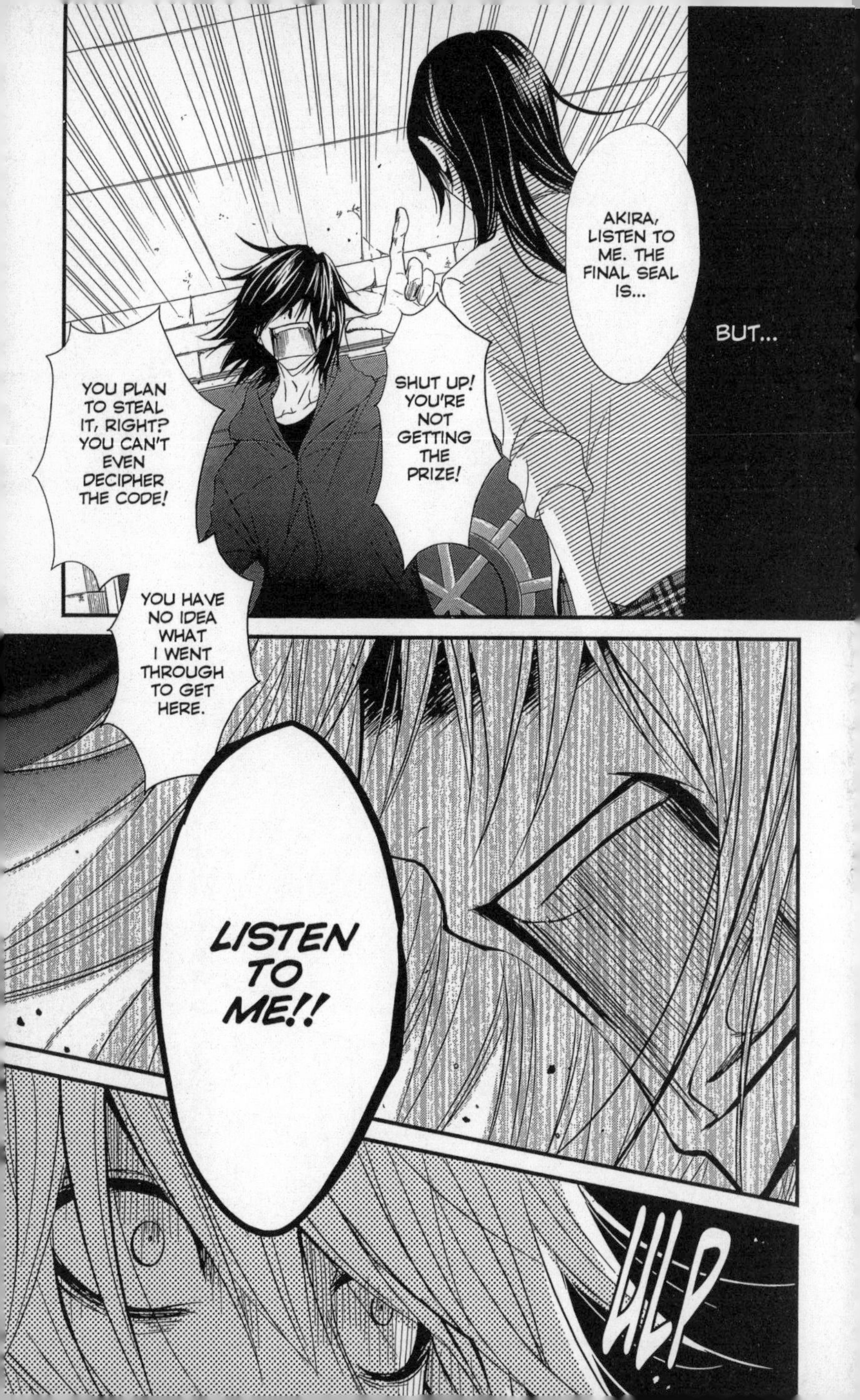
BUT...
AKIRA, LISTEN TO ME. THE FINAL SEAL IS...
SHUT UP! YOU'RE NOT GETTING THE PRIZE!
YOU PLAN TO STEAL IT, RIGHT? YOU CAN'T EVEN DECIPHER THE CODE!
YOU HAVE NO IDEA WHAT I WENT THROUGH TO GET HERE.
LISTEN TO ME!!
ULP

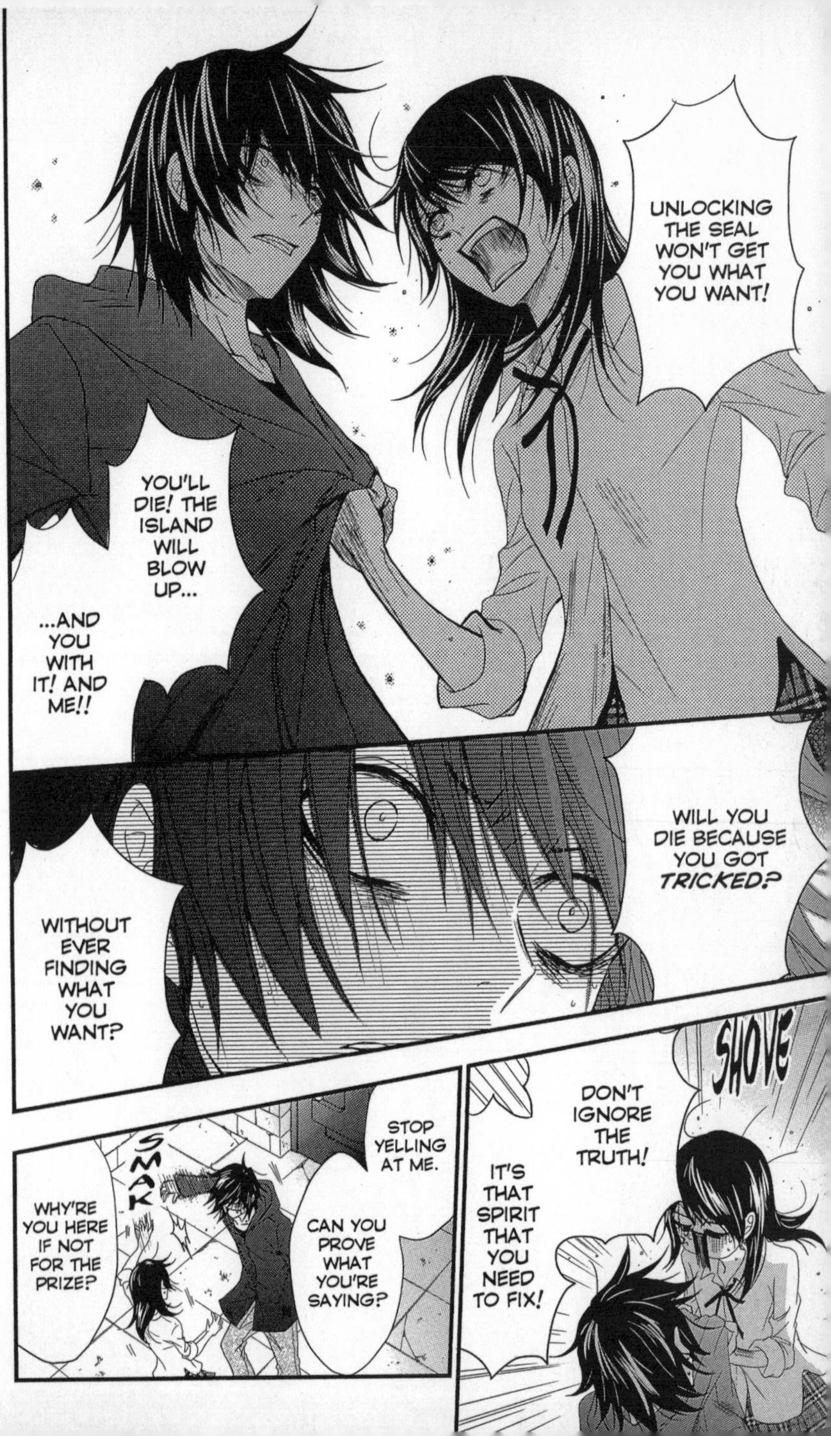
UNLOCKING THE SEAL WON'T GET YOU WHAT YOU WANT!
YOU'LL DIE! THE ISLAND WILL BLOW UP...
...AND YOU WITH IT! AND ME!!
WILL YOU DIE BECAUSE YOU GOT *TRICKED?*
WITHOUT EVER FINDING WHAT YOU WANT?
SHOVE
DON'T IGNORE THE TRUTH!
IT'S THAT SPIRIT THAT YOU NEED TO FIX!
STOP YELLING AT ME.
CAN YOU PROVE WHAT YOU'RE SAYING?
SMAK
WHY'RE YOU HERE IF NOT FOR THE PRIZE?

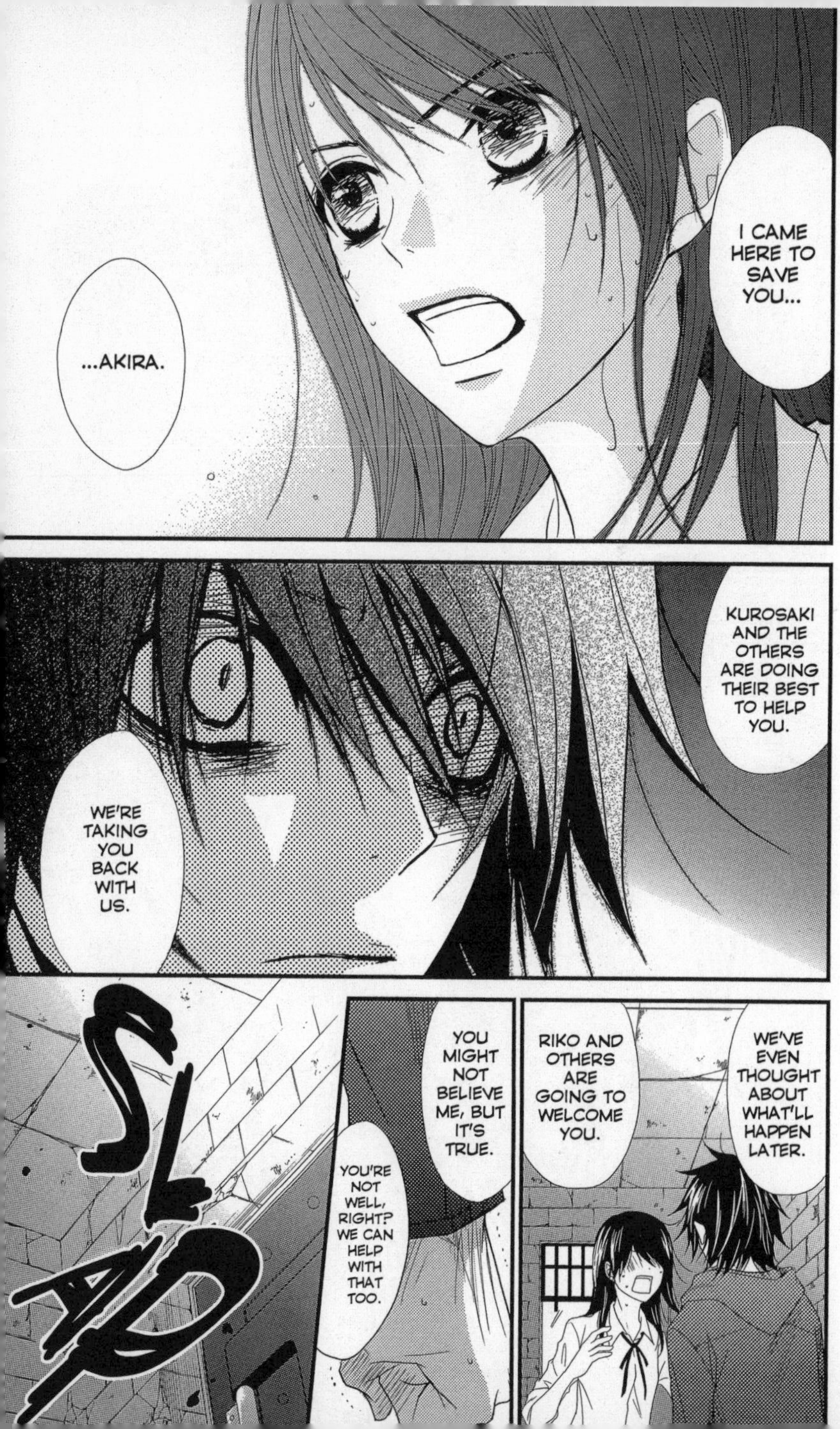
I CAME HERE TO SAVE YOU...
...AKIRA.
KUROSAKI AND THE OTHERS ARE DOING THEIR BEST TO HELP YOU.
WE'RE TAKING YOU BACK WITH US.
WE'VE EVEN THOUGHT ABOUT WHAT'LL HAPPEN LATER.
RIKO AND OTHERS ARE GOING TO WELCOME YOU.
YOU MIGHT NOT BELIEVE ME, BUT IT'S TRUE.
YOU'RE NOT WELL, RIGHT? WE CAN HELP WITH THAT TOO.
SLAP

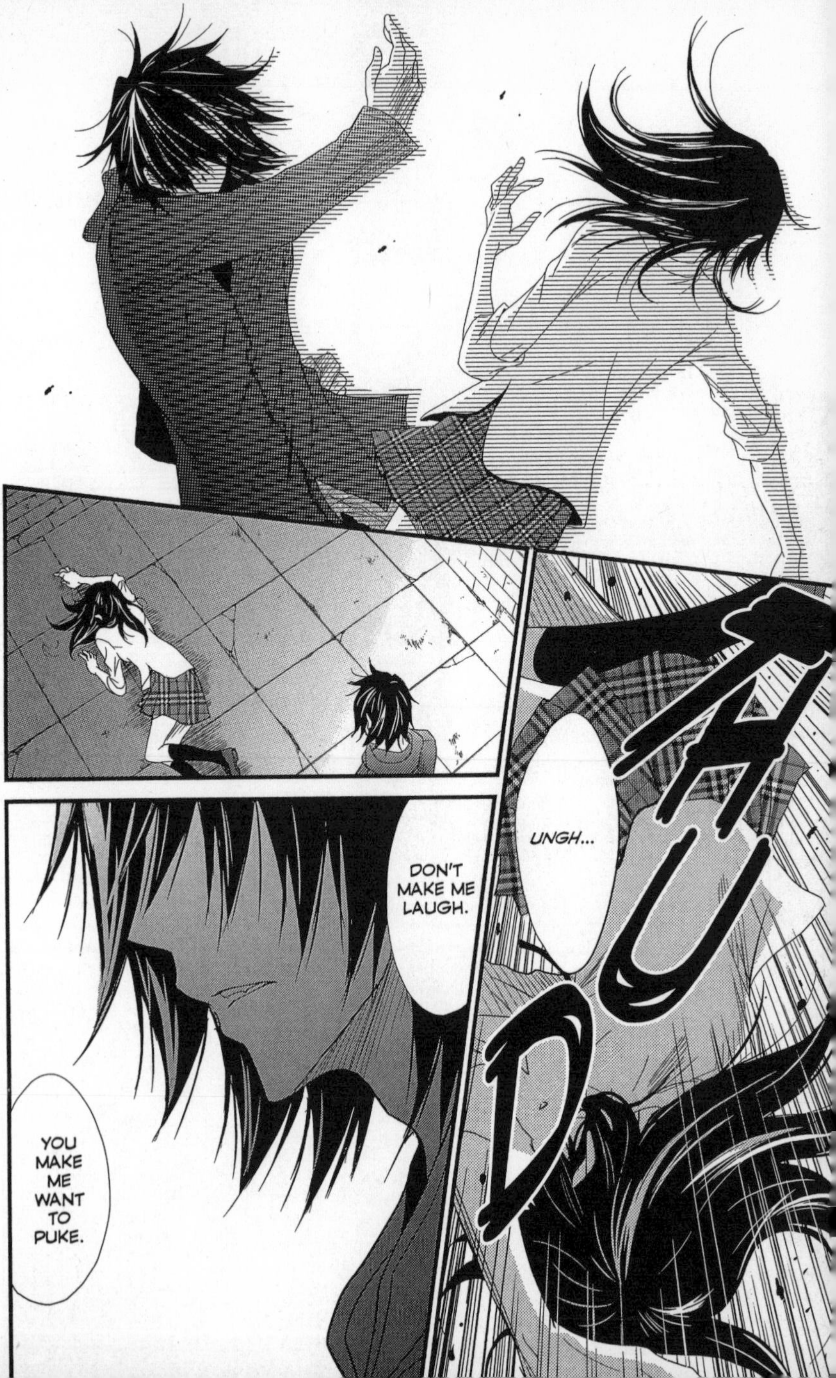
UNGH...
DON'T MAKE ME LAUGH.
YOU MAKE ME WANT TO PUKE.

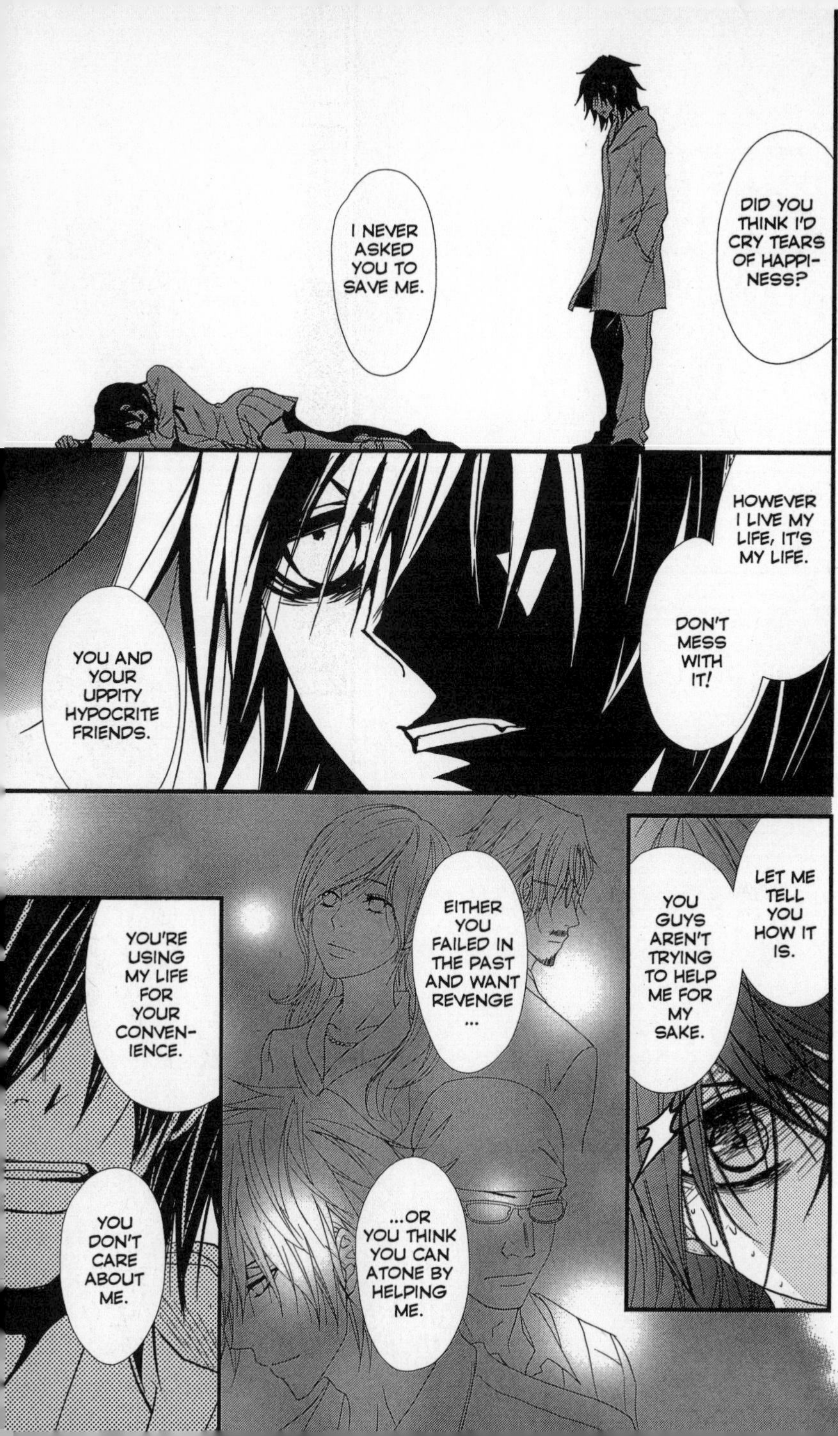
DID YOU THINK I'D CRY TEARS OF HAPPINESS?
I NEVER ASKED YOU TO SAVE ME.
HOWEVER I LIVE MY LIFE, IT'S MY LIFE.
DON'T MESS WITH IT!
YOU AND YOUR UPPITY HYPOCRITE FRIENDS.
LET ME TELL YOU HOW IT IS.
YOU GUYS AREN'T TRYING TO HELP ME FOR MY SAKE.
EITHER YOU FAILED IN THE PAST AND WANT REVENGE ...
...OR YOU THINK YOU CAN ATONE BY HELPING ME.
YOU'RE USING MY LIFE FOR YOUR CONVENIENCE.
YOU DON'T CARE ABOUT ME.

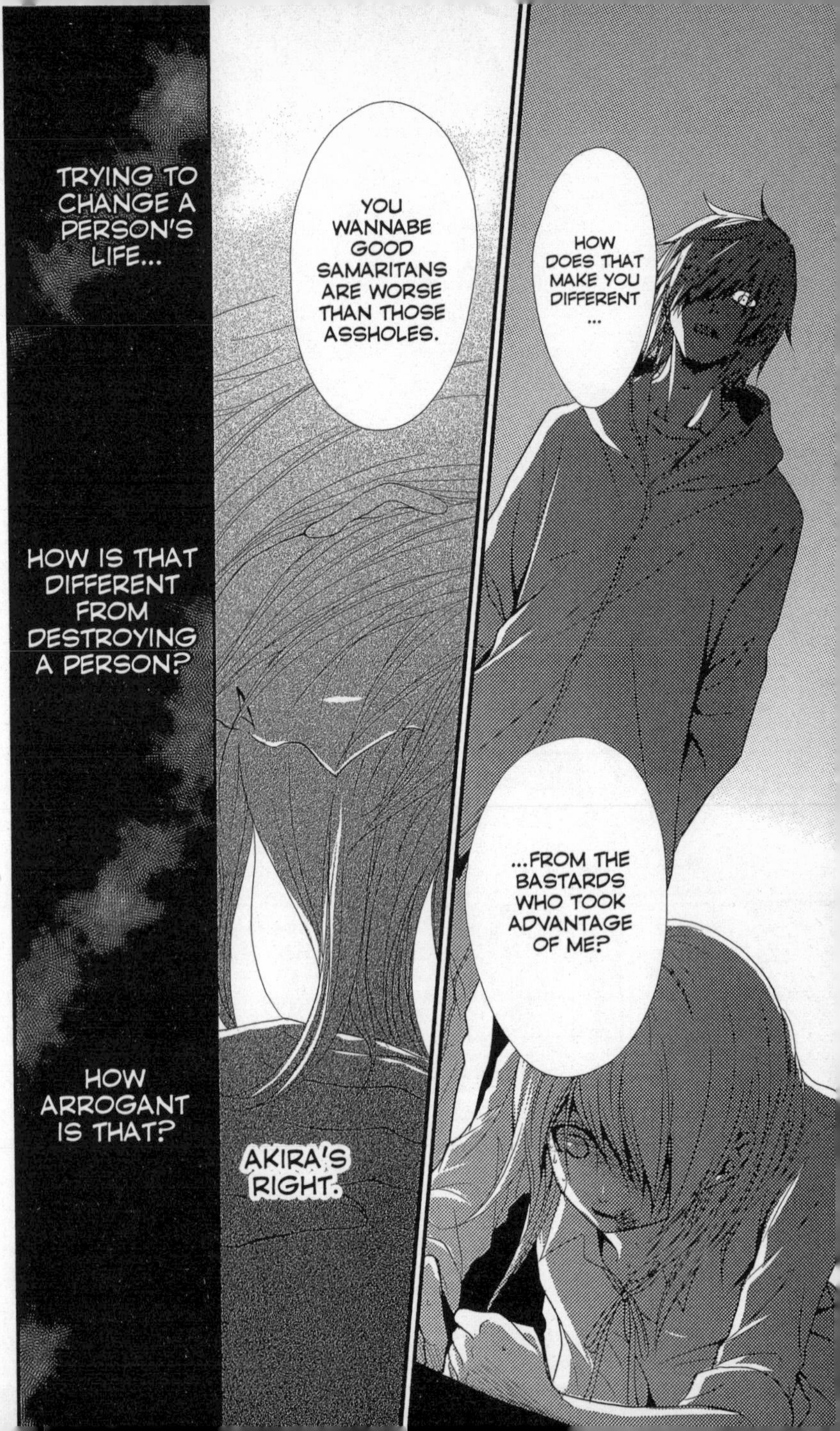
HOW DOES THAT MAKE YOU DIFFERENT ...
...FROM THE BASTARDS WHO TOOK ADVANTAGE OF ME?
YOU WANNABE GOOD SAMARITANS ARE WORSE THAN THOSE ASSHOLES.
AKIRA'S RIGHT.
TRYING TO CHANGE A PERSON'S LIFE...
HOW IS THAT DIFFERENT FROM DESTROYING A PERSON?
HOW ARROGANT IS THAT?

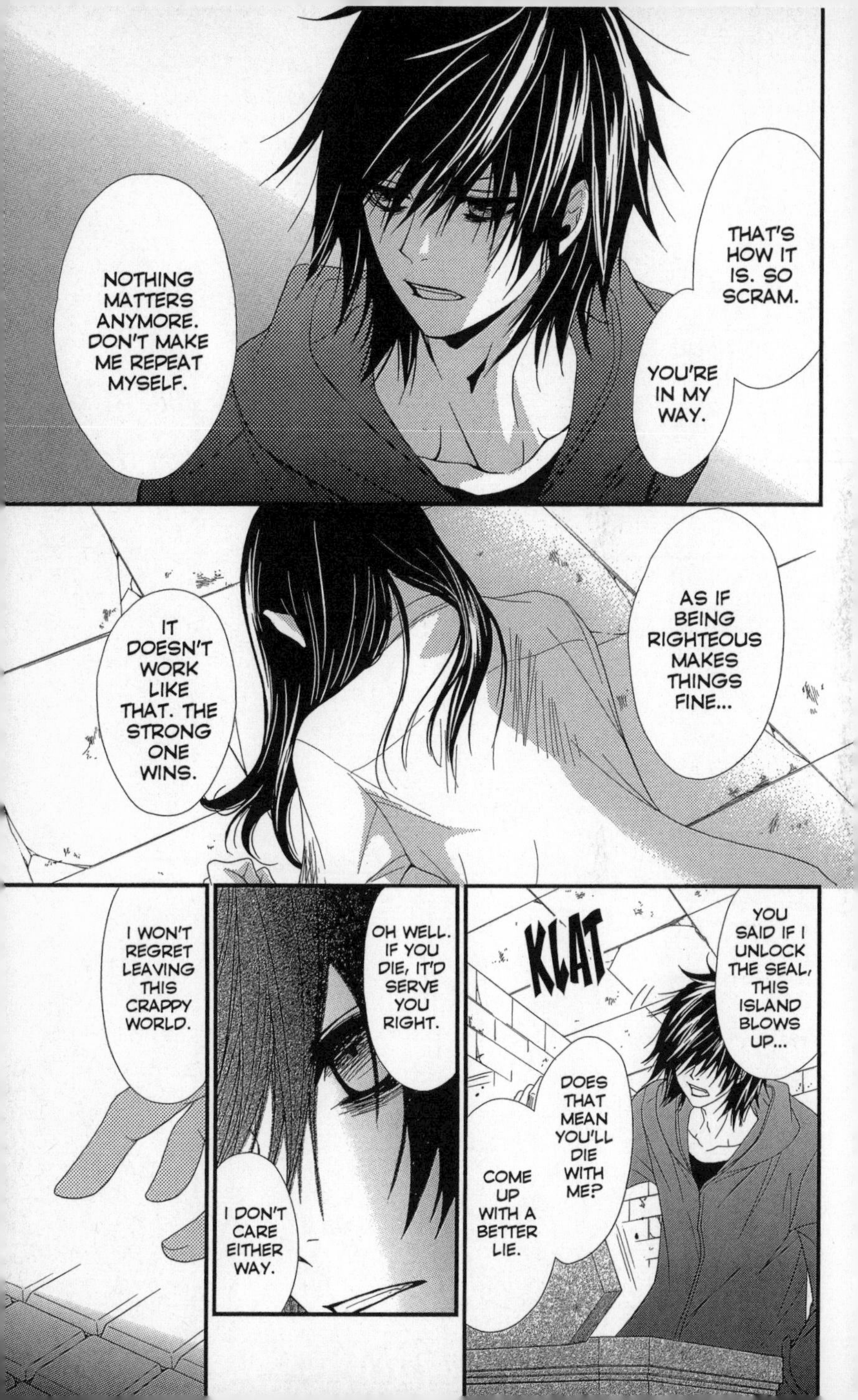
THAT'S HOW IT IS. SO SCRAM.
YOU'RE IN MY WAY.
NOTHING MATTERS ANYMORE. DON'T MAKE ME REPEAT MYSELF.
AS IF BEING RIGHTEOUS MAKES THINGS FINE...
IT DOESN'T WORK LIKE THAT. THE STRONG ONE WINS.
KLAT
YOU SAID IF I UNLOCK THE SEAL, THIS ISLAND BLOWS UP...
DOES THAT MEAN YOU'LL DIE WITH ME?
COME UP WITH A BETTER LIE.
OH WELL. IF YOU DIE, IT'D SERVE YOU RIGHT.
I DON'T CARE EITHER WAY.
I WON'T REGRET LEAVING THIS CRAPPY WORLD.

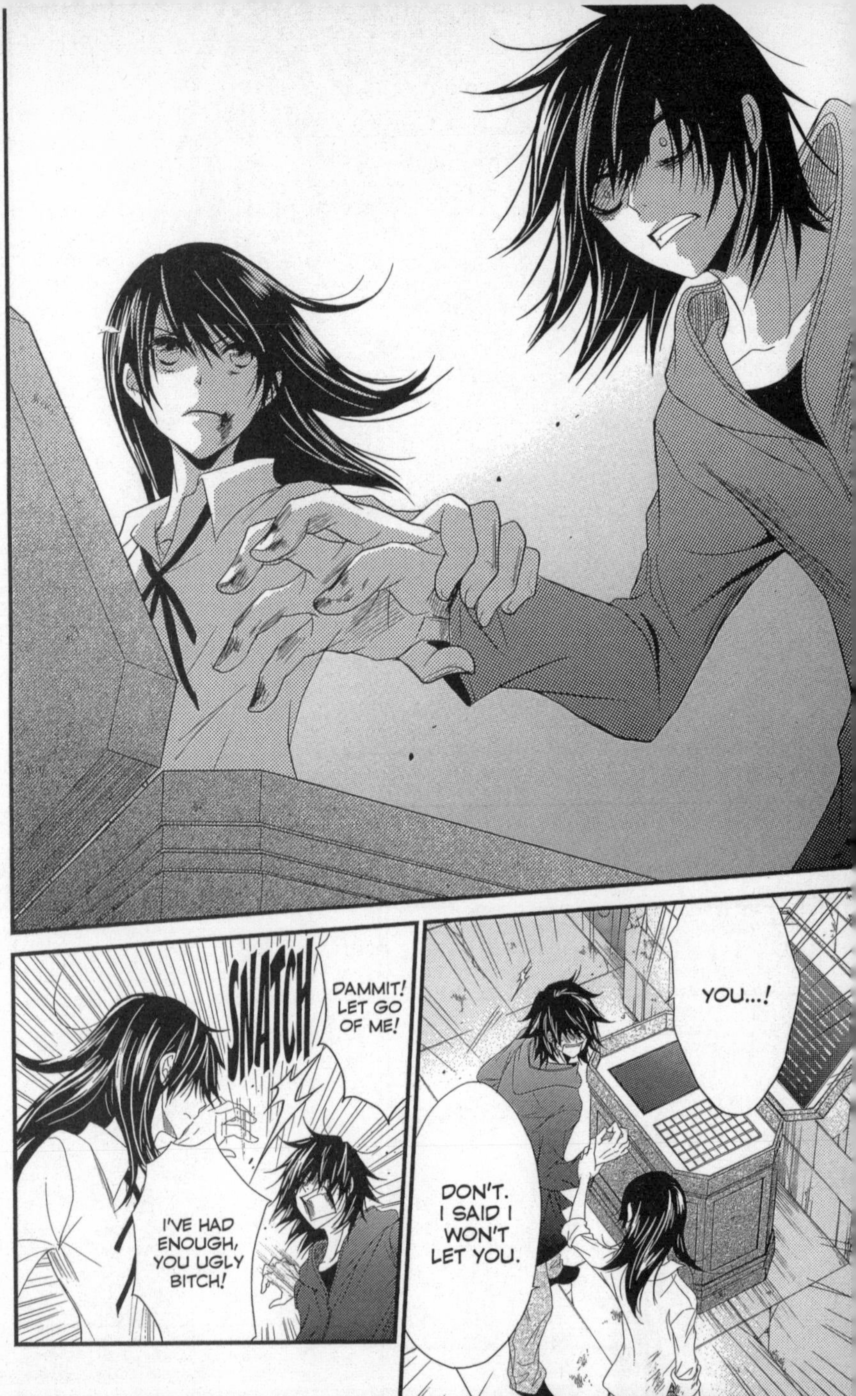
YOU...!
DON'T. I SAID I WON'T LET YOU.
DAMMIT! LET GO OF ME!
SNATCH
I'VE HAD ENOUGH, YOU UGLY BITCH!

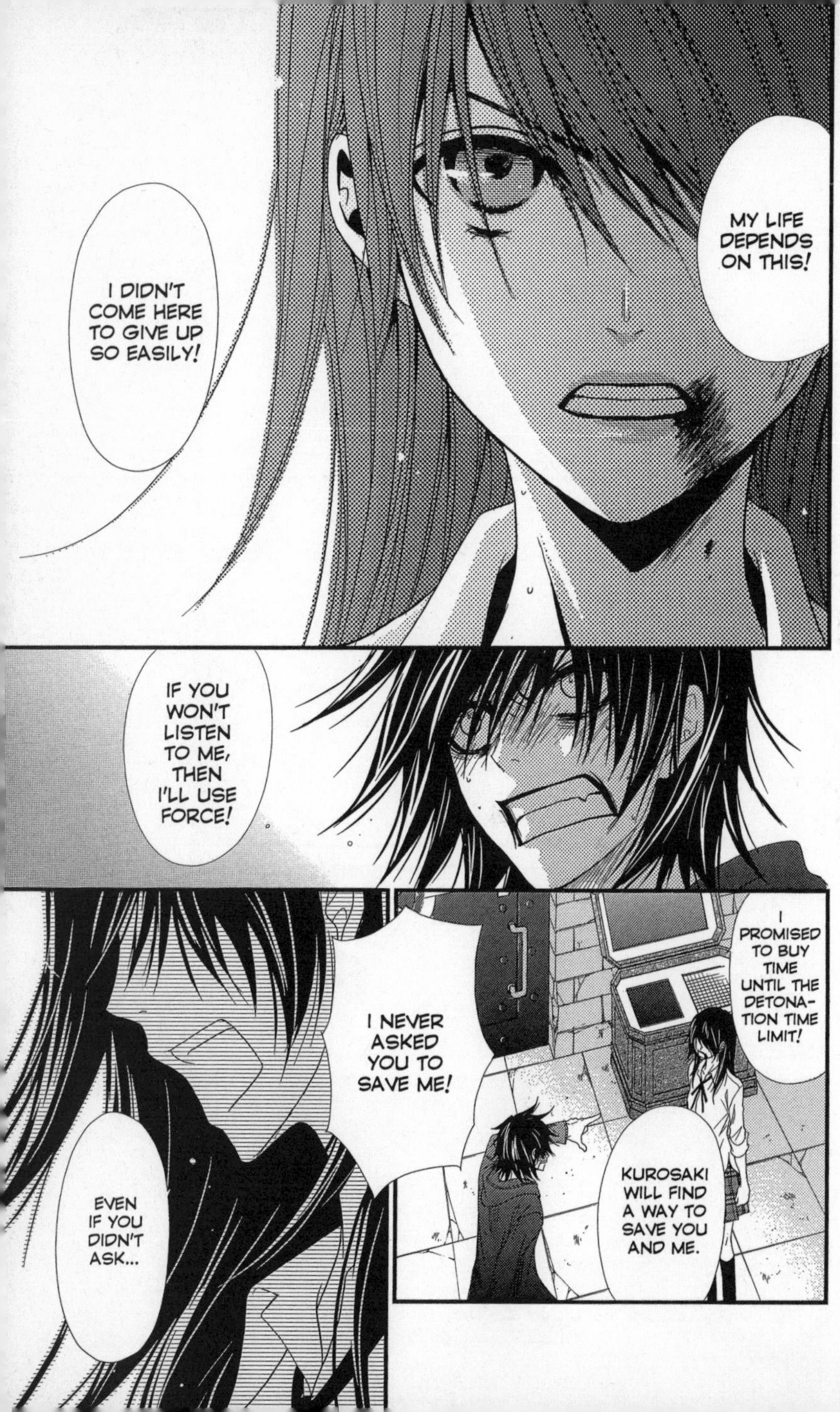
MY LIFE DEPENDS ON THIS!
I DIDN'T COME HERE TO GIVE UP SO EASILY!
IF YOU WON'T LISTEN TO ME, THEN I'LL USE FORCE!
I PROMISED TO BUY TIME UNTIL THE DETONATION TIME LIMIT!
KUROSAKI WILL FIND A WAY TO SAVE YOU AND ME.
I NEVER ASKED YOU TO SAVE ME!
EVEN IF YOU DIDN'T ASK...

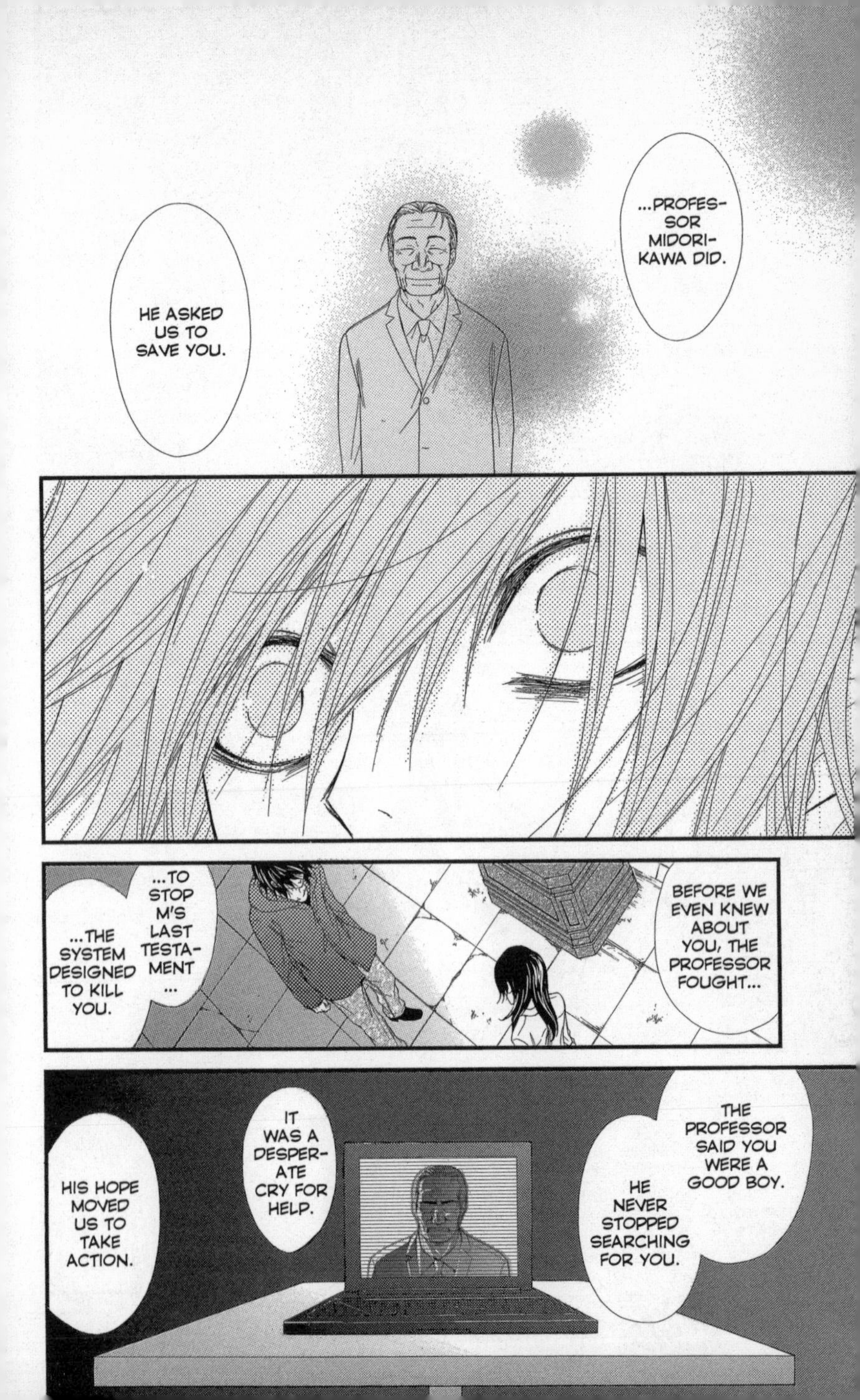
...PROFESSOR MIDORIKAWA DID.
HE ASKED US TO SAVE YOU.
BEFORE WE EVEN KNEW ABOUT YOU, THE PROFESSOR FOUGHT...
...TO STOP M'S LAST TESTAMENT...
...THE SYSTEM DESIGNED TO KILL YOU.
THE PROFESSOR SAID YOU WERE A GOOD BOY.
HE NEVER STOPPED SEARCHING FOR YOU.
IT WAS A DESPERATE CRY FOR HELP.
HIS HOPE MOVED US TO TAKE ACTION.

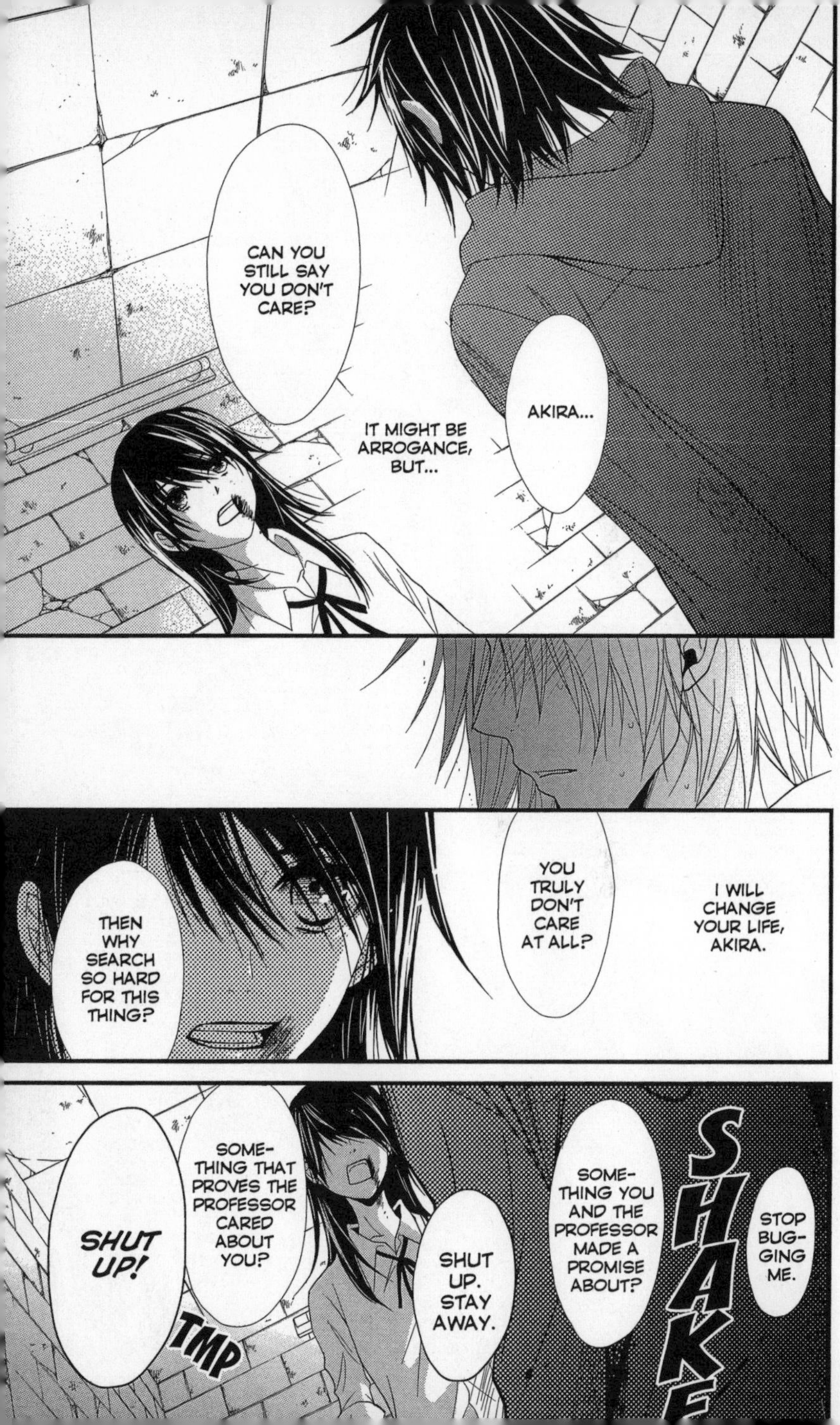
AKIRA...
IT MIGHT BE ARROGANCE, BUT...
CAN YOU STILL SAY YOU DON'T CARE?
I WILL CHANGE YOUR LIFE, AKIRA.
YOU TRULY DON'T CARE AT ALL?
THEN WHY SEARCH SO HARD FOR THIS THING?
STOP BUGGING ME.
SHAKE
SOMETHING YOU AND THE PROFESSOR MADE A PROMISE ABOUT?
SHUT UP. STAY AWAY.
SOMETHING THAT PROVES THE PROFESSOR CARED ABOUT YOU?
SHUT UP!
TMP

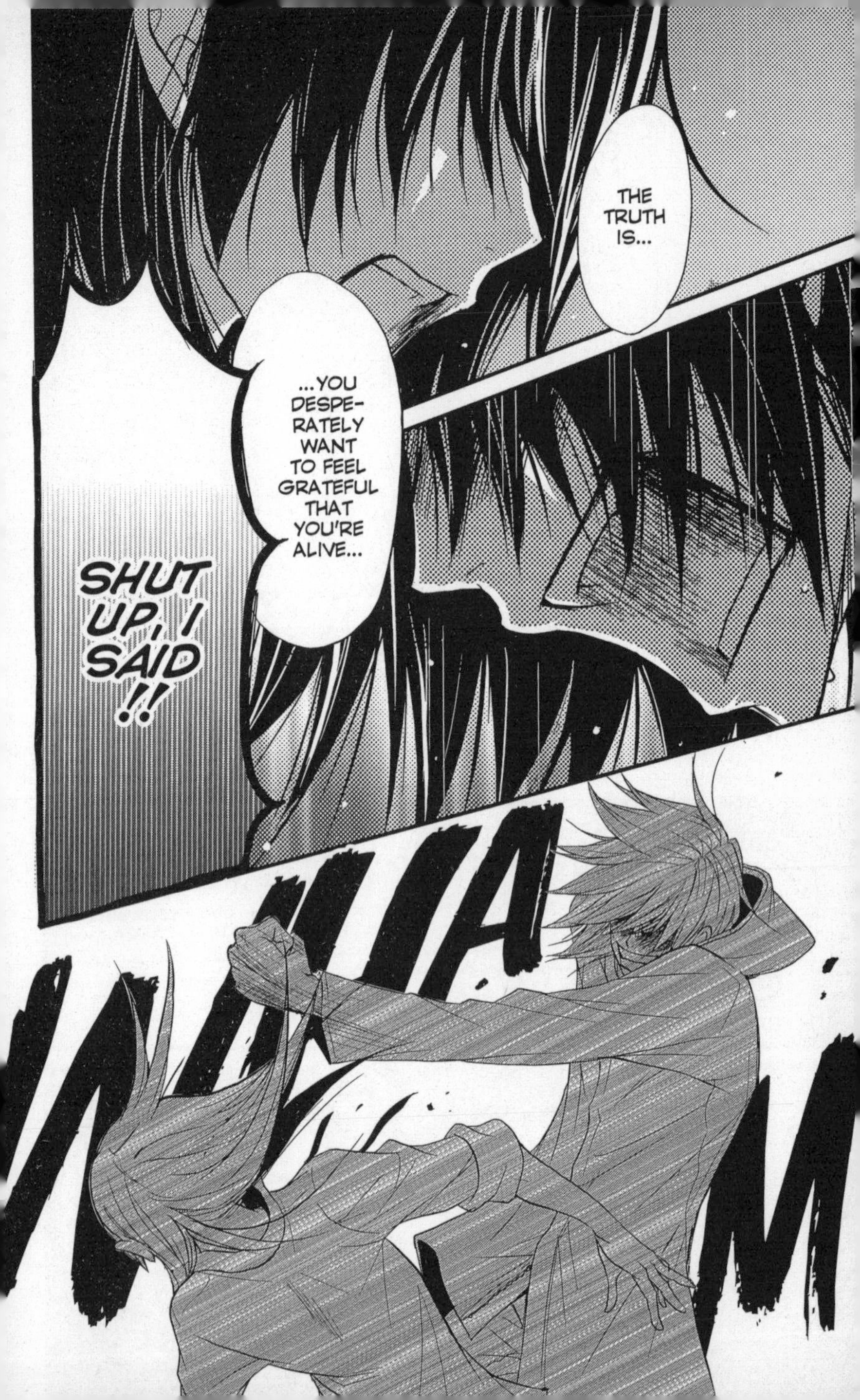
THE TRUTH IS...
...YOU DESPERATELY WANT TO FEEL GRATEFUL THAT YOU'RE ALIVE...
SHUT UP, I SAID!!
WHAM

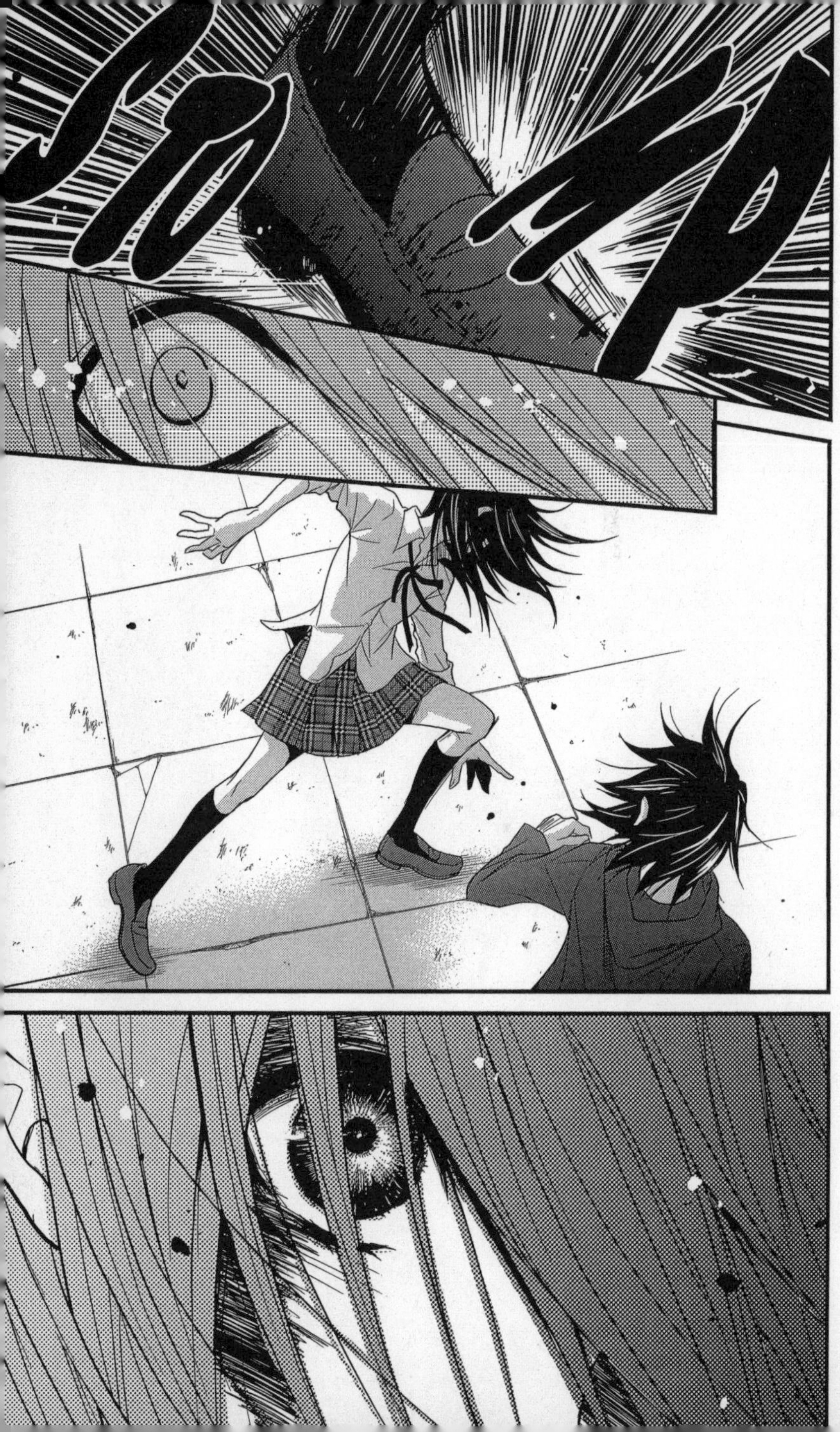

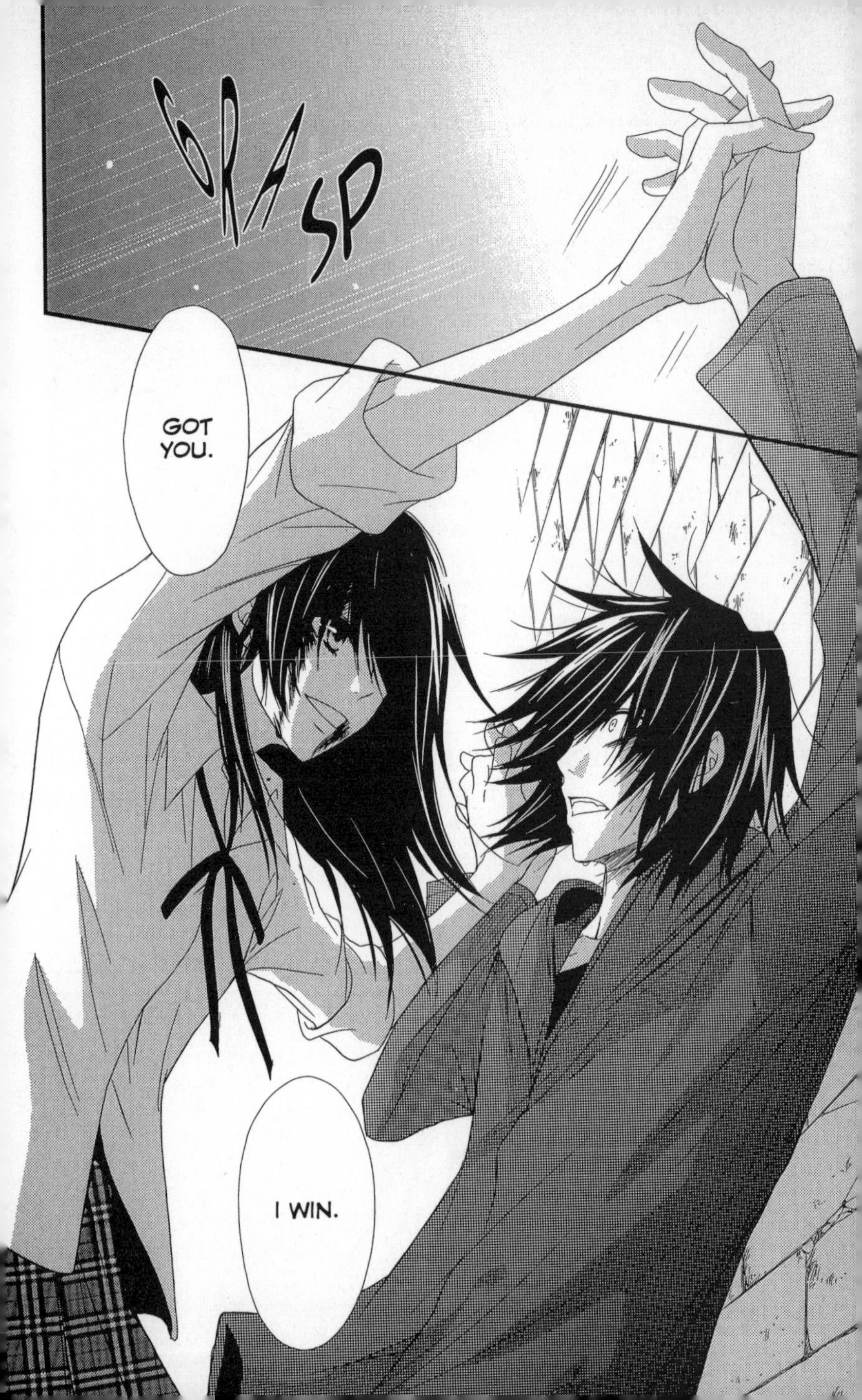
GRASP
GOT YOU.
I WIN.

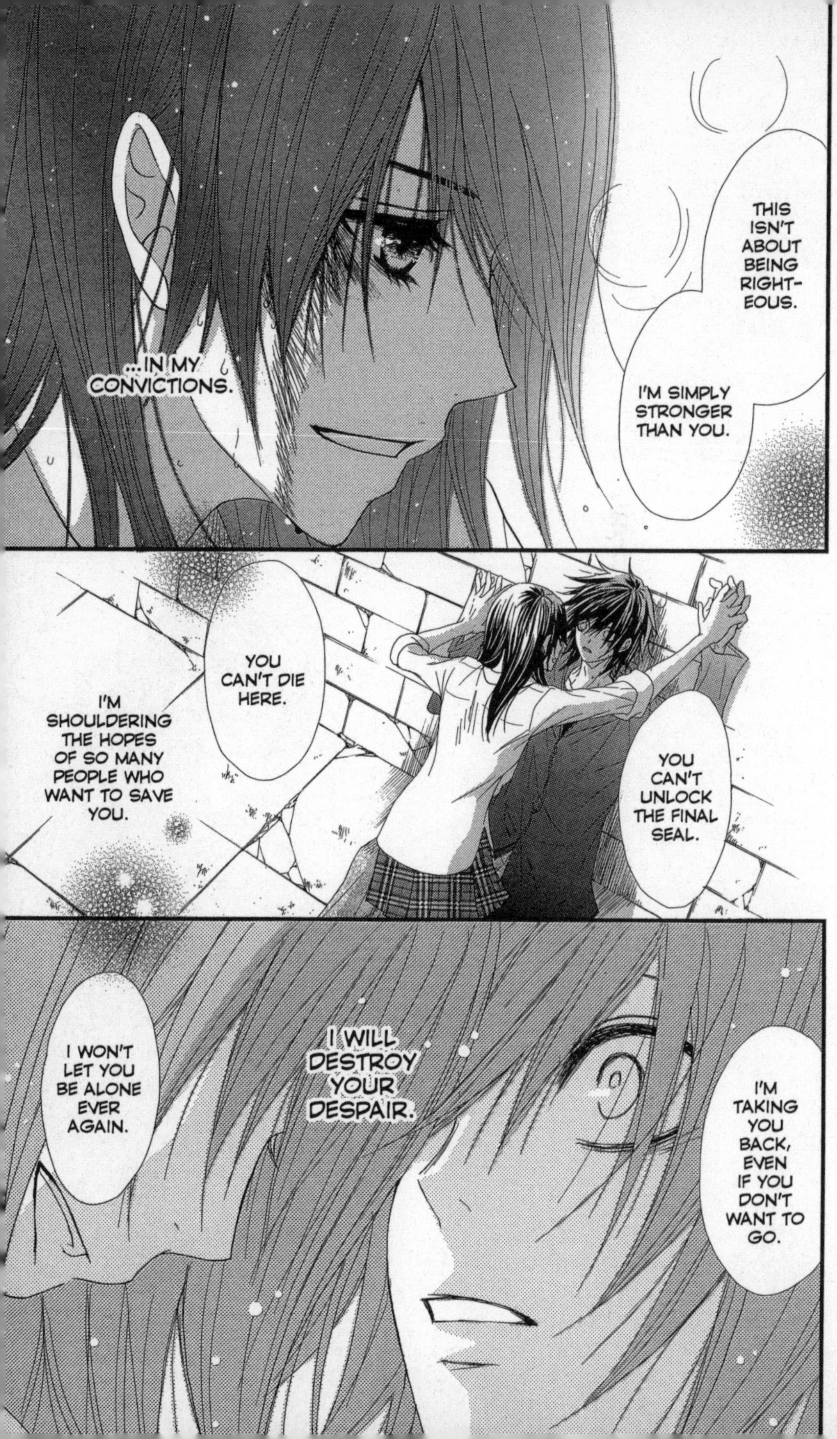
THIS ISN'T ABOUT BEING RIGHTEOUS.
I'M SIMPLY STRONGER THAN YOU.
...IN MY CONVICTIONS.
YOU CAN'T UNLOCK THE FINAL SEAL.
YOU CAN'T DIE HERE.
I'M SHOULDERING THE HOPES OF SO MANY PEOPLE WHO WANT TO SAVE YOU.
I'M TAKING YOU BACK, EVEN IF YOU DON'T WANT TO GO.
I WILL DESTROY YOUR DESPAIR.
I WON'T LET YOU BE ALONE EVER AGAIN.

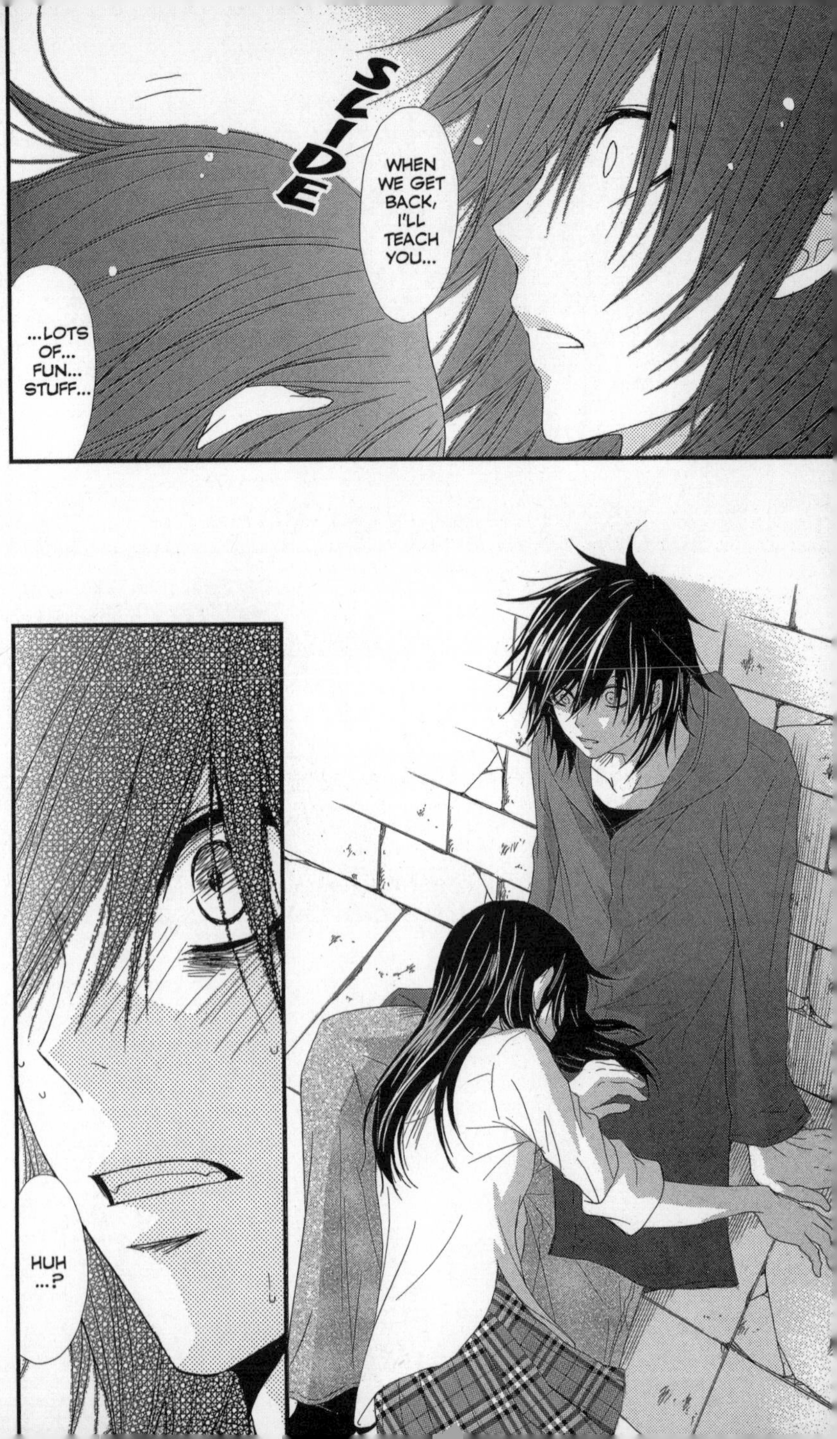
SLIDE
WHEN WE GET BACK, I'LL TEACH YOU...
...LOTS OF... FUN... STUFF...
HUH ...?

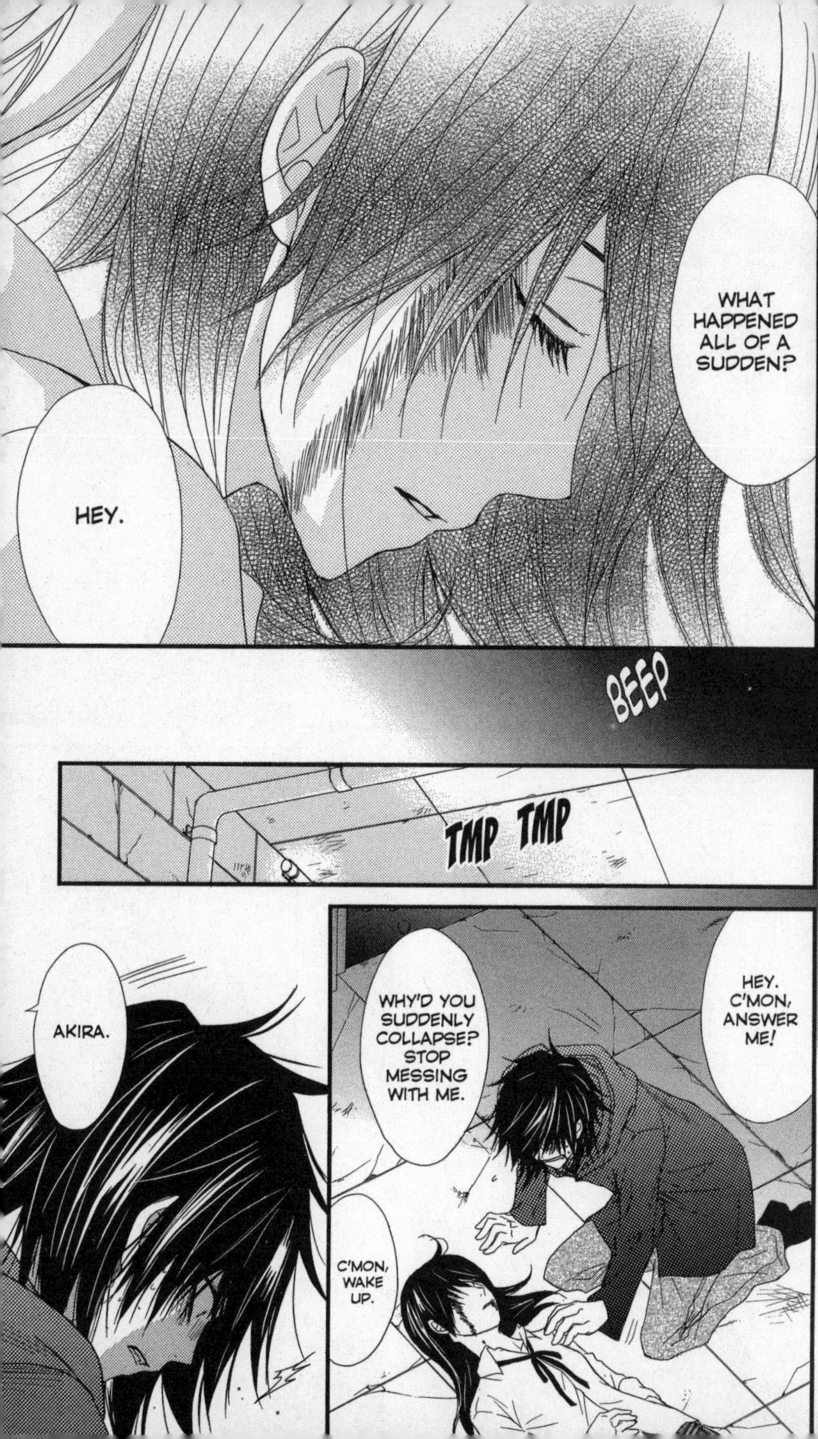
WHAT HAPPENED ALL OF A SUDDEN?
HEY.
BEEP
TMP TMP
HEY. C'MON, ANSWER ME!
WHY'D YOU SUDDENLY COLLAPSE? STOP MESSING WITH ME.
C'MON, WAKE UP.
AKIRA.

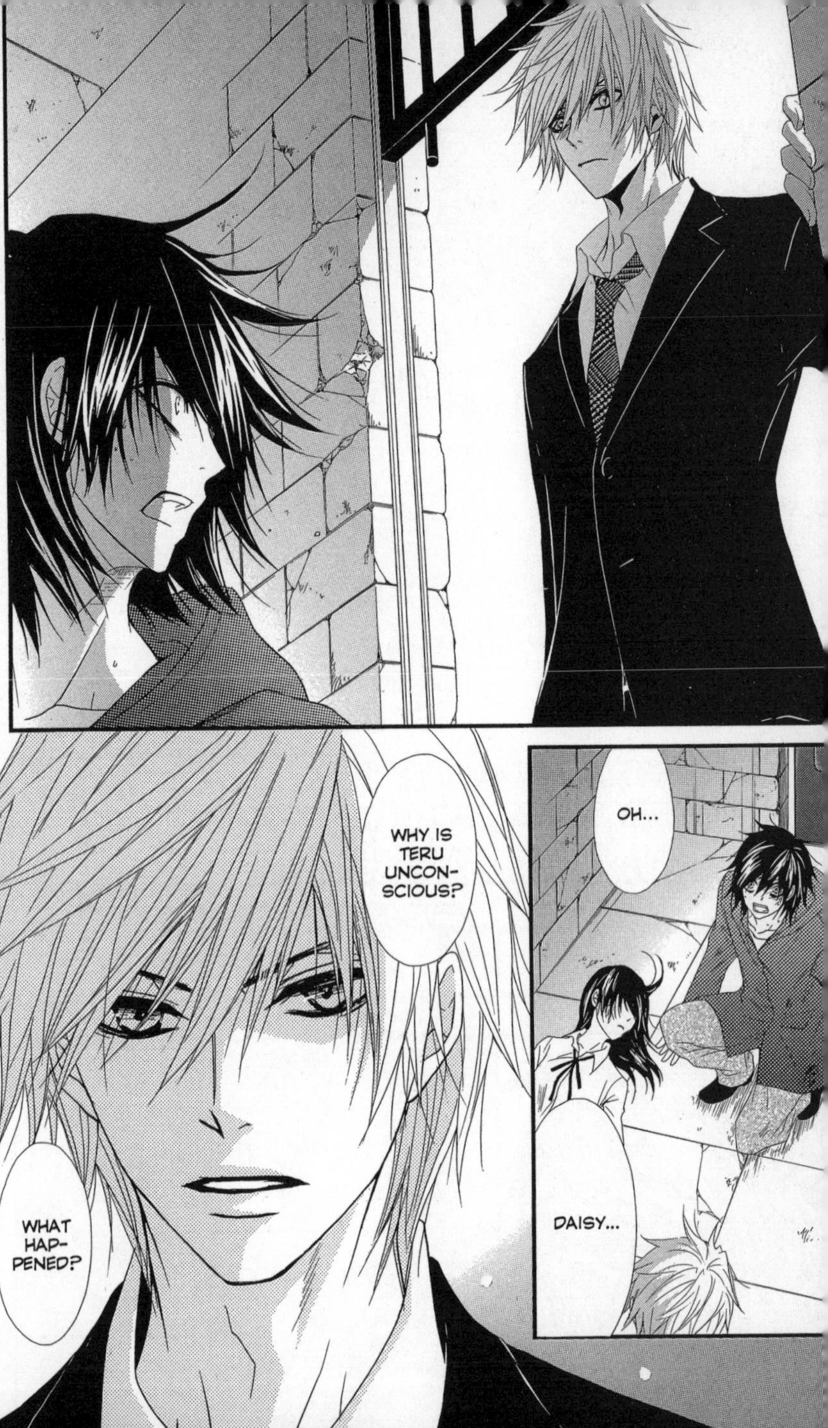
OH...
DAISY...
WHY IS TERU UNCON-SCIOUS?
WHAT HAP-PENED?

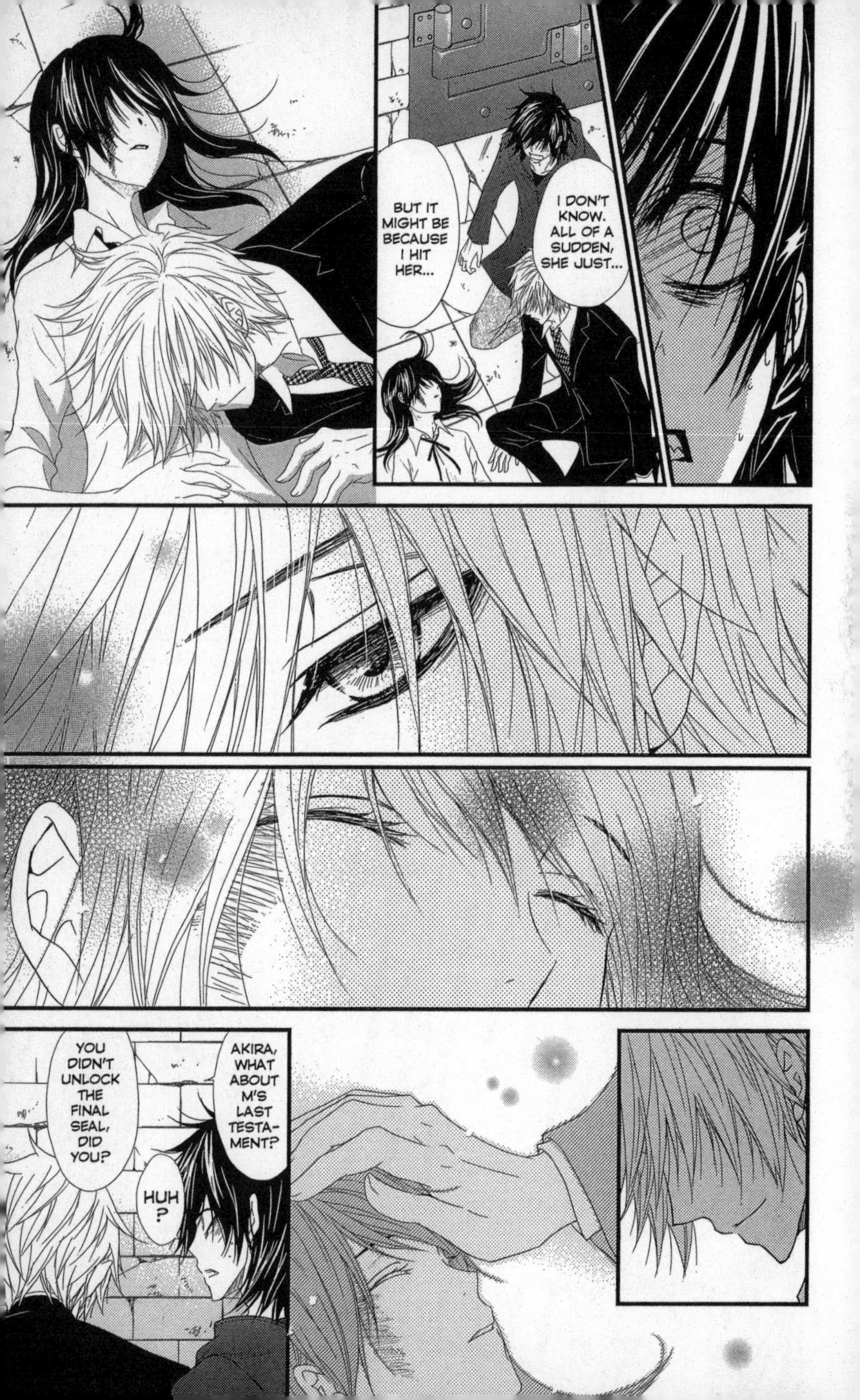
I DON'T KNOW. ALL OF A SUDDEN, SHE JUST...
BUT IT MIGHT BE BECAUSE I HIT HER...
AKIRA, WHAT ABOUT M'S LAST TESTA-MENT?
YOU DIDN'T UNLOCK THE FINAL SEAL, DID YOU?
HUH?

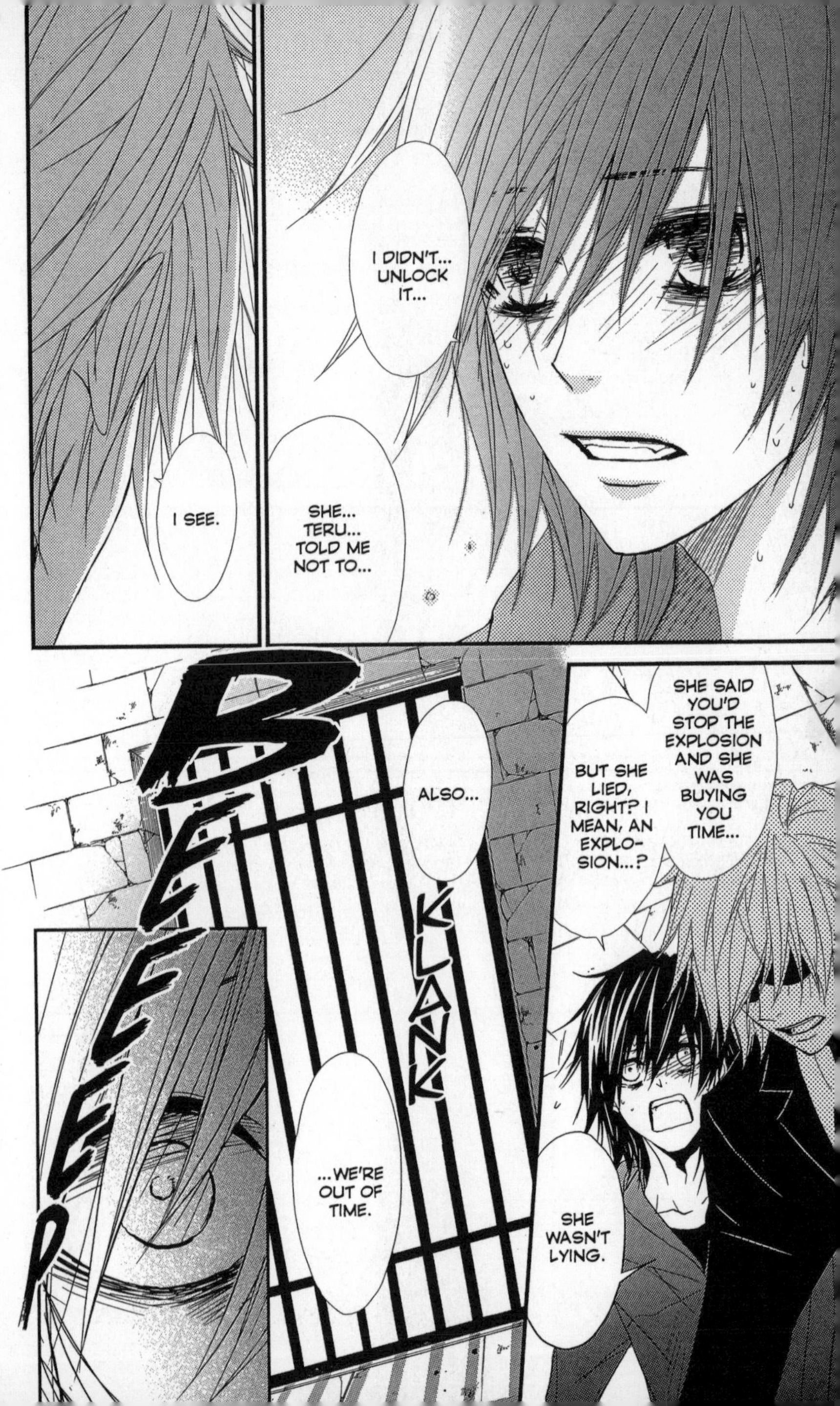
I DIDN'T... UNLOCK IT...
SHE... TERU... TOLD ME NOT TO...
I SEE.
SHE SAID YOU'D STOP THE EXPLOSION AND SHE WAS BUYING YOU TIME...
BUT SHE LIED, RIGHT? I MEAN, AN EXPLOSION...?
SHE WASN'T LYING.
ALSO...
KLANK
...WE'RE OUT OF TIME.
BEEEEEP

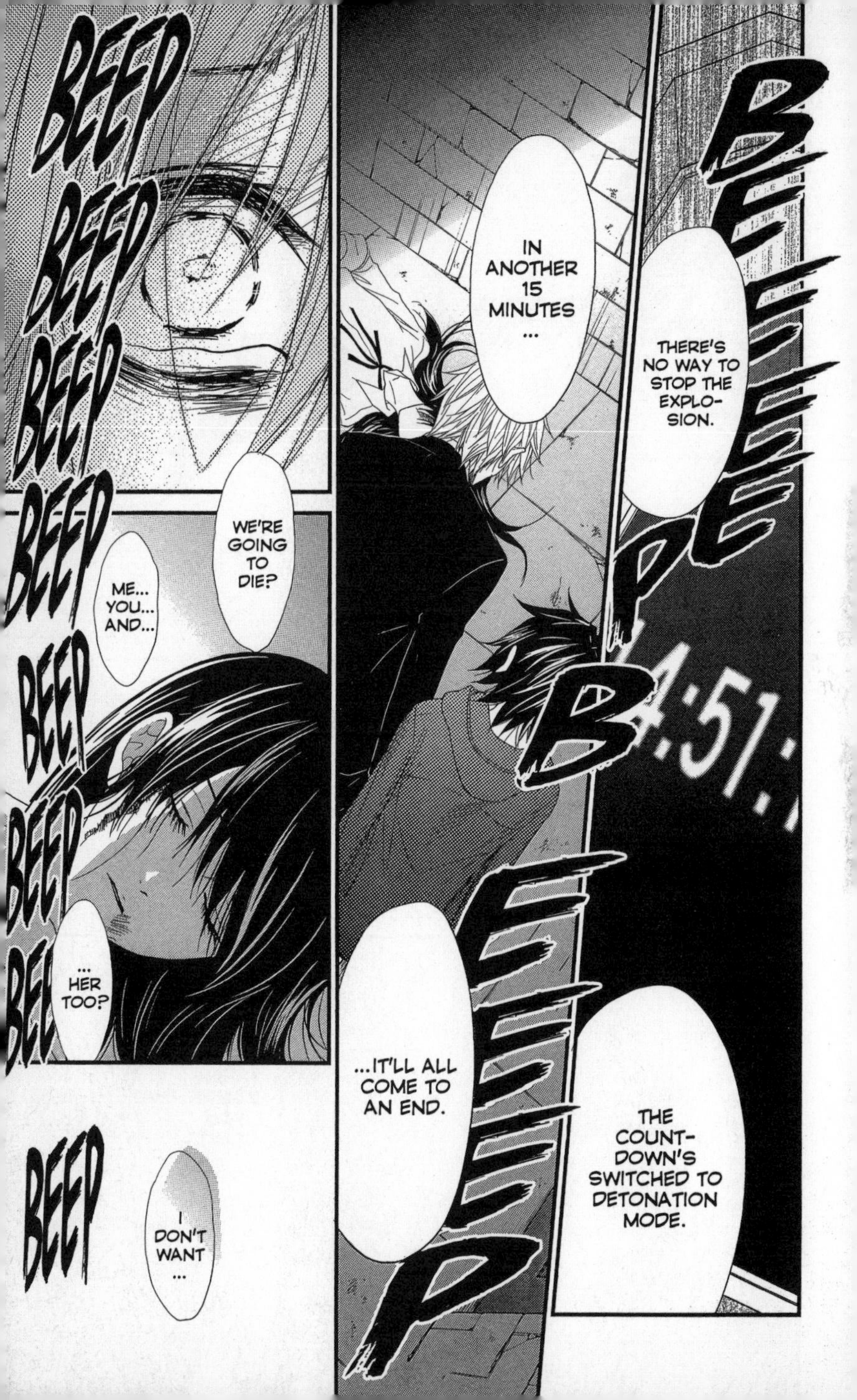
BEEEEEP
THERE'S NO WAY TO STOP THE EXPLOSION.
4:51:
THE COUNT-DOWN'S SWITCHED TO DETONATION MODE.
IN ANOTHER 15 MINUTES...
BEEEEEP
...IT'LL ALL COME TO AN END.
BEEP BEEP BEEP BEEP BEEP BEEP BEEP BEEP BEE
WE'RE GOING TO DIE?
ME... YOU... AND...
...HER TOO?
BEEP
I DON'T WANT...

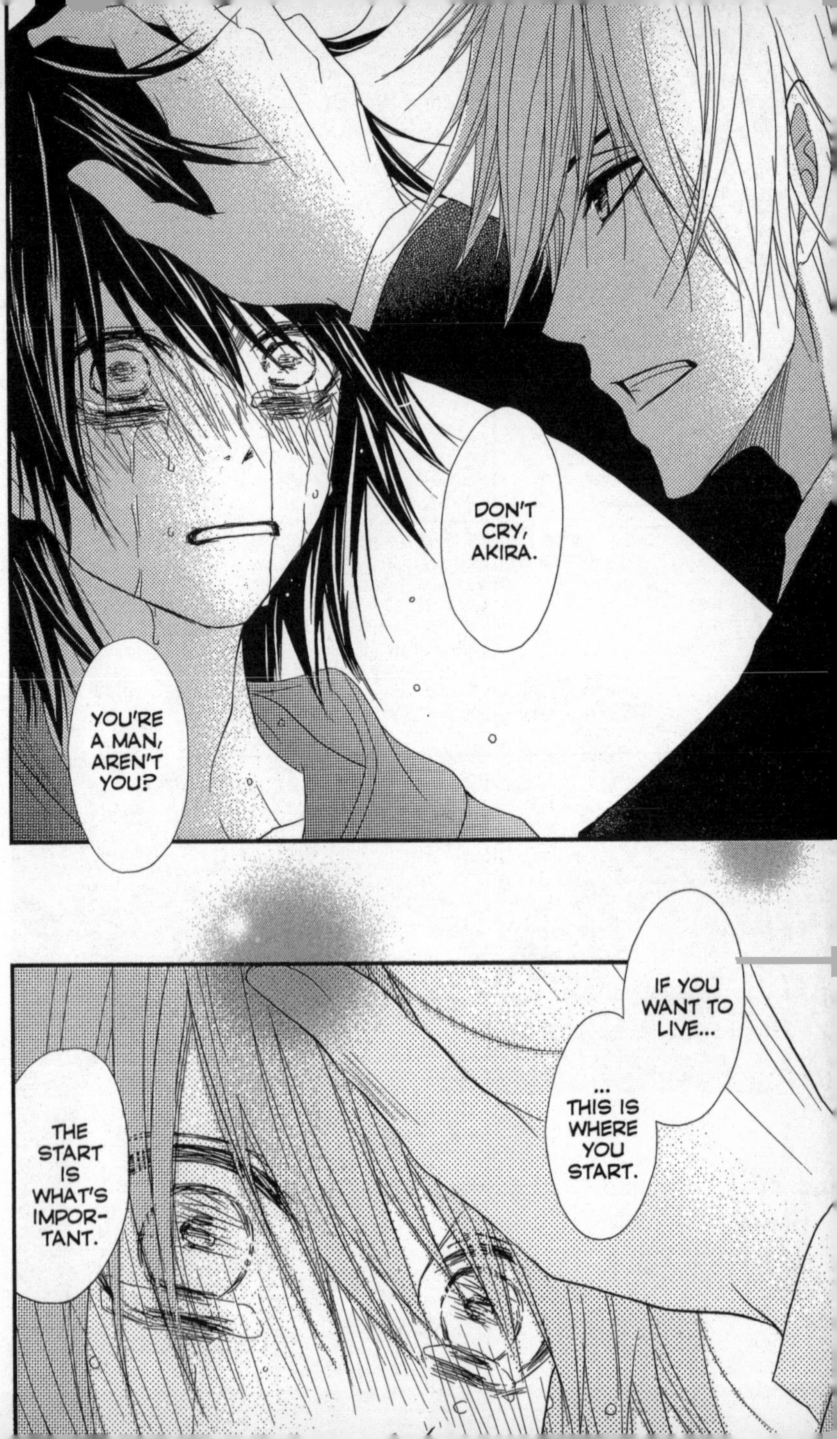
DON'T CRY, AKIRA.
YOU'RE A MAN, AREN'T YOU?
IF YOU WANT TO LIVE...
... THIS IS WHERE YOU START.
THE START IS WHAT'S IMPORTANT.

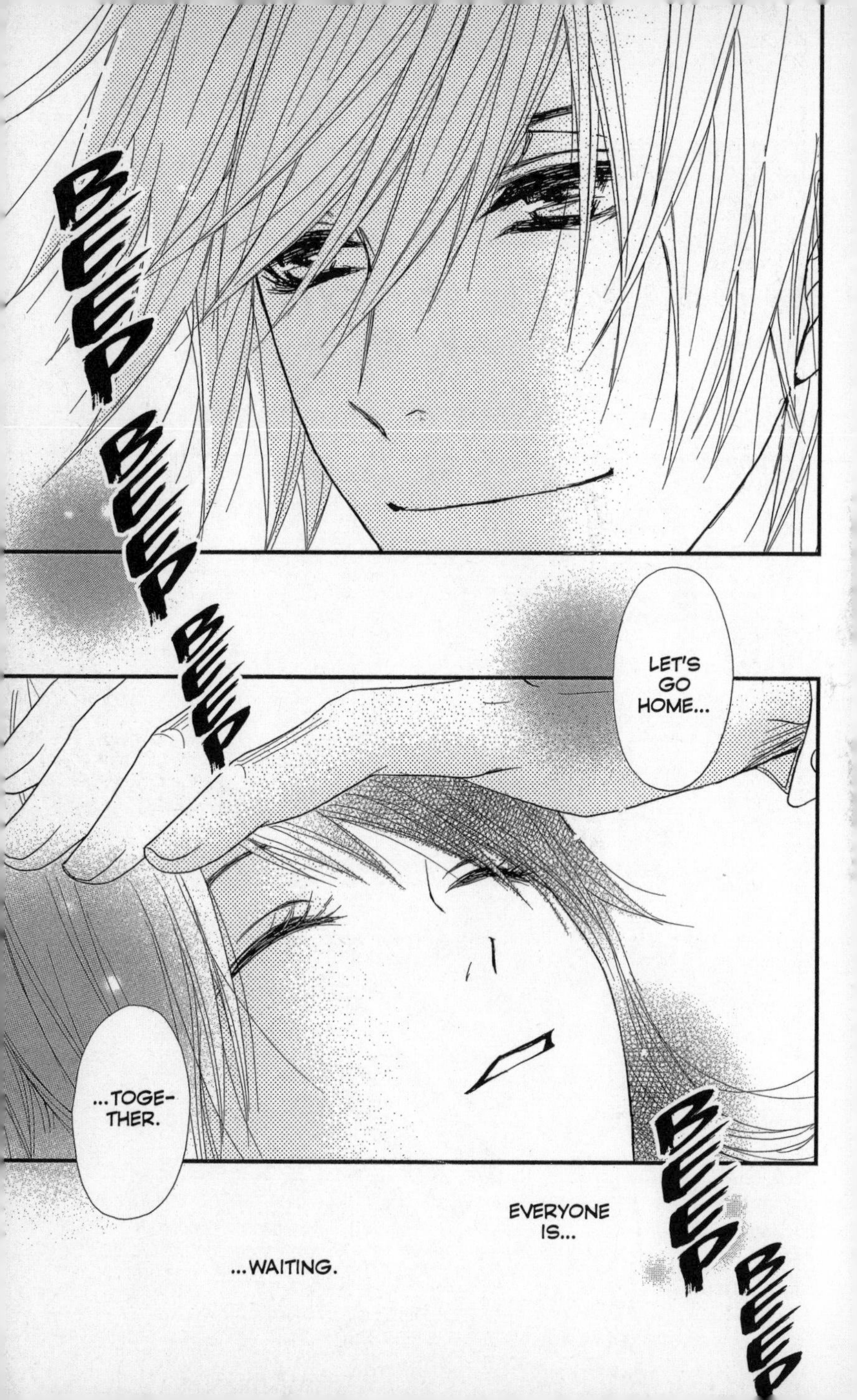
BEEP BEEP BEEP
LET'S GO HOME...
...TOGE-THER.
EVERYONE IS...
...WAITING.
BEEP BEEP

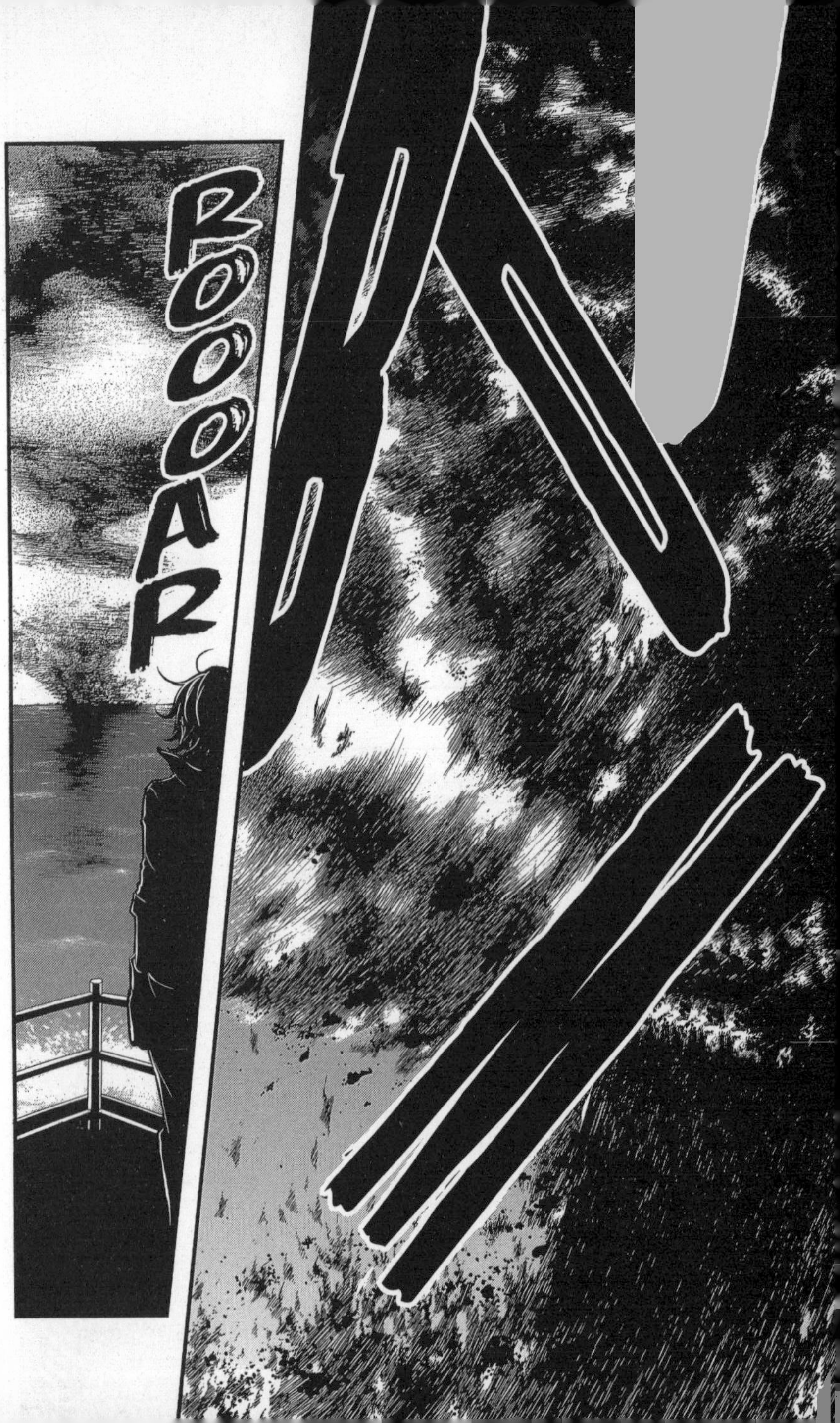
ROOOOAR

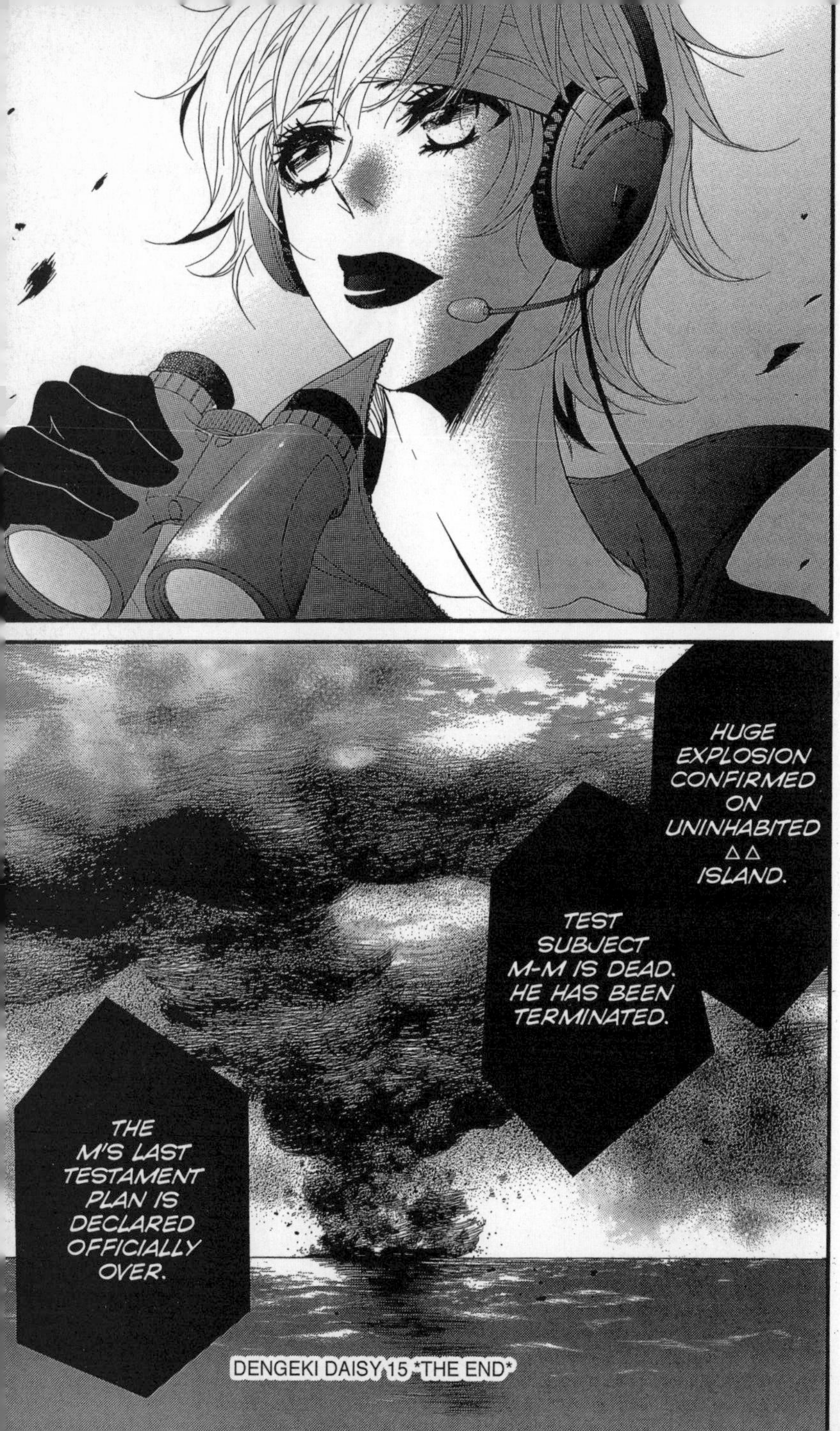
HUGE EXPLOSION CONFIRMED ON UNINHABITED ∆∆ ISLAND.
TEST SUBJECT M-M IS DEAD. HE HAS BEEN TERMINATED.
THE M'S LAST TESTAMENT PLAN IS DECLARED OFFICIALLY OVER.
DENGEKI DAISY 15 *THE END*

AFTERWORD

YES, *DENGEKI DAISY* VOLUME 15 ENDS HERE. THANK YOU FOR STAYING WITH ME UNTIL THE VERY END.

WELL, WELL. THE STORY OF *DENGEKI DAISY* WILL CONCLUDE IN THE NEXT VOLUME. I'D LIKE TO SAY, "I'M OVERWHELMED WITH EMOTION," BUT I'M NOT DONE JUST YET. I INTEND TO KEEP ON WRITING WITH EVERYTHING I'VE GOT JUST AS I ALWAYS HAVE SO THAT IT BECOMES A FINAL VOLUME BEFITTING *DENGEKI DAISY*—ONE THAT LEAVES NO REGRETS.

ANYWAY, SEE YOU NEXT VOLUME!!

KYOUSUKE MOTOMI

最富キョウスケ

DENGEKI DAISY
C/O VIZ MEDIA
P.O. BOX 77010
SAN FRANCISCO, CA
94107

← IF YOU HAVE ANY QUESTIONS, PLEASE SEND THEM HERE. FOR REGULAR FAN MAIL, PLEASE SEND THEM TO THE SAME ADDRESS BUT CHANGE THE ADDRESSEE TO:

KYOUSUKE MOTOMI
C/O DENGEKI DAISY
EDITOR

...AND THAT'S IT. THANK YOU VERY MUCH!!